This book is dedicated to the thirty-seven...

First published in Canada by
Fortress Publications Inc.
P.O. Box 9241
221 Barton St. E., Unit B
Stoney Creek, Ont.
Canada L8E 2K3

Canadian Cataloguing in Publication Data

Bashow, David L., 1946-
Starfighter

Includes index.
ISBN 0-919195-12-1

1. Starfighter (Fighter plane). 2. Aeronautics, Military - Canada. 3. Canada - History, Military - 20th century.* I. Title.

UG1242.F5B38 1991 358.4'3 091-093604-8

Colour profiles by Ron E. Lowry
Line drawings by Bob Migliardi
Typing, proofreading and special assistance, Heather Bashow
Design & layout by S. R. Taylor Publishing
Printed & bound by Kim Hup Lee Singapore

David L. Bashow

Toronto • 1990

Fortress Publications Inc.

Starfighter

A loving retrospective of the CF–104 era in Canadian fighter aviation

1961 - 1986

Table of Contents

The Canadian Fighter Pilot

Say what you will about him; arrogant, cocky, boisterous and fun-loving fool to boot; he has earned his place in the sun. Across the span of seventy years, he has given this country some of its proudest moments and most cherished military traditions. But fame is short-lived, and little the world remembers.

Gone are most of the fighter pilot forerunners; the "airborne cavalry" of the skies over Europe during the First World War. Almost forgotten are those who fought the Battle of Britain as Sir Winston Churchill's immortal few, and in his words gave England "its finest hour"... you were of them. Gone from their hardstands are the aircraft with which you further humbled the finest squadrons the enemy had. Dimly remembered are they who gave Canadians their proud moments in the skies over Korea. Unheralded are the hundreds who have not been required to fire in anger but who contribute unselfishly to world peace, patrolling the skies of Europe and North America.

So here's a "nickel on the grass" to you my friend, for your spirit, enthusiasm, sacrifice and courage... but most of all, for your friendship. Yours may be a dying breed. However, should you go, the world will be a lesser place.

- Interceptor Magazine

Photos (above and opposite page) by Bill Johnson

Preface

For nearly a quarter of a century, from 1962 until 1986, the CF-104 Starfighter roamed the skies in defence of western Europe as part of Canada's contribution to the NATO Alliance. This diminutive erstwhile interceptor, which so capably donned the mantles of low-level Nuclear Strike and Reconnaissance, then, in the latter years, Conventional Attack, became the centrepiece of a proud Canadian military aviation era: an era that would touch the lives of thousands of Canadian servicemen and their families in a very special way.

The constant that was the banshee wail of the Starfighter thundering over the German landscape spanned many of the momentous events that have shaped our times: the Camelot years of the Kennedy administration, Trudeaumania, the Wall, Vietnam, the Czechoslovakian Crisis, Middle East wars, Détente, and the birth of Glasnost... and was a story unto itself.

The changing nature of the Starfighter program during the Strike/Reconnaissance period lends itself to dealing with events of those years in a largely chronological fashion. From 1970 onwards, although the aircraft, tactics and roles were periodically updated, operational conditions remained relatively static. For this reason, the last 15 years of the era are covered in a more subject-oriented manner. The structure of the book thus reflects the history of the CF-104 era, a combination of the audit trail of a piece of military hardware and a human history made up of a host of personal recollections of the aircraft, people and events... some my own, many contributed by others.

The vignettes and stories recounted in this book are true; their veracity has been meticulously cross-checked and the events have been related without embellishment or exaggeration. Sources remain anonymous only when events were of a particularly sensitive nature and when participants could not be contacted. There has been no attempt to glorify this era, but rather to chronicle the life of the CF-104 in an honest, yet affectionate way - warts and all.

A few words on perceptions. When viewed from the more moderate and socially responsible 1990s, some readers may feel that the behavioral patterns exhibited by a few of the principals in this documentary were a bit excessive. They may be right. The Starfighter community of the sixties, seventies and, to a lesser extent the eighties, was a microcosm of the society that it pledged to protect. In those days, group acceptance and approval generally assumed a more important position in the hierarchy of needs than it does today. Perceptions vary with time as well. After all, my generation viewed the social antics of our predecessors in the forties and fifties as being practically beyond belief. Most of the specific stories recounted in this book consist of the spectacular, the unusual, and the remarkable; the routine and commonplace, which comprised the vast bulk of events in the Starfighter era, tend to fade into obscurity with the passage of time. On balance, I feel that the Starfighter community had things in perspective, didn't allow pleasure to interfere with professionalism, and in many ways showed considerably more social responsibility than their peers in the "outside society" of the day.

Support for this book was provided by many agencies within the Department of National Defence, most particularly the Directorate General of Information and Directorate of Flight Safety at National Defence Headquarters, CFB Cold Lake, the Aerospace Engineering and Test Establishment, and the Aerospace Maintenance Development Unit at Trenton. The Royal Danish Air Force, the Royal Norwegian Air Force, and the Turkish Air Force have been particularly helpful in tracking the present whereabouts of the remaining CF-104s.

Many people have given unselfishly of their time in providing a wide variety of valuable contributions, either to the text or by photos and art work. Special thanks to Marty Abbott, Ralph Annis, Tom Archer, John Bagshaw, Pat Barrett, Jim Baxter, Frank Birchall, Gary Blake, John Blouin, John Bradley, C.F. Carrington-Smith, John Christie, Blake Clark, Andy Cline, Keith Cotner, Larry Crabb, Leona Day, Jack Desbiens, Ray Dunsdon, Mark Fairley, Blaine Feltmate, Sam Firth, Jack Frazer, Jim Gale, Dave Ghyselincks, Neil Gillespie, Dave Girling, Dave Granger, Jim Grecco, Steen Hartov, Gord Hatch, Laurie Hawn, Gary Hook, Dave Huddleston, Al Hunter, John Hutt, Bill Johnson, Nancy Johnson, Vic Johnson, Stan Jones, Dave Jurkowski, Doug Keall, Garry King, Tom Klassen, Gary LaCroix, John Laidler, Tom Lawson, Ken Lett, Mic Mayr, Mike McCarthy, Jim McCullough, Mac McGregor, Dave McIntosh, John McKee, Bill McWilliams, Larry Milberry, George Miller, Hank Morris, Bill Paisley, Wally Peel, Phil Perry, Harald Riedel, Pierre Rochefort, Bryan Rollason, Dan Rooks, Ivan Sanford, Ronnie Sanford, Ernie Saunders, Mike Savard, Al Seitz, Lawrence Sianchuk, Thomas Slavicek, Al Stephenson, Al Stewart, Jan Stroomenbergh, Ian Struthers, Brian Sturrock, Larry Summers, Ken Thorneycroft, Eric Thurston, Bill Turnbull, Kevin Vaillant, Rick Wall, Jack Waters and Jon Williams.

Finally, a very special thank you to my dear wife, Heather, for whom this book has also been a real labour of love. Not only did she type and proof-read this entire manuscript, but she also helped with the research, and provided many invaluable suggestions and improvements regarding the content and structure of the text.

Every effort has been made to verify names, places and dates. Should any inaccuracies have persisted, my apologies are sincerely tendered.

Dave Bashow
Toronto 1990

AT RIGHT AND INSET: *The first... Two views of a pristine '701 immediately after rollout from the Cartierville plant, 18 March 1961.*
- Canadair photos

You love a lot of things if you live around them, but there isn't any woman and there isn't any horse, not any before, nor any after, that is as lovely as an airplane. And men who love them are faithful to them even though they leave them for others. A man has only one virginity to lose in fighters, and if it is a lovely plane he loses it to, there his heart will ever be.

Ernest Hemingway

Conceived in the fertile mind of Lockheed design legend Clarence "Kelly" Johnson during the early 1950's, the F–104 Starfighter would go on to win a very special place in the hearts of airmen and aviation enthusiasts the world over. Johnson, who gave the aviation world a whole stable of thoroughbreds, ranging from the P–38 of World War Two fame to the sleek, menacing SR–71, had a design game plan for the F–104 that was both a product of the technological times and a perceived need from those wearing air force blue. Johnson had painstakingly interviewed returning Korean War fighter pilots to solicit their views on what would constitute the ideal fighter aircraft. The majority wanted a "no frills" lightweight, fast-climbing steed, capable of out-turning the opposition and hopefully leaving them in the dust as well. Most were willing to eliminate some sacred cows, such as armour plate, backup flight systems, and even ejection seats in order to keep the weight down.

Taking these views to heart, Johnson decided to produce a small, fast fighter aircraft that would reverse a growing trend towards larger fighters. He reasoned that the diminutive dimensions of his design would permit a maximum speed in the neighbourhood of twice the speed of sound. Also, he envisaged the use of a single engine, which would drastically cut the cost, size, and complexity of the aircraft. At that time, aircraft designers were constrained by the limited power available from the early jet engines. However General Electric, true to their motto, were about to "bring good things to life" in the aviation community by tooling up to produce the mighty J–79, which would eventually become the Merlin of the jet engine world.

Genesis

Johnson proceeded with his design, planning a marriage of his airframe and General Electric's latest propulsion progeny. He reputedly investigated over 300 design shapes in his quest for an optimum compromise between factors such as maneuverability, range, speed, and landing characteristics. Aerodynamicists of the time felt that extensively swept wings of conventional thicknesses would produce excessive drag at Mach 2. Johnson therefore elected to use a tiny, straight wing that was only four inches thick at the widest part. Rumor has it that Johnson *conceived* the F–104 on a restaurant napkin. Apocryphal or not, it must have been a cocktail napkin because he obviously didn't have room for the wings. Nevertheless, what emerged was a sleek, timeless design that looked like it was going twice the speed of sound, just sitting on the ramp.

In reality, the projected drag fears of the aerodynamicists were somewhat unfounded, and although the radical wing design produced very little drag at high speeds, its smallness resulted in high aerodynamic wing-loading (around 95 pounds per square foot). This turned out to be a double-edged sword. While it doomed the aircraft to relatively poor maneuverability, since wing-loading is such an essential ingredient in turning performance, it also provided a measure of unparalleled stability in the low-level, high speed environment; a realm in which it was to excel. In all fairness to Johnson and his design team, the '104's initial role was envisaged as a high speed, high altitude point defence interceptor against the relatively poor maneuvering manned bomber threat. Low and fast would come later…

The first flight of the F–104 took place on February 7, 1954 under the skilled hands of Lockheed test pilot, Tony Le Vier. Subsequently, the USAF displayed cautious enthusiasm for the aircraft, placing orders for 676 of the jets, with which they planned to equip Air Defence Command. However, a somewhat alarming accident rate which was blown out of proportion by the press, coupled with a limited all-weather capability and early teething troubles with the engine resulted in the decision to relegate all USAF F–104s to Air National Guard units. In all, only

296 F–104s were actually built for the USAF, of which 44 had been lost by the summer of 1960. A number of these aircraft were returned to Air Defence Command during the Cuban missile crisis and served as well with Tactical Air Command in Southeast Asia during the early days of the Vietnam war. They also performed yeoman service with the Puerto Rico Air National Guard until 1975.

Though official interest in the aircraft by the American military was chilly by the late 1950s and had reached an impasse by 1960, Lockheed was convinced of the quality of their product and the viability of a world market for it. Accordingly, they mounted an extremely aggressive and successful sales campaign to promote the aircraft as the answer to a NATO consortium of fighter requirements. Led by Germany, these NATO nations wanted a fast, multi-mission attack fighter to replace a plethora of largely obsolete types. The result was the significantly enhanced F–104G, which featured the world's first highly-accurate inertial navigation system, an uprated engine, improved flight controls, and a proper fire control radar with a ground mapping capability.

During this time frame, Canada placed her long-term defence commitment to NATO under a magnifying glass and concluded that the way ahead was best served by Nuclear Strike bombers based in Europe in a deterrent scenario. To that end, competition for a suitable aircraft type had been fierce, and included the Fiat G–91, the Republic F-105 Thunderchief, the Blackburn Buccaneer, the Dassault Mirage III, the F–104G and the Grumman Super Tiger. Though the Republic offering was Canada's first choice, the cost of producing it in Canada with the Canadian Iroquois engine proved to be prohibitive, and accordingly it was eliminated as a contender. For one reason or another, the others fell by the wayside as Canada, in consultation with her NATO neighbours, reasoned that the same low drag, high acceleration and speed properties of the F–104 interceptor applied to the low-level Strike/Reconnaissance roles would indeed be formidable. Minister of National Defence George Pearkes made it official on July 2, 1959, when he took the floor of the House of Commons to announce that the Starfighter would replace the aging Canadian Sabre fleet in squadron service with NATO. Differences with the production F–104G would be relatively minor, but would include a radar optimized for air-to-ground navigation and radar bombing, removal of the M–61 Vulcan cannon and its replacement with extended range fuel cells, a modified undercarriage, and improved instrumentation. Although the original bill had been estimated at approximately one million dollars per aircraft, the final tally was nearly twice that at 1.95 million per unit. The entire production run of 200 single seaters (CF–104) and 22 two seaters (CF–104D) would cost nearly $464 million, a not-inconsiderable sum at the time. In August, it was announced that Canadair in Montreal would build the single seaters, while the duals would be purchased directly from Lockheed. Orenda Engines of Toronto was contracted to build the J–79 engines under license, which Canadair would then mate with the airframe at their Cartierville assembly plant.

Immediately following the first rollout of a stock production CF–104 (12701) at Cartierville in March 1961, it was whisked away via Hercules transport to Lockheed's Palmdale, California facility for extensive performance testing. (Lockheed had been contracted under the licensing agreement to do performance tests on the first two production aircraft.) There, test pilot Ed Brown "slipped the surly bonds" with '701 on May 26, 1961 for her maiden voyage aloft. The first CF–104D would fly shortly thereafter on June 14, 1961.

Meanwhile, back in Canada, the Cartierville plant was a beehive of activity as they geared up for full production. '703 would fly on August 14th, and on the same day Lockheed testing luminary Glen "Snake" Reaves, who would later become so well known to CF–104 pilots through squadron visits and his SURE Reports on Starfighter flying characteristics, launched in '704. By mid-August, the first ten production Starfighters had been completed and by early 1962, the Cartierville production line was turning out '104s at the rate of 14 per month. Although the last CF–104 (12900) rolled out in June 1963, the company would go on to build 140 F–104Gs for Turkey, Greece, Taiwan, Denmark, Spain and Norway under the aegis of the U.S. Mutual Aid Program. Production of these aircraft, including a supply of wings, aft fuselages, and empennages for European, Japanese and Lockheed built F–104s kept the Starfighter production line at Canadair open long after the CF–104 production run had become historical. The last F–104G of this contract was completed by Canadair on November 19, 1965.

The first production CF–104s and the majority of the Lockheed built CF–104Ds were destined for CFB Cold Lake in the wilds of Northern Alberta. Cold Lake would accommodate #6 Strike and Reconnaissance Operational Training Unit (6 ST/R OTU); the "school house" for CF–104 pilots. In total, the base would receive 104 CF–104s, including 22 duals (631 - 652) and 82 singles (701 – 711, 722 – 760, 762 – 791, 872 and 886). Many of these aircraft would eventually see service in Europe.

ABOVE: *Eager anticipation as '701 approaches completion. Note the schedule day display board on the hangar wall.* **BELOW:** *First flight. Test pilot Ed Brown "slips the supply bonds" with '701 at Palmdale, California on 26 May 1961.*

Big Plans, First Steps

As production of the CF–104 went into high gear, the RCAF turned its attention to the other side of the equation; namely, preparing a small cadre of experienced pilots to form the nucleus of the Operational Training Unit. Originally, eight seasoned RCAF fighter pilots under the able command of Wing Commander Ken Lett, and Squadron Leader Bill Paisley, who would be the first Chief Flying Instructor, were selected for training. Their ranks at the OTU were later augmented by two USAF exchange officers and a further four Canadians, who collectively formed the initial instructor cadre.

John Hutt was one of the original eight. He would serve a long and distinguished portion of his career in the CF–104, culminating in the command of 441 Squadron from 1975 to 1977. John vividly remembers the attitude of RCAF brass at the outset that insisted on day fighter as opposed to interceptor experience as a prerequisite for flying the CF–104.

When the '104 program started back in the early sixties, it was determined that the people they wanted had to have previous fighter experience, and fighter in that context was pretty well Sabre or Vampire; that kind of time, as opposed to CF–100 fighter time. Of course, a great deal of rivalry almost bordering on ill-feeling developed as a result of that basic determination.

Ottawa decided that "the Originals" needed a short requalification course in the Sabre, emphasizing the need for low level practice, but were rather vague and mysterious about its application to nuclear deliveries and the planned role.

In two groups of four, we went down to Chatham and got back into the F–86 again, racing around at low level. We weren't really sure why so much at low level, although that later became quite obvious...

It was also decided that the original group would need intermediate training in a century-series aircraft and some experience in practice nuclear weapons deliveries prior to tackling the CF–104. Accordingly, "the eight" were sent in two groups of four to Nellis AFB, Nevada in the spring of 1961 for a 20-flying-hour program in the F–100 Super Sabre.

Bill Paisley, who would culminate a very distinguished fighter career in the Starfighter and eventually rise to the rank of Major General as Commander Fighter Group, was selected as the first Chief Flying Instructor for the embryonic CF–104 OTU. He recalls life and high-speed flight back at Nellis in 1961...

In May we arrived in the gambler's mecca, Las Vegas, Nevada where three of us installed our families in apartment motels/trailer parks

Above: *The originals...some of the initial instructor pilot cadre of the CF-104 era. From left to right, John Hutt, Ernie Saunders, Bob Gillilland (Lockheed), Don McGowan, Bill Paisley, Jake Mulhall, Ken Lett.*

mid-way between the "Strip" and Nellis AFB. Al Weixl was living in the luxury of on-base Visiting Officers' Quarters (VOQs).

*After a few days of relaxed F–100 ground school from 0700 hours until 1600 hours, we were rapidly indoctrinated into the ways of daily USAF squadron routine. At that time in USAF Tactical Air Command (TAC) history, the word of the day was **central maintenance**, which meant complete centralization of scheduling and control of all levels of maintenance, including first-line servicing. The first flight of the day was scheduled for 0600 hours "power-on"; the time when pilots were to be ready to start engines. To ensure the aircrew didn't screw up the centralized system, there was a TAC Flying Order that stipulated that **all pre-flight briefings will commence two hours prior to scheduled power-on time.** It didn't matter that the briefing would take 15 minutes maximum, it **MUST** start two hours before power-on. This meant an 0300 hours wake-up for those not living on base if you were lucky enough to draw the "dawn patrol".*

I found my first flight in the Super Sabre a memorable affair. It was a mid-morning take-off with a runway temperature of just over 100° F and the aircraft was an F–100F (two-seater) with external tanks. The "boot in the rear" and rapid acceleration of my first afterburner take-off was really exciting, but my heart stopped when, after reaching the appropriate speed and altitude, I reduced power to Military. My initial thought was that everything had quit, that the speed brakes and flaps had somehow been extended and that we were dropping straight down to old terra firma. Fortunately my IP, Captain Graham, assured me that we were still flying and I would have to wait for another day to try the ejection system. After four transition missions, we flew about a dozen trips in F–100C aircraft doing weapons delivery at one of several ranges and Combat Mission Profiles with a weapon delivery on a tactical target. It was during this period that we learned that the RCAF would be given retarded nuclear weapons for carriage on the CF–104. It took some time for this information to filter down to our mentors at Nellis, so our first weapons training was based on the false premise that we would be carrying free-fall weapons on the CF–104 and using the bomb-toss-computer that was being installed in our aircraft. The method of delivering free-fall weapons from the F–100C was a gyro-based system of tossing the weapon "over the shoulder" during a high speed looping manoeuvre. We were happy when our training focused on LADD and Laydown as we didn't set any records for accuracy doing the over-the-shoulder deliveries. Our stay at Nellis lasted eight weeks and we gained some exposure to nuclear weapons planning and delivery methods, enemy SAM capabilities, mission planning, low level radar navigation, prediction and planning, and radar navigation utilizing the NASAAR equipped Sabreliner, - as well as the night life on "the strip".

However, Ernie Saunders, another of the initial group of four, recalls some bureaucratic problems associated with the short stay at Nellis...

We found that the bright lights downtown managed to keep our pay accounts in disarray. We were paid from Washington who didn't know who we were. On one occasion you would get a cheque for $8.30, and the next time you would get one for $1200. By the time we arrived at Cold Lake in September, the Pay Accounts Officer couldn't believe the mess he was seeing when he looked at what we had, and it took almost a year in my case to get it straightened out. But Las Vegas was a great time...

Meanwhile, the second group of four, including John Hutt, had arrived at Nellis. John Hutt recalls his impressions of flying "the Hun"...

The year was 1961 and the time of year was around May when our group arrived at Nellis. Al Weixl was already there, as was Ernie Saunders, Bill Paisley and Jake Mulhall, and so Don McGowan, Ken Lett, myself and Don Williamson got there as the second group. At any rate, May in Las Vegas was a pretty welcome break from frigid Canada.

We did the usual "here's the book and here's the exam - write it " on the F–100, and then off we went. My recollection of the F–100 was that it was like the F–86, only all kinds of knots faster...

However, you can imagine what kind of handling difficulties an airplane that didn't have any flaps would exhibit, because that's the way the F–100C was built. When you wanted to turn final from base turn, you actually used more rudder than aileron. If you just used aileron, the damn thing just wouldn't handle it. It would waddle across the horizon and was extremely uncomfortable... The first film that they showed you at Nellis was the F–100 "behind the power curve", literally walking the whole length of the runway on its tail before it hit and exploded. That left a lasting impression with me and I don't think that I have ever since pulled the nose up on any airplane before I put the power on, so there were some valuable lessons to be learned at Nellis.

I don't think any of the eight ever got to the point where they could handle the airplane with any degree of confidence at all. It was a very disturbing point in time, because we thought that if this is what the "century series" of aircraft were all about, then maybe the '104 would be four times as bad.

*We were introduced to some strange bombing methods after the basic transition. There were low and high angle pull-up bombing modes, and there was over-the-shoulder bombing, all of which was completely strange to us. These were obviously methods of delivering nuclear weaponry... You can just picture dusting along the bombing range at full speed in this beast and at a predetermined time "pickling", then pulling up, and when the Angle of Attack reached 35 or 40 degrees for low angle bombing, the bomb went off as if by magic - but in reality due to the manual release timers. The bomb went straight ahead and we went back to the starting point. There was a higher angle of bombing, and I think the thing came off at 75 or 80 degrees. Then there was the one which we employed a fair bit called over-the-shoulder. We set the release gyro at around 110 degrees and we roared in over the target almost, did a sort of a loop and at 110 degrees pitch, this flaming bomb went off and it kept on going. While you exited, completing a type of half Cuban Eight or a Roll Off the Top, the bomb peaked and headed off towards the target. I say the target with tongue in cheek because I was surprised that we even hit the **ground** on some occasions. It was an extremely inaccurate means of weapon delivery, even for nuclear weapons. Everybody was so bad that probably the safest place to be was anywhere within 100 yards of the target...*

When the Nellis experience was at an end, the two groups proceeded to Lockheed's production and test facility at Palmdale, California for their first taste of the Starfighter. John Hutt continues...

The first group went on to Palmdale for the '104 checkout ahead of us, but they did little if any flying before our arrival. We probably got there two to three weeks later. We were assigned to some of the Lockheed acceptance and check pilots to get checked out in the '104D, the dual model. Naturally, rank had its privileges and Lett was first, Paisley second, and guys like McGowan and I brought up the rear, but it was still a really exciting time.

We had some strange working habits...we would usually be in the air by six in the morning to take advantage of the coolness of the day. This was because Palmdale, which was just south of Edwards, was just as bloody hot as Las Vegas. If it was a bit of an "iffy" day, usually for wind, the Americans just didn't fly, and naturally neither did we. This was because they were at that time having some trouble with their drag chutes and 25–30 knots of wind would ground them. There was a little place we used to stop in at called "The Royal Palms". We'd pop in there the odd day for a beer, if you can imagine, at ten in the morning. On good flying days we were home by noon, but the bad days...

Palmdale was an ideal location for proving the radar, because right at the factory floor they were really peaked up well. We would fly the valleys through the coastal mountain ranges and it was just great. It was here that we met up with some of the support trades. They were down there learning that side of the operation while we flew.

In sum, we didn't get very much flying at Palmdale. A lot of our time was spent learning systems and reading and writing exams; learning all the funny things that kept the airplane in the air. We never dropped anything from it; just did general handling exercises.

Bill Paisley recalls his impression of the Palmdale phase and meeting the Starfighter for the first time as well…

For me, the big day for which I'd been waiting so long came on August 31 when I went for my first encounter with the Starfighter in aircraft '633 with Bob Gilliland. The afterburner takeoff and climb left me gasping for breath even though it was a hot (100° F) day. After levelling off at 37,000 feet, we headed northeast into the Edwards AFB supersonic corridor, re-lit the afterburner and galloped out to Mach 1.8, which was the limit on the CF–104D with tip tanks. I was also amazed at how quickly our fuel was being used with the afterburner engaged and at supersonic speed. So it was out of 'burner and back to shoot a few circuits, with a full stop becoming mandatory after about 35 minutes of flying. It would be a gross understatement to say that I was somewhat impressed with the performance of this aircraft. I cannot say the same about the nav/attack systems, because they were hopelessly outside allowable tolerances during most of my 15 hours flying time at Palmdale. In fact, the Litton LN–3 inertial platform toppled on all but one of my first four flights. Despite this, we were having the time of our lives flying this wonderful aircraft.

During their brief stay at Palmdale, "the Originals" had a chance to rub shoulders with some legends in the flight testing business. Ernie Saunders recalls a rather prophetic encounter with Lockheed test pilot, Tony Le Vier…

During our training at Lockheed, it was interesting to meet Tony Le Vier, a very famous racing pilot who was then their Director of Flight Operations. I remember him walking in and saying, "You'll love the '104 except for the stupid nosewheel. I'll bet you any money you will have nosewheel shimmies with it. Lockheed have never built a decent nosewheel, and this goes back to the Lightning." Not two days later, Kenny Lett and I were taking off from Palmdale in a dual and had the first of the nosewheel shimmies and every circuit breaker popped... a million of them. We had so many lights on and the stick shaker going, that we literally didn't know what to do. We kind of just flew around and landed without any idea what was wrong with the aircraft. It took some time - almost a year - before they got a dampening system built in to overcome this problem.

The Palmdale exposure to the CF–104 was over by the end of September. John Hutt's log book records 13 missions, totaling 15 hours 40 minutes flying time. It is interesting to note that all the flying was done in either CF–104D '632 or '633, which were fresh off the Lockheed production line. These two particular aircraft would have remarkably active and varied flying lives, and we will meet them again much later in this book.

With the completion of the Nellis missions and the '104 familiarization course, the RCAF had acquired its nucleus of CF–104 Nuclear Strike pilot experience with which to "get the ball rolling" at the OTU back in Cold Lake. A point of interest is that "the Originals" had not yet soloed in the CF–104D, let alone flown the single-seat version of the aircraft. Bill Paisley recalls the rather humble beginnings of the OTU that fall…

After all the thrills of Nellis and Palmdale, it was a real letdown during our initial days in Cold Lake. The CF–100s had departed some months before and the Station personnel had been enjoying a relaxing summer and fall. We new arrivals were something of a "thorn in their sides"; an unnecessary hindrance to their continued tranquility because we were anxious to get the many essential preparatory actions completed before the CF–104 aircraft started arriving. Therefore, we commenced the intensive training necessary to get ourselves qualified to instruct our first course, which was scheduled to commence in late summer 1962. We did have a few T–33 aircraft, so we were at least able to familiarize ourselves with the weapons range and to pick locations for our tactical targets within the range boundaries. My main task initially, as Chief Flying Instructor, was to utilize all the vast talent and experience of the excellent aircrew that had been selected for the OTU

Above: *Prior to 1969, all CF-104 pilots received their fighter lead-in training on the Canadair Mark 5 Sabre, based at Chatham, New Brunswick.*

Staff to develop our training syllabus, training materiels, training routes, and targets. Although everyone was eager to contribute to the success of our collective assignment, the excessive amount of talent and experience embodied in the OTU Staff (and in fact the first seven courses) presented its own difficulty. Every person selected for the OTU Staff and and the first seven squadrons had the talent and experience to be at least a flight commander, if not a squadron commander. In short, "too many chiefs and not enough indians". This, combined with the inevitable program delays was frustrating for many in the early days of the CF–104 era.

Notwithstanding, we managed to get the syllabus developed, the training materiels prepared, the low level routes designed, the main ranges constructed, and all the tactical targets built in plenty of time. What was late in arriving was the main actor - the aircraft. Although we did not have one person in the group who gave less than his best to assure the success of the OTU, I would be remiss if I did not mention the extraordinary efforts of some outstanding members of this group - without their individual contribution, the OTU training would not have been nearly as effective.

My first thoughts turn to our two USAF exchange officers, Mark Cook and Bill Leitch. We had met Cook at Nellis where he was the F–105 expert at the Fighter Weapons School. Cook provided the depth of knowledge and experience in the application of the CF–104 weapons system that we had yet to acquire. He was instrumental in developing our approach to all-weather operations and radar weapons delivery. Leitch, on the other hand, had extensive knowledge and experience flying the F–104C and came to us from George AFB. He was the driving force behind the development of our main bombing ranges and the construction of our tactical targets. In fact, Leitch led many crews in bitter sub-zero weather, waist deep in snow, building tactical targets during the winter months of 1962. Both were graduate Fighter Weapons Instructors (FWIs), both had extensive experience in Tactical Air Command, and each had his own personality and demeanor. My second thoughts turn to three RCAF Navigators assigned to our Ground School - Flight-Lieutenants Jerry Hunn, Peter Desmedt, and John Allison. They each did a remarkable job of helping us understand the nav/attack systems in the CF–104 and the most practical and effective ways of applying the systems.

John Hutt recalls the events and personalities of those first few months at Cold Lake as well...

We came back from Palmdale at the end of September, 1961. The Base Commander was not fond of fighter pilots, and we had a fair bit of trouble with him. Possibly because of Lett not getting any support, a new Base Commander, Group Captain Mussels, eventually arrived on the scene and was a breath of fresh air. He called Lett into his office and said, "Look, I may be the Base Commander, but I am here in support of you. Anything you want, you will get," and he was true to his word, providing for (in the point of view of Ottawa) some of the most outrageous equipment and people. We got everything we asked for. We were working approximately 90 hours a week and when the first course arrived, the airplane deliveries were all backed up. We still had to get the job done, so we were working Saturdays and Sundays as well. Meanwhile the Supply and Pay Sections were all working their standard eight to ten hours a day, with breaks for lunch, inventory, etc. We explained to Mussels that we couldn't arrive at the wicket between 11:00 a.m. and 12:00 p.m. as we might be 500 miles north trying to find ourselves, and the Base Commander arranged to keep these sections open all day. While they might not have been open on Saturdays and Sundays, they were sure as hell open just about any time we wanted to go over on Monday to Friday. That kind of thing could not have been done without the tender mercies of a guy called Mussels.

On arriving back in Cold Lake we found that eight guys were not sufficient to handle all the OTU requirements. We had previously arranged for Captain Bill Leitch and Captain Mark Cook, both USAF to join us, and they were to be of immeasurable assistance as they had been involved both with the aircraft and in the nuclear kind of flying that we were getting ourselves set up to do. Bill Leitch had flown a fair bit of '104 time. He had been in Vietnam and I believe that when he later volunteered to go back to Vietnam for his third tour, they gave him an appointment with the local psychiatrist. He had also done a lot of Starfighter flying in Spain and had bailed out of a '104 and had lost either portions or all of his kneecaps... we were never too sure if it was this or the Canadian Whisky that caused his walking problems. Bill and Mark were the real diggers around the range. We would set up a route to a target , and Bill would go into the range, disappearing for days on end, and would construct visual targets and reflectors, a skill of which we knew very little. Bill was also instrumental in acquiring old tank hulls, jeeps, and surplus Army junk for the range.

Also augmenting the Squadron were J.T. Price, Ron Russell, Scott McKay, Jack Newsom, Frank Farr, Doug MacLeod, Wes McEwen, Glen Hollingshead...all posted to the OTU after we got back. We were required to train them, and thereby had a pretty sizeable squadron.

All through October and November we flew T–33s, as there were not any '104s available. As a matter of fact, it wasn't until February 3rd that I flew a '104 dual, and March 7th that I flew a single. Paisley had brought the first dual back from Palmdale in January 1962, and we used to use Hill AFB as the staging base for the duals we ferried back with regularity after that. As a point of interest, I had to go down to Customs and explain what we wanted to do because we didn't want to go to Edmonton on these trips, and Cold Lake wasn't a Port of Entry. That was the only time I have ever been treated civilly by Customs. They indicated they were not concerned about the odd package of cigarettes and the odd bottle of wine that came back; they were after the dope and the diamonds. Nonetheless, the system we set up is that we would call as we went by Edmonton just to let them know that we were there, and they reserved the right to bring us in to Edmonton for an inspection on each occasion...but they never did. They probably ***would*** *have had they known how* ***much*** *wine we were bringing back, and how many cigarettes!*

Those were also the days of the Crud game, and we played it pretty rough. In one particular game, Base Commander Mussels was refereeing and using a pool cue to make his point. When J.T. Price began ranting and raving about a particular call that went against him, Mussels broke the pool cue over J.T.'s back just to reinforce his ascendancy. In another game, one of the pilots taking a wide turn to avoid a crushing body check, slid and took Lett and two or three other people right out of play. It was a shambles out there on Friday nights, and it was surprising that no one got seriously hurt.

Ernie Saunders also has some very clear memories of Mussel's term as Base Commander during the early OTU days...

There was a freezing rainstorm during Mussel's tenure, and that storm was followed by an immediate plunge in the temperature to about -40° for weeks on end. We had this 11,000 foot long, 200 foot wide curling rink out there of absolute glare ice. After a couple of weeks of not flying, Mussels had a bright idea and, by God, he would fix this lousy situation. He went out and dumped about 1000 gallons of JP–4 on the runway and threw a match in it, and then we had this huge conflagration. When all the smoke and flames subsided, they had actually polished the runway, and it was even more slippery. Finally they put some plows on it and scraped it and scraped it, and it was well over a month before we had enough bare runway that we could work on. We couldn't handle a cross wind at all because if you ever drifted off the asphalt with your drag chute out, you would be in ***real*** *trouble.*

Arriving in Cold Lake from Palmdale, we were very short of

Permanent Married Quarters (PMQs). It was so bad that some of our airmen were actually living in garages with their families. When Mussels came in, being a "doer" and knowing how to beat the system, he sat on the phone one morning in our flight and called Air Marshal Campbell, who was then Chief of the Air Staff. Mussels said he had made arrangements with a private developer in Calgary to come in and put up PMQs. I understand he had already done one of these Co-Op things at Uplands. Whatever he had done, this sure lit a fire under the Chief of the Air Staff and we had the first 200 of the mobile home-type houses put in some months later. I think all of us who wore light blue can take our hats off to Mussels for getting that job done for us.

As has already been mentioned, the OTU received its first dual on January 16, 1962. Although the first single (12709) was actually delivered in September 1961 for use as a ground maintenance trainer, the first single (henceforth to be referred to as CF–104) for *flying* purposes should have arrived on January 16 as well. However, the ferry pilot undershot the runway on landing in Duluth, Minnesota, causing significant damage to the underside of the aircraft. This aircraft was airlifted back to Canadair, re-inserted into the production line, given a thorough rebuild, and was eventually delivered in May. The first OTU CF–104 (12707) touched down at Cold Lake on March 1st, with '711 and '724 arriving later that month. 6 ST/R OTU now had its first mounts and was ready for business. However, just **getting** the first of the single seaters had been something of an odyssey, as Bill Paisley explains...

On February 8th, I flew to Cartierville to ferry our first Canadair built single seat aircraft to Cold Lake. The aircraft (number '707) had been accepted by the RCAF and was ready for a pre-ferry local flight on February 10th. I had strict instructions from the Commanding Officer RCAF Station Cold Lake, Group Captain Cam Mussels, not to leave Canadair unless all systems were operating to specifications. The Senior Air Staff Officer in Air Defence Command HQ, Group Captain Ralph Ashman, had directed me to get the bird to Cold Lake with haste as we were already over two months behind schedule, and not to be too concerned with the systems as long as safety was not compromised. I test flew the aircraft in the afternoon of February 10th and found both radar and inertial systems were well outside acceptable limits. While I was signing in, I received a telephone call from Cold Lake inquiring about the status of the aircraft. I was given unmistakable direction not to bring it to Cold Lake until the systems performed as advertised. I finished signing in, made arrangements with the line crew to have the unserviceabilities corrected, and returned to my hotel room across the street from Canadair. The telephone was ringing as I entered my room so I rushed to answer it, only to realize that it was Group Captain Ashman, asking why I was not on my way to Cold Lake with '707. My explanation of the defects satisfied him that there were genuine safety concerns, but the next time I got in the cockpit of '707, I was to be on my way. Eleven days later, on February 21st, the aircraft and weather were ready for another flight. The results and the post flight telephone calls were all nearly identical to that which had transpired on February 10th, except that my two superiors agreed that when the aircraft was next serviceable, I would take off with the intention of proceeding to Cold Lake and not return to Cartierville unless there were safety considerations. So it was that on the first day of March, I flew aircraft '707 to Cold Lake with a fuel stop at Duluth. It was a most enjoyable trip - the radar and inertial systems both performed well, and the only problem encountered was an unorthodox afterburner light-off at Duluth. By the end of March, we had aircraft arriving at Cold Lake on a regular basis and the program was really starting to roll.

But Bill Paisley was not the only member of the OTU to have an eventful ferry mission of a new jet out of Canadair. Ernie Saunders recalls...

An amusing incident, although very scary at the time, happened when I was bringing a single back from Montreal and was on takeoff with Jake Mulhall on my wing. As I selected gear up (you can imagine how close I was to the ground) the stick kicker fired full forward. At that time, we had the kickers set to 110 pounds and I just about went in with it - it took two hands to pull the stick back. I flew it holding it with two hands all the way to Cold Lake where I got hold of tower. Bill Leitch told me to switch off the APC switch (which shows you how much I knew about the aircraft) and then it was fine. They subsequently found that there was a computer card problem and this incident was certainly not unknown in the US Air Force.

While 6 ST/R OTU was responsible for proliferating the ranks of qualified CF–104 pilots, another unit at Cold Lake was receiving the aircraft as well. This was the Central Experimental and Proving Establishment (CEPE), predecessor of the present-day Aeronautical Engineering and Test Establishment (AETE). Their fleet originally consisted of the five CF–104s (12701 - 12705) and one CF–104D (12652), and their mandate was to evaluate CF–104 structural modifications and to test weapons deliveries from the aircraft. Over the years, they provided invaluable experience to the Starfighter operational community exploring the edges of the jet's performance envelope in a host of different aircraft configurations as the CF–104 program evolved, matured, and changed.

In order to ease student transition from the venerable T–33 to the sophisticated technology and performance of the CF–104, Ottawa decreed that all potential Starfighter pilots would first complete a three month, 50-hour fighter pilot lead-in course in the trusty F–86 Sabre. This course, consisting of low-level navigation training and air-to-ground weapons familiarization, was conducted at CFB Chatham until Sabre phase-out in December

Above: *12770 keeps American and German Starfighters company during early trials at Lochheed's Palmdale facility. Note the highly streamlined DC-3 in the background.*

1968. After a brief interim period of flying WT–33s, the mantle of fighter lead-in training was ably donned by the CF–5; an aircraft which, in terms of performance, much more closely resembled the Starfighter than its two predecessors.

Ottawa recognized the technological sophistication of the '104 and deferred to it, as we have already seen regarding selection of "the Originals". They further decreed that only experienced fighter pilots, and a few hand-picked "wings" graduates (known as "pipeliners") would fly the aircraft. While the ratio of experienced to inexperienced CF–104 pilot trainees would diminish over the years, the demand for a high entry level of flying skills by the pipeliners would remain constant. Simultaneously with augmenting their aircraft fleet during the early months of 1962, the original fourteen instructors (including the two USAF officers on exchange duties) set about augmenting the flying staff of the OTU. They checked out an additional twenty pilots and one navigator (for radar navigation systems training) before the official commencement of student flying. The first eight student courses were completely dedicated to the formation of a specific Air Division CF–104 squadron. In other words, Course One became 427 Squadron, Course Two became 434 Squadron, and so on.

Since the "learning curve" for both students and staff was quite steep during Course One, the OTU was not yet running like a well-oiled machine, and deadlines for the establishment of the first squadrons in Europe were looming. Indeed, some "shortcuts" were taken in order to graduate this first group of pilots on time. Sam Firth, one of the truly colourful characters of the era,

was a member of Course One. He would later command both 439 and 417 Squadrons, and would become a world-class champion eater of floral centerpieces at a myriad of social functions. He distinctly remembers the somewhat-rushed manner in which that first course was treated...

In late 1961, I and nineteen other pilots received messages to report to the STU at Chatham for Sabre training in the low-level regime. Following that, we went on to Cold Lake, completing the '104 course in November 1962. I think I got about 67 hours. Obviously the Canadian Government, or Hellier, who was then the Minister of Defence, had made a promise that Canada would have a '104 squadron in Europe by the end of 1962, and that was to be done come hell or high water. Our course at Cold Lake was split in half, and I was in the first group which went to 427 Squadron, while the second group went to 434.

Bill Paisley recalls the rationale for these early manning and establishment changes...

At least three factors impeded the acceleration of the program and prevented us from making up lost time. These were (1) runway resurfacing at Cold Lake and the forced deployment to Edmonton; (2) afterburner nozzle bracket failures (Jack Aitken had to eject from dear old '707 just after takeoff from Edmonton); and, (3) by mid-to-late summer, we had so many aircraft on the base at Cold Lake combined with the

Above: *Straight flush - the first five production CF-104s were AETE's stable of Starfighter thoroughbreds in 1963. Note the Sabres on the other side of the apron.*

number of special inspections and shortage of spares that the work load was far in excess of the number of technicians. It became evident that the only way we could come close to meeting the target dates for our commitment to NATO would be to reduce the number of pilots per course by fifty percent. Although Course 1 had already been named and posted to Cold Lake, they were split into two courses to form the nuclei of 427 and 434 Squadrons. The training for these pilots commenced close to the scheduled date, but by that time we had completed less than half the training of OTU staff, so staff training proceeded in parallel with training pilots for the Air Division. From the very beginning of CF–104 flying at Cold Lake, we adopted a policy of flying the serviceable aircraft whenever they were ready for flight, and ground crews were available for start and recovery. This meant early morning starts, long days and seven of them in each week. After a year or so, this grew a little wearisome for some of our staff since they always got "the short end of the stick" with priority going to regular course members. Nonetheless, most of us enjoyed the flying and spirits were generally very high. It was always a challenge to equal or out-shine the course members in a variety of recreational activities.

One of the favourite recreational pastimes was trying to figure out the complex psyche of the succeeding Base Commander to the much admired and respected Group Captain Mussels. John Hutt explains...

Dudley used to lie in wait, and when he saw an aircraft land inside the first 3000 feet of runway, he became extremely upset. He would roar down the taxiway after the pilot in his car, subsequently balling him out. He was so concerned about landing short that he had a yellow line painted on the runway, and God help anyone landing short of it. We used to think it would be fine to run off the other end, but not to land short.

He also had a fetish about cigarette butts on the floor of the Mess, and couldn't understand why pilots couldn't walk across the room to a table and butt their cigarettes in the ashtray. He therefore had about six large ashtrays built and placed them strategically around the Mess, feeling this would clean up the situation. Well, at the next Friday night thrash, the guys saw all these ashtrays, but of course if they were not standing by one, they dropped their butts on the floor as they always had. What really had to be done was to provide one ashtray per pilot to eliminate the problem. However, when Dudley came in the next Saturday morning to look around, the place was a disaster, and in fact the expense he had gone to in order to provide these ashtrays had done absolutely no good at all. So somebody pointed out, "Well, it's because the ashtray's over there, and the pilot's over here!", so Dudley thought, "I'll fix that," and he put wheels on the ashtrays so that as a pilot walked around the lower bar, he could drag this ashtray behind him. What he didn't reckon on was the native skill and cunning of a fighter pilot, and especially a pilot who has had a number of drinks, and who is intent on chasing the nurses and school teachers that used to infiltrate our Friday nights. What ended up happening was that we thought that these things would make ***great*** *seats for racing. We would put a school teacher in each ashtray and then race them across the floor. This went on for about several hours. The next morning when Dudley came in, all his ashtrays were broken. He was beside himself, and I don't think he ever really recovered from Cold Lake. I can imagine that he would have gone bonkers if he had actually seen some of the races... teachers with their legs and skirts high in the air being propelled with great speed and no dexterity across the floor by the liquor-enhanced pilots.*

Dave McIntosh's flying time in the CF–104 spans almost the enitre service life of the aircraft itself. His first flight was on July 19, 1962, as a lowly Flying Officer and member of the first student course. His last, however, was on July 19, 1985, as Base Commander, CFB Baden-Soellingen. Dave recalls the early "teething troubles" associated with Course One back in 1962, which resulted in the Course being split into two squadrons, and the requirement to respond to a truly flexible flying schedule...

The fact that Courses One and Two graduated with even as many hours as they did [1] *was at the expense of the OTU staff. Many of them, who were upgrading and not directly involved in instructing us, spent a lot of frustrating time just sitting around and waiting. Even just getting four aircraft together for a four plane formation mission was a scheduling officer's coup. We flew seven days a week. I can recall our Flight Commander, Ernie Saunders, combing the barracks early on a Sunday morning, trying to find a course member to fly a fourth aircraft on a formation trip which had suddenly evolved. None of us were feeling the best - it was a sunglasses and dark visors morning - and we were hoping that Ernie would not be able to find anyone. Unfortunately he did, and led by our fearless staff pilot John Hutt, I took off along with course mates Pudge Marshall and Pete Russell. It was a maximum 60° of bank, 2 "G" "gentleman's trip". However, when we landed, we all looked like we had been in a constant two-hour dogfight.*

To say that the daily routine of a student Starfighter pilot was full would be an understatement. From dawn to dusk, and often after dusk, the students were bombarded with aircraft operating instructions, inertial navigation theory, emergency procedures, radar navigation, bombing, and reconnaissance. They also studied a myriad of academic subjects relating to nuclear weapons theory and delivery, and other tactical considerations. Before students could be expected to cope with radar navigation at "seven plus" miles a minute in the CF–104, they got a chance to practice it at approximately two miles a minute in a specially converted DC–3. In all, three hybrid Dakotas were modified with CF–104 nose cones and equipped with the aircraft's radar and inertial navigation systems. One of these aircraft was aptly named "Pinocchio"; one of the few printable monickers this bizarre aircraft would earn over the years. About the time that students were beginning to despair of ever seeing a CF–104 "in the flesh" during the six month conversion course, it was time to head down to the flight line and log what would be at that time the first of approximately 90 hours of syllabus flying. It is at this point that the love affair between man and machine, if not already in full bloom, would begin.

And so by the end of 1962, the OTU was well and truly on its way, with the first graduate Starfighter pilots Europe bound. It is only appropriate that Bill Paisley, who as Chief Flying Instructor had been so instrumental in establishing the program, should have the last word on these earliest of CF–104 days...

Regrettably, all was not happiness. We lost a number of the RCAF's finest post-WW II fighter pilots during those early years at Cold Lake. Some due to aircraft malfunctions, like Jake Mulhall who experienced an oil pump failure and ejected just after lift-off during a touch-and-go, only to be consumed by the resulting fireball after a successful ejection and chute deployment. Others lost their lives as a result of the hazards of low level, high speed flight and a fraction of a second of inattention. Notwithstanding these tragic losses of first-class Canadians, I believe that the CF–104 program from start to finish was a great success and a memorable part of Canadian military aviation history. The aircraft was inappropriately dubbed "the widow-maker" by the press. It was a great aircraft, a pilot's aircraft; it fit like a glove and was respected and loved by all who flew it. I am very happy and proud to have been associated with CF–104 operations from the beginning to the end, at 6 OTU as Chief Flying Instructor and Officer Commanding, in 1 Air Division as CO 430 Squadron and as a Staff Officer, and in both 1 Canadian Air Group and Fighter Group as Commander.

[1] Many of the students on the first two courses were significantly short-changed in flying hours and syllabus missions, in order to expedite their arrival in Europe.

Down to Business

After successful completion of the OTU course, the new graduates were posted to Europe for duties with NATO and the Canadian Air Division. As was mentioned earlier, 427 Squadron was the first student course to graduate in November, 1962. While the pilots were honing their flying skills at Cold Lake, their aircraft were already arriving at their home base in Zweibrucken, West Germany. In an operation known as Rho Delta (Greek for 104), RCAF C–130 Hercules transports had delivered 19 CF–104s to Zweibrucken by New Year's Day, 1963. In fact, all CF–104s delivered to Europe, with the exception of a staged flyover in the aircraft's twilight years, would be delivered by Hercules from the Canadair plant. In order to make the journey, technicians removed the empennage, wings, and nose cones of each jet, *squeezed* it into the belly of a Herc, and delivered it to Zweibrucken approximately 10 flying hours and 3200 nautical miles later. By summer 1965, the Air Division's strength would consist of 133 CF–104s and 19 CF–104Ds; 18 European-based Starfighters having been lost by that time in accidents.

The "big picture" game plan for CF–104 operations in Europe envisaged basing at four Wings; two each in France and Germany. The primary role of all squadrons was Nuclear Strike, with a limited secondary capability in Reconnaissance.

In order to have a proper reception committee waiting for the Starfighter at the European end of the Rho Delta airlifts, the RCAF shipped the first CF–104 technicians to Zweibrucken during the fall of 1962. John McKee was an airframe technician at that time and a member of the initial Starfighter maintenance cadre. John recalls a rather bumpy flight overseas and some of the earlier problems associated with establishing the '104 at its new German home…

We left for overseas the last weekend of September 1962 from Trenton. That particular Yukon damned near wound up in the North Atlantic. West of Ireland, we fell 10,000 feet; from 19,000 feet to 9000 feet! Wally Norton had been sleeping and I had been dozing when this occurred. With his eyes the size of saucers, Wally looked at me, then out the window to see the wing coming back to normal. Those wings had flexed about twenty degrees… who says those times were uneventful! We continued on to Marville, France, where buses were waiting to

Above: *Sometimes it was successful…CF104 12721 unloading at Zweibrucken on 12 October 1962 as part of Exercise Rho Delta. This was the first CF-104 to arrive in Europe.* **Inset:** *And sometimes it wasn't…the loading ramp of RCAF Hercules 10301 tries to amputate the radome of CF104D 12634 at Marville in September 1964.*

whisk us off to 3 Wing at Zweibrucken.

3 Wing wasn't prepared for us, or even aware of our exodus from Canada...we literally descended on the place. We were actually settled into quarters fairly quickly, but signing on the Base created a problem. As a group, we had to go to the Supply Section for a Base Defence Force kit and other bits and pieces. A sergeant greeted us with, "We weren't expecting a group like this." Sergeant George Watier was standing at the supply desk in the front of our group. Standing towards the back, I piped up, "Hey, George, you better tell him there's another 400 behind us." You could see the supply sergeant wilt. One had to give him credit though. Within weeks we had our supplies fairly well set up.

Then the first of the '104s started coming in, tucked in the bellies of Hercs, and I was there to put the first of them together. When they were completed, all systems checks had to be carried out... hydraulics, communications, avionics, and then an engine run-up.

Now the '104 is not a normal aircraft on run-up, and Zweibrucken was in for a rude awakening! The first run-up occurred on a weekday at nine o'clock in the evening, and involved myself as the airframe tech, Clive Whelton and Stormy Blizzard as engine techs, and Sam Parcher as the avionics tech.

After refuelling, the aircraft was towed to its run-up spot, which happened to be on the west side of the Base by the snag hanger. With no noise suppressor, the tail was facing west over the top of the hill and the city. It was one of the few spots where the aircraft could be tied down for run-up.

The four of us were grinning. We knew what was going to happen. I said, "It will take half an hour or so; then we'll know."

We started the run-up at low throttle settings, so I could carry out all my hydraulics and flight control checks, and avionics could carry out all their checks. As for the engine, things were just beginning...

With all primary checks done, the engine tech started his checks. The throttle advanced, the variable blades on the first stage of the compressor took their bite, and then the god-awful screaming started. It's a racket one has to hear to believe. For fuel system flow checks and oil system checks, the throttle is slowly advanced to 100 percent, then dropped back for stabilization and temperature checks. Following that, the throttle is advanced to approximately 70 percent, and then slammed forward beyond 100 percent to full afterburner for the Emergency Nozzle Closure System (ENCS) check. A tremendous bang occurs, with a sound like Hell breaking loose! An absolute banshee scream! That was the '104s arrival to 3 Wing. True to form, when we started the run-up at nine, Squadron Leader Clarke, the Station Aircraft Engineering Officer, arrived at 9:30 p.m. and we had to shut things down. We found out that the Zweibrucken mayor had caused quite a fuss. Within time, he was to raise absolute hell with the evening run-ups, and we were eventually given a time beyond which run-ups couldn't be done.

On December 16, 1962, Wing Commander P.B. St. Louis formally handed over 427 Squadron to Wing Commander R.G. Middlemiss at Zweibrucken. While the first CF–104 Squadron in Europe was now officially "in place", their fleet of aircraft had not yet completely caught up with them. Middlemiss and his eleven pilots were very keen to establish themselves, as well as to develop and refine many new techniques and tactics, including high speed low-level radar navigation and various types of nuclear weapons deliveries. However, the miserable winter flying weather, combined with limited aircraft availability, various mechanical "teething troubles", and the necessary Wing orientation to the new aircraft would preclude an immediate all-out assault on the new Strike/Attack role. The aircraft, once assembled, lacked some weapons systems and in fact, the weapons to use them with, since Canada had not yet finalized the terms of the nuclear custody agreement with the United States, and no conventional weapons (including a gun) were available for Canada to use as an interim measure with the aircraft. Thus, the Lions of 427 Squadron were temporarily "toothless lions". Their CF–104s were warplanes without a war load of any nature, armed only with practice bombs. Sam Firth recalls these lean times at Zweibrucken...

ORIGINAL BASING PLAN FOR CF-104S IN EUROPE

WING	SQNS.	SYMBOL	COURSE	ACTIVATION DATE	ROLE
#1 Wing Marville, France	439	Sabre Tooth Tiger	8	March 1964	Strike/Reconnaissance
	441	Silver Fox	7	January 1964	Strike/Reconnaissance
#2 Wing Grostenquin, France	421	Red Indian	6	December 1963	Strike/Reconnaissance
	430	Silver Falcon	5	September 1963	Strike/Reconnaissance
#3 Wing Zweibrucken, West Germany	427	Lion	1	December 1962	Strike/Reconnaissance
	434	Bluenose	2	April 1963	Strike/Reconnaissance
#4 Wing Baden-Soellingen, West Germany	422	Tomahawk	4	July 1963	Strike/Reconnaissance
	444	Cobra	3	May 1963	Strike/Reconnaissance

*Twelve of us arrived at Zweibrucken two weeks before Christmas in 1962. Accommodation was very scarce, and many of the chaps lived in one-room hotel rooms with their young kids over Christmas. Things were not very pleasant, but I suppose that's no never mind...the thing that bothered us most of all was that there were no airplanes to fly. We sat around Zweibrucken for a month as the aircraft were being flown in by Hercules from Canadair, and of course they had to be put together, checked, airtested. We **did** begin limited flying in mid-January, and it built up slowly after that. However, all we were doing was flying... no bombs, no guns, no gun sights, as the Canadian Government wrestled with the perceived problem of acquiring nuclear weapons. It was at least a full year that we flew around Europe as essentially unarmed warriors. I don't know what we would have done if a war started...the flight line joke was that we were over there to ram other aircraft. It was not until late 1963 or early 1964 that the Canadian and U.S. Governments signed a nuclear agreement, and we began serious training and learning of procedures to accompany the arrival of nuclear weapons.*

Soon, however, the hurdles facing the Lions were overcome, and they were going aloft with ever-increasing frequency. They were joined at Zweibrucken in January by the second half of the original split course, otherwise known as Course Two, and now known as the reconstituted 434 Squadron. Under the able command of Wing Commander O.B. Philp, the Bluenosers flew their first European sortie in the CF–104 on February 4, 1963; and after the official handover on April 8th, they joined their brothers at 427 in going about the business of becoming combat ready in the demanding low-level Strike role.

Dave McIntosh recalls those earliest of days with 434 Squadron at Zweibrucken...

I arrived at Zweibrucken in January'63, with my wife Mado and the two oldest boys, who were both still in diapers. Europe was in the throes of one of its worst winters in the past 100 years, and all of us had to stay at Marville for three or four days because the roads were ice-covered. The Squadron pilots travelled with their families as a group, and most had young children. Needless to say, by the time everyone got to Zweibrucken and moved into their respective quarters, all were beat. As usual, it was the wives who bore the brunt and coped with the new environment, the kids, and the husbands.

*I vividly recall some of the early radar CPM trips that we flew. We were still using the tracing paper, do-it-yourself radar predictions...and the majority of us got lost and **stayed** lost until we could sight the ground and figure out where we were. There were a few, very few, that had it aced right off the bat - even to the extent of "breaking out the barges on the Rhine". On one trip, I was paying more attention to the radar and other instruments than the clock, and when I **did** see the ground and the cloud broke away, I passed an airfield with some fighter aircraft that I instantly recognized as "not ours". I left for home ASAP, as fast and as low as I dared. There was no reception for me when I taxied back into the dispersal, nor was anyone waiting for me when I signed in. For the next two weeks, my heart thumped every time the phone in the flight room rang, or the boss called me. I got away with it, but I never forgot it - another lesson learned. The early days of radar CPM proficiency flying were best summed up by one of the pilots who, after landing, said, "Well, I think I broke out Germany today."*

Phil Perry spent a long and distinguished portion of his career as an Aircraft Engineering Officer on '104s. Arriving at Zweibrucken in April 1963, Phil vividly recalls some of the earlier teething troubles with the aircraft...

It was great to see so many familiar faces in the pilots of the two squadrons from Sabre days in Europe, and during their training in Chatham. This was the start of another great tour with the best pilots and groundcrew in the world; and for what lay ahead in this new program, we certainly required both.

*In the maintenance program were two old friends; Flight-Lieutenant Gordie Pitts in charge of Maintenance and Repair, and Flight-Lieutenant Gerry Cuttance, who headed Servicing and Snags. I was assigned to Servicing and Snags, which looked after the flight line (launching and recovery) and "de-snagging", or repair after flights. There were very few recoveries done at the flight line as most aircraft returned directly to the Snag Hangar for repair after flying, and many **before** flying. This, of course, is normal for a new aircraft, however, the '104 was a lot more demanding than most. It was so bad for awhile that our Snag crews couldn't believe it when an aircraft taxied back to the flight line after a flight, in which case they would either give a cheer, or mumble, "Bloody pilot is probably lost."*

*I have never seen groundcrew work as hard as they did during the early days of the '104 program. Our Snags crews worked both a day and a night shift; the latter of which was scheduled to end at midnight. We had two NCOs in charge of these shifts - Flight Sergeants Gil Gilcrest and Sam Hupka; two very dedicated and knowledgeable senior technicians, backed up by prime tradesmen. They worked for maximum serviceability, and it was not unusual for the night shift to be still at work when the day shift came in. We finally had to put a curfew in effect; no work after 0300 hours unless we were below a certain serviceability rate. I can still see Gil and Sam telling me what they thought of **that** one, and what the so-and-sos could do with it.*

The shortage of spare parts was one of our major problems, and resulted in a "rob" program. However, this was closely controlled with a maximum number of items permitted for removal off any one aircraft. There was a lot of engine swapping back and forth, which kept our Maintenance Test Pilot, Bob Ayres, busy each morning.

An unfortunate incident took place during this period, when we lost a CF–104 aircraft which caught fire during an engine ground run-up in a modified Zulu[1] *hangar off the end of the runway. The aircraft was tied down with a cable for the run-up and it was impossible to disconnect it because of the fire, which was difficult to fight in the hangar. Nonetheless, they **did** save the front section of the aircraft, much to the joy of Corporal Jake Frizzel, our Navigation System expert who immediately grabbed the LN–3 computer. Oh yes, we also got a spare tail section which was not on the aircraft during the engine run-up, so all was not completely lost.*

At first the former Sabre pilots from both squadrons were "having their eyes watered" by the bad weather, poor visibility, and extreme density of traffic in their new low-level environment. Since there were very few restrictions to low-level flight in Europe at the time, the Zweibrucken CF–104s roamed the skies at 500 feet (or less) with relative impunity, passing over many of the landmarks that others had seen from Spitfires and Lancasters a generation earlier. In order to hone their bombing skills, 3 Wing Starfighters became regular visitors to several European practice bombing ranges, such as Vliehors range in the Netherlands and Suippes range in France.

Ralph Annis, who flew '104s with both 427 Squadron, and later as CO of 421 Squadron recalls the early days of the Starfighter era at Zweibrucken...

At Zwei, the true test of our expertise began. We had our fair share of snags in the early going, but the most frustrating problems were associated with the gyros of the LN–3 inertial navigation system. They didn't seem to last more than 25 hours before the whole unit went tits up. In fact, the situation got so bad that it was suggested that the gyros be hand-carried in special boxes from Canada to Germany to ensure that no damage would occur in transit.

I was Deputy Squadron Commander of 427 for only a short time before being appointed as the Wing Tac Eval Officer. In addition, I was appointed Operations Officer of the Operational Capability Trails Unit for the CF–104 in Europe, and those jobs were both challenging and most interesting. As part of the Trials Unit, one of our duties was to evaluate the inertial system in all its modes. During one of those trips using the Dead Reckoning Mode, I inadvertently made it into East Germany. My exit was just under supersonic speed, and as low as I could get the machine. Nothing came of this little incident, probably because I did not report it.

One other incident frightened the daylights out of me, and that occurred on my third trip of the day when I was feeling mighty chipper. I asked for a low pass by the tower, and as I was screaming over the taxiway, who taxied out but Group Captain Laubman, our Base Commander. I eyeballed him for split second, pulled up, and meekly joined the circuit. Group Captain Laubman made me shake in my boots for a full 24 hours before he called me about that bit of low flying.

*One of my most enjoyable jobs at Zweibrucken was demonstrating, along with my old Golden Hawk buddy John Price, the capability of the aircraft; and it **was** a capable aircraft. With takeoff flap and full bore, I could turn that sucker within the length of the runway by holding it in shaker, with only a rare kick of the stick! I recall on one trip meeting two Mirage IIIs at 35,000 feet who were willing to play. They were **no** match for the '104 at making supersonic passes and a vertical yo-yo where you came over the top at 50,000 feet plus.*

We designed and flew our own routes all over West Germany, the Low Countries and France, both day and night. During the day, it was

[1] Alert hangar

eyeball and LN–3, but at night it was mostly radar and LN–3. The mission started with a strip map, manufactured by the pilots with the help of the Intelligence Section. We started using many hundreds of maps in cut-and-paste exercises, but before long had built a bank of route maps covered in plastic that we could use over and over again. This is when radar prediction came into its own since our individual efforts at using a grease pencil on the plastic overlay to give a radar shadow effect was, at best, woefully amateurish.

One of my many interesting jobs was to evaluate the gold visor coming into use for nuclear warfare to prevent flash blindness. I was given the first gold-plated visor, threatened with my life if I damaged it, and told to evaluate it…but only in the CF–104D and never solo. Of course, they wanted the results in a rush, and in those days our dual aircraft were mostly unserviceable. Naturally, the trial was done in the single seat machine with no problems encountered.

With the new radar predictions, our squadrons became as accurate in cloud or on the darkest night as we were in the daytime. Before going to Germany, I thought, "Oh boy… 500 feet at 540 knots in the middle of the night is going to be a real terrifying experience," but we did it, and most of us really enjoyed it. One major advancement that came along was the Ground Speed Readout. When the LN–3 was working as advertised, we merely had to crank open the throttle so that the ground speed was the same as the flight planned speed, and ergo, we were at our turning points and on target well within the allowable ten seconds.

Even though lights on the ground looked mighty close on many occasions, one night while flying along near the Vosges Mountains, I noticed out of the corner of my eye that the lights were ***unusually*** *close. I pulled up to my safe altitude and began to check a few things. Two of the pages of my strip map had stuck together when I had flipped into a new course. Another minute or two and I would have been splattered all over the French countryside. A sobering moment.*

Dave Girling was a Sabre pilot with 427 Squadron at Zweibrucken in 1962, and he was caught in the throes of the Starfighter transition. Since at that time he was ineligible for the CF–104 program, he was assigned to the Operational Capability Trials Unit with Ralph Annis. Dave recalls a Zweibrucken-hosted event at which the guests of honour undoubtedly later wished that they had stayed at home…

The Great Zweibrucken Helicopter Caper

When the first '104s began operating out of Zweibrucken, Search and Rescue service was provided by a U.S. Army helicopter outfit located about 14 kilometers down the road at Pirmasens. Someone suggested that it might be a nice thing to invite the pilots to a beer call at the Mess in Zwei. An invitation was duly issued and accepted, and at about 1630 hours on the appointed day, a beautiful sunny Friday in

Below: *John Hutt defies gravity in a heavily-laden '895 at Zweibrucken in 1963.*

June, the U.S. Army pilots arrived by bus. They were joined at the Mess by their Canadian hosts, and the early round of drinks began. At about 1800 hours, the sound of an approaching helicopter was heard in the bar. The U.S. visitors explained that their standby crew had been authorized to fly over for the beer call when their standby period was over; they would then fly the aircraft back to Pirmasens the next day. As the noise increased, it became obvious to all that the helicopter was about to land on or near the Mess parking lot. The bar of the Mess emptied, everyone with drink in hand, slipped through a rear door which gave unlimited view of the parking lot, and sure enough, there was a helicopter on approach to land.

The captain of the helicopter was a U.S. Army Captain; the co-pilot was a U.S. Army Major, qualified on type, but new on the squadron. They had been cleared to hold on a visual fix off the airdrome until some CF–104 traffic landed. However, the Captain, who had been to the Officer's Mess before, hatched the following plan: they would land on the Officers' Mess parking lot where the Captain would disembark. The Major would return to the holding fix and land on the Helipad when cleared. Meanwhile, the Captain would organize transportation for the Major from the Helipad to the Mess. The Captain landed the helicopter on the Mess parking lot according to plan (and to the applause of the gallery assembled behind the Mess), passed control to the Major, and hopped out. The Major increased power and commenced his takeoff. However, as he transitioned to forward flight over the parking lot, he saw out of the corner of his eye, a cable. What he did ***not*** *see was that the cable ran to the edge of the parking lot where it ran down a pole and continued underground. Thinking that he was going to hit the cable, he instinctively pulled up and lost control of the aircraft. The helicopter then rolled over to the inverted position, and fell to earth on top of Al Hoar's and John Hutt's cars.*

The main rotor shattered, and the tail rotor broke off and circulated around the parking lot inscribing cars at random. The parking lot was, of course, awash with 80/87 Avgas[1]. Fortunately, however, the cockpit was suspended between the two cars. Furthermore, the pilot was suspended upside-down in his harness, his head only inches from the pavement, dazed, but miraculously unhurt.

Needless to say, the gallery was stunned. The first person to swing into action was Dr. Lorne Gazely, the Station Medical Officer. He ran through the fuel to the aircraft and rescued the Major from the cockpit. (To my knowledge, Dr. Gazely's courage during this incident was never recognized.) The beer call was quickly replaced by MP cordons around the crash site, and as far as I know, the invitation to the fine folks at Pirmasens was never renewed. The U.S. Army court-martialed the Major and Captain, then reduced both by one rank, and life went on.

An example of the zany crowd that populated the place at the time was found at the quarterly Mess meeting, which was held on the Friday following the helicopter accident. At the end of the meeting, the President of the Mess Committee (PMC) asked if anyone had any other items of business to bring up before a motion of adjournment was invited. Flight-Lieutenant "Pudge" Marshall rose and said that he would like to take the opportunity to congratulate the Mess Entertainment Committee on the spectacular exhibition staged in the Mess parking lot last Friday, and could the rumour be confirmed that a mid-air collision was scheduled for the beer call following today's Mess meeting!

Early during the tenure of the CF–104 at Zweibrucken, it became apparent that the occasionally fickle, often downright atrocious, low level flying weather (particularly in winter) was going to pose a serious threat to aircrew operational effectiveness. The Sabre jock of the '50s was not as affected by the weather as his CF–104 counterpart, since the bulk of Sabre training was done at high level. Conversely, the Starfighter pilot's regime was "in the weeds", and in order to maintain a continuity of training and expertise in weapons deliveries throughout the year, something had to be done.

Accordingly, Canada "bought into" a time-share plan of air-to-ground weapons ranges at Decimomannu on the island of Sardinia. For many years, the Canadian detachment at Decci witnessed memorable events and a whole succession of mellow aircrew and support groundcrew, as all CF–104 squadrons in the Air Division took turns deploying there for their annual "gun camps", called Exercise Sardinia Salvos, which were conducted on the Capo Frasca range.

Dave Girling would later serve an operational tour on CF–104s with 441 Squadron at Baden-Soellingen, but during the early '60s, he was posted to Decci as the Personnel Administration Officer, and remained there for over two years. Dave recalls life at that time as a member of a happy group of expatriate Canadians braving the wilds of Sardinia...

The Base at Decimomannu was built with NATO funds, and also served as an alternate/diversionary base for the U.S. Sixth Fleet. The Air Weapons Training Unit (AWTU) was operated at Decci by the Italian Air Force (IAF). The cost of operating the base was paid by Germany (50%), Canada (25%), and Italy (25%), and the air and ground range time was theoretically apportioned in accordance to these percentages. I say theoretically because it was usually possible to find extra range periods from one or other of the users. The Base Commander was an Italian Air Force Colonel; the German and Canadian detachments were each commanded by Lieutenant Colonel equivalents and considered by their respective services to be "self accounting" units.

The Canadian Detachment (known in the RCAF as the Air Weapons Unit, or AWU) was comprised of about 80 permanent personnel, almost all of whom were married and accompanied by their families. These personnel were augmented by about 45 groundcrew, deployed from the Air Division Wings to provide the line servicing crews. Barrack accommodation and messing facilities for the deployed air and ground crews were at the Base, while almost all families lived in rented civilian accommodation in the Poetto area, about 22 miles from the Base, but close to the public beaches just outside Cagliari. Poetto was easily identified by the prominent rock formation at one end known as "The Devil's Saddle".

The Poetto apartments occupied by the Canadian families were designed and built as summer beach accommodation. With their high ceilings, marble floors and complete lack of any built-in heating systems, they were a challenge to heat during the wet and blustery winter months. This challenge was usually met with the ubiquitous Aladdin heater with its circular kerosene wick, guaranteed to spew sooty smoke unless trimmed daily with surgical precision. The kerosene was obtained in either Jerry cans or drums, with special coupons from the local Esso bulk distributor, whose regular business hours remained a mystery, even to the Esso staff, I believe.

One other memorable feature of the Poetto area was the frequent power failures. More than one family found themselves groping around a strange apartment in the dark on the evening of their arrival, and quickly found that emergency candles and flashlights were standard equipment.

The cold and inconvenience of the short winter were more than offset by the truly fabulous summers. From the beginning of June until the end of September, every day was perfect beach weather. The Poetto beaches were usually very crowded on weekends, so many Canadian families drove an hour or so from Cagliari, where two or three families could share a mile or more of pristine beach with fine white sand and azure blue water. Many beaches were framed by rocky formations which provided outstanding snorkeling and scuba diving.

Canadian visitors and residents alike will remember the Maple Leaf Club, a very small former hotel building leased by Non-Public Finds (NPF) to provide an all-ranks Mess. In addition to a bar and snack bar, it also housed a small grocery store, a library, and rooms for Guides and Scouts, as well as a very persistent cockroach colony that just wouldn't quit. However, it was the only place in town where one could find a hamburger and french fries, and was therefore also popular with the crews of ships of the U.S. Sixth Fleet which were sporadic visitors to the Port of Cagliari.

Also located in Poetto was a U.S. Coast Guard Loran monitoring station. This was commanded by a Master Warrant Officer (MWO) and manned by a total of about nine enlisted U.S. Coast Guard personnel, all of whom were accorded membership in the Maple Leaf Club as well as provided with car licensing, gas coupons, etc. It was nice to be able to extend to this group some of the "creature comforts" extended to us so generously by the U.S. forces in other parts of Europe.

Another unique feature at Decci was the "Pilot's Bus". In about 1964, all Air Division pilots made a one-time contribution of $10 to a fund set up to provide an alternative to the Italian Air Force (IAF) bus service. A VW van was purchased and licensed, and made available to each group of Air Division pilots deployed to Decci. A small mileage fee was paid for actual use. When the RCAF finally withdrew from Decci, this van (rebuilt and replaced several times) was moved to Baden-Soellingen where it continued to provide yeoman service as Friday night Mess transportation, as well as a casual moving van and temporary transportation for whoever needed it.

One incident that comes to mind from the times in Decci was on July 5, 1965, when Dave Thom experienced an engine failure while downwind in the air-to-ground bombing pattern at Capo Frasca. Unable to restart the engine, he ejected, and both he and his aircraft

[1] Fuel from the helicopter

entered the water. He was quickly rescued by one of the range rescue boats, but the lost aircraft posed a frustrating problem. It was thought that the engine failure was caused by a faulty Main Fuel Control Unit (MFCU), a component suspected of causing at least one other earlier aircraft loss. This couldn't be proved, of course, unless the suspect component could be retrieved and inspected.

The main problem was to locate the wreck on the ocean floor, as no accurate fix had been made on its position. Fortunately, the water was not deep off the west coast of Capo Frasca, but the wreck could have been anywhere in a fairly large area. Flight-Lieutenant Phil Perry, the Maintenance Officer at the time, Corporal "Newf" Faulkner, a Metal Tech and improvisor extraordinaire, and several of the RCAF Sardo Squids scuba club, designed and built a tubular metal sled with control surfaces which allowed some underwater maneuvering while the sled was towed behind a boat. After several days of trolling, the wreckage was finally located. The engine was subsequently raised, and the MFCU definitely identified as the cause of the engine failure. There is no doubt that this dogged persistence resulted in preventing future '104 engine failures.

Phil Perry also remembers the frustrations of this particular incident...

Underwater Recovery

In May of 1964, I was posted to the Air Weapons Unit at Decimomannu, Sardinia. My position was Chief Technical Officer, which included Aircraft Maintenance, Motor Transport, Construction Engineering, and trying to keep peace with the Italians through my NCO in-charge workshops and interpreter, the late "Newfie" Graham Faulkner. This was a great tour... interesting work, great people, and living on the Italian Riviera. You could plan every weekend at the beach from March through until November.

One of the incidents I well remember was a voluntary salvage operation of a crashed CF–104, July 5, 1965, off Capo Frasca, Sardinia. Rough seas, language problems, international rivalries and unmarked locations were among the problems encountered.

F/L Dave Thom's aircraft suffered a flame-out on that day over the Mediterranean. He ejected and parachuted to safety in the sea, where he was picked up by an Italian Air Force (IAF) rescue helicopter.

Later the same day, I was taken to Capo Frasca by IAF helicopter, but was unable to check the crash scene because the IAF ops officer wouldn't clear the range of aircraft for the chopper. Consequently, the crash scene was not marked by a buoy.

The next day when we carried out a short air search, we could not spot any wreckage or oil slick. On July 7th, LCol. Fatagati, LACs James, Lukawitski, and I travelled to the village of Tumnaria, where the colonel interviewed local residents and got information from the two eye-witnesses to the crash. We went to the crash scene in fisherman Armando Poma's 15 foot boat. The fisherman had attempted to rescue F/L Thom, but was beaten to the scene by an IAF helicopter. LAC James and I carried out a 30–minute dive to depths ranging from 80 to 100 feet without any results.

So it went through several days, while the divers constructed an underwater sled at Decci which could be towed behind a boat and would permit a controlled depth and direction of underwater searching.

Since Air Division had decreed that the Italian Air Force would be the lead agency in the search, the Canadians had to wait for the arrival of the Italian Navy, who were supposed to be fully equipped for the operation.

Photo: *'799 overflies the flightline at Decimomannu, Sardinia. The aircraft parked directly below this CF-104 are Luftwaffe F-84s.*

When the navy (three mine sweepers) arrived, using Italian Navy Scuba divers we discovered that the navy started work when they felt like it and quit every day at 1400 hours. Our divers would have liked to work later.

On July 17th, the fisherman, Armando Poma, who had been an eyewitness to the crash, caught some wreckage from the aircraft in his net, and the Italian Navy raised the engine from a depth of around 100 feet. LCol. Fatagati had offered a 50,000 lire reward for finding the wreckage, and this was subsequently paid to Poma.

CFHQ requested further salvage efforts to recover the fuel control components on July 26th, and a week later, three qualified volunteer scuba divers from the Salvage Section at 1 Wing arrived to help in the search. Again, the operation was to be carried out under the control of the Italian Navy, which was due to arrive on August 4th. Finally on August 6th, after further delays, the divers (LACs Shaw, Stock, Bowman and Lukawitski) married up with the Italian Navy at Capo Frasca.

Unfortunately, the crash site was not marked, so again a search had to be carried out to locate the wreckage. The divers carried out a 20–minute dive to a depth of 100 feet in the area thought to be the crash scene, but no wreckage was found. Although the same Italian Navy personnel were on the boat as were involved in recovery of the engine, none of them seemed to have any idea of the location of the crash scene; nor would they take advice from other people, including the fisherman, Poma. The RCAF personnel were becoming very disgusted and morale was very low.

On August 10th, LAC Faulkner joined the divers' group as interpreter, and I joined as co-ordinator and volunteer diver. LCol. Fatagati went out in the boat with us in an attempt to pinpoint the crash location, as he had been on the Italian Navy boat when the engine was recovered.

LCol. Fatagati said that the aircraft could be seen from the surface, so all the divers carried out a very extensive surface search using snorkels and masks. Two of the divers became seasick in the rough sea. Later, LACs Shaw, Stack, and I carried out 20–minute dives to a depth of 120 feet, but no wreckage was sighted.

The next day, we hired a smaller boat with a motor to tow the underwater sled. This proved an excellent method of searching, as the boat kept the diver on course and a larger area was covered. All five divers carried out two dives each at depths ranging from 60 to 100 feet, and the canopy and seat pack were found.

On August 12th, I contacted AWU Ops and advised the Chief Ops Officer where the canopy and seat pack had been located. By knowing the speed and direction of the aircraft at bail out, we were able to determine a more accurate crash site. But the Italian Navy people did not agree, and insisted that we search in the area where the ejection materials were found. We all carried out two dives to a depth of 70 feet, but found nothing.

The Italian Navy failed to show on August 13th - they later said they had missed the boat when it left the dock at Capo Frasca - so I hired Armando Poma as a guide. Using the underwater sled, we located the wreckage in less than two hours. The wreckage lay on a flat reef at a depth of 75 feet. All divers carried out one dive each, but no wreckage was removed because the sea became too rough. The site was marked with two buoys, and operations ceased for the day.

The next day the buoys had disappeared; however, a short search using the sled found the site again. LAC James had joined us, so all six divers carried out two dives each, and all the required parts were found and salvaged.

Photo: *On final approach at 50 feet on Capo Frasca range for a bombing pass. Note that the practice bomb dispenser doors are open.*

The salvage of this aircraft had been very interesting, and eventually led to establishing the cause of the accident and the probable cause of previous CF–104 accidents - the fuel pump drive of the Main Fuel Control Unit.

All six of us eventually received the Flight Safety Good Show award for our efforts.

In spite of the frustration of that salvage operation, Phil has fond memories of his tour in Decci...

The CF–104s deployed from the Wings to Decci for a two-week period, supported by groundcrew on a monthly "vacation". Well, the serviceability had improved by this time, and we were able to get our range sorties in (when the Italians had the range open), and the fellows still had time to enjoy the beach. We took advantage of the deployed CF–104s from the Wings to supplement some items which were not too readily available in our local shops or the store in the Maple Leaf House.

I was fortunate in that my contacts at 427 and 434 Squadrons would call down and get my meat order. This was then carried in the bomb dispensers of the aircraft. It always was a joke for the pilots to threaten to open the doors of the dispenser prior to landing, or on arrival at the flight line... "Oops, sorry Phil "

We lost two CF–104s while I was at Decci, but fortunately no pilots. The second accident involved an aircraft which was being flown back to 4 Wing by Flight-Lieutenant Al Seitz when he had an engine failure during his climb-out. He ejected and landed in the sea, which was very rough and gave him a bad time before he was picked up by a fishing boat. Later, an Italian helicopter returned him to Decci. I greeted his return with some smart-ass remark about it being a hell of a time to take a swim, which didn't go over too well as Al was somewhat the worse for wear from all that sea water. The aircraft unfortunately missed the sea and came down on a small island which was an Italian prison just off the coast. It hit solid rock and just disintegrated, the largest piece left being about a foot square. The amazing thing was that no one was injured, nor were any buildings damaged by the impact. Nevertheless, it created a real problem with all those pieces of metal laying around with which the prisoners could make weapons! This was a tough salvage job to clean up, but there was no lack of manpower as we used the prisoners and their guards. We had to go back a number of times, as they would call to tell us that they had found more pieces, and insisted that we take them away.

While the Italian Air Force provided the operational support required to keep the base running, it was the Canadians and the Luftwaffe that did the bulk of the flying. The Capo Frasca range, located on Sardinia's west coast, was used both to provide pilots with concentrated weapons delivery practice as well as the opportunity to re–attain the NATO annual weapons delivery qualifications in various modes. Unlike the capricious weather on the Air Division's home turf, the generally fine weather in Sardinia made Decci an ideal location for these exercises.

A Salvo deployment usually began on a Monday morning when eight-to-ten aircraft would arrive for a two–week stay. They would be met at the flightline by their own Wing's groundcrew, who were cycled through at four-week intervals. The flight down took roughly one hour and forty-five minutes and normally passed over Strasbourg, Dijon, Lyon, Nice, Corsica and finally Decimomannu. Usually the trip down was uneventful, however, sometimes it was not...Al Seitz, an experienced fighter pilot who converted early in the Starfighter program (Course Four), would acquire a lot of '104 experience both with 422 Squadron in the Air Division, and also as an instructor at the OTU. Al's memories of the "Decci haul" suggest that pilot frustration may have been high on a fairly regular basis...

European air traffic control, patterned after North American and ICAO-approved procedures, doesn't always reach expectations. Interpretation varies, I guess, but some French, Italian and Greek controllers interpret air regulations in ways completely incomprehensible to outsiders. We were exposed to the first two nationalities five or six times annually on flights to Decimomannu, Sardinia where we did our weapons training, and to the third only occasionally on flights to Athens or Cyprus.

The Decci haul was in the vicinity of 700 miles, and meant an IFR flight plan at altitudes between 30,000 feet and 35,000 feet. Two-thirds of the flight was over France, the remainder over the Mediterranean and Sardinia under Italian tolerance. France control would usually assert its authority soon after contact by giving us a change of cruising altitude, quite often to an unacceptably high or low level, like 50,000 or 10,000 feet. When the new flight level was declared unacceptable, the reply from the controller would be, "Your flight plan is cancelled!"... then silence. Only a MAYDAY call could evoke further conversation. The first time it happened you wondered whether you were expected to bail out, go home, or continue. After that first time, it became the preferred way to travel, weather permitting.

After passing Corsica, ATC clearances were given reluctantly by the Italian agency, Rome Control. Responses to radio calls were invariably slow in coming, but could sometimes be hastened if one said loudly and distinctly, "Roma Controla, this is..." An exasperated pilot's voice was once heard to say, "Luigi, answer the goddamn phone!" No answer; but a few days later a NOTAM[1] came through to all NATO flying units which stated, "Henceforth, Rome Control is not to be addressed as Luigi..."

The general routine of a deployment consisted of two practice bombing missions per day to the Capo Frasca range, and that left a good deal of time for recreation, exploration, and even occasional mischief. After their morning arrival, the incoming pilots would usually fly their first range mission that very afternoon. On each trip, a four–ship formation would launch and proceed to the range by a standard, preplanned ten-minute route. Obviously, the boys were there to do the very best they could, and the expressions "Skip Hit" and "Bull's Eye" were music to their ears. On the other hand, altitude violations resulting in assessed fouls and a curt "Number Four, you fly too low, you go home" transmission ended the day for many an overly zealous pilot. A level pulloff (as opposed to climbing) after delivery would raise the hackles of the Italian range controllers as well, and reputedly prompted one exasperated controller to say; "Hey Number Three, you pulla the stick back before you benda the wings or else you gonna busta your ass!"

Although the rooms in the quarters were quite spacious, the lack of adequate heating did make the winters a bit less than ideal. Further, the plumbing was generally poor and the water undrinkable, forcing a regular liquid diet of, amongst other things, "Aqua Minerale". There was not a great deal on the Base in the way of facilities to hold the interests of touring Canadians, other than the Combined Mess and the Airmen's Club, which showed a different movie every evening. A much more popular place was the Maple Leaf House in nearby Cagliari, which, as mentioned, served as a social centre for the small Canadian community in Sardinia. The rest of the town was not without its attractions either, as has been documented in the 4 Wing Closing Commerative History...

There were wild, horn-honking drivers going in every direction, led by a large group of seemingly drunk fellows in a Volkswagen bus. There were also many restaurants serving various seafoods or the "Pizza Canadazi", along with red Sardinian wine or Zambuca. However, for a good portion of the year the beaches around the island provided the chief attraction. These were blessed with clear water, fine sand, hot

[1] Notice To Airmen... Aviation advisories found in flight planning centres the world over.

sun and many bikinis. The beach at Cagliari also provided a location for the RCAF Sea Survival School which opened in the Spring of 1967. All CF–104 pilots in Europe plus some from Canada attended this course. It consisted of one half-day of lectures followed by an afternoon on the "Med", where a pilot was towed in his parachute straps by a powerboat and was required to extricate himself and climb into a dingy. There was considerable horse-trading with the scheduling officers in the respective Wings in order not to be sent to Decci in the winter because of this aspect of the course.

However, the raison d'etre for Decci was bombing qualifications, and at the end of each year results of all camps held during the year were totalled. The squadron with the best bombing average was presented with the Bradshaw Trophy.

Morale was particularly good at Decci for the most part, and life was full of a clear sense of purpose. George Miller, who flew CF–104s in the mid-sixties, comments on operations there during his tenure as Weapons Officer...

Probably the most outstanding aspect of the Decci operation was the prevalent high spirits and sense of mission that pervaded the camp, including personnel deployed and those on permanent strength. Teamwork was essential, as over each period up to ten aircrew had to qualify in all bombing modes, and participate in a sea survival course. It was an operation of deadlines and milestones, but goals were easily defined and evident, and success easily measured...an ideal small unit operation. From supply clerk to Station Commander, all were aware and fully supportive of the operational need for keeping the aircraft flying. Groundcrew who deployed for periods of up to three months were top-notch, with always a core of Decci volunteers who, as veterans of many deployments, could be counted on to keep the aircraft on the line. Among the aircrew, competition never ceased. Pilots had little difficulty qualifying to SHAPE accuracy standards, but kept a focus of intense effort on lowering individual, and thereby, squadron CEP averages. Individual and collective pride and reputation was at stake. Results reflected on squadron averages and were yet another measure among pilots of relative standings among peers. An air of friendly rivalry heightened the spirit and quickened the pace of activity.

Flying weather was normally excellent for practice bombing at Capo Frasca range, a peninsula on the west coast of the island, free from built-up areas and with a "run-in" track that permitted a long, very low approach and good radar returns. This also made it ideal for night bombing, an innovation introduced into the Sardinian syllabus in 1967 to acquaint CF–104 pilots with this possible wartime tasking. The introduction of night bombing was met with some skepticism by the Italians as they were convinced it could not be done safely. The experience was also a first for Italian base and range personnel. The first full scale night flying schedule drew great interest from the Italians. The control tower became full of base brass watching sections of CF–104s taxi out and takeoff individually a few minutes apart. The initial operation had to contend with flame pots to serve as taxiway lights and to mark the ends of the runway. No approach or threshold lights were available for some months. Needless to say, landings were interesting. Probably the most memorable evening of night flying was the time when, just at nightfall following mission briefing, the Italians, without warning, collected all the flame pots. Before the matter could be sorted out, it was too late... flying had to be scrubbed. The Italian operations staff had authorized their Officers' Mess to use the flame pots to mark the entrance to the base and line the road leading to the Mess to create an impressive touch for their annual Officers' Ball.

When the Strike role was terminated in 1971, the squadrons briefly honed their fighting skills in the air-to-air range at Decci. However, it soon became apparent that with the CF–104 in its new Conventional Ground Attack role, simulated air-to-air combat had taken a back seat to the air-to-ground work needed. Due to the limited tactical air-to-ground training facilities available, the utility of further Decci deployments was called into question, and they were eventually cancelled on May 19, 1971; the event being marked by a thirteen plane flypast tribute. Much later, 1 Canadian Air Group would re-establish weapons camps at Decci, but this would not occur until the waning years of the CF–104 era, and would never be conducted with the same intensity of effort that had characterized these deployments in the sixties.

Meanwhile at 3 Wing, the CF–104 phase-in was both literally and figuratively having its ups and downs. Mercifully, no mid-air collisions occurred at Zweibrucken during this intense readjustment period, though the role and the new aircraft were beginning to take their toll. On July 23rd, 1963, ironically enough at Decimomannu, Flight Lieutenant R.J. Prescott of 427 Squadron was killed while on a bombing run at the Capo Frasca range. It was thought that a slow topple of the LN–3 inertial navigation system coupled with very hazy flight visibility were responsible for his demise. Back home at Zweibrucken, 434 Squadron was having problems of their own when one of their aircraft caught fire on an engine run-up in a hangar and was essentially written off.

As autumn approached, a particularly gloomy series of misfortunes befell the 427 Lions. On September 11th, Flight Lieutenant D.O. Schneider experienced an engine exhaust nozzle failure and a subsequent failure of the Emergency Nozzle Closure System (ENCS). To crown a tragic set of circumstances, he apparently had a seat malfunction on ejection and died in the wreckage of his aircraft, due to the late bailout. Then on October 24th, Flight Lieutenant B.G. Sheasby flew his aircraft into the ground on a night TACAN penetration; due in all probability to a misread altimeter. Further, on December 30th, Wing Commander Middlemiss and his family were returning from a vacation when the Bristol freighter in which they were travelling crashed on radar final approach at Marville, France. Mrs. Middlemiss was killed instantly, while both the Wing Commander and his daughter sustained severe injuries. In February 1964, Wing Commander H. R. Knight officially took command of 427 as Middlemiss was still hospitalized and likely to remain so for an indefinite period of time.

Ralph Annis comments on the 3 Wing accidents that had plagued the early months of the transition program...

Our early days in Zweibrucken were marred by three fatal accidents and a few more bailouts. It seemed that I was the only Squadron Leader eligible to do Boards of Enquiry, and I had the first three accidents to investigate - none of which were fatal. We were able to exactly pinpoint the cause of two of them, even though we only recovered a little over half of the wreckage. We got every last piece of the third one, but couldn't come up with the cause, and it is still a mystery to me why Rocky Van Vliet's nozzle would not close.

However by June 1964, the Zweibrucken Wing was performing in a somewhat more positive manner when they eked out a pass on their first annual Tactical Evaluation. Though the evaluation results were disappointing and would rapidly be improved upon, both 427 and 434 Squadrons were declared combat ready, and got on with their nuclear alert job of "babysitting the bomb". Quick Reaction Alert (QRA) meant that pilots had to be continuously available on fifteen–minute readiness to launch with a 2000 pound nuclear weapon strapped to their backsides. 3 Wing was once again manned by warriors with weapons, and a second Tac Eval in November would add considerably more prestige to their credentials when they would pass with a substantially elevated overall grade of "two".

Zweibrucken though, was not the only Wing in the Air Division. Jack Waters would later go on to fame as the Red Knight solo demonstration pilot for Canada's centennial celebrations in 1967, but in 1963 he was a Sabre pilot with 430 Interceptor Day Fighter (IDF) Squadron at Grostenquin. Jack remembers the arrival of the '104s that summer...

At RCAF Grostenquin in France, the arrival of the '104s was muted. It was 1963, and we Canadians were clearly becoming persona non grata in the eyes of President deGaulle. In June, we flew our trusty Swords into retirement at Prestwick, Scotland, then returned to 2 Wing to await the arrival of our 430 Squadron replacement '104 aircraft and pilots. During that summer of '63, the aircraft arrived in bits and pieces, but it soon became clear that a move was in the cards. To my recollection, the characteristic moan of the Starfighter was seldom heard at Grostenquin.

The arrival of the '104 pilots was less muted...we were all in a bit of awe at these types who had "earned their spurs" the hard way. Some had flown Sabres or Vampires in the mid-fifties, during the halcyon days of the Air Division. Some had even been operational World War Two pilots. ***All*** *had just been through the toughest flying course then known in the Air Force. We instinctively knew that they deserved to swagger a bit, but they swaggered in a strange way. Whereas your average Sabre jock could be likened to a pup who yelped his presence, the '104 types we saw were like old dogs who growled their authority. I remember that a lot of people in the Wings at the time remarked, "We knew the young Sabre drivers. Now, here are their fathers." In fact, a few of them looked like grandfathers!*

Above: *These guns for hire...PR "hero" shot on the Zweibrucken flightline during the early days. Left to right; Gord Joy, Bob Prescott.*

Meanwhile at Baden-Soellingen, the Sabre squadrons had been disbanded in the spring of 1963, and flying operations at 4 Wing had effectively ground to a standstill. While many of the Wing's personnel had been repatriated back to Canada, a great many others had come to replace them; to prepare 4 Wing for the new role, the new aircraft, and the new operation. Almost simultaneously with the last of the Sabres being ferried to England for scrapping, the first CF–104s began arriving in the bellies of Hercules on March 19, 1963, with the fleet gradually increasing in size throughout the spring and summer. The first 4 Wing CF–104 pilots, part of the recently reformed 444 Cobra Squadron under the command of Wing Commander Ken Thornycroft, arrived in late May. As Jack Waters has already mentioned, far from being for the most part "young tigers", the 4 Wing Commemorative History records a very telling observation on their age and experience level, along with the eventual fate of the few bachelors...

Generally, they were older and more experienced than the pilots of the Sabre squadrons. The CF–104 was a new aircraft and much more sophisticated than the older generations of RCAF jet aircraft. The role and the operational procedures were also new. Nearly all the pilots arrived accompanied by their families. It was only in later years that significant numbers of "pipe-line" pilots began arriving at 4 Wing. Although relatively young, many of them were already married, and if not, the majority of them soon gave up their bachelorhood. The large colony of female school teachers at the Officers' Mess was the primary cause.

In July, the Cobras were joined at Baden by 422 Tomahawk Squadron under Wing Commander Bill Bliss, who flew the squadron's first CF–104 sortie in Europe on July 27th. 4 Wing, like their brothers at Zweibrucken, now got down to the serious business of attaining Combat Ready (CR) status. In order to reach this benchmark, each pilot had to demonstrate proficiency at flying to a target from low altitude, both visually and on radar. Just to keep smiles on faces, there was also a host of exams pertaining to aircraft and weapons systems, low level procedures, and mission knowledge. Like their peers at 3 Wing, they also had to demonstrate bombing credibility in all possible modes of delivery, and that of course meant frequent trips to various bombing ranges. Part of each pilot's training was instrument practice in the venerable T–33 aircraft, and emergency systems practice in the hated and dreaded CF–104 simulator. By November, Wing CR training was sufficiently advanced to the point where the squadrons could partake in other activities, and thus both squadrons sent pilots to participate in an Escape and Evasion exercise in "la belle France".

On the other side of the Rhine, trouble with the deGaulle government was coming to a head. In 1963, France had decided to acquire an independent nuclear force for reasons of prestige, control of her own destiny, and for the guaranteed protection of French territory. This meant that nuclear weapons on French soil would be subject only to French authority. In December of 1963, a Special Committee of Defence reported to the Commons that even French squadrons armed with American nuclear warheads were not permitted to operate from bases in France, and thus were stationed in Germany until their own home-grown air-portable nuclear arsenal could be developed. What hope then for four squadrons of Canadian Starfighters to be based at Grostenquin and Marville respectively? The answer from the French government was not long in coming... CF–104s based in France would **not** be permitted to store their American-acquired nuclear devices at French bases, and would consequently have to obtain these warheads outside of France. In terms of presenting a credible deterrent posture, this situation was unsatisfactory. Something had to give, and the Special Committee recommended that NATO be petitioned to immediately relocate the Starfighter Strike squadrons based in France to more hospitable soil. Again, action was swiftly forthcoming, and the upshot of it all was that Grostenquin was closed

down in February, 1964. 430 Silver Falcon Squadron (Course 5) was sent to Zweibrucken in the Strike role, and 421 Red Indian Squadron (Course 6), who had only arrived in time for Christmas and had barely had time to unpack their bags, headed east to Baden-Soellingen.

* * * * * *

Years later, in the mid-seventies when I was serving as a pilot with 439 Squadron at Baden, the name of Grostenquin would resurface and it would acquire a new claim to fame in the Air Group...Grostenquin was at that time being used by the French Air Force strictly as a storage facility and an inactive one at that, and although the extremely robust runway was still in splendid condition, there were absolutely no air traffic control facilities available. 439 Squadron, like all such units, had a very large aircrew statistics board near the operations desk that contained each pilot's name and a breakdown of flying hours and sorties in a myriad of different categories. The stats board also listed numerous annual and semi-annual requirements, usually in columns headed by some form of acronym. For example IRT stood for Instrument Rating Test, AOI for Aircraft Operating Instructions, PPFL for Practice Precautionary Forced Landing, and so on. One day, Roy deWolfe, a Squadron pilot, unobtrusively and silently added a new column to the board, labelled TGLGTN, and put the number 1 beside his name. Wolf was often somewhat enigmatic, so no one gave it much of a second thought. About a week later, Wolf walked in and quietly changed the "1" in his new column to a "2". Now Wolf was an outstanding pilot, but his utter disregard for keeping records was practically legendary, so it was most unusual to see him tracking this supposedly new requirement so assiduously. Nevertheless, after a lot of puzzled looks and shrugged shoulders, we let it go. Wolf would unravel the mystery in his own good time...About three days later, when he had further changed the board from 2 to 3, one of the pilots could stand it no longer and said, "Hey Wolf...what does TGLGTN stand for anyway?" "Touch and go landings at Grostenquin," came the laconic reply. We never did find out if he was serious or joking...

* * * * * *

Above: *The leading edge and the trailing edge of technology. The "living lawn mowers" get close to this Zweibrucken CF-104 in 1968.*

It should be noted that all the Strike squadrons were nominally dual-roled in Conventional Attack as well, but it would be several years before practice weapon deliveries for the latter role were done on a regular basis. Also, the conventional munitions to support this role (BLU–1B napalm, CBU–2B/A cluster bombs and 2.75 inch rockets) were very slow in coming to the bases. Meanwhile, 1 Wing at Marville in the northeast corner of France was to garrison both 441 Silver Fox Squadron (Course 7) and 439 Sabre Tooth Tiger Squadron (Course 8), albeit exclusively in the Photo Reconnaissance role.

Dave McIntosh recalls the impact of the French decision on the CF–104 basing plan regarding the Reconnaissance role...

*The original concept called for the recce pods to be spread throughout the Strike squadrons, and each unit would have a **very** small reconnaissance capability. How practical this would have been is questionable. Subsequent experience in the recce business demonstrated just **how** specialized this field was. However, having the pods available early on proved a godsend because when France declared that no nuclear weapons-equipped squadrons would be allowed in their country, collecting the pods and forming specialized reconnaissance squadrons was a natural solution. Even after these units were formed, all reconnaissance pilots continued to complete the Strike syllabus at Cold Lake, then do their recce conversion on squadron. The original group of pilots assigned to the two reconnaissance squadrons were sent to Shaw AFB to receive the USAF reconnaissance ground school. It's interesting to note that one option being bounced around Air Force Headquarters (AFHQ), when options were being examined for the French-based squadrons, was that of arming them with Shrikes and using them in a radar-suppression role. It is also interesting to reflect on how our tactical fighter community and our tactics would have developed if this role had been pursued.*

Meanwhile, 430 Squadron made the move to Zweibrucken, and Jack Waters went with them, attached to Wing Instrument Flight (WIF) at 3 Wing as an Instrument Check Pilot. Jack recalls these early days at Zweibrucken...

Over the next two years, I got to fly with all the old, grizzled types from 427, 430, and 434 Squadrons. Apart from "riding shotgun" for their instrument flying training in the T–33 (and occasionally the CF–104), I took them to places where they might, perchance, have to take their Starfighters... lunches from Naples, Italy to Stavanger, Norway; and from Furstenfeldbruck, Germany to Prestwick, Scotland. Pete Russell from 434 and I even tried for lunch one day at one of the new

French "Force de Frappe" nuclear bases. Unfortunately, the air traffic control system pooched, and we arrived unannounced. The reception was decidedly cool... We passed lunch hour in the French equivalent of "Crowbar Hotel", and departed, lunchless, some time later. As we were being hustled to our "T–bird" for departure, I was handed a fuel voucher to sign. Only after we were climbing out through 15,000 feet did I notice that I had signed for 3500 litres of fuel... for an aircraft which could hold less than 3000 litres. Some "accounts type" in Metz paid the bill anyway, and as yet nobody has asked me to pay the difference.

These were paradoxical times...On my last '104 trip, I accompanied Flight Lieutenant Bob Ayres on an Air Division acceptance airtest out of Zweibrucken; then we delivered the aircraft to Baden-Soellingen. On the return trip to Zweibrucken, Bob, (who was a crack '104 test pilot) and I (a Sabre and T–33 pilot) flew home as pilot and co-pilot in our humble C–45 "bugsmasher" at a sedentary 140 knots.

There were also uproarious times. Old as they were, these '104 pilots were still full of highjinks. In one instance, the incorrigible J.T. Price (of Golden Hawk fame) had flaunted his "50 mission", grease-stained RCAF "Gieves" flat hat once too often in the face of our Station Commander at 3 Wing, who had repeatedly told J.T. to replace it. One day Group Captain Berg finally made his point by incinerating J.T.'s hat at the bar in the Mess in front of a disbelieving audience. Lighter fluid, a match... poof! J.T. got the message.

When I left in June 1965, the era of the "old guys" was ending. Very capable pipeliners like Bob Hyndman and Jack Partington were starting to take their places. The growing pains were over. The "old guys" had firmly established a place for Canada in the Strike role.

In January 1964, 4 Wing's role was changed from Strike/Reconnaissance to Strike/Attack. With the deletion of the recce role came the requirement for a revised training program and, you guessed it, accompanying mountains of staff work. They also gained another lodger unit when 421 Red Indian Squadron under Wing Commander Bud Lawrence arrived from Grostenquin, France in February. During the spring and summer months, the construction of the nuclear alert Quick Reaction Area (QRA) was completed. The Air Force Police section was expanded and friendly neighbourhood sentry dogs were acquired who, after being put through an extremely demanding training period of their own, generated respect from even the regular visitors to the QRA. The 4 Wing History recalls some of the intense activity of this period...

On March 16, 1964, the Operations Centre commenced operating on a twenty-four hour basis, providing command and control throughout the Wing during alerts. Later, it provided the vital link between the QRA and higher headquarters. The Wing was subjected to frequent base exercises such as Alerts, Quick Trains, and Capability Inspections. Finally, on the eleventh of June, # 4 Fighter Wing had its first formal Tactical Evaluation. The Tac Eval, conducted by the Fourth Allied Tactical Air Force was successful, and the Wing settled down to a CR status maintenance program.

The Wing's primary function, aside from providing crews and aircraft for Quick Reaction Alert, was to maintain a sufficient number of combat ready pilots and aircraft to be used in the event of an actual Wing Alert. To accomplish this, the squadrons established a daily flying program consisting of low level navigation, bombing, forward air control and low level night navigation missions. The pilots were also expected to fly 24 instrument proficiency missions a year in the T–33 aircraft. Eighteen simulator missions per year in the Operational Flight Tactical Trainer (simulator) were required to practice such things as emergency procedures, radar navigation, radar bombing and instrument flying.

Besides daily monitoring of the flying program by supervisory personnel, a total of twelve written examinations, two CF–104 dual aircraft check rides, a T–33 aircraft instrument rating ride, and four qualifying bombing missions had to be completed annually. Throughout the year, a continuous ground school program was maintained, covering such subjects as intelligence, aircraft systems, weapons systems and flight safety...

Sounds pretty sterile, doesn't it? Cold facts often are, but the 4 Wing History contains an excellent anonymous recapitulation of the average daily routine for a CF–104 pilot during the Strike days at Baden, as seen through a pilot's eyes. Since it tends to make a statement in its own right, that portion of the history is repeated here in its entirety.

A Day in the Life of a Fighter Pilot

Not 0530Z[1] already; it seems as if I just went to bed. Those three beers after night flying were really unnecessary. What time was it when I got home, midnight? Met briefing at 0615Z. I'd better get going. Perhaps I can leave without waking Ginny. That class of Grade 4 children at school certainly seems to tire her. Maybe she won't be so anxious to teach next year.

This may still turn into a nice day if the fog lifts. Five...six, if I see another pheasant it will be a record. Only two rabbits though. There, the farmers are already working in the fields. It isn't such a ghastly hour to get up after all. And the spargel pickers have already finished an hour ago and are on their way to work. Where is the squadron going to dinner tonight? I seem to recall the Cheval Noir. We're not likely to have fresh spargel over there... more likely schnecken or frogs legs.

The guys living in PMQs may get a bit more sleep, but this twenty minute drive through the Rhine Valley with its picturesque villages, patchwork fields dotted with fruit trees and the deer that I just might see

[1] Z (or Zulu) is Greenwich Mean Time (GMT).

today is a more pleasant way to wake up.

My pass! Where is it? If I have to go home to fetch it I'll be late, and phoning from the guardhouse for a pilot to come and escort me into the restricted area is embarrassing. Oh, it's in my wallet after all.

0600Z. Enough time for two pieces of toast with peanut butter. Coffee is made; I wonder who made it? The Ops O must have been early this morning.

"All pilots met briefing."

"Good morning, gentlemen, this is the 0300Z surface chart. There is a high pressure system situated over England, resulting in a weak northerly flow of cool and relatively dry air over our flying area. The sky is clear, and the present shallow fog in the valley should lift around 0900Z giving us 2– 3 miles in haze for the rest of the morning. At 0600Z the visibility was .8 of a mile with a 500 ft. ceiling. Minimum altimeter in Germany is 29.90 and in France 30.00. The primary alternate [1] is 3 Wing and the secondary is Bitburg. Any questions?"

"Ceiling and visibility at Helchtern please?"

"Presently, one mile vis and 300 ft. ceiling, expected to lift after 0900Z."

There goes my bombing trip, third day in a row, and tonight I go into Q, and then a day off and next week 421 is the bombing squadron. Not very many pilots around, perhaps someone in the bombing section to Suippes at 1100Z is U/S [2]. Maybe I can get on it!

"...compressor stall, Melvin?"

"Me? Compressor stall? Throttle off...70% start switches... throttle on...land as soon as possible."

Those emergency questions are not like bombing trips; I never escape them.

"Gentlemen, since the weather won't allow us to go bombing, we'll fly low level routes for the first launch and go bombing on the second. It is a good opportunity to practice hitting some equivalent targets. Remember that we are aiming for a maximum lateral error of 300 ft. and a time accuracy of better than 3 seconds. An Air Division Top Gun is scheduled two weeks from now and unless we can be within these criteria on the EQs, the squadron could lose the Top Gun trophy. Have we any French routes, Ops O?"

"Only two penetrations are filed for this morning, Sir."

"OK, the first four on the priority list go into France in two sections."

Shucks, I don't get a French route. Well, let's see...next best routes for weather are routes 408 and 404. These I could probably fly without a map, and perhaps the EQs also. Here are some EQs for 407...I can't remember those. I haven't flown that route very often. What restrictions? Parachute jumping on the 6 minute mark and gliders at the 20 minute mark. There shouldn't be any gliders this early in the morning and the last time I saw parachutes they weren't NOTAMed.

Spurs, mae west, knee pad, helmet, parachute, got my maps...all set.

"Hey, Melvin...you forgot to sign out!" "Thanks."

Now I must be all set to go to the line shack to sign out.

"Good morning, Sergeant. L–14 for 833, please."

Everything is signed out...there are no outstanding minors and the last major U/S's look standard.

"Where is the A/C parked, Sergeant?"

"On DLA23 [3], Sir. The start crew is there waiting for you."

Good. Maybe the LN–3 heat has been on long enough. Everything looks good on the walk around, but what a dirty aircraft. Spurs hooked on, dinghy lanyard attached to mae west, harness on, helmet on, and

Above: *Part of the Zweibrucken flightline in March, 1963.*

---

[1] Diversion Airfield.
[2] Unserviceable.
[3] Aircraft Designated Launch Area; an aircraft parking space.

oxygen hose connected.

"Have a good trip, Sir."

All switches in the right place, and the gauges look good. Signal to wind up. Everything normal. Five finger check complete, seat pin is out and LN–3 is in NAV. All set to go. Chocks away.

"Soellingen tower, Jacket 79, TAXI."

"Jacket 79: TAXI R/W 22, wind 220/5, altimeter 29:94, time 05."

R/W 22 in use...that means a right turn after takeoff and hacking over the autobahn junction at 7:30 min. after take off. Must remember to call approach control before crossing the 040° radial.

Pre-take-off check complete...everything looks okay.

"Tower, Jacket 79 for take-off."

"79, you're cleared for take-off, Departure 1 to VMC,[1] call VMC."

"79."

Run-up check. Throttle full mil, RPM 100%, all instruments look good, 80% no stall, idle 600 lbs. Throttle full mil; 6 sec., good. Clock punched, brakes released and throttle around the horn... feels as if I'm decelerating!

"Tower, 79 aborting, no A/B."

"Roger, 79, can you take the first exit?"

"Roger."

Wouldn't you know it. For once I'm on the first launch!

"Alouette, Jacket 79."

"Go ahead 79."

"I'm on my way to snags. Will you send Sputnik to pick me up? Any other A/C available?"

"Roger for Sputnik, but negative for other A/C. But Bart Brady is U/S... you can take his slot in the bombing section."

All this trouble because the torch wouldn't work. It's nice to see Sputnik here.

"Wie geht's, Sputnik?"

"Alles ist OK."

I wonder how Sputnik managed to drive for us since 1953 without having an accident, and why is it that we still can't communicate? Let's hope there is someone left at the squadron besides the Ops officer so that I have someone to play darts with. It is almost 0800Z. Briefing for bombing at 0930Z - that should allow three cups of coffee and a half dozen games of darts.

"Why did you have to give me a U/S bird, Ops O? What's wrong with Bart?"

"I don't think there is anything wrong with him. He had to take his little lad to the hospital at Lahr or something. Are you an element lead? OK. Then you're number three for bombing at Suippes, with power on at 1000Z. Why don't you prepare the briefing since lead should land shortly before the power on time. And give a call to met. They called a while ago with a different forecast for Suippes."

"Met, COR[2]."

"Go ahead, COR."

"What is the latest WX at Suippes, and the winds please?"

"The fog is lifting more slowly than I anticipated; however, you should have 4 miles vis by 1100Z and no ceiling. The surface wind is light and variable, at 1000 ft. it is 080/5, and at 2000 ft. 070/8. Surface temperature should be 14° by 1100Z."

"Thanks."

I hope I can bomb better than I throw darts. First I lose 2 out of 3, so I make 3 out of 5, and now 4 out of 7.

"Let's brief for Suippes, Melvin."

"Roger Lead."

"Our call sign is COMET INDIA, and the line up is as on the board. Start and take-off will be as SOP's. Weather is VMC. We'll do two LADDs, two lay-downs, and two EMRS[3]. Timer settings are on the board. Is everyone familiar with the range pattern? Good. Sorry for the rush...it's almost power on time. Any questions?"

"How do we depart from the range?"

"I'll do one more pattern after calling last pass; two, you make a somewhat tighter pattern; three, make a 360°, and four turn left after your last pass. Beer's on the worst bomb. Don't forget to sign out. See you on seventeen."

"Lead, India three is ready to go."

"Lead checks, Indias go channel 8."

"India two" ..."India three" ..."four"

"Lead, Tower, Indias four A/C taxi."

Pre-take-off check done, everything looks good.

"Comet Indias, take-off clearance"

There go one and two. Our turn to wind up. Engine instruments look good. Number four nods telling me he is all set. I nod my head, and release the brakes, throttle around the horn, that feels much better, full A/B and then reduce .5 of a nozzle for number four. He's keeping in nicely. Two thousand feet, 140 kts., good. One hundred and eighty knots, nose coming up. Gear coming up. Four hundred and fifty knots, A/B out. There's number one and two at twelve o'clock, high, as we're through the haze layer.

"India three and four coming on board."

"Indias, go channel one three."

A Call to Menthol Red, and it should be smooth going for the next fifteen minutes. Happiness is being number four in a bombing section. Number three isn't bad either. We're in loose formation and lead doesn't need any assistance to navigate on a day like this. One can spend a good part of the trip looking at the red roofs of the villages on either side of the track.

"Indias two A/C at 2 o'clock, same altitude, right to left."

Looks like two Mirages, and a little bit too close. Maybe a little less looking down at the countryside is in order.

Frequency change to Suippes range control tower. Contact on first call... that's unusual. Lead's pulling up, ten seconds to go for my turn.

"Suippes Range, Indias' clearance to arm."

"You're cleared to arm."

All arming switches are done. I'll open the doors after final.

"India three is base."

Full power on, and into a left turn. Lead's bomb went short. Two's just called final. Where's the church? It should be about half a mile on my left as I roll out on 020°. Airspeed still low. Leave full power on. Where's that pylon marking the run-in?"

"Number two, two hundred at six o'clock."

Again? I'll add 2/10ths of a second to the run-in timers.

"India three, final."

"You're cleared."

Should pass just right of the water tower in that town. I wonder how these people put up with us flying at about 100 ft. at Mach .85. Airspeed too high, throttle back. Wish I could see the run-in line...I'm getting quite close. Airspeed looks good. Green light, red light, doors... forgot the damn doors! There's still enough time for them to open. Somewhat left of the run-in line, 5° right should do it. Pickle over the railroad. Airspeed still good. Looks like a good heading. There goes the buzzer. Full power and control column back for 3–1/2 g. Solution light back on, roll to the left and the nose is coming down to the horizon.

"India three off wet."

"Roger, India three, three hundred feet at one o'clock."

Second pass; 200 ft. LADD. Third and forth passes; laydowns at 250 ft. and 100 ft. Fifth pass; 700 ft. This last one had better come closer.

"India three is base for last pass."

That EMR looked good. Now for a hard left turn. There goes two at my nine o'clock. Perhaps I can maintain visual contact with him.

[1] Visual Meteorological Conditions, i.e., clear of cloud.
[2] Central Operations Room.
[3] Emergency Manual Release. A surprisingly-accurate "that looks about right" form of backup delivery.

"India three, shack."

That's better, but I've lost number two. I wonder whose smoke that is. Must be lead. And there's two and four. Looks like a smooth join-up. Straight and level for fifteen minutes to base. By that time I should be a little less wet. Have to order that steak before debriefing, so that it will be ready right after. Frequency change to Soellingen Tower.

"Soellingen Tower, Indias land four."

"Indias, Runway 22 in use. Altimeter 29:90. Call initial."

Break looks good. 260 knots, gear down, three greens, land flaps down. 210 knots, rolling out, speed brakes, Germans watching us again on the bunker. Over the button, 170 knots. Touchdown, good chute.

"Indias go channel one on your own time. See you inside."

If it hadn't been for that 700 ft. bomb I'd have had the best average. Now I'll have to buy a round on Friday night. That steak should be ready by now. I like those short debriefings.

"Melvin Gallagher, telephone in the pilot's room."

"Hi, Melvin. This is Gilles Lapointe in Q. They're after me for being late on the stock check. Could you replace me early at around three o'clock?"

"Replace you early in Q today...? It's a good thing you called. I had completely forgotten about that Q. I remember now Bart just changed it a few days ago. And all day I have been thinking about those schnecken. Oh well... at least I won't have a hangover tomorrow. I think I would be able to make it by three. I'll finish eating here and then rush to the PX for those two speakers I've been talking about. Would you believe they called yesterday and suggested that unless I picked them up today they will sell them to someone else? Apparently they arrived here two weeks ago and they called me while I was in Decci, but of course it was never passed on to me."

"Thanks, cheers."

Wouldn't have thought it was so hard to get rid of one's money. First the parking problem, then all those foreigners at the counter, but they did have the speakers still. Ginny will be glad. Now to get back into the flying suit and to fetch the helmet, and I'll be almost on time for Gilles. Don't envy that stock check.

"Ops, Jacket 79 DLA 1B, A/X 999 accepted."[1]

A peaceful twenty-four hours ahead. I'm glad I'm not scheduled with one of the snorers. It's a good thing the party's on tonight so they won't call me for night ops and I can watch a movie... and if we're lucky the Boss will bring in some popcorn. I suppose I'm scheduled for a simulator ride tomorrow... it's a good excuse to leave the "pen".

* * * * * *

The year 1964 continued to roll by in Baden at a fast clip. Along with mingling with the locals at such august events and the Buhl Plum Festival parade, the number of operational commitments continued to increase. In October, the Wing bore the brunt of a second Air Division Tac Eval. Earlier that summer, two Canadian fighter pilots from 4 Wing had participated in the 4 ATAF Tactical Weapons Meet at Chaumont, France. On November 12th, upholding the winning traditions of past Canadian airmen, Flight Lieutenants Cunningham and Seitz were presented with the Broadhurst trophy in recognition of being the winning 4 ATAF team at the Meet.

1964 was also a year for the display of considerable innovation at 4 Wing, as noted in the 444 Squadron History...

At right: *When all else failed... This CF-104 has had a successful runway departure end barrier engagement. Note how far the arrestor cable has reeled out.*

[1] Aircrew acceptance of the aircraft and nuclear weapon on alert status. It's important to note that the aircraft was never actually flown with a nuclear device uploaded.

Radar Shadow Prediction

In 1964, Flight-Lieutenant J.S. Eggenberger, the CO of 4 Wing's Radar Prediction Unit devised a new system of Radar Shadow Prediction that was both economical to produce and accurate enough to allow flight of the CF–104 in all weather conditions. This method was adopted by several other NATO Air Forces and later lead to Flight-Lieutenant Eggenberger receiving the Canadian Aeronautics and Space Institute's Romeo Vachon Award in recognition of his achievements.

This process utilized terrain relief models that had an exaggerated vertical scale. A light source was then placed at a scale height above the model and the resulting shadow pattern photographed. A montage of successive images taken along a planned route yielded a continuous strip prediction that could be laid beside a similar strip of a conventional map of the route. Though this technique was improved and modified over the years through use of plaster models, John Eggenberger must really be given credit as being the father of modern radar prediction. His pioneering spirit resulted in a considerable improvement in combat capability for CF–104 pilots with regard to all-weather navigation.

On the domestic side, the unprecedented influx of personnel and dependants during the year caused significant problems such as insufficient housing and lack of sufficient school and recreational facilities. These problems, like those encountered on the operational side, were quickly remedied through extensive construction activity. In South Dispersal, serious overcrowding had resulted from the unexpected addition of 421 Squadron to Central Dispersal, the move of 444 Squadron from Central to South, and the growth of the Wing in general. An all-out effort was made to move existing hangars, construct a concrete flight line and new maintenance buildings, and to install new high intensity runway lights on the airfield. The Wing also received a significant boost in morale during 1964 with the creation of a nine-hole golf course on the west side of the runway.

Morale was also kept at a very high level at 4 Wing because of a never-ending state of playful banter and friendly rivalry that was fostered among the three squadrons. For example, 444 Squadron's front entrance was dominated by a sign which read:

444 Strike/Attack Squadron
The Pride of 4Wing
The Protectors of 421Squadron
The Envy of 422 Squadron

444 Squadron's official History makes note of the particularly special relationship that existed with 422 Squadron at the time, and the Cobras never missed an opportunity to "rub salt in the Hatchetmen's wounds"...

Needless to say, Triple Four's tenure at Baden-Soellingen did not consist solely of exams and check rides. Time could always be made available for parties and harmless pranks. For instance...

The rapport between 444 and 422 was always very close. It was a continuing saga of trying for one-upmanship and it contributed a great deal to the morale of both outfits. 422 celebrated its birthday on New Year's Eve and The Snakes from 444 always gave them a super present to commemorate the occasion. The presentation always included large amounts of salt, a commodity we used liberally in any dealings with 422. For example, in 1963 the Squadron presented 422 with a truly handsome clay urn, appropriately decorated with Indian designs and (of course) full of salt. The following year, the 444 presentation was a CF–104 tip tank totem pole. Because of the size of this magnificent gift, the presentation had to take place in the courtyard of the Mess. When the CO of 422 pulled the cord to unveil this masterpiece, he was showered with salt!

During Wing Commander Thorneycroft's tenure as CO 444, he acquired a beat-up old Opel to get to and from work. To be honest, the car lacked the class normally associated with Triple Four, and the Squadron pilots decided to remedy the situation. W/C Thornycroft had occasion to be absent for three days attending a Squadron Commander's Conference and when he returned he was presented with his "new" car, appropriately painted staff car black and handsomely decorated with a replica of Cecil[1] on both front doors.

Because the CO 422 didn't have a personal "staff car", and the Chief Snake did, the 444 folks felt it necessary to correct this undesirable situation. At great expense, an antique wheel chair was acquired, completely reconditioned, and presented to the 422 CO on New Year's Eve. It was necessary to use a toilet seat as the base of the "driver's seat" and below it, in case of accident, was positioned a potty - full of salt.

* * * * * *

And so, the second full year of CF–104 operations in Europe drew to an end. Significant milestones had been reached, but not without cost. During 1964, the Canadian government had been hard hit by a series of financial worries and setbacks, which had been translated to the RCAF in the form of a $70 million cut in the budget. A follow-on purchase plan of an additional 24 CF–104Ds from Lockheed (the so-called Mark 2 duals) was impacted by this austerity move when the order was reduced to 16. The CF-104 loss rate was beginning to turn some heads... Jake Mulhall had been the first in the Starfighter program to die, on August 10th, 1962 at Cold Lake. John Hutt has vivid and poignant memories of the loss of Mulhall...

In August we lost our second aircraft, this time with the pilot, Jake Mulhall. This was particularly traumatic for me for a number of reasons. He had started with us, and those kinds of fatalities seem to hit closer to home. Secondly, he was a fine pilot and he had ejected safely, but on what seemed to be the only day ever with no wind in Cold Lake, he came right down in the middle of his fireball with the chute vaporizing above the ground. Thirdly, he lived next door to us and the four of us had become fast friends, to the point where we had discussed putting a turnstile between the two houses and using the proceeds for a party each week. I had a lot of trouble handling that loss.

All told, to the end of Calendar Year 1964, 21 Canadian Starfighters had been lost, of which seven separate accidents had resulted in fatalities. Eleven crashes had occurred in Europe since the phase-in of the new aircraft; and though the loss rate was not particularly alarming when compared with that of the Sabre era, the combined factors of the introduction of such a sophisticated weapons platform along with rather glum economic realities were making some very senior brows perspire. The future would have to get brighter...

[1] Cecil the Snake was the brass Cobra "mascot" of 444 Squadron.

In Full Stride

1965 would prove to be another year of significant milestones for the CF–104 in Europe, and not all of them would constitute successes. In Marville, 439 and 441 Squadrons were wrestling with their newly-acquired Reconnaissance role, supported by equipment and an infrastructure that was in a word, embryonic. At the time, 1 Wing pilots received no formal recce training at the OTU prior to being posted overseas. They were fully Strike trained and qualified like their peers in the other Wings, and in fact were expected to maintain a Combat Ready status in nuclear weapons deliveries throughout their European tours. Like their Strike peers, this meant frequent visits to Decci for concentrated periods of weapons practice, where they would occasionally raise the hackles of the professional killers by beating them at their own game. Getting firmly established in the recce role was another matter... Unlike other NATO neighbours who had bought a reconnaissance system integral to the Starfighter, Canada's answer was an externally-mounted afterthought, the Vinten Vicom camera pod. This detachable system was mounted on the fuselage centreline rack, and contained four 70 mm cameras in forward oblique, side oblique, and vertical configurations. It proved to be a much better system than that of the RF–104G, which was adopted by the Luftwaffe, the Italian Air Force and the Royal Netherlands Air Force. Specifically, the side oblique cameras of the Vinten system permitted the pilot to offset photograph a target while flying straight and level and simultaneously completing a visual reconnaissance report; a supplementary procedure that was considered very important at the time. It is interesting to note that the Dutch eventually developed a reconnaissance pod of their own for the Starfighter, replacing the internal system.

Reconnaissance to Canadian fighter aviation was, at that time, something of a "black art". While a considerable amount of expertise had been gained by Canadians flying Spitfires with 39 Wing of the Second Tactical Air Force during the Second World War, postwar application had been limited to a short-lived fighter reconnaissance squadron of P–51 Mustangs in the late 1940s. Consequently, there was very little resident photo reconnaissance (PR) expertise in the RCAF in 1965, both from a pilot viewpoint and from that of the indispensable photo interpreters. 1 Wing recce training was conducted through procedures that were established locally by the squadrons; a sort of evolutionary on-the-job training program. However, from these humble beginnings, the PR expertise would flourish and before many years had passed, Canadian crews would be besting their NATO allies at the annual Royal Flush reconnaissance competitions held in Europe.

From a pilot viewpoint, Dave Huddleston had an extremely successful career in CF–104s, and would go on to command 1 Canadian Air Group at the time of the Starfighter close-out in 1986. However in 1964 and 1965, he was just one of the few pipeline pilots of the time with 439 Squadron at Marville, and was trying to come to grips with the exciting new world of photo reconnaissance...

I was fortunate to end flying training as the first '104 pipeline postings appeared. We were to be four on Course 5 which, as each course was divided, became Course 9. Although we were well received at Cold Lake, a certain skepticism had developed as to the wisdom of trusting neophytes with such a complex piece of machinery in such a hazardous flying environment. When even CF – 100 pilots were referred to as "test cases", this was hardly surprising. My own initial instructor, Bill van Oene, displayed no such outward concern and was the epitome of the cool, confidence-instilling professional. In fact, as a group, our four did rather well on the course and any stigmas which might have existed were quickly dispelled. Young pilots need good supervision, but are generally quicker than their seniors to adapt to new equipment and ideas. Besides, squadrons full of senior pilots, as existed in the early '104 days, lacked balance and tended to foster frustrations rather than **esprit de corps**.

When I arrived in Marville, it was as the sixth member of 439 Squadron. 441 Squadron also had six pilots at this time. As the Strike squadrons had priority in manning because of their alert commitment, the two recce squadrons grew very gradually. Indeed, our seventh pilot arrived nine months later. There was no such shortage of aircraft, however, and we quickly acquired a "flying club" reputation. Mostly "sour grapes" from the Strike boys! Until additional facilities were built, we had all the outward appearance of two flights of one squadron, although Wing Commander Edwards and Squadron Leader Frazer, the two COs, had no intention of allowing that to develop, and with Ernie Gardiner, master practitioner of one-upmanship on 441, the calm was frequently punctuated by bouts of open warfare.

Opposite page: *Photo by Bill Johnson.* **Above:** *It almost always worked... The drag chute was usually a very effective breaking device.*

The initial challenge was to re-adopt the tactical reconnaissance role after its effective absence from the RCAF for almost twenty years. There was no lack of expertise in low-level navigation or in technical photo matters, but this expertise had to be applied in a manner and on a scale which was new. The "book maps" of Strike training were too labour-intensive for quick mission planning and soon gave way to the cut-and-paste methods we know today. Having devoted endless hours at Chatham and Cold Lake to the precise construction of these route maps, it was a pleasant change to have an army of mission planning assistants to expedite the process. Our instruction in recce came from two "augmentees" - Flight-Lieutenant Noel Funge and Major Mike Nicholas. Noel, a navigator, had just completed an exchange tour on Canberras at RAF Wyton, and between that and his time with 408 Squadron, he was an expert in aerial photography, with self-taught majors in tactical reconnaissance and photo interpretation. He was our ground instructor and producer of training materials. Mike was a USAF pilot detached from an RF–101 squadron at Ramstein, and he introduced us to recce flying techniques. He had flown early F–104s in Air Defence Command. He later became the American pilot in a Canadian aircraft based in France who locked wing-tips in a head-on collision with a British Canberra over Germany! Fortunately, all he lost was two tip tanks.

The recce team became complete in September 1964 with an invasion of ten photo interpreters from the school in Rockcliffe. They were all pilots and navigators from ADC; "green" in their new occupation but eager to learn. Noel, of course, was their instructor too, but at least he didn't still have to debrief every mission, and could devote more time to assembling his Aircrew Reconnaissance Manual, a labour of love which served as a basic text for those who followed.

The recce mission offered a freedom, variety and intellectual challenge which I found continually stimulating. We were obliged to learn an enormous mass of detail on transportation and communications systems and structures, on airfields, dams, and military installations. Even if carried to excess, as we frequently suspected, it made the product of each mission a genuine team effort of the operational, intelligence, and technical communities which was extremely satisfying. Furthermore, as we tended to fly two "missions of the day" with everyone flying the same missions in succession, there was an inherent element of competition to get the best picture, or in-flight report, which kept us on our toes. Perhaps the most enjoyable aspect of all, however, was the challenge of getting to know the whole of Central Europe well enough to treat it as a large, familiar flying area where, except for the final few miles to each target, a line on a map was an aid rather than a path from which deviation was discouraged. From this perspective, Marville was ideally situated. If weather permitted unrestricted low level flight, our radius took in the Benelux, Central Germany, most of Bavaria, the Jura, Burgundy, Champagne, and Normandy. If that area was weathered in, we had Hi-Lo-Hi options covering all of West Germany and all of France excluding the Pyrenees, Bordeaux, and the western tip of Brittany (but including the Riviera). Enroute, Air Traffic Control was advisory, so that every pound of fuel could be applied to its intended operational training purpose.

Vic Johnson was one of the stalwart photo interpreters during the reconnaissance heydays of the CF–104. He was posted to 1 Wing in July 1965 and would eventually move with the squadrons to Lahr in March 1967, remaining there until the summer of 1969. During those four years, he worked in all aspects of the CF–104 recce operation. Vic recalls the early days at Marville…

Since the Second World War, most of the lessons learned by the RCAF in the photo reconnaissance field had been forgotten. Photo recce had become a lost art that had to be re-learned by the Canadians. New equipment had to be designed and techniques had to be developed that would take advantage of the technology of the day. Thus was born the Vicom photo-reconnaissance system, designed and built to RCAF

Below: *'854 shortly after takeoff at Marville, France in April, 1964.*

specifications by Computing Devices of Canada especially for the CF–104 Starfighter... Essentially, the system consisted of four Vinten 70 mm electrically driven, high precision cameras fitted with data recorders. The recorders were wired into the aircraft's inertial navigation system and registered certain position and heading information onto the film through an optical link. The cameras normally took eight pictures per second and with an aircraft speed of 450 knots at 500 feet altitude gave optimum frame overlap for stereoscopic viewing of the photos.

A typical photo recce mission would consist of locating and photographing three assigned targets which were usually widely separated. These targets could be dams, factories, bridges or any number of things, and might be anywhere in western Europe. Opportunity targets, such as an unexpected column of tanks hiding in a forest, would be bonuses like candy to a baby for any aspiring recce pilot. Other targets of opportunity included the occasional nudist colony such as at the Isle of Sylt where pilots would sometimes inadvertently stray off track and accidentally hit the camera button while recovering from a low pass!

At the height of the recce program, we numbered almost 100 photo technicians at 1 Wing, and were involved in all aspects of the CF–104 photo support operation. For the first time, photo techs became fully integrated with "hard" aircraft tradesmen. We found ourselves working on line servicing crews, in snag recovery, aircraft maintenance and overhaul, repair, and at all levels of command and supervision. This was a new experience for most of us who had come from static units or base photo sections. The veteran riggers, fitters and armourers were a bit skeptical at first, but generally we adapted well and enjoyed the operational lifestyle. Occasional deployments to other NATO bases for squadron exchanges made life even more interesting.

Our film processing facilities at Marville consisted of four large moving vans that had been converted into mobile photo labs. They were well equipped but basic and certainly contained no space-age hardware. A three-ton truck, with a smaller van on the back that served as a debriefing room for the pilots and photo interpreters following a recce mission, was parked alongside each photo van. The operation used hundreds of thousands of feet of 70 mm film over the years and in the days before environmental consciousness, we simply burned the unused negatives in an outdoor incinerator. The ashes in the incinerator are probably still there, and if one went to reclaim them today they would likely contain a small fortune in residual silver.

While intense reconnaissance activity was being conducted at Marville, the other Wings were busy as well. At Zweibrucken in May, 3 Wing was subjected to yet another Tac Eval, and this time they "poured on the coals" in their efforts to excel and came up with the coveted "one" rating. In June, success came to the Wing in another manner, through one of its 427 Squadron pilots, Flight Lieutenant Hyndman. From the 21st to the 27th of that month, Hyndman and his fellow team members, (Flight Lieutenants Dow, Hull and Frioult, led by Wing Commander Bill Bliss), represented Canada at the annual AFCENT Tactical Weapons Meet at Chaumont, France; the annual competition between the two Allied Tactical Air Forces. The results were very satisfying for the Canadians. 4 ATAF won the Meet itself, the RCAF won the Best Nation award, and Flight Lieutenant Frioult was the top individual scorer.

During the year, 434 Squadron acquired a significantly more nautical air when Rear Admiral Welland, on a visit to the squadron, accepted the appointment of Honourary Flag Officer. Shortly thereafter, the "Bluenosers" began RCN infiltration procedures by making exchange visits with personnel from Canada's aircraft carrier, HMCS Bonaventure. These visits resulted in the accumulation of a great deal of nautical lore and memorabilia, and prompted one visiting navy pilot to quip; "It's a pleasure to be visiting the best Strike squadron in Europe and the finest naval establishment in the RCAF."

1965 provided numerous highlights in Baden-Soellingen as well. On the 15th of February a significant change occurred for 4 Wing and Canadians as a whole, when the Air Force Roundel with the Union Jack as well as the Canadian Red Ensign were lowered for the last time. Their replacement with the new Canadian Flag on the Starfighters was immediate. Initially, a large Flag was superimposed directly over the Ensign, but in due course the Ensigns were removed and a smaller Flag was employed.

In Baden and throughout Germany, a problem precipitated by this new supersonic era was the increased frequency of noise complaints caused both by low flying aircraft and by sonic booms. 4 Wing and the Air Division waged a countering campaign through articles in the local newspapers and television appearances. The Wing also encouraged familiarization visits by local civilian groups in order to further educate them in the role of the CF–104s in Europe and the imperative of these noisy, low-level, high speed missions.

Ken Thorneycroft, who would not only command 444 Squadron during the '104 era, but in 1967 would also assume command of the OTU, reflects on early Starfighter operations out of Baden-Soellingen...

Flying in the low level environment proved to be very challenging. The visibility was never very good at the best of times, and often the industrial haze cut the forward visibility down to two or three miles. Swarms of gliders seemed to congregate over many hill tops and small helicopters were everywhere. It really is amazing that there were no mid-air collisions... there certainly were many near misses! Weather was a continuous problem as well, with extended periods of dense fog in October and November which created havoc with the flying programs.

When General deGaulle kicked the NATO folks out of France, 4 Wing took on another CF–104 Squadron, namely 421. The Standard Operating Procedure was to pool the Base aircraft... two Squadrons operated during the day with the third Squadron utilizing the aircraft for night flying operations. The '104 was working in well. We usually had sufficient aircraft to meet our requirements, and almost everyone managed to get at least 200 hours a year. Time hogs did even better!

Radar prediction was perfected in the early days of operations. Routes could be flown with confidence on radar maps prepared by Mission Planning. This system was "invented" by Flight-Lieutenant John Eggenberger, who was a hell of a good type... even if he **was** *a Navigator!*

On one Tac Eval, the Wing generated and launched 39 aircraft for the initial "scramble"...one hell of a lot of aluminum getting airborne in quick succession! I don't know of any Wing anywhere in the system that equalled or bettered this record launch.

The QRA alert commitment called for two aircraft and crews from each Squadron; a total of six aircraft on fifteen minutes. Duty at the QRA came up about every five or six days, and after a day spent "captive" in the Q, we found people came out mean as bears, and it was almost a must to give the outgoing folks a day off to give them time to become relatively human again.

In sum, the Wing maintained a high level of operational efficiency throughout the Nuclear Strike period. All Tac Evals were successful, and indeed, the Canadian Wings enjoyed an enviable reputation for operational effectiveness.

The "down side" of 1965 was the continued high CF–104 loss rate. Twelve more Canadian Starfighters fell during the year and the only solace that the RCAF could draw from this record was that the number of fatalities had been reduced from 1964's total of seven, to two. Flight Lieutenant James N. Stacey of 421 Squadron was not to be one of the lucky ones... On February 8 in CF–104 '894, he struck the ground during a low level navigation mission over France and was killed instantly. Then on May 16, Flight Lieutenant I.W. McKnight disappeared over the North Sea while on a maintenance test flight out of Prestwick, Scotland. Some wreckage, including the pilot's helmet was found, but the cause of the accident was undetermined.

For some time, the RCAF had viewed the CF–104 accident history with considerable concern. While a substantial number of the accidents were attributable to mechanical problems - problems that would be largely rectified - a disturbing number of the accidents carried some implication of pilot shortcomings. Furthermore, senior staffs were beginning to question the wisdom of generally placing only experienced fighter pilots in command of the aircraft. There was an increasingly-widespread feeling that the youthful reflexes of the younger pipeliners might be at least compensatory when flying this demanding aircraft where split-second decisions and actions in critical situations were absolutely necessary. Accordingly, starting with Course 9 (the first "steady state" CF–104 course) there would be an increased presence of pipeline pilots who had graduated with distinction from the undergraduate pilot training program.

Nonetheless, even some of the accidents had their lighter aspects. Jack Frazer had a distinguished career in CF–104s as CO 439 Squadron and later as Base Commander at Baden-Soellingen. Jack remembers the events surrounding the loss of '659 on September 16, 1965, when both pilot and passenger "jettisoned the aircraft"...

This story concerns the 1 Wing Marville days and a slow, soft spoken Texan, Captain Chuck Summers. Chuck was a 7th US Army officer (Ground Liaison Officer) assigned to our Wing. A GLO wasn't required to fly, but some took the opportunity to see the job from the pilot's viewpoint. After having been with us for a while, Chuck decided that he would take the plunge and go for a ride in the CF–104. His pilot on the mission was Flight Lieutenant Ed Griedanus, a Wing Simulator Instructor who was well qualified and regularly flew our aircraft.

It was a warm, sunny day and the mission, a low level recce sortie, went swimmingly until they took a birdstrike which destroyed their engine and made an ejection inevitable. Chuck had been properly briefed, so he knew what he was supposed to do even if, like most of us, he wasn't overjoyed at the prospect. However, rather than assuming the correct ejection posture when Ed told him to eject, Chuck leaned forward to pull The Handle. Thus he was bent over when the rocket boosted him out of the aircraft and he suffered some minor back injuries. Whether as a result of this or because he was understandably fraught at what was going on, Chuck lost consciousness after pulling the handle. Fortunately, the automatic ejection sequence operated exactly as advertised, pushing him clear of the seat and opening his parachute.

His parachute descent to a landing in a cow pasture was observed by a young French woman who rushed to give him assistance. Finding him alive and unconscious but otherwise uninjured, she sat herself down, put his head in her lap, and held her open parasol to shade him from the bright sun.

When he "came to", the first thing that Chuck saw was a cow standing nearby, slowly munching its cud and observing him with great interest. From there, his gaze moved to the parasol and then to the face of an attractive young lady looking down at him with great concern. As he gradually remembered the circumstances which had brought him to where he was, it was perhaps understandable that Chuck's first thought was, "I've died and gone to Heaven." In the meantime, Ed had landed, found a phone, and informed the Base of the circumstances. Shortly thereafter, he and Chuck were recovered.

There is always great relief when the good word is received that aircrew have survived a "prang"; but in this case, Chuck's story told at the bar in his Texas twang, just broke all of us up!

1966 would also prove to be a year of considerable upheaval and change to Canadian Starfighter operations in Europe. As has been mentioned previously, there had been considerable high-level concern over the perceived high accident rate, and several steps were implemented in 1966 with a view to extending the longevity of both the aircraft and the pilots that flew them. Along with the introduction of a greater number of appropriately-qualified pipeline pilots into the CF–104 training scheme, technical staffs focused on what could be done for the jet. They determined that the Starfighter had backup systems for everything *except* its one engine, and since adding a second means of propulsion was deemed out of the question, ways were sought to make the J–79 more reliable and predictable. The result was a Spectrometric Oil Analysis Program (SOAP test); a preventative maintenance procedure targeted at detecting excessive wear and possible engine deterioration. This program would prove instrumental in preventing the loss of valuable equipment and possibly further human lives throughout the balance of the CF–104 era.

In June, another AFCENT Tactical Weapons Meet was held in Chaumont. Again, Canadian representation was in the vanguard of the honours parade. 4 ATAF won the Meet overall, the RCAF was the second-best team, and Flight Lieutenant LB Marion of 421 Squadron won the top individual honours for having the highest single score in the competition.

By this time, the CF–104 had been operating for over three years with the Air Division, and several pilots were rapidly approaching the coveted 1000–hour mark on type. Before the year was out, such notables as Con Platz, Bill Worthy, Dick Spencer, Stu Deacon, Ed Rozdeba, Gerry Walker and Ron Potter would achieve this plateau, then turn their log book over to the next page and keep on writing...

Baden-Soellingen had its social and support hands rather full this summer when, in an operation named appropriately enough Tight Squeeze, 434 and 427 Squadrons deployed to 4 Wing through July, August and part of September. The Silver Falcons of 430 spent their time away from Zweibrucken either in Marville, in Decimomannu, or on leave. The reason for all this uprooting was the resurfacing of the Zweibrucken runway. By September 16th, all the wandering nomads of 3 Wing had returned, some rather more auspiciously than others. In fact, the 427 Lions with their eight deployed aircraft were the only unit able to find the home aerodrome for the traditional flypast on their return.

In September, CF–104s were also flown for the first time to Norway and north of the Arctic Circle. On this occasion, Squadron Leader Deacon and Flight Lieutenant Clayton paid a visit to RNoAF Station Bodo. This would mark the beginning of many Canadian Starfighter excursions to "The Land of the Midnight Sun", and several squadron exchanges with the Norwegians.

Over in France, Marville was experiencing what would turn out to be its last full year of CF–104 operations, and remarkable progress had been achieved since the Wing transitioned in 1964. Bill Turnbull flew Starfighters in the recce role with 441 Squadron, and has vivid memories of Marville and the reconnaissance business at that time...

My first view of Europe from the window of a Yukon aircraft left a lasting impression - a crazy-quilt of fields as far as the eye could see. Even after nine months of low-level navigation training, that crazy-quilt was to prove a formidable challenge.

The airfield was located just west of the village of Marville. Designated historic, the buildings could not be altered by their occupants, and still bore bullet scars from one or other of the World Wars. One of the first things you noticed about the base itself was the flock of sheep grazing in the infield. They were most efficient at keeping the grass cut, and never once strayed onto a taxiway or the runway.

Marville was a NATO standard airfield with a single, 8000-foot runway and unrevetted circular dispersals. The Wing Instrument Flight's (WIF) T–33s occupied one dispersal, while 441 and 439 Squadrons shared another. My squadron's crew area was a small blister tacked onto the single hangar in the dispersal. 439 was housed in a somewhat temporary-looking building along with our mission planning facility. Film processing and interpretation were carried out in modified van-bodied trucks which technically gave us a deployment capability. The vehicles were rumoured, however, to be less than roadworthy.

The recce CF–104 retained all of the Strike variant's navigation and weapons capability. The only cockpit difference was the presence of a camera control panel in the right console, replacing the nuclear weapon enabling panel of the Strike aircraft. The right side was an unfortunate location, however, since changing camera selections required removing one's hand from the control column. The panel had on-off selector switches for the four cameras, a two-position frame rate selector, and an indicator light which blinked with film advance. A steady light usually indicated a film jam, but one didn't see that too often, the Vintons being quite reliable.

Some other nations had purchased an RF–104 variant which was less than satisfactory on two counts. The GAF version had no forward looking radar. Most importantly, its tri-camera arrangement was mounted in the belly with the oblique cameras set at an extreme depression angle. Consequently, at low altitudes one had to bank away from the target in order to capture it on film. This made it difficult to gauge where the cameras were pointing and denied the pilot much opportunity for target viewing.

The CF–104's left, right, and nose-facing oblique cameras set at very shallow depression angles were a much better arrangement for low level tactical operations. The fourth, vertically-oriented camera, was of limited practical value since (as with all vertical, non-panoramic cameras) its narrow field-of-view required relatively high overflight altitudes. This in turn demanded clear weather and a benign environment, neither of which was anticipated in the European theatre. In any case, the side-oblique cameras were the favourites since they permitted a low altitude pass, easy estimation of where the cameras were pointed, and a good view of the target to the pilot. Adjacent frame pairs usually provided overlapping coverage which, when viewed through a stereoscope, yielded an exaggerated three-dimensional image, a significant assist to interpretation. There was no sighting device for the cameras, but it only required a few practice runs to learn the approximate frame boundaries for varying stand-off distances and bank angles.

Originally all cameras were fitted with 3-inch lenses made by Zeiss Canada. A 12–inch telephoto was available for the nose oblique position, but was rarely used. Eventually a 1.75–inch lens was fitted to the vertical camera to provide a wider field of view. The side oblique and

Photo above: *Shortly after adoption of the Canada Flag in 1965. Note the enormous flag on the far aircraft, which was initially applied to completely cover the Red Ensign. The aircraft in the foreground have had the initial flags removed and smaller versions applied.*

vertical coverage still did not overlap, however. All three obliques were needed to provide horizon-to-horizon coverage, but this combination was not ideal since the forward and side-facing perspectives were so different, and the "nose-facer" would not provide stereo frame pairs.

Standard Kodak Tri–X film was used. Several hundred frames were carried in detachable, two–spool magazines accessed through doors in the camera pod. Film economy was deemed important since fewer exposed frames meant less time processing and searching for the target imagery. Ideally, the pilot would plan his mission to use a single camera so that only one magazine had to be downloaded and processed. This presupposed a good knowledge of target location (variously called "plot" or "plot position"). If the target could not be visually acquired on the run-in, one usually ran the camera(s) based on timing, perhaps even selecting all three obliques as a hedge.

We never experimented much, if at all, with colour, infrared (IR), or false-colour IR films. We probably should have, since standard black and white film is not the best for detecting and analyzing camouflaged targets. Of course, an infra-red line scanner would have been a welcome addition, but our staff officers (all fighter pilots to whom reconnaissance was not a manly activity) got us out of the business about the time IR scanners could be purchased for a few thousand dollars.

By the mid-60s, tactical recce had not changed much since WWII. Day photo was still the primary technique. The USAF was operating the RF–101, the Danes the RF–84, the British the Hunter, the Germans and Dutch the RF–104 described above. RAF Canberras and early USAF RF–4Cs had a night capability based on photo-cartridges, although advertising one's position with a string of flares was not a very survivable technique.

In any conventional photo operation, the return, processing, and interpretation of exposed film slows the delivery of useful intelligence information to the requesting agency. A camera or processing malfunction could even ruin the film. As a hedge against either eventuality, great stress was placed on the pilot's obtaining (and relaying by radio) accurate visual reports on his assigned targets. Much of our training was devoted to learning the standard nomenclature used to describe a matrix of some two dozen target types and their key features (Essential Items of Information or EIIs).

Our mission planners would draw 1:250,000 and 1:50,000 scale maps for the mission and plot approximate target locations on the former. The pilot, from information contained in his "frag order", would plot the precise target locations on the 1:50,000 maps, which we found were essential for the target run-in phase. These positions were then transferred by eye to the 1:250,000 maps on which the route would eventually be drawn. Careful perusal of the maps would usually yield a preferred direction of approach, and track lines were drawn to provide what was estimated to be the best offset for photography.

A standard training mission comprised three pinpoint targets, and one line of communications (LOC) search ("line search" for short). The latter might be a segment of road, rail line, canal or river along which we were to photograph and record details of, say, vehicular movement. As an aside, trying to manhandle a '104 along a twisting LOC while looking for and recording sightings required more hands, eyes and flying skills than most of us possessed.

All pilot observations had to be written down. We carried a set of log card-sized forms for this purpose, one for each target, printed on card stock. The recce CF–104 was originally equipped with a wire-type voice recorder which turned out to be an idea before its time. Because it was so difficult to locate the correct portion of the wire during playback, these units were removed from the aircraft. Remember, the original installation pre-dated today's compact audio cassette. In later years, we talked about installing an audio cassette recorder but the price of a mil spec unit, reportedly around $1000, seemed astronomical.

In retrospect, our failure to push for relatively inexpensive modifications seems funny, but not as funny as the occasional directive from on high that we were using too many maps. The notion that expending, say, $5 worth of maps for each mission involving an aircraft which then cost $2500 per hour to fly was ludicrous, and no doubt reflected the fallacy of managing money in discreet little pots. In any case, whereas the 1:250,000 maps were inevitably cut with a utility knife into a kind of crude strip map, we carefully folded the precious 1:50,000 maps into clear plastic folders on which we marked our track and timing data with grease pencils. This allowed the maps to be re-used many times.

At one time, our stock of 1:50,000 coverage for France was rather spotty. A good substitute turned out to be 1:200,000 scale Michelin road maps which portrayed cultural features in exquisite detail. The French 1:250,000 maps were among the finest I have ever seen, comparable to the Canadian maps used in our training. In fact, they resembled Michelin road maps with the addition of contour relief. For whatever the reason, we used American maps, and they were lousy. Even the JOG series, which appeared in the late 1960s and which is still in use, proved inferior in readability to the French and Canadian maps. The makers just didn't seem to realize that dark colours overlaid on dark colours become a blur when you're being bounced around in high speed, low level flight.

I mentioned that I had received no recce training in Canada. It took about three months of training on squadron to become "combat ready" in the role. Frankly, it took me at least that long to feel reasonably confident that I could complete an entire mission without getting lost. The nine months' training in Canada really hadn't prepared me for low level navigation in Europe, which had none of the lakes and few of the distinctive terrain features to which I was accustomed. Moreover, the landscape was a clutter of look-alike settings and the maps which we originally used were woefully out of date. They were based on immediate post-war survey data and showed few contour details.

Radar navigation in Europe proved almost impossible without predictions, and the continuous strip prediction developed at 4 Wing did not exist in the early years. At 1 Wing, we only practiced low level radar missions as a means to meeting our mandatory night flying requirements. Needless to say, we had no luck correlating the radar picture with maps which lacked contour information, and tended to follow the INS. Given its inaccuracies, we often wandered rather badly. One pilot, returning from a night mission, remarked that, at one point, he had observed many "flares" being fired from the ground. We later figured that he had flown through an active artillery range located close to his planned track!

One big advantage of being based in France was ready access to the largest and least crowded flying area in Europe. Only if we could not find good weather in France would we look to Germany or the Benelux countries. On one of my first trips to Germany, I felt that the cockpit was getting progressively warmer, although I wasn't sure whether this was real or an illusion attributable to the difficulty I was having navigating in unfamiliar terrain. The first confirming clue came during a line search when the INS failed. The standby compass couldn't keep up with the twisting and turning. I wandered off on an incorrect heading, became lost, and decided to head for home, figuring I could always request radar vectors. Then the slight background hiss normally present in the headset stopped. I keyed the UHF, but it was dead. One by one, electrical systems were dropping off line and warning lights were coming on. I still couldn't decide whether the heat in the cockpit was imaginary or real. I had no idea where I was.

It turned out that I was near Zweibrucken, and repeated calls on the emergency radio eventually elicited vectors to that Canadian airfield. Afraid to select the electrically-driven flaps beyond the takeoff position and anxious to get on the ground, I touched down at a pretty

Photo captions: ***Above*** *– '899, the second-last production CF-104 enroute to work and above the weather, at least for the moment;* ***Below*** *– a photo pod equipped CF-104 taxis for take-off at 1(F) Wing, Marville in 1966;* ***At right, inset*** *– a typical formation takeoff. Photo by Bill Turnbull.*

good speed. Never having been to this base before, I did not know that the runway had a pronounced hump at its centre. Naturally, this created the illusion that I was quickly running out of runway, and I braked harshly, coming to a stop at the crest of the rise.

Sheepishly jettisoning the drag chute on the runway (a no-no according to the creed), I taxied to the dispersal feeling a bit foolish for having become lost, still wondering whether I had over-reacted to the electrical failures. Therefore, I was somewhat gratified when the groundcrew warned me to stay clear of the aircraft's fuselage, which they reported was too hot to touch! It turned out that the inlet duct to the air-conditioning unit had become loose, porting 17th stage compressor air into the Electronics Bay (E-Bay). The temperature in the bay had risen to the point that the circuit breakers located there had begun to trip.

It rained a lot at Marville, and the wind always seemed to be 90° to the runway. It was one of those places where you could have strong winds and low ceilings, and the two seemed to go hand in hand - inevitably accompanied by driving rain. Sometimes, landing with a crosswind well above drag chute limits, you simply had to ride out the hydroplaning phase, travelling perhaps half the length of the runway before the tires would make contact with the asphalt... a most helpless feeling since nothing - not brakes, not even nosewheel steering - would do anything. One was along for the ride in this 17,000 pound collection of aluminum, titanium, and JP–4.

Taxiing in after one of these hair-raising experiences, I had a close up view of the most spectacular CF–104 arrival I have ever seen. One of my confrères seemingly forgot about the crosswind limit and promptly deployed his drag chute after landing. His aircraft immediately turned into the wind, which happened to be 90° to the runway. Going sideways, it must have decelerated quickly thereby allowing the tires to bite, for it then abruptly snapped 180° to face the opposite side of the runway. I was enthralled by the immense rooster tail of spray and the way the airplane was rocking from one main wheel to the other. As quickly as the pirouettes had begun, they ended with the aircraft pointing straight down the centreline. After shutting down my aircraft at the dispersal, I waited for the other pilot to taxi in. Recalling his face, I can truthfully say that I have never seen a *"whiter shade of pale".*

Fortunately, the CF–104 accident rate took a dramatic turn for the better in 1966. The number of "A" Category (write-off) accidents was reduced to five, and fatalities were again limited to two. On March 4th, Flight Lieutenant D.C. Lawson of 427 Squadron was killed in'789 while attempting to remain in visual contact with the ground on a low level navigation route not far from the city of Freiburg. On a happier note, there were some spectacular saves during the year. In May, Flight Lieutenant Roy Barnes of 4 Wing received the Queen's Commendation, for landing his crippled Starfighter near Munich under adverse weather conditions rather than risk danger to civilians by ejecting over a densely populated area. On November 30th, Flight Lieutenant V. Peppard of 427 Squadron was aboard'826 on a low level route when the oil low level light came on. He promptly transmitted a "Mayday" and in a beautifully choreographed series of actions with German Air Force radar controllers at their Lechfeld base, got the aircraft safely on the ground there in an absolute minimum of time. On shut down, it was determined that only *one pint* of oil remained in the engine. For his quick reactions and superb airmanship, Flight Lieutenant Peppard received a Good Show Award from the Directorate of Flight Safety.

As 1966 drew to a close in Zweibrucken and Baden-Soellingen, changes of a significant nature were occurring within the respective Wings that would officially come to pass in the following spring. In a nutshell, 434 Squadron at 3 Wing and 444 Squadron at 4 Wing were placed on the chopping block after another fiscal review, due in no small measure to the fact that the first four years of CF–104 operations had severely attritted the fleet (37 "A" category accidents), and in order to keep unit strengths at a respectable level, it was decided to reduce the number of squadrons at both bases to two apiece. Though the Bluenosers of 434 *officially* deactivated on February 28, 1967, in reality they ceased operations at Zweibrucken at year's end, 1966. Along with the augmented aircraft fleet acquired by the two remaining squadrons, the pilots of the now-defunct 434 Squadron were also distributed to 430 and 427 Squadrons in an equitable manner. A similar procedure would occur at Baden–Soellingen on March 31st when 444 Squadron officially disbanded. The Silver Falcons at Zweibrucken "made out like bandits" during this reorganization process... As the junior squadron at 3 Wing, they had the worst job accommodation environment; but with the shut-down of 434, the Falcons purged the last vestiges of nauticalness from the Bluenosers digs and moved in for an extended stay. The Starfighter era had been a relatively brief one for 434 Squadron. In its four years of CF–104 operations, the unit had flown approximately 15,300 hours, and although three unit Starfighters had been lost, there was no loss of life. They had certainly left their mark at Zweibrucken and had contributed a host of memorable experiences. Few there at the time will ever forget Dave Thom's thrilling rescue by an Italian helicopter at Decci after his ejection, when they plucked him out of the brine and then took off for home with him still dangling at the end of the hoist. Who also could forget John Ayres' remarkable feat of two takeoffs and two consecutive "nylon let-downs". Though their tenure in the CF–104 era was brief, the excellent record of the Bluenosers with the Starfighter speaks for itself.

Enroute at altitude; pilot's eye view. - photo by Gary Hook

Halcyon Days

1967 was a year for momentous events on the world stage. In China, Mao's Cultural Revolution rocked the nation; in the Middle East, Israel stunned world onlookers with a blitzkrieg-type victory over Egypt in what is now known as the Six Day War; in the United States, there were huge demonstrations against the Vietnam war; in South Africa, Dr. Christiaan Barnard performed the first human heart transplant. Meanwhile, in Canada, it was a year of feasting and merriment as the nation celebrated its one hundredth birthday. Montreal hosted Expo '67 - the World's Fair, while for Canadian servicemen and their families in Europe, many parades, functions and flypasts were held to celebrate the century of confederation, growth and expansion. However, the winds of change were once again blowing for the Air Division...

Throughout 1966, France had become progressively more disenchanted with the existing structure of NATO, and ultimately elected to pursue her own nuclear and conventional strategy while maintaining a special status of self-determination within the Alliance. Part of France's newly-defined policy called for the elimination of all foreign troops from French soil, and accordingly, 1 Wing at Marville and the Air Division Headquarters at the Chateau in Metz had to search for new homes in a different neighbourhood. After due consideration, Lahr, about 30 miles south of Baden-Soellingen in the Rhine valley, was chosen as the new location for both the Wing and the administrative hub of the Air Division.

Bill Turnbull recalls the actual departure of the aircraft from Marville...

As the deadline for leaving France approached, we still had no word on where we would move. Reportedly, the French Air Force was under pressure to vacate their base at Lahr. Indeed, they eventually did accede and, in March and April, first 439 and then 441 flew their aircraft there.

Our departure from Marville was an emotional event for many, especially the French citizens who had worked at the Base for up to 13 years. I can still see the tears streaming down the face of our squadron driver, although I can't remember his name. He was the stereotypical Frenchman of the wartime movies - rather short, always dressed in a slightly seedy dark suit and a dark beret. He drove our black Peugeot 403. It was a terribly uncomfortable car, and he was a terrible driver, but he was always there to take us anywhere we wanted to go on the base... an almost forgotten luxury. Every day he would come to work with a loaf of French bread, a hunk of cheese wrapped in wax paper, and an unlabeled bottle of red wine. This he would carefully ration over the day - at morning break, lunch, and afternoon break - so that all was

Above: *Doug Fenton "mounts up" at Marville in 1966. Note the spurs on the heels of his flying boots. These spurs, connected by cables to the ejection seat, prevented leg flailing on ejection.*

consumed by mid-afternoon.

Each squadron planned a 12-plane departure flyby. The morning of 439's leaving Marville was sunny but misty, and the 4-plane elements had some difficulty joining up. In fact, they put on a spectacular, if dangerous, airshow as sections criss-crossed the airfield at low altitude, sometimes encountering each other head on. From our vantage point on the ground, various derisory remarks about the "pussycats", our usual term for the 439 Tigers, could be heard, although the situation was more scary than funny. Their equally less than affectionate name for us was "anteaters"... a reference to the most unfortunate rendition of a silver fox which adorned the official 441 badge.

Our own flight to Lahr was uneventful until we were running in for the overhead break in 4-plane sections. I was number three in the third echelon. For some reason, my section lead thought he was too close to the other elements and slowed to around 250 knots, at which speed the CF–104 was very sluggish. He then managed to drop us into the wash of the sections ahead. That was the one time I can recall actually being out of control in a '104. One moment I was rolled 90° left and was staring at the canopy of number two; the next moment the roll had reversed 180° and I had a close–up view of number four's canopy. Full stick deflection did seemingly nothing. Suddenly we were all upright, still in tight formation.

All of our equipment was moved by truck, courtesy of the U.S. Army. It was said we could not have managed the move without American assistance. Perhaps that was the origin of the local joke to the effect that what Charles deGaulle had really said to the Americans was, "Leave France, and take your cheapskate Canadian friends with you." That may have been the one occasion when our photo vans were actually driven anywhere. I say "may", because I'm not certain they made the trip under their own power.

Speaking of the photo vans, obviously they had to head down the road along with the rest of the support equipment in advance of the aircraft transfer. This they did, just days prior to the first Starfighter arrivals at Lahr. Thus, in March, 1 Wing ground personnel packed their bags and headed east. Vic Johnson recalls this transition period and the early days at 1 Wing's new home in Germany...

Our centennial project would be to move a base. Rumours buzzed as to where we might relocate the Marville operation - Holland...? Belgium...? Back to Canada...? Finally we were told it was to be Lahr, a base in the Rhine Valley of southern West Germany.

Lahr had been a Luftwaffe base during the First and Second World Wars and a French Air Force base since. I was part of an advance party that arrived in Lahr in March of 1967 to find the base in a pitiful state of disrepair. It was as if the clock had stopped in 1945. The barracks we moved into were decrepit, unheated, and several windows were broken. There were no facilities for hot water, and the toilets consisted of holes in a concrete floor. (This particular building is now called the Europahof and is used as a transient accommodation centre for service families.) When our detachment commander, Wing Commander Jim Dunlop, saw the conditions, he hit the ceiling and stormed off to do battle with the French base commander. Not long after, we were moved to better quarters at the Menard Caserne, a headquarters complex on the other side of town.

We immediately began to prepare for the arrival of the squadrons, but because the French Air Force occupied the main base, we were only given one dispersal area - the north marguerite - in which to run the flying operation. As soon as all the support facilities were in place, rudimentary though they were, 439 Squadron flew in. Following a formation fly-past, they landed, refuelled and flew sorties that afternoon. The photo recce operation never skipped a beat!

Meanwhile the job of moving the base itself was gaining momentum. Trucks rolled in around the clock and had to be unloaded at all hours of the day and night by the same people who supported the flying operation. Eighteen-hour working days were not uncommon. Most of the airmen had left their families behind in Marville because of a severe housing shortage in the Lahr area. The French military still occupied all the married quarters and were in no hurry to leave. The crunch came in July when the Canadians living in married quarters at Marville were

Above: *One of the many iterations of "Tiger Birds" that flew out of Baden-Soellingen and Lahr with 439 Squadron during the '104 era.*

ordered by French authorities to vacate. A crisis was averted when most of these families voluntarily moved into camping trailers and tents in camp sites around the Lahr area. Luckily, 1967 boasted one of the balmiest summers on record, and most people simply enjoyed it until more permanent accommodation became available in the fall.

Soon, the French military began to pack up and leave according to the terms of the agreement, and things started to improve. The "grown-ups" began throwing great bunches of money our way and the Base soon began to come up to RCAF standards. Flying operations moved to the main Base, and the photo operation acquired a permanent building near the flight line.

Lahr, we had discovered, was a delightful town in a marvellous location. After northern France with its dismal climate and backward way of life, the Black Forest area with its fairytale villages, festivals, gasthausen and "gemütlichkeit" was a paradise. The local people, who were apprehensive at the first influx of unaccompanied Canadian airmen, soon came to realize that we were not the bunch of drunken lumberjacks that a disinformation campaign had led some of them to believe. There were more than enough gasthausen and cafés in the area to accommodate everyone, and we were soon made to feel welcome. Given the situation though, it is a credit to both the local Germans and the Canadians that no serious incidents occurred early on that could have soured what was to become an excellent relationship over the years.

Bill Turnbull recalls the recce operation at Lahr, as seen from a pilot's perspective...

Our new home at Base Aerienne 139 was its North Dispersal. At one time, the French Air Force had held U.S. tactical nuclear weapons there. The weapons bunkers, guard dog kennels and double fencing were silent testimony to those days. 441 Squadron was housed in what had been the dog keepers' building. For the first six months of our occupancy, the base remained under French control, and a Mirage III squadron occupied the South Dispersal.

The French aircrew invited us to a welcoming get-together. Under reversed circumstances, Canadians would have laid on beer. The French served champagne. I always thought that said something about our respective cultures.

There was no published approach for Lahr. The French used random radar recovery methods, and we were always impressed by the speed with which they could get us all down, especially since Lahr was surrounded by controlled airways. After about three months of operating this way, we sent our own ATC people out to the French approach facility to see how this feat was managed. It turned out that the French controllers were only looking at discrete secondary (IFF) returns, descending us through airways in blissful ignorance of any civil traffic which might be there... further proof that the "big sky" theory works, I guess.

Squadron Exchange was a mandatory exercise, and 441 hosted two exchanges while housed at the North Dispersal. The first was with a USAF RF–101 squadron which had just returned from Vietnam. As if to confirm our own survival doctrine, this unit, during a year's operations, had lost only one aircraft and no pilots using high speed, low level techniques.

Our second exchange was with a Danish RF–84 squadron. The RF–84 carried two enormous drop-tanks which the Danes could not fill and still get off Lahr's 8000 foot runway on a standard day. The French

Below: *This mighty J-79 engine gets a run-up after routine maintenance at Baden-Soellingen.*

had a self-erecting net barrier for the Mirage IIIs, triggered by photoelectric detectors about 1000 feet from the end of the runway. When lining up for takeoff, the Danes would call to have the barrier "put on manual" since they would otherwise have triggered it on their takeoff rolls.

Lining up for a stream takeoff with an RF–84, I could hear the odd low frequency moan of its engine over the noise of my own aircraft. Blue smoke was emanating from every panel and the only confirmation of brake release was a slight extension of the nose strut. After a seemingly interminable delay, the aircraft began to move, finally disappearing in its own exhaust plume. About the time I began to think it must have failed to get airborne, it appeared... barely clearing the rooftops of Langenwinkel, a small village about 1/2 mile off the end of the runway. I lit the '104's 'burner and rolled, catching the RF–84 before it had completed a 180° turn downwind. Later, leading this jet down a twisting line search, I discovered that at least one aircraft was inferior to the '104 for that kind of exercise...the poor old RF–84 simply lacked the power to maintain speed during sustained turning manoeuvres.

I missed the return exchange to Aalborg because I was called to participate in a Board of Inquiry into a fatal accident at 4 Wing. While the Squadron was away, I met one of the 441 pilots in the Lahr PX with a shopping cart full of steaks. I was surprised to see him there when he was supposed to be in Denmark. He grinned, and said he had come to pick up steaks for "the barbeque". When I asked how he was going to transport them to Denmark, he said, "In a '104". When I asked where he was going to put them in the aircraft, he replied, "In the E–Bay...we took all the black boxes out". Now, the Lahr PX carried only Danish beef. The irony of flying a '104 from Denmark to Lahr to buy Danish meat because it was cheaper there (given the cost of operating the aircraft) seemed lost on some people in those days. As to the Saturday night barbeque, I guess the boys had a good time, for they swore a pact of secrecy to never talk about it. Years later, I still could not get anyone to tell me what it was I'd missed.

One story that did get retold several times concerned two Canadian '104s going after the same submarine target. The Danes had a real-world intelligence mission to keep tabs on Warsaw Pact shipping in the Baltic. Their method involved dead-reckoning their way to an estimated target position and then commencing an area search. They were fascinated with the CF–104's INS which rendered this task immensely easier. During exchanges, the visitors usually flew some of the host unit's daily missions. Two CF–104s were out looking for a submarine which they both acquired on radar about the same time. For safety's sake, it was our practice to maintain radio contact and to call "on" and "off" targets with a view to avoiding mid-air collisions. On this day, as on many others, the air was very hazy and the visibility limited. The radio calls indicated both Canadian aircraft were converging simultaneously on the submarine. Being clever fellows, and still unable to see each other, the pilots agreed that one would pass to the left of the target, the other to the right. There was only one thing that they forgot to establish - the direction from which each was approaching; which turned out to be opposite. Needless to say, the aircraft came very close to colliding head on.

To proclaim our ownership of the dog keepers' building, a couple of the boys decided to paint its large chimney in the 441 black-and-white checkerboard scheme. Sometime later, one of the departing pilots donated his huge 1960 Ford stationwagon to the squadron, and it too acquired a checkerboard paint scheme. It was also equipped with a drag chute which could be deployed, although the poor old thing could barely muster enough speed to blossom the chute.

Other than decorating the chimney, we had to await the landlord's departure before refurbishing the Base. The French didn't waste any money on cosmetics. In fact, through a combination of benign neglect and design, Lahr was an almost impossible place to find from the air without a serviceable TACAN. The infields were farmed which meant there was no apparent break to the surrounding crazy-quilt of fields. The dispersal areas were obscured by trees and shrubs, and the buildings were a patchwork of olive-drab paint, patching compound, and rust. In fact, the only thing which gave away the airfield's location was our white Yukon and Hercules aircraft parked on the small transient ramp.

To provide meals for the aircrew, one of the outbuildings was turned into a kitchen. Our cook was an expatriate Spaniard who spoke only Spanish and had been hired as a cleaner. His credentials as a chef were questionable but, to our amazement, no one contracted food poisoning. As is so often the case, a close, affectionate bond developed between the Spaniard and the pilots. Thus, there was a note of sadness to our eventually leaving the dispersal for better quarters across the field since it meant losing our newest adopted member of the Squadron.

After taking over the Base, we set about to destroy its beautiful camouflage, planting bright green grass on the infield, cutting down much of the foliage, and painting the buildings lovely pastel shades. When I asked the Base Commander why he was doing this, he replied that camouflage didn't matter when a nuclear weapon detonating within a three-mile radius would flatten the place. There you see again our mentality at the time - nuke or nothing.

Those were also the days of centralized maintenance. The Base Aircraft Maintenance Engineering Officer (BAMEO) insisted that he did not have enough people to operate from the dispersals, and so we poured a concrete pad on which to park our shiny silver aircraft in two geometrically perfect lines. The aircrew called this our "Egyptian Line", referring of course to events of the 1967 Middle East War. Eventually the Base Operations Officer (BOpsO) forced the issue, and we did successfully operate for several months from the South Dispersal, just to prove a point.

The aircrew were always furious at the maintenance organization's telling them when they could fly... "the tail wagging the dog" was an oft-heard phrase. In all fairness, we never stuck to any predictable schedule during the early days at Lahr, and the CF–104's avionics were a maintenance headache. Ultimately, we adopted a flying routine whereby "waves" of five aircraft were launched at five-minute intervals. The launch cycles were repeated several times over the course of the day, alternating between the two squadrons. On a good day, an individual pilot had a reasonable chance of getting two missions, although by late afternoon most of the aircraft were unserviceable.

Typically, the pilot proceeded to Mission Planning about 1–1/2 hours before the scheduled takeoff time. It took about an hour to "cut and paste" a mission. Collecting his safety equipment, signing out, and getting airborne took about 30 minutes, and a typical mission was 1–1/2 hours long. Upon recovery, he taxied by the photo processing facility (we finally retired the vans) where the film was downloaded. By the time the pilot had shut down and signed in, the processed film was usually on the light tables. He then spent about another half hour selecting frames for printing and interpretation, debriefing the photo interpreters (PIs), and comparing his visual reports against what showed up in the imagery.

I don't know why we insisted on building an operationally questionable parking area, and then made it so narrow. Clearances between aircraft were minimal, and it's surprising that we never had a taxiing or towing accident there. Nevertheless, one night an unlit portion of the ramp that was used as a run-up pad was witness to a close call for one of our groundcrew. In one of those Keystone Cops scenarios, he stood right in front of a CF–104 intake. In the darkness, the run-up crew had neglected to ensure the intake screens were installed. The fellow was sucked into the intake where he became wedged with only his feet sticking out. Eventually he was missed and extricated. To my knowledge, he was uninjured.

Though Lahr was probably the most disrupted Air Division base during 1967, a lot was happening elsewhere as well. Just a short distance up the autobahn at Baden-Soellingen, 444 Squadron flew their last CF–104 sorties in a formation flypast over the Chateau at Metz. The Squadron then officially disbanded on April 1 and marked the occasion by a farewell function in the Baden Officer's Mess, with the Commander of the Air Division, Air–Vice Marshal Lane, in attendance. The aircraft and pilots were distributed between the two remaining squadrons, and Wing Commander Ralph Annis, the outgoing commander of 444, changed offices, squadron patches, and allegiances when he moved over to take command of the 421 Red Indians shortly thereafter.

To this point in time, the Attack role had been considered so secondary that the squadrons basically were not even practicing a Conventional option. However, with the gradual arrival of suitable Conventional munitions, soon to be supplemented with stocks of the MK–82 General Purpose 500–pound bomb, and in line with NATO's evolving policy of Flexible Response, Conventional Attack weapon deliveries were gradually becoming more popular with the squadrons.

The centennial activities and the deactivation of 444 Squadron did not tarnish the operational efficiency of 4 Wing. This was amply demonstrated in May when, during the annual Tac Eval, the Baden component again attained an overall "one" rating. Also in May, the mission planning process at 4 Wing received a true boost when the new Colour Reproduction Centre opened its doors. This process proved to be an invaluable aid for rapidly reproducing training route maps complete with the previously-mentioned radar predictions. An excerpt from the 4 Wing Commemorative History provides a taste of the variety of other activities that took place at Baden Soellingen during centennial year...

Excellent weather in 1967 allowed the squadrons to fly maximum hours. The large number of hours flown had to be supported by the Wing. That this was done was evident by the number of servicing records broken during the year. During March and April, the refuelling section dispensed over one million gallons of fuel each month. This was a record high in the output of the section and is especially significant in that, during the month of April, only two squadrons were flying. Coinciding with the high number of hours flown, the Air Traffic Control section recorded 6,048 aircraft movements in the month of March and 50,387 aircraft movements for the year. Both these figures were the highest monthly and yearly totals since 1958.

The opening of our sister Wing at Lahr presented a grand opportunity for a flypast to mark the occasion. On October 7, six 421 Squadron pilots participated in a giant 36–plane flypast at the official opening of the 1 Wing Lahr base.

Things were busy over at Zweibrucken as well... At 430 Squadron, Wing Commander Fern Villeneuve, like Ralph Annis at Baden, dropped his 434 "Speedbird" flying suit patches and took command of the Silver Falcons in May. Also in May, Squadron Leader Mac McGregor had been seconded on temporary duty to Lahr to carry out some airtests. On May 21, he experienced a complete power loss on takeoff just after raising the landing gear. He "jettisoned the aircraft" just in the nick of time by ejecting at an altitude of **25 feet**, then spent a near-world-record minimum time in the parachute, landing on the runway in the subsiding fire caused by the ignition of fuel splashed along the path of the wreckage!

In June, Flight Lieutenants McKay and Rozdeba represented 427 Squadron at the AFCENT Weapons Meet, held that year at Wildenrath in Germany. They were joined in their efforts by Flight Lieutenant Robbie Robertson from 430 Squadron and Flight Lieutenant Duffy McCallum from 4 Wing . This time the Canadian national team outdid itself by placing first in the Meet. Duffy McCallum also won the Visual LADD trophy, and Ed Rozdeba walked away with top honours in the Laydown delivery category.

The 4 Wing Commemorative History, published in 1971, provided an excellent overview of what it was like to participate in an AFCENT Meet, and what it meant to the competitors...

One of the most exciting and challenging tasks a Strike/Attack pilot may encounter during his European tour is to participate in a NATO AFCENT Weapons Meet.

Introduced in 1962 by the Commander of AFCENT, Air Chief Marshal Sir Harry Broadhurst, the Meet is a competition between 2ATAF and 4ATAF, made up of teams from the Belgian, French, German, US, British and Dutch Air Forces. In 1964, a team from the Royal Canadian Air Force took part in the competition for the first time. The Canadian team promptly chalked up the highest national team score, contributing decisively to the 4ATAF victory.

The teams are scored on the totality of the mission: aircraft serviceability, mission planning, accuracy of navigation, time on target, and bomb score. This requires an elaborate set of rules whose application is not easy. The national character of the teams added to the difficulty of scoring because it resulted in keener competition, and frequently an enterprising team captain would find ways to circumvent some rule. Thus, year after year the body of rules grew and became more specific, and the missions more closely monitored. This has resulted in nearly as many judges, scorekeepers, and arbitrators as participating pilots.

A national team had to be completely self supporting, providing its own aircraft servicing, it own mission planning, and often including a meteorological and medical officer. A few months before the Meet, a

Above: *Border incursions, though infrequent, worked both ways, and this one was obviously intentional. A defecting Soviet pilot belly landed this MIG-17 in a West German farmer's field circa 1966.*
– photo courtesy of a CF-104's photo reconnaissance pod

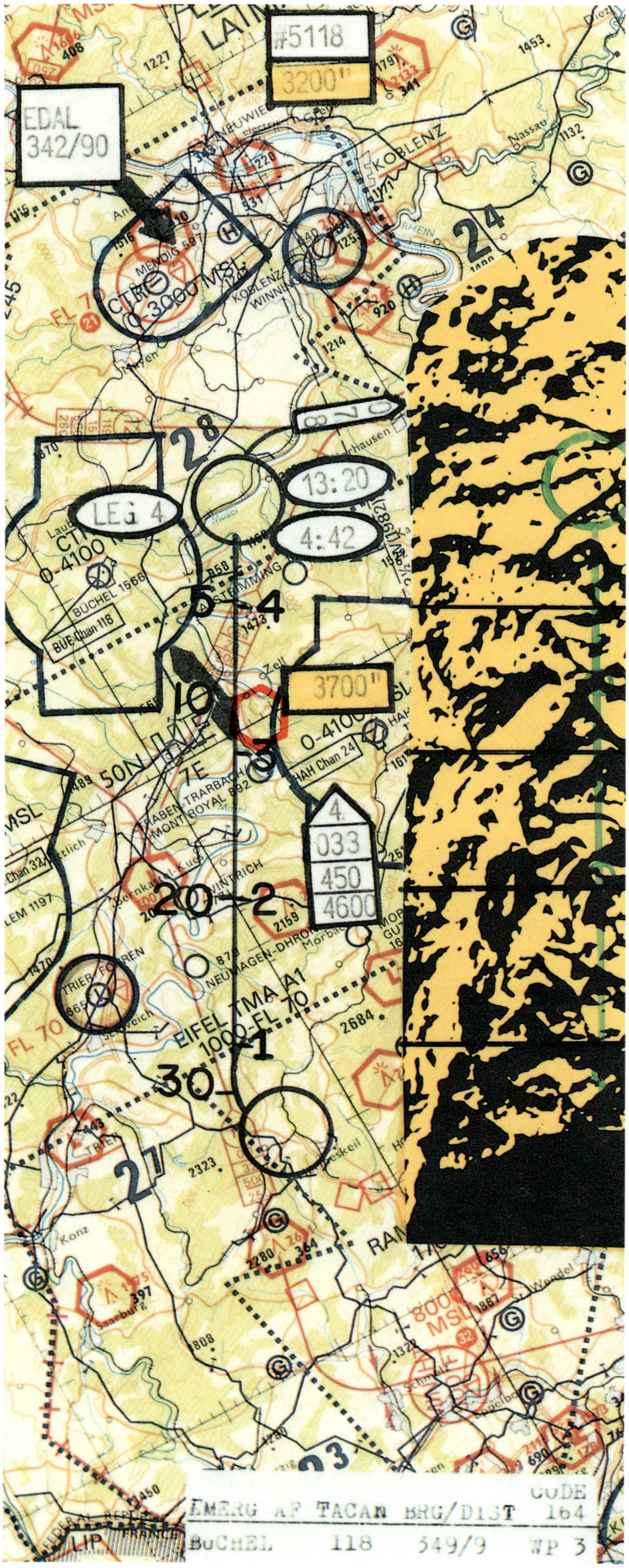

team captain (usually a pilot with the rank of Major) and a technical officer would be selected by Air Division H.Q. These two officers would then organize and select the support personnel for the team. Efforts were made to find the most qualified personnel. The aircraft servicing group comprised about 26 NCOs, three or four mission planners, the all-important Weapons Officer, and an Intelligence Officer.

The pilots were selected on an entirely different basis. The intent was not to form a national team with the best pilots, but rather to select the team which reflected the squadrons' operational capability. To meet this aim, the squadron commanders were instructed to submit to 4ATAF a list of at least 50% of their combat ready pilots. Approximately four weeks before the Meet, four names would be picked at random. These four pilots would form the team and a fifth name was drawn to provide the team with a spare pilot. The four weeks provided sufficient time to prepare the team, but this time period would not allow dramatic improvement in pilot proficiency.

However, in the four weeks available there was indeed concentrated training. Each pilot, including the spare, would fly approximately seventy hours. While Decimomannu was being used by No. 1 Air Division, the pilots would spend a week there practicing "close-in" bombing. A shorter timer reference point to target distance than normal is used in the Meet to increase bombing accuracy. If the bombing range to be used for the Meet was far from home base, the team would deploy to another air base for about a week to allow the pilots to familiarize themselves with the range. Much flying time would be spent to practice hitting "equivalent targets" (EQ), and night navigation and bombing were emphasized. During this period the national team would operate as a unit, providing training for the support element. A few days before the Meet, the team captains accompanied by the team support personnel and equipment arrived at the host base. The participating pilots flew in the day before the opening of the Meet. After a brief ceremony on the first day, a briefing was held where the rules were specified, and then the pilots would each fly a familiarization mission. The competition would commence in earnest on the second day, and continue for ten days.

A typical mission profile consists of an equivalent target that has to be hit at a predetermined time, followed by a bomb drop at the range. The pilot receives a frag order and a briefing on the particular mission four hours before the time-on-target. The "map-makers" immediately start plotting the coordinates of the EQ target, choose the best run-in to the EQ target, and make the map. The servicing people are given a

At left, *an example of a '104 pilot's navigation strip map with the innovative radar prediction of the leg on the right-hand side.*

Below, *Dusk patrol.*

- photo by Bill Turnbull

power-on time. Meanwhile the pilot, assisted by the weapons officer, calculates the timer setting for the particular bomb delivery using the meteorological officer's wind and temperature forecast. The route is carefully studied and calculations are rechecked. Finally, allowing sufficient time for engine start and taxiing to meet the calculated take-off time, the pilot walks out to his aircraft. A back-up aircraft is simultaneously started in case the first becomes unserviceable at any time up to the calculated take-off time. On these missions, the EQ target usually presented the greater challenge. It might be a railway or railway crossing, a small bridge, a fork in a road, etc. Located at the EQ is the targeting judge, assisted by two spotters positioned 100 meters on either side of the EQ. The aircraft was required to pass between the two spotters, otherwise the EQ was considered "missed", resulting in zero score. The pilot then proceeds to the range for the bomb delivery. The bomb score counted heavily for the total mission score, and all points for bombing would be lost if the bomb was unscoreable, failed to drop, or failed to detonate. The pilot then returns to base to nervously wait for the score to come in. Similar missions were flown at night also. There were also pure day and night bombing missions at the range.

The cumulative results of all missions were continually tabulated and posted, both on an individual and collective basis. As the Meet neared the end, the results were scrutinized more and more frequently, particularly when the scores were close. This resulted in great stress on the individual pilot, and a missed EQ or no–spot bomb could mean an irretrievable set-back. Towards the end of the Meet, a pilot who suffered this misfortune felt particularly unhappy about it, in spite of the fact that a "no–spot" early during the Meet was just as significant.

The Meet was officially brought to a close by a ceremony attended by all participating team members and guests. CINCENT or his deputy presented the Broadhurst trophy to the winning ATAF and the honours to the individual pilot and teams. Flag lowering and an aerial flypast would close the ceremony. The inevitable retreat to the Mess for refreshments followed.

1967 was a great year for squadron exchanges; an institution that would stand the test of time with the European squadrons. The idea was to spend approximately a week visiting another NATO squadron of a different nationality, swapping techniques, procedures, lies, etc., and then hosting them at a later date on a reciprocal visit to home base. A variation on this theme was the simultaneous exchange of contingents from each unit at the other's home field. During centennial year, 430 Squadron had exchanges with both the Italian Air Force at Ghedi, Italy, and with 214 Squadron of the Royal Air Force from RAF Bruggen. In June, 427 Squadron visited and were visited by the 55th TFS from Weathersfield, England. At 4 Wing, both 421 and 422 Squadrons spent part of the summer getting to know the 91st TFS from Bentwaters, England. These squadron exchanges were tremendously popular, and did a great deal to further excellent relations between all members of the NATO fighter community. Probably the most famous of the *collective* mixed-nation fighter gatherings was the annual NATO Tiger Meet, which was hosted on a rotational basis by each national fighter/recce/attack squadron in Europe that had the tiger as its symbol. Naturally, the tigers of 439 Squadron were very active participants in these Meets, and would host several of them over the years. This was also an opportunity to paint a CF–104 in *very* distinctive markings, much to the disgust and ridicule of the other CF–104 squadrons who referred to the special paint job as, amongst other things, "the bumble bee" and "the flying radar prediction". More on Tiger Meet later...

Back in Canada, a very special CF–104 event was being scheduled during the centennial year. The RCAF had earlier decided that an appropriate centennial project would be an all-out assault on the world altitude record of 113,892 feet; held at that time by the Soviets in a modified MiG–21. In lieu of using a stock operational aircraft, it was decided to modify the original CF–104 prototype (12700) for the project. '700 was, in fact, a reworked F–104A–15–L0 of the USAF. It possessed standard CF–104 flight and fire control systems, but lacked the strengthened airframe of Canadair production examples. Consequently, it was somewhat lighter than the operational CF–104, and it was further modified to carry only the instrumentation essential for the attempt. Other modifications included an extension of the air intake inlet shock cones, which made the supersonic shock wave position across the intakes at high mach numbers more aerodynamically efficient. The air conditioning and pressurization systems were also improved, and the aircraft was stripped of most of its external paint. On December 14, 1967, Wing Commander R.A. "Bud" White, flying out of RCAF Station Uplands and with AETE's '702 in chase, firewalled '700 to a blistering Mach 2.4, then zoomed to 100,110 feet. Although this attempt fell far short of the Soviet record, it set a new Canadian national record which remains intact until this day. '700 had, however, outlived its usefulness and was placed in the National Aviation Museum in Ottawa; its sleek lines now gracing the foyer of the new building opened in 1988.

While centennial year was marked by extensive accomplishments in the CF–104 world, the accident rate was somewhat higher than the previous year. There were eight "A" category accidents; two in Cold Lake and the balance in the Air Division. These accidents resulted in three fatalities, and it is interesting to note that four of the eight cited either birdstrikes or Foreign Object Damage to the engine as the major contributing factor to the accidents. One could well speculate that regarding the 1967 CF–104 accident history, and indeed in many other cases throughout the era, a second engine would have resulted in an aircraft save rather than a total loss.

On a lighter note, the CF–104 pilot community really broadened itself in '67 by opening its ranks to the other services when Lieutenant (N) Larry O'Brien became the first Royal Canadian Navy pilot to join a Starfighter squadron. Larry was welcomed aboard 430 Squadron in October, and initially caused a tremendous paper shuffle, particularly in the nuclear custodianship procedures, as *all* the orders were written with specific reference to RCAF personnel, leaving no provision for the anomaly that was Larry. A little better stage management by the RCAF might have seen him as an ideal flying mascot for the Bluenosers...

1968 was an extremely violent and troubled year throughout the world. Unprecedented civil unrest in the United States culminated in the assassinations of Reverend Martin Luther King Jr. on April 4th in Memphis, and Democratic presidential candidate Senator Robert Kennedy on June 5th in Los Angeles. Across the Pacific, the United States called an end to Rolling Thunder, the strategic bombing campaign against North Vietnam in the hopes of prodding the Hanoi government towards peace negotiations. For the Air Division, relative stability reigned, as the Wings settled down to business in their reorganized state. However, on February 1st, an event occurred that would profoundly affect the Canadian military at large; that event being the integration of the three military services into one Canadian Armed Forces. Though intended to be a cost-reducing policy change, integration was to a great extent an economic disappointment, and instead produced a significant decline in the morale of service members due to a perceived erosion of their respective service traditions and ethos. Overnight, the traditional air force rank structure was converted to a system more army oriented than otherwise. For example, Wing Commanders became Lieutenant-Colonels; Squadron Leaders became Majors; Flight-Lieutenants became Captains, and so on. Also, the distinctive environmental uniforms were to be gradually replaced by a green uniform common to all three services. It would be nearly twenty years before the individual services would revert to more traditional, distinctive attire, and this would not be accomplished during the remainder of the Starfighter era. Though integration was a bitter pill to swallow, the vast majority had a brief hiatus of bidding adieu to the old ways, then got on with the business at hand. However, the RCAF was not ushered out without many rousing farewells, and Phil Perry remembers the aftermath of the January 31st RCAF/RCN/RCA Farewell Mess Dinner at Zweibrucken when things got just a little out of hand, and some of the more stalwart of 3 Wing's warriors found themselves in the Base Commander's "dog house"...

The following day, we got the word from the Base Commander (Group Captain Ken Lewis). He was a great guy, but we all knew that we had shit in the buckwheat. Believe me, the heat was on and lasted, I think it was, until Eric Mould asked him in the Mess after an excellent Tactical Evaluation[1] *if we were off the "shit list" yet. Even Kenney couldn't hold back on that one...it was a great party.*

Integration hit and made a few changes, and we became Captains and Majors, etc. I had difficulty with that one and, like a lot of others, took an inward stand against it. I continued to answer the phone as "Flight-Lieutenant Perry here", not "Captain Perry here". ..stubborn or just pride. This was brought to my attention by some of my senior officers on more than one occasion, and my answer was that I had lots of aircraft but no ships. Well, Colonel Ken Lewis fixed that on my farewell party from 3 Wing in July '68 when he presented me with a model kit of a boat and the statement, "Here is your boat, now you are a Captain." Still have that model but it hasn't been built yet. However, when I was posted to 434 Squadron at Cold Lake, I was promoted to Major, and fortunately no one gave me a tank.

While the Air Division was soldiering on in Europe's Central Region preserving the status quo, studies were being conducted in Ottawa that would have deep ramifications for the CF-104 squadrons. Canadian public sentiment was increasingly favouring non-nuclear defence roles. In the spring, Mr. Trudeau's government initiated a review of Canada's foreign and defence policies, and determined that Canadian political and military commitments with respect to NATO were due for a fundamental revision. In keeping with a new commitment to NATO's northern flank, mobility was predominating the rationalization of a new force structure. The incompatibility of an air-portable, Canadian based non-nuclear air fighting arm with the nuclear armed, permanently garrisoned European Air Division was be-

Below: *Intense pre-launch activity at the 1969 AFCENT Tactical Weapons Meet in Norvenich, Germany. Note the 4ATAF team crest on the air intake.*

[1] This took place in May.

coming increasingly pronounced. The Starfighters were thus felt to be nearing obsolescence in the Strike role, and the government was faced with the problem of justifying alternative employment for the aircraft. Air Defence was deemed unsuitable since the European nations favoured a policy of territorial air defence, and the CF–104 was in any event totally inadequate for that task. Conventional Attack was felt to be the only viable role for the aircraft, and even this had to be caveated with some rather formidable restrictions on tasking due to limited maneuverability, limited stores carriage capability, and limited range. In short, the Air Division would have to make do with an aircraft that was less than optimally suited to the new tasking until such time as the Starfighter could be replaced by a more capable aircraft. These limitations would demand a great deal of innovation from the entire CF–104 community during the aircraft's waning years in order to preserve its operational viability. Thus, in 1968 the political dye was being cast that would significantly affect the Air Division over the ensuing several years.

Operationally, 1968 was a quiet year for the Air Division. Both the Strike Wings again excelled in their annual Tac Evals, achieving the overall "one" rating in all areas. Meanwhile, the Reconnaissance squadrons in Lahr were more than holding their own at the annual Royal Flush NATO recce competitions. Their capabilities had evolved with great rapidity, and in a mere four years of operations, they had earned their position at the vanguard of NATO reconnaissance expertise. Vic Johnson recalls these gatherings...

For several years, an annual competition was held among reconnaissance squadrons of NATO's 2ATAF and 4ATAF. The contest was called "Royal Flush", and in 1966 the two Canadian recce squadrons were invited to participate for the first time. The three-day competitions entailed maximum effort on the part of everyone involved and points were awarded or subtracted by umpires using a complex scoring system. Being the new kids on the block, we were all pretty naive as to the finer points of the game so, not unexpectedly, the Canadians did not fare well the first year. But we learned a lot from that and spent the next 12 months polishing up our performance for the next year. After all, national pride was at stake!

Speed was the name of the game and the processing and photo interpretation vans became scenes of frenzied activity. Immediately upon aircraft engine shut-down, the film magazines were removed from the cameras and were delivered on foot, lickety-split, to the waiting processing crew.

Umpires started their stop watches. A machine was used to load the rolls of film into special spiral reels and the film was hand developed in our specially concocted "soup".

After a quick fix bath, the film was hastily washed, dipped in alcohol, then spun dry in a powerful Sirocco dryer that duplicated a mini hurricane.

The rolls of negatives were quickly passed to the photo interpreters for initial assessment. They would then select negatives for printing and pass them back to the darkroom where enlargements were printed and developed using a rapid processor. Meanwhile, the interpreters received a verbal debriefing from the pilot and prepared a written report on what

the pilot had seen.

Target information was annotated onto the photographs. The photos, negatives, and reports were then sealed in an envelope and handed to an umpire.

Total elapsed time from engine shut down - 30 minutes.

Given this scenario, our goal was to refine our techniques. Fractions of seconds counted and - like Olympic competitors - we rehearsed and re-rehearsed every step of the process. Every second shaved off the photo process meant an extra second for photo interpretation.

Against all laws of photo chemistry, we would boost the temperature of our chemicals to 90°F, as opposed to the manufacturer's specifications of 68°F. Any more heat and the emulsion would melt right off the film. Ten minutes was the recommended developing time; however, in that liquid dynamite, we cut the time to 60 seconds.

The results were astounding.

We would take these razor-sharp negatives and blow them up into mural size display prints that caused Kodak technical representatives and visiting competitors to shake their heads in wonder.

The pilots also refined their techniques.

On one occasion, I checked the film brought back by Squadron leader Jack Frazer, a former member of the Golden Hawks air display team. I noted that some of his negatives were upside down relative to the others. He explained that when he saw he was approaching a target on the wrong side and didn't have time to turn, he snap-rolled the aircraft on its back and took the pictures inverted! "That way I could keep all my pictures on one roll of film", he said.

This was the sort of "no sweat" approach that eventually made the Canadian recce squadrons front runners in the Royal Flush competitions.

Bill Turnbull also recalls the Royal Flush gatherings from a pilot's perspective...

The big event for all recce squadrons in the Central Region was the annual Royal Flush competition. In its original form, each squadron competed from its home base. Under Royal Flush rules, 70% of a unit's Combat Ready aircrew had to compete. Many umpires were required at each base and at selected targets, either in the air or on the ground. Many army formations were asked to put units in the field under camouflage, specifically for the exercise. This was a large scale event.

Every participating crew was to fly three missions of three targets each over the course of the three-day exercise. At least three of the nine targets flown were to be "army" targets. The fixed targets were usually of the pinpoint variety, but the army targets might be "fragged" as a pinpoint or a line search. In later years, a "strip search" was introduced. Here, the target was considered to lie somewhere within a narrow rectangle a few kilometers long. Over time, the emphasis on army targets increased. These were certainly the most challenging to both aircrew and PIs alike.

For the day missions, all pilot visual reports were radioed to home plate. The PIs had to complete all of their target reports and print annotations within 30 minutes of aircraft shutdown. A squadron was given a target list to work with and was free to select the number of targets it needed within areas of suitable weather. Once an aircraft was airborne, its mission was scored. If no results were obtained due to bad weather or a technical malfunction, too bad - the mission scored zero. Thus the pressure was on everyone - aircrew, groundcrew and PIs alike - and the flying pace was reasonably intense, especially if weather cut into the available time. In that sense, it was a good exercise.

When 1 Wing first competed in Royal Flush in 1966, its squadrons, not surprisingly, came last. By 1968, we were starting to win. In that year, I placed fourth overall and my squadron won first place. That was also the year we hosted the awards ceremony in Lahr. The following year, 441 and 439 placed first and second.

Policing the "big base" version of Royal Flush was a problem, and accusations of cheating were rampant. One air force did particularly well at finding its own national army targets which, in our experience, were seldom on plot. Moreover, that air force's visual reports invariably matched their army's submitted solutions, even with the targets were heavily camouflaged or hidden in woods. Naturally, collusion was suspected. With such a large target list, umpires could monitor only a few targets. Thus, multiple passes at the same target, forbidden under the rules, were unlikely to be detected.

Because squadrons did not necessarily fly against the same targets and because they perceived wide variations in the marking standards, there were debates over the results. Granted, with the large number of targets flown, team scores were probably a good "on average" indication of proficiency. But if you happened to be based in an area hampered by weather when others were not, or if you received more than your share of poorly plotted targets, or if you happened to have several targets scored by a harsh marker, then you had some grounds for complaint.

Beginning with the 1970 competition, the modus operandi changed. Squadrons sent hand-picked teams to a single base where all flew identical missions. I believe each team comprised four crews and aircraft, plus one spare machine. Limitations were placed on the number of groundcrew. The majority of the targets flown were deployed army units. Much greater emphasis was placed on night capability.

In that year, 439 Squadron won the day competition, but the handwriting was on the wall for day-only units. We wanted to get into night reconnaissance but had to convince Ottawa to buy us an IR line-scanner. In my view, we had the other essentials - an all-weather navigation system, and the techniques developed by our confréres in the Nuclear Strike game. All we needed was a sensor.

The Strike squadrons acquitted themselves with pride in competition during 1968 as well. From the 10th to the 21st of June, Captain Jack Partington of 427 Squadron led the Canadian Forces team to a second place finish at the AFCENT Tactical Weapons Meet held at Jever, West Germany. It was a very close competition, both for team and for individual honours. 4ATAF won the Meet by 13 points. The Royal Air Force of 2ATAF took both Top Team and Top Pilot awards, but not without a photo finish. Jack Partington narrowly missed being overall best individual by a mere 0.5%.

There were also a significant number of squadron exchanges in 1968. Memorable among them was the May deployment of 427 Squadron to visit the 55th TFS in Weathersfield, England. August was also a busy period in the exchange business. On the 19th, a number of 421 Squadron pilots and groundcrew deployed to Rygge, Norway on exchange with 332 Squadron, RNoAF, while eight Norwegian pilots deployed to 4 Wing for the reciprocal exchange. During the visit, Soviet tanks under cover of their air support forces, invaded Czechoslovakia in the wake of liberal reforms in that country. Though the incident caused some anxious moments and an intense period of international political awareness, the Wings were not brought to an increased state of readiness. Also during August, the "Fighting 55th" got together with the 427 Lions in their home den of Zweibrucken for the second phase of the squadron exchanges.

In September, it was party time for the Silver Falcons as they hosted the 92nd TFS from Bentwaters, England. During this exchange, most 430 Squadron pilots were given familiarization rides in the F-4 Phantom. A reciprocal visit to England occurred later in the month. But the year was not over for the Silver Falcons, as their official History notes...

Come October, 430 Squadron members once again showed their worth with HMCS Bonaventure 90 miles offshore in the North Sea. The team - Major Liukko, Captain Dunsdon, Lieutenant (N) O'Brien, and Lieutenant French - performed a number of passes to show the Navy "flyboys" what real flying was all about.

Ray Dunsdon, who flew with both 430 Squadron and later as an instructor at the OTU, remembers the event in a slightly different vein...

Larry O'Brien was one of the first Navy pilots to join the CF–104 operation. A friend of his was Deck Officer aboard HMCS Bonaventure during its last cruise, so Larry planned and led the formation. We also had a recce CF–104 to take pictures. I can remember thinking two things about the flight. The first was, "What in hell was Mother Dunsdon's boy doing this far out over the cold North Sea in a CF–104?". The other was that the Bonaventure flight deck looked miniscule and that I was damned happy nobody expected me to land anything on it.

A most unusual event happened to a member of 427 Squadron in 1968. On March 14, Captain C.F. Carrington–Smith was returning from a low level mission and subsequently became involved in some "yanking and banking" with an American Phantom from the 8th TFS, based at Spangdahlem. In the words of the 427 Squadron History...

...the F–4 was seen to pitch up and spin into the ground. The crew ejected safely. This rests as the first Squadron "kill" since 1945.

In 1984, Carrington-Smith wrote a letter which provided considerable amplification to this rather bizarre occurrence...

I was returning from a target in the Ardennes and was in the area of Spangdahlem when I spotted a contrail well above. Airspace restrictions were not at that time the dampening influence that they were to become later, and so I had no hesitation in putting on full power and climbing up to investigate. Somewhere around 30 to 35 thousand feet, I passed by an F–4 on a 180 degree heading, and because of my rate of climb and airspeed I was able to execute a quick wing-over, which put me close in at his 6 o'clock. A couple of 360 degree turns ensued in which I was able to maintain position with the help of takeoff flap, and I was then greatly surprised when the other aircraft suddenly pitched up and departed over my head. For an instant I thought that this was some devilish new manoeuvre, but I soon regained contact and saw the F–4 in my 8 o'clock low position in a flat spin. He was obviously in trouble since fuel/exhaust was coming straight up from the tail pipes, and shortly thereafter he tried drag chute deployment with no effect. I followed the aircraft down, but stayed above and watched the crew eject. I did not see the aircraft crash because of a layer of cloud topped at about 8000 feet. While returning home I reported on squadron frequency that I had seen a crew ejecting and gave a position relative to the Bitburg TACAN. I later found out that I had been over Spangdahlem and that the aircraft had crashed on the Base golf course.

The whole episode came as quite a surprise, particularly as there was no training in air fighting in those days, although quite a few of the pilots took an interest in the subject. In fact, when flying from Zweibrucken, there were quite a few encounters with F–102's and Mirages, and I even remember one day when pilots were able to come down, refuel, and rejoin the mêlée.

The incident was kept quiet because we did not want to involve the USAF pilot in the trouble that would surely have come his way if the truth had come out. Also, unfortunately there were several CF–104 losses at about that time which were attributable to mishandling during airfighting. I believe that the official USAF story was that the F–4 crew had suddenly seen an airliner ahead of them and that with split-second decision making and in the true spirit of military pilots, they had sacrificed their own aircraft to save the lives of many innocent civilians.

History later would effectively repeat itself, though with disastrous consequences, when on December 20, 1979, a CF–104 engaged two German Air Force F–4F Phantoms from Pferdsfeld in practice air combat, resulting in the loss of control and crash of one of the Phantoms. Kevin Vaillant, a stalwart of 439 Squadron and later the OTU during the twilight years of the Starfighter, was the CF–104 pilot that day. Initial moves, both offensively and defensively against targets of opportunity, were commonplace; standard operating procedure in Europe during the CF–104 era. They provided valuable, realistic tactical training, which included the need to keep a keen eye peeled for an approaching enemy aircraft at *all* times. Occasionally, however, events of this nature had their dark side. Thus it was that Kevin, through no fault of his own, bore witness to the last moments of two unlucky NATO allies...

The date was December 20, 1979. At 10:55 a.m. I was returning from a low level navigation flight over the American sector and had kept a sharp lookout to avoid being "bounced" by fighters in that area. Fortunately, I had been lucky and had come through unscathed. I had only arrived in Germany six months previously, and had been combat ready for only three of them, so I considered myself lucky as today I would not show up on someone's gun film.

As I flew over the Reinphaltz area near the town of Landau, I picked up two F–4 Phantoms flying in line-abreast formation, 7000 feet apart at 500 feet above ground. They were at my left 11:00 o'clock, heading north toward the American sector. A quick assessment of my

Above: *The hybrid '700, in which Wing Commander "Bud" White set the Canadian national altitude record in 1968.*

fuel state told me I had enough for a quick engagement. I was outnumbered but I had the element of surprise, and by now the advantage of position as I lit the afterburner and pulled hard into the right-hand man. As I closed on him, the left-hand man pulled hard into me. *I could see from his both the aggressiveness of his initial reaction and his paint scheme that he was German Air Force. I immediately abandoned the thought of gunning the right-hand jet, and turned left to meet the attacking wingman. As we passed, the best I could achieve was a high angle gunshot with a very low probability of a "kill". The tables had now turned. Not only had I lost the advantage I once had, but I was still outnumbered, flying against a superior pilot, out of fuel, and flying in the wrong direction from my home base. My only choice was to try and escape without being "gunned" by my pursuer. As I pulled hard toward base, I could see my opponent across the circle continuing to pull hard into me. I was so involved with the attacking F–4, that I almost ran into the ground. In the following dive recovery, I missed ground impact by less than 100 feet, and overstressed my aircraft in the process. I quickly looked over and realized that my opponent was not so fortunate. He had stopped lead-turning me and was attempting to recover from the dive. Although his nose was pointing above the horizon, the vapor trails coming off his wings were telling a different story. His sink rate was too high...he hit the ground with his nose still above the horizon, and exploded on impact.*

I slowed down to 400 knots and flew over the crash site, hoping I had missed seeing the ejections. I had not; there were none. After formating for a short while on the other F–4, there was nothing further I could do as I was now critically short of fuel and had to return to base.

At Pferdsfeld Air Base, 130 nautical miles away, a woman and her son waited in the control tower. Her husband was a German fighter pilot who was on his last flight before retiring. He never came home.

Another significant event occurred for the Air Division when on June 30, it was officially announced that 3 Wing Zweibrucken would disband the following summer. The "keys" were to be handed over to USAF representatives, who would become the new tenants, on July 1, 1969. This move, done in the name of cost-effectiveness, would consolidate the Air Division into two full -strength Wings of three Squadrons each, based respectively at Baden-Soellingen and Lahr. It was decided that 427 would go to Baden, while the Silver Falcons would join 439 and 441 at 1 Wing.

1968 was a rather typical accident year for CF–104 operations at the time. There were eight "A" Category crashes; five in Europe and three at Cold Lake. Unfortunately, four of the five European accidents resulted in crew fatalities. If the loss rate appears excessive, it should be noted that these were the halcyon days of CF–104 operations, and that over 45,000 operational and training hours were flown that year. This translates into an accident rate of 2.44 accidents per 10,000 hours of flying time; one of the better years of the nuclear period for the CF–104.

It was also a year wherein several Canadian Starfighter pilots distinguished themselves by demonstrating superior flying skills in extremely difficult circumstances, probably saving aircraft and more importantly, lives in the process. Perhaps the best example is that which happened to Captain J.P. Desbiens on September 11th. According to the 427 Squadron History...

On the 11th of September, while on a low level trip in the Soest area, Capt. J.P. Desbiens suffered a bird strike in aircraft 12796. The bird damaged the left windscreen causing Capt. Desbiens to lose his helmet and mask and sustain facial cuts and bruises. Despite his injuries and loss of communications, Capt. Desbiens returned to 3 Wing and landed safely. He was quickly rushed to hospital and undoubtedly upset his wife who was a nurse on duty at the time. Fortunately much of the "blood and gore" proved to be that of the deceased bird and after a few hours he was released to share his adventures with other members of 427. For saving a valuable aircraft under difficult conditions, Capt. Desbiens was given a well-deserved "Good Show" award.

Jack Desbiens subsequently wrote a letter in 1985 which "flushes out" his participation in the event, which he describes with disarming modesty...

I was flying a low level mission not too far from Soest. I had just completed my final turn into the "target" and decided to engage the auto-pilot in "altitude hold" (which ultimately saved my life) when I heard a large "bang". The bang was produced by a duck which decided to pay a visit into the cockpit! As he entered, he broke the canopy and tore off my helmet and knocked me out. When I came to, (about 15 seconds later) it was very loud in the cockpit and I noticed the canopy was shattered and I was still flying straight and level (thanks to the auto-pilot!).

I remembered that the first item in the checklist for "loss of canopy" was "visor down", so I reached up to lower my visor and all that was there was my head *which was covered in blood and guts which I thought were* **mine**! *I then decided to set course for Zweibrucken, and as I did so, I also slowed down to reduce the horrendous noise which was a result of the wind blast. As I slowed down I heard a distinct "rumble" which I thought was the engine failing, so I reached for the ejection handle and was about to eject when I decided to perform a quick engine check, only to find it operating normally! So I sped up a little, and the "rumble" disappeared. I later learned the noise was caused from turbulent air around the ejection seat itself.*

The trip back to home base was relatively uneventful apart from the fact that it seemed to take forever. As I approached the Zwei area I squawked emergency and pressed the mike button several times (I couldn't talk to anyone as I had lost my helmet and mask). The action

Above: *Mother Dunsdon's little boy and his friends overfly HMCS Bonaventure; October, 1968.*

was picked up by Ramstein Air Base who advised Zweibrucken that an apparent NORDO[1] *was proceeding in their direction, and as such Zweibrucken cleared the area and I proceeded with a straight-in approach and landing, despite having an "unsafe gear" indication for some unknown reason. I was subsequently presented with a "Good Show" award, of which I am very proud...*

To end this chronicle of 1968 on a light note, it must be remembered that rivalry between the two Strike Wings was nothing if not intense. Gord Hatch recalls a classic case of "Initiative - 10, Judgment - 0" in this regard...

In the 1960's, 4 Wing had a version of central maintenance that apparently controlled the aircraft to the point that routine snags could bring a squadron's operation to a halt. This compared to the 3 Wing system that gave the squadrons a little more control of the aircraft and their snag recovery. In April 1968, an inter-Wing Top Gun weapons competition gave points to both the aircrew's efforts to hit the target, plus the efforts of maintenance to generate aircraft. As the hectic day wore on, the word got back to Zweibrucken that the Baden Squadrons were running out of aircraft. In a fit of one-upmanship, 3 Wing launched a sixteen-plane formation to over-fly the rival's quiet base. Once overhead, the formation lead apologized for only having sixteen aircraft, but explained that a good number were still flying Top Gun sorties to the range.

It was a grand flypast that left everyone feeling warm and fuzzy, and for recovery the gaggle headed North to line up for Runway 21 at Zweibrucken. The lead, obviously thinking of those behind, made a fairly wide turn and it was only when he was heard on guard saying, "Sorry about that, Ramstein", that it was realized that we had just inadvertently flown through the Ramstein Control Zone.

1969 would be yet another year of tremendous upheaval and uncertainty for the Air Division as the departure from Zweibrucken loomed nearer. The "pecking order" for the move dictated that 430 Squadron would head for Lahr in February, then 427 Squadron would move to Baden-Soellingen in June. Practically coincidental with the move of the Silver Falcons to Lahr was the arrival from Canada of a new pilot named Dan Windeatt. Lahr was accustomed to playing host to the Division's two Reconnaissance squadrons, and so had to "gear up" substantially to house a Strike unit complete with alert facilities. Perhaps Lahr's lack of a previous Canadian Strike commitment resulted in a somewhat cavalier attitude toward things nuclear at first, as recalled by Sam Firth...

The nuclear role brought with it all sorts of American procedures and methods of doing things which were quite foreign to us. I think it's a truism to say that the American Air Force really operates by rules and regulations, but in the nuclear business there was some reason for that, and of course the Canadians had to go along with whatever the Americans wanted us to do. Nuclear safety was paramount. With such things as "no lone zones", you could not for example, cross over to an armed aircraft without two of you crossing at the same time, and one would have to be an American. There would have to be an American guard there as well. This caused some minor paranoia among us as the RCAF was pretty much free and easy in comparison to the US Air Force, and we got along pretty well by doing things that way. What I am leading up to is that, while there may have been others, the most humorous, (and yet at the time it was serious) incident happened at Lahr, not all that long after 430 Squadron moved there from Zweibrucken. A fellow named Dan Windeatt was checking out his new sports car around the north marguerite at Lahr, and was showing individuals how fast it would corner, etc. Unfortunately, Dan lost control of it and rammed the Q Fence, crashing through the first gate. You can imagine the outcry and concern that the Americans had over this incident, because anything like that in their own outfit would have resulted in the dismissal of the Base Commander and Lord knows who else.

Meanwhile, over in Baden the exchanges started early, with 421 Squadron hosting 725 Squadron of the Royal Danish Air Force for twelve days in February. However flying activities ground to a halt in early March when the squadrons moved temporarily to Zweibrucken for another Operation Tight Squeeze. This time, it was the runway at 4 Wing that was resurfaced, and simultaneously taxiway extensions were constructed at each end of the runway. During this period of refurbishment, the taxiway was kept open as an emergency runway. Nonetheless, the deployment was not without inconvenience as there was a requirement for 421 Squadron pilots to hold "Q" (quick reaction alert) out of Baden-Soellingen, and this necessitated a lot of transit time between 3 and 4 Wings in the venerable Dakota. All training flights were flown from 3 Wing, and both 421 and 422 remained there until the renovations at 4 Wing were completed on June 9th.

On March 23rd, a simple ceremony took place in the Rosengarten in the heart of the city of Zweibrucken. German civil authorities were presented with a gift of seven maple trees, which would be supplemented on May 31st by a commemorative totem pole to mark the Canadian tenancy of 3 Wing for over sixteen years. For this event, sixteen Starfighters from both 427 and 430 Squadrons provided a suitable flypast. A simple plaque at the base of the totem pole reads as follows...

> "The maple trees and totem pole are presented to the citizens of Zweibrucken as a token of friendship from the Canadians who served here during the period 1953 to 1969. This gift is made in the name of those airmen who gave their lives in defence of freedom during those years. "
>
> *- May 31, 1969*

May would be a month for more than one memorable CF-104 air display. Larry Summers flew the Starfighter with 422 Squadron from 1968 to 1970 and again with 439 Squadron while posted to Group Transient and Training Flight (GTTF) in Baden from 1976 to 1979. He recalls a remarkable flypast over Holland that occurred on the 3rd of May...

The Starfighter event that always sticks out in my memory was a formation flypast at Gross Beek Cemetery in Holland as a remembrance service for Canadian servicemen. 422 Squadron was tasked for this event and due to the shortage of flying hours, the only practice was going to be during the flight to Holland. The formation was scheduled to fly up the day before, RON[2]*, then do the flypast and continue home on the same flight. The formation was led by Major Carl Mattson in a dual, with Lieutenant Luedemann in the rear seat. The formation was to be a nine plane with one spare to act as a spotter if not needed. A number of different formation shapes were tried, but a Nine Plane Cross was finally settled on with Captain Russ (Fuzzy) Challoner as spotter. I was Number Two, immediately line astern to lead, and as far as my poor memory recalls, the rest of the formation consisted of Lieutenant Red Millar and Captain Merv Kuruluk flying line abreast off my right wing, Captain Bill Nesbitt and Lieutenant Dale Andersen line abreast off my left wing, with Captain John Callahan, Lieutenant Carl Steff and Lieutenant Terry Humphries line astern of me.*

As we were settling down into this formation with Fuzzy 1000 feet above checking us out, I saw an airliner pass right in front of us and slightly high. What Fuzzy saw was the huge nose of an aircraft with both of the crew looking down at our formation. Fuzzy estimated the miss in

[1] Aircraft in a "no radios" condition.
[2] Remain Overnight.

yards. The airliner crew never saw ***him****, but did report* ***us****.*

We eventually arrived in Vokel, Holland, were met by the base commander who bought us all a drink, and then asked us what we would like to do as he had a bus and driver laid on. So we all decided on Amsterdam. The evening went well for everyone except for Fuzzy, when he was escorted away with a very firm grip on his arm by the local police. He had decided to argue with one of the ladies of the evening.

The next day the actual weather observations and the forecast were fairly good. At Vokel it was clear as was our join-up point, with clouds around the 2000 foot level at the cemetery. It was also forecast for 3000 feet and 3 miles back at Base, so a ten-plane flypast was planned and briefed.

On the start-up, I initially had some radio problems but they cleared up only to have them return after becoming airborne. The radio did not fail totally as it turned out - only the receiver-amplifier, which meant all I was receiving was a faint whisper in my head set. I naturally assumed that my transmissions were the same. So I hollered whenever I did transmit, much to the chagrin of the rest of the formation.

At the join-up point, we formed our Cross, orbited 'til the run-in time, and then proceeded. Fuzzy broke off at about four miles back and then climbed on top of the cloud. It was topped at 10,000 feet and very thick. The weather at the cemetery was bad, so bad that the people on the ground didn't think we were coming. Lead was navigating on heading and airspeed and only saw the cemetery seconds before it disappeared under the nose of the aircraft. We then started our climb to the sun with nine silver 104's through some of the thickest clouds I have ever seen. Because of my radios, I did not hear anyone call out of the formation. All I knew was that the stove pipe ahead of me became very dim and sometimes would vanish for a second or two. I slowly moved closer and froze whenever it vanished, and then moved closer again when it came back into sight. I was also developing a very bad case of the leans. In fact, it got to the point I felt I was upside-down with about ten degrees of bank. I could not pull up out of the formation because of the overlap I had on Lead, and I could not depart in any other direction because I did not hear any call of anyone else departing. I could not take the gamble of departing the formation into anyone. Little did I know of what was really happening...

As it turned out, the wingmen from both sides lost sight of the formation, then called out and climbed. The last two aircraft line astern lost sight at the same time and turned away, but both in the same direction. As the last man line astern rolled wings level, he saw a tail flash past his pitot boom.

Meanwhile, Fuzzy was on top circling, waiting for us to appear, and appear we did, all over the place; six of the aircraft in burner and climbing. The last to come out was Lead, with two aircraft in the closest line astern Fuzzy said he ever saw.

We slowly got back together in a very loose formation and continued back to Base. As we approached, the weather was updated to 200 and 1/2, so no flypast. Of course, I had no inclination of this, but knew something was wrong because Lead wanted me to go with him on a two plane approach (via hand signals). The 200 and 1/2 turned out to be more like 100 and 1/4, but due to low fuel and nowhere to go, we had no choice. Everyone got down in pairs, and no-one said a thing about the whole trip. That is until everyone signed in and met at the pilot's bar at the Mess. Then with a beer in hand, all the stories came out and the trip was thoroughly debriefed...

As summer approached, the tenure for the Canadians at Zweibrucken ended, and 427 Squadron departed for Baden in fine form on June 16th, as their official History notes...

June 1969

The highlight of this month was the move of 427 from 3 Wing to 4 Wing. The Squadron flew down to Soellingen in a sixteen-plane formation led by LCol. R.E. Carruthers. The Lions arrived in 4 Wing complete with Manes and Tails, and were welcomed by Col. F. Kaufman, the Base Commander, and the two residing Squadrons, 421 and 422. A few difficulties were encountered settling in, but in a short time the 427 building was in order. While there was a slight slow down in flying due to the move, it continued at a steady pace. On the social scene, it was sufficient to say that 4 Wing was well aware that the Lions had arrived.

During July, 421 Squadron reciprocated 725 RDAF Squadron's February visit with a sojourn to Karup, Denmark. The Danes, flying aging F–100s, were very impressed with the Canadian Starfighters, but were probably somewhat less overwhelmed when Captain John Dunlop was forced to jump out of his ailing '104 during the visit...

Still during July, 427 headed south to Cameri, Italy to visit the IAF 21st Gruppe. This was the first time that squadron pilots found themselves 500 to 1000 feet above ground level at an indicated altitude of up to 14,000 feet, but they all agreed that low level flying in the Alps was a most invigorating experience. In August, 422 Squadron was graciously hosted by the 334 Squadron Polar Bears of the Royal Norwegian Air Force at Bodo. The predominantly-bachelor Tomahawks really enjoyed their visit to what was referred to as "north of the moral circle", and noted in their ten day visit that not once did the sun disappear below the horizon.

In the summer of 1969, the recce squadrons really "went for the gold" at Royal Flush. Vic Johnson explains...

Each year our scores improved, and at Royal Flush XIV in 1969, 441 and 439 Squadrons finished first and second respectively. Photo interpreter teams assigned to them walked off with all the top prizes in the interpretation category.

Also that year, Captain (now Major-General) Scott Clements of 439 Squadron was top pilot out of 108 competing, finishing with a score of 1055 out of a possible 1200 points. The win was a remarkable achievement and was particularly gratifying since most of the competing squadrons had been in the recce business uninterupted since the war. And even with our primitive "dip and dunk" processing methods,

Above: *Cpl Gordie Gilbert uploads a photo pod with full film magazines. Circa 1964.*

nobody, including the Americans with their shiny mega-dollar equipment, came close to us for quality of the finished product.

But the real bombshell of the year came in September when the government announced that 422, 427 and 430 Squadrons were to be disbanded in July 1970, Lahr was to cease functioning as an operational Wing, and 421 was to be joined at Baden-Soellingen by 439 and 441 Squadrons. Furthermore, while the Tigers would remain the "eyes" of the CF–104 world, 441 was to shed its Reconnaissance role and join 421 in the Strike/Attack business. As a crowning touch, the Air Division and the Wing structure would officially cease to exist in July 1970, to be renamed #1 Canadian Air Group, or 1 CAG for short.

The sense of unease about the future of the Air Division had been percolating for some time, as was noted in the 4 Wing Commemorative History...

The initial few months of the last year of 4 Wing were filled with uncertainty about the future of the Wing and its personnel. The rumours, like always, played a large part in providing the answers, but the fact remained that there was a possibility of the disbandment of 4 Wing and the Canadian Forces in Europe in general. There was talk of the Army moving down from the north and the closing of all Wings except one, on which there would be a reduced number of personnel at each of the remaining squadrons. Everyone was asking the same questions: "Would the air element with their '104s remain in Europe; if so, would 4 Wing remain, what squadrons would remain, and probably most important to the individual, would ***he*** *remain?"*

It must be remembered that in keeping with the results of the 1968 study, there was considerable doubt at that time as to whether Canada should even remain within the NATO Alliance. The final decision, which was in brief to remain within NATO but to cut the Canadian commitment in half, was a compromise decision, and it trumpeted a serious division of feelings on the matter in Cabinet. Prime Minister Trudeau staunchly defended the new defence policy, stating that NATO had in the past played too great a role in the determination of Canadian foreign policy, and that Canadian defence policy, which was a logical offshoot of the NATO influence *"was more to impress our friends than to frighten our enemies."*[1] He also felt that the nation should not restrict itself to a military policy that existed solely to support NATO.

Canada's NATO neighbours were not impressed with the decision to slash in half the European-based commitment. In fact, the original intent had been to reduce the squadrons from six to two, but that decision had been revised upward due to intense NATO lobbying. It was also at this time that Canada officially announced its decision to terminate the Nuclear Strike role in January, 1972. Though the original intention was to convert 421 and 441 Squadrons to the Conventional Attack role while leaving 439 with its Reconnaissance duties, the 1971 White Paper would later note that *"due to a perceived need for a substantial conventional ground-support capability in Europe, a major element in ensuring that any hostilities could be contained without escalation to nuclear war, the plan has been changed. The Government, after consultation with NATO, intends to employ all three squadrons in the Conventional Attack role in which the CF–104 is an effective aircraft. This role involves providing the tactical ground support for NATO forces in the area. The intention to task all three squadrons in this role will require minor modifications to the aircraft."* [2]

So at long last, the proverbial cat was out of the bag. However, in the fall of 1969, there were still a great many unanswered questions, the preponderance of which entailed who would remain in Europe and who would be repatriated. What it meant was that a great many personnel, both pilots and groundcrew, were going to be "short toured", and very few were keen on leaving.

There were some that still felt the Starfighter should be extensively modified and placed in an Air Superiority role, but for reasons of cost, limited suitability and European national territoriality, that idea was discarded.

Though originally designed as an interceptor, the CF–104 had poor capabilities as an air superiority fighter due to its particularly noteworthy lack of turning ability, limited endurance, and most importantly the lack of a suitable air-to-air radar and missile fitment. Time and circumstances had quite literally passed it by, and although Air Superiority is vital in a war, it is also academic if a Soviet Army tank commander is eating a hamburger in your snack bar. Thus it was felt that the Starfighter could make a meaningful Conventional role contribution in other, more appropriate ways.

Dave McIntosh recalls 1970 as being an extremely busy period for the operational staffs, since a great deal of work needed to be done to find appropriate Conventional roles and tactics for the CF–104...

When the big cut came in the spring of 1970, I was transferred to the Headquarters at Lahr, and for the next four years spent most of my time working on the development of 1 CAG's Attack role. Initially we did a lot of experimentation. The Air Division had been involved in the 4ATAF Close Air Support program for a number of years and, although the CF–104 was not suited to the role, our pilots gave a good account of themselves. However, we had a lot to learn about going after airfields...

The basic tactical philosophy that all agreed upon was that we should try and concentrate the maximum number of aircraft over the target in the shortest possible time. Our American exchange pilot, Billy Sparks (who had Vietnam combat experience) was a proponent of medium altitude tactics. Nevertheless, in the end these tactics did not

Above: *It was traditional during Royal Flush that the squadron COs would run the last film magazine of the competition to the waiting processing crew. Here, LCol (later General) Paul Manson of 441 Squadron puts on a burst of speed during Royal Flush XIV in 1969. The cheering section includes Capt Marc Dumontet, left, and Capt (later BGen) 'Sky' King, second from left.*

[1] Excerpt from a speech by Prime Minister Trudeau to the Alberta Liberal Association at Calgary, 12 April 1969.
[2] Defence in the 70s. The White Paper on Defence. Donald S. MacDonald. August 1971. Pg. 35.

apply to the 1 CAG operation as we did not have the heavy Electronic Countermeasures (ECM) and suppression support required. We ***did*** *however practice medium level tactics for awhile, and I can recall a twelve-plane attack at Lahr where we constantly changed heading and altitude, then finished up with a 30° dive bombing attack - en masse. We looked like a swarm of drunken bumble bees moving through the sky, who suddenly discovered the hive, then all tried to get in the door at once! We experimented with attacks using up to 24 aircraft. LCol. Ben Oxholm led a 24-plane raid during a Tac Eval which flabbergasted the German airborne evaluator along in a dual.*

LCol. Sam Firth was Senior Air Staff Officer (SASO) at the Headquarters. We decided that the best approach would be to see how other air forces approached the Counter-Air role. We formed a small team consisting of Headquarters representatives and a senior pilot from each squadron. Together we visited American, German, Dutch, Belgique, Danish and Norwegian Attack squadrons with a Counter-Air role. They all told us what their tactics were, how they had evolved, and the effect weapons and aircraft limitations had on those tactics. The American pilots with recent Vietnam experience leaned towards medium level ingresses and egresses, with heavy ECM support. However, American pilots with both Vietnam experience and *a couple of years in the European theatre tended to stick with low level all the way. Poor weather and an aggressive enemy air defence force seemed to be their primary considerations. All of the Europeans felt that staying low level and avoiding detection was the key to success. Everyone was concerned with the strength of the enemies' air defences - and equally concerned about trying to make their way safely back home through our own air defence system.*

Mass attacks became the order of the day, and they were practiced and refined constantly. I feel we were lucky in that we did not have a major accident during this evolutionary period. God knows, we had enough close calls! We quickly learned that a 24-plane mass attack was not a practical option and that coordinated attacks by smaller force packages was the way to go. An eight-plane force seemed to be the best option. It was easy to plan - only one squadron was involved - the tactics could be kept simple and detection was minimized. However, everyone agreed that the big mass attacks sure were exciting...

CF-104 OPERATIONAL DISPOSITION - 1969

Wing	Squadrons	Role
#1 Wing	439	Reconnaissance
Lahr,	441	Reconnaissance
West Germany	430	Strike/Attack
#4 Wing	421	Strike/Attack
Baden-Soellingen,	422	Strike/Attack
West Germany	427	Strike/Attack

The flying activity in the Air Division during the early months of 1970 was sustained in a "business as usual" fashion, in spite of the fact that the Division would be cut to half strength on the 30th of June. The Silver Falcons got off to an early start as world travellers by exchanging with 144 Squadron of the Turkish Air Force from Murted, near Ankara during the period February 1st to 9th. Many Squadron members furthered their own personal cultural awareness programs through side trips to Istanbul with transport and guides very graciously provided by the Turks. This exchange was almost "the end of the line" for 430 Squadron as a Starfighter unit. On the 30th of April, the Falcons were disbanded and squadron members were scattered to the four winds. Nevertheless, there was a rather interesting side to the glut of experienced pilots that this disbandment made available. South of the border, our American allies were approaching an Air Force manning crisis, due to the great number of pilots required to prosecute the Vietnam war. Not knowing quite what to do with their temporary surplus of experienced aircrew, the Canadian Forces volunteered their services to the USAF Air Training Command for exchange duties as flying instructors. And so it came to pass that 430 Squadron's Al Currie, Bob Huxter, Glen Heaton and Bob Morris were sent to various USAF bases flying both T–37s and T–38s.

On May 19th, Lieutenant-Colonel Bendt Oxholm, CO 421 Squadron, led a farewell flypast of 13 CF–104s at Decimomannu to honour the closeout of the Air Weapons Unit there. In this manner, a very colourful portion of the Air Division history came to a close, and it would be many years before the Canadians would return to the sunny shores of Sardinia in Starfighters.

Also in May, the "Red Devils" of the Italian Air Force, Ghedi, played host to and were hosted by the "Red Indians" of Baden in reciprocating simultaneous exchanges. In June, it was 427's turn as the Lions conducted a similar reciprocal exchange with the 43 Squadron "Fighting Cocks" from Leuchars, Scotland. While the Brits were royally wined and dined at various local gasthausen in the Black Forest, 427's deployment team was replacing divots all over the fairways at the prestigious Saint Andrews Golf Course.

June 1970 would also see the last Tactical Weapons Meet in which CF–104 pilots would participate as members of the Air Division. Held this time at Spangdahlem, Germany, the Canadian team, led by Major Ed McKeough and consisting of Lieutenant Grant Dunn and Captains John David, Dale Andersen and Dave Leier, once again emerged successful. At this ninth Meet, the Canadians won the Canberra Trophy for placing first in the Strike event, and thereby significantly helped 4ATAF to defeat 2ATAF in the overall final standings.

However, fair play and good sportsmanship were starting to take a back seat to healthy competition at the Meets... at the 1970 gathering, the leading Canadian pilot had been given a "miss" by the 2ATAF judge at one of the EQs, thus putting him out of competition for top honours. Nonetheless, his N–9 gunsight film of the target flyover verified that he was "right on the money". Technically, the camera film was not to be used, since after landing it could theoretically be developed and EQ photos shown to another team member who had not yet flown the mission, thereby giving him an unfair advantage. A sound regulation... in principle. But the reality of the mission scheduling was such that all team members were airborne and would overfly a particular EQ before the first team member landed; a condition which would make the foregoing concern unrealistic. This particular team member had just happened to photograph his target as a matter of routine procedure. When he was able to confront the 2ATAF judge with this indisputable evidence of his success, *not* only did the judge not reverse his decision, he had that team member disqualified for using the gun camera! All this from a nation whose team members *used lead-in lights to a target for their pilots, and yet were not disqualified.* This "win at all costs" attitude would cast a very dark pall over future

Weapons Meets, and the persistence of these childish games would eventually lead to the Meet's devolution.

Obviously, the keystone event of the year was the closure of 4 Wing and the disbandment of 422 and 427 Squadrons at Baden-Soellingen on June 29th. The 4 Wing Commemorative History capsulizes the ceremony...

The end of seventeen years at 4 Wing, Baden-Soellingen, and the disbandment of two of the squadrons that contributed to its distinguished history, were marked by formal ceremonies here on June 29th, 1970. With the establishment of Canadian Forces Base Europe on July 1, 4 Wing became 1 Canadian Air Group, Baden Detachment, and thus no longer a separate base in its own right.

Unfortunately, low clouds and rain showers forced the final parade to be held in the arena rather than outside. Nevertheless, the roar of a 4–plane formation passing overhead greeted the arrival of the Base Commander, Colonel F.J. Kaufman, at the dias to review the parade.

Many visitors, civilian and military, from Canada, Germany, France and the United States, were present as the two retiring squadrons, 422 and 427, made their final appearance. The handing over to Col. Kaufman of 422's Tomahawk and 427's flag symbolized the passing of yet another two of Canada's famous fighter squadrons. And so, 4 Wing faded into history to be replaced by 1 CAG, CFB(E) with 421, 439 and 441 Squadrons to carry on the roles of Strike, Attack and Reconnaissance in the new Canadian Forces Europe structure.

In spite of the fact that, being a flying operation, public attention was largely focused on the aircraft and the aircrew, the groundcrew and support trades were truly the unsung heroes of the Air Division. Their professionalism and pride of membership were every bit as intense as that of the fliers. They worried with them, shared their triumphs and defeats and, yes, they shared their anguish when a pilot was killed. It was a closely-knit family, the likes of which one does not find in the civilian world. Occasionally in their mind's eye, they would wistfully accompany their pilots aloft, to which this anonymous poem of the period testifies...

Fantasy Flight

Today I flew through cloudless heights
And scanned a world unfolding,
Saw towns and farms, all nature's sights,
A joy to be beholding.

I suffered not the loss of men
Who, locked upon the earth
Rely on worlds the author's pen
Describes of meager worth.

I saw the Rhine, this mighty course,
and barges with their loads,
I saw cathedrals, spires' source
And teeming, seething roads.

Below me, forests, dark and black
With castles on the hills,
And fancy often took me back
To days of knighthood's thrills.

I flew in dazzling sunlight bright,
While storms beneath me raced,
I flew in cloud all milky white,
My flight on instruments paced.

Then power ceased, my engine died,
Should I eject, or stay?
And then with skill, a relight tried,
I kept the earth at bay.

I coped with ease, emergencies,
Where lesser men would fail,
I courted death, disaster teased,
And knotted my contrail.

Approaching home, I flew in low
To touchdown, coasting landlocked.
Deployed the chute, used brakes to slow
And soon was parked and chocked.

My snags are fixed, so's destiny,
I've never tried to fly,
This flight was not but fantasy,
A groundcrew clod am I.

- *Anonymous*

Photo at left: *Multinational formation practice when RNoAF F-5s from Rygge, Norway visit 421 Squadron and Baden-Soellingen. August 1968.*

1970 was obviously a year of significant restructuring for the CF–104 force. While a number of pilots from the three disbanding squadrons were posted to the remaining squadrons within the newly-formed Air Group, the vast majority were repatriated. A significant impact of the restructuring was felt by the OTU back at CFB Cold Lake, as the 417 Squadron History explains...

1970 marked a number of changes for 417 Squadron, brought about mainly by two political decisions. First, Canada's contribution to NATO would no longer include nuclear weapons, and second, the Air Division compliment would be reduced from six to three CF–104 squadrons. The last "Q" (nuclear alert) was to be held on December 31, 1971.

Because of the cutback, there was no student training on 417 after Course 36 graduated in January 1970 until Course 37 startedin January 1971. Naturally, there was an overflow of "zipper" drivers, and a certain number of lieutenants, such as Orr, Molnar, Burroughs, Folks and Beaulieu, tacked on to 417 as supernumeries and spent much time flying between base and Jimmy Lake range. One or two of the aforementioned pilots were heard to say that, for them, the squadron was a "flying club" during that time of no students.

Throughout 1970, the expertise in Strike and Reconnaissance was maintained, while at the same time much work was being done to develop tactics for the Conventional role. In June, a 1 CAG pilot hit the trees on a target delivery and subsequently bailed out with minor injuries. In July, command of the Squadron changed from LCol. K.J. (Thorney) Thorneycroft to LCol. H.L. (Herb) Graves. In the fall, the first "CAG Course" was held. These continuation courses were designed to train current operational Strike pilots in the Conventional role, and from March 1971, Air Combat Maneuvering (ACM) was also part of the program.

It is certainly safe to say that '104 drivers of the period needed some formal instruction in the intricacies of air fighting the Starfighter, since it was much more demanding in this arena than fighters of the Sabre era. Al Seitz remembers the early days of the '104 program, before practice air combat was officially sanctioned. These observations were made by Al when the Canadian Forces was still flying the Starfighter, back in the early seventies...

Some of us occasionally, and against orders, played at air combat. Some suspected shortcomings were confirmed and others discovered. Rearward visibility, one of the most important desirables in a fighter airplane, is lousy. This is a common failing in most modern fighter designs, collective density of brain apparently having taken possession of the creators of combat aircraft the world over. All were apparently convinced that their own particular Mach 2 brainchildren could never have equally speedy opponents sneak into their 6 o'clock killing positions. Of course, all had eagerly subscribed to the theory that the death-knell to the old fashioned dogfight had long since sounded. Vietnam has brutally disproved that ever-lingering, ever-surfacing bit of wishful thinking. It is interesting to note that the third generation of supersonic fighters, exemplified by the F–14 and F–15, are sporting all-round vision canopies, last seen in the F–86 Sabre.

We very quickly confirmed that the old Sabre-style rat racing, scissoring and buffeting right on the stall, or in gut-wrenching turns sometimes right down to the deck, was not the '104's lifestyle. When both attacker and evader have to pay more attention to flying than fighting, then both have slipped out of their steed's best performance envelope; a fatal error in real combat against different fighter designs. In any case, simulated combat between identical aircraft hardly ever proves anything beyond relative pilot abilities.

It was not until we had completed our training sojourn at Cold Lake and had been organized into a squadron at Baden-Soellingen that we had the opportunity to try our "Wingless Wonders" against more conventional hardware. Since we had been formed as a Nuclear Strike unit, we carried neither guns nor rockets, nor the associated sighting equipment.

Toothless though we were, we pretended armament, and took turns at anything military that intruded into our sky... There are damn few airplanes that cannot out-turn the '104. The F–105 is in the same wing loading category, but with its low mounted tailplane it can hang in there at low speed and full burner turns at angles of attack that would have kickers activated in the CF–104. The F–4 and the F–5 are blessed with more wing per pound of weight and therefore have shorter turning radii. Compared to our stub-winged "missile", the delta-wingers, the F–102 and F–106, and the French Mirage III, can take square corners. Our only advantage over these is better acceleration and less airspeed loss at high "G" loadings when at very high speeds, like supersonic.

It goes without saying that '104s don't get into turning contests with transonic or subsonic fighters. When contending for a piece of sky against these, the name of the game is to indicate speeds of 600 knots or better at low altitudes and Mach 1 Plus when higher up. Some of these slower birds can display mongoose-like agility if they spot an attacker in time. If the jockey of a supersonic hot-rod allows himself to be lured into a ring-round-the-tail chase at anything below Mach .95, he very quickly finds himself leading the conga line.

Regardless of the calibre of opposition, the F–104's only real forté is speed. When Mach 2 is the base figure and combat is actually joined, a speed advantage of 100 to 200 knots can be easily neutralized by gun and missile. Positioning at time of contact counts for everything for the attacker, as evasive maneuverability does for the attackee. Positioning is a matter of luck, eyesight, and/or radar control or warning. Combat at Mach 2 would be decided in seconds.

When not chained to a rigid flight profile, supersonic flight can produce some pretty delightful kicks. In Canada, supersonic corridors are rigidly controlled and limited to unpopulated areas. In Germany, at that time, as long as we were at 30,000 feet or higher, the area didn't matter. In one of my early free romps after arriving at our base on the Rhine, I was lurking just above the contrail level at about 36,000 looking for a victim on whom to pounce. I spotted one, a little lower, about thirty miles away, the white condensation vapor trailing him for miles. I went full burner and went after him, sliding directly under his 'trail, in his blind area. The setup happened to be perfect, I was hitting Mach 1.95 just as I passed him. It is fortunate that I didn't have a proper gunsight with which to do a simulated firing pass, because I'd have gone through him. It was a two-seat F–100D, cruising at a genteel Mach .9, that I steered to miss by thirty feet. I knew my bird's performance even though this was one of the first times I was playing at the top end of its envelope. But I hadn't really thought about, let alone visualized, an overtake speed in the vicinity of 700 knots! I passed that F–100 when I was mentally a mile back! My mental jolt was at least as great as that of the guys in the '100. The shock wave of my passage must have had them thinking they'd been in a collision.

As I was recovering from my surprise, my instincts took me into a hard climbing turn to establish a perch from which to launch another pass. Naturally, my eyes were over shoulder to keep my victim in sight. I still had their 'trail when I arrived in the desired position, parallel to their heading and 4 o'clock high. The Stick Shaker rattled, and I glanced into the cockpit. Airspeed - about 280K, Mach - just over 1.0.Altitude nudging 66,000 feet! Je–sus!

I forgot my simulated hostility, rolled inverted, and gently pulled the nose down toward more hospitable climes. I returned to base resolved to do a lot of studying and thinking on this machine's max performance envelope. A flameout in those higher regions where engines can starve for air, would result in loss of pressurization and extreme danger to pilot, ME, since "Moon Suits" were not on issue. I recalled horror stories 'way back in my intake of aviation lore that blood boils at altitudes in the sixties of thousands of feet, invariably with fatal consequence. You can do yourself an injury by flying too high, as well as too low, in this airplane.

Al Seitz's comments about tactics would become prophetic, and for some time after the start of the CF–104's Conventional life, the Air Combat Tactics being taught at the OTU were not doing any favours to either the aircraft or its pilots. It was only after the Canadian fighter community formally adopted the Double Attack system and also started to practice realistic tactics for a multi-threat environment such as Central Europe that this discipline was optimized for the Starfighter. More on that later...

The year 1971 pushed the 1CAG squadrons inexorably closer to their scheduled role change. Though all the squadrons participated in squadron exchanges and various meets, the pilots could not help increasingly focusing their attention on matters Conventional. In fact, during this latter portion of the Strike period, training was being split about evenly between nuclear and non-nuclear operations. Let's face it - a nuclear weapon, even a small one, is an incredible force multiplier, and both the Strike and Reconnaissance squadrons had become very ingrained in the ways of operating as combat single penetrators. However, the carrying capacity of the Starfighter for Conventional ordnance was such that formation tactics would now be required in order to mass firepower and to do significant damage to an enemy target. Flying together in groups and bunches for tactical reasons required a considerable readjustment for the Strike/Reconnaissance airmen, and tactics development was very much an evolutionary process. As with the development of meaningful air combat procedures for the '104, ground attack tactics would also get off to a slow, conservative start. A great number of concepts were borrowed from our American allies, since appropriate, recent Canadian expertise was largely lacking. A lot of these borrowed tactics would shortly prove to be inappropriate for the Starfighter, her ordnance loads and the high-threat Central European theatre. In the fullness of time, ground attack tactics would be adopted that optimized the CF–104 for the ordnance available, the environment, and the threat.

On December 31st, the "Last Supper" of the Strike period was held in the "Q", and the next day, the Air Group became Conventional Attack squadrons. An awesome responsibility had been lifted from the shoulders of 1 CAG, only to be replaced by the formidable challenges of making the Starfighter a viable contributor to NATO's Conventional Attack force. Larry Summers succinctly sums up the attitude of many of the Strike pilots as they reflected back on the ten years of nuclear operations...

The sitting of QRA during the nuclear days took some adjustment, as you had to realize, respect, and yet not let it bother you, that that small cigar on the centreline position made Little Boy and Fat Man look like toys...

The formal Reconnaissance role for the CF–104 was drawing to a close as well, though the Tigers of 439 Squadron would be tasked with official recce missions until mid-year. Several of the Vicom pods would then remain in the Air Group, and locally-qualified pilots would do some "odd job picture taking" for some years to come, as the occasional requirement presented itself. Dave Huddleston gets the last word on the Reconnaissance period for the Starfighter...

From a standing start, we quickly learned the recce "trade" from our NATO allies and, as has been typical of our Air Force in any role, became a force to be reckoned with. To excel demanded individual effort, teamwork and speed. Two years after the small nucleus had formed, we were generating 150 sorties in a three-day Royal Flush competition scenario, and the following year were taking our share of the top honours. Prominent among the top performers were such "pipeliners" as Romeo Lalonde, Ken Mowbray, Gord Wallis, Scott Clements, "Sky" King and Phil Engstad, four of whom have stayed in the Air Force and filled a wide range of senior operational positions.

The "Fangs of Death" and "Stalk and Kill" mottos of 439 and 441 Squadrons were always the subject of comment from our Strike brethren. They preferred "Killum with Fillum". The mottos are quite appropriate today, of course. We are right in a small Air Force, I believe, to be focusing almost entirely now on the basic tactical fighter roles, but a country of Canada's strategic importance disposes of a reconnaissance capability at its peril, and those of us whose operational careers started in that role with the CF–104 have nothing but fond memories of it.

The bill for the Strike/Reconnaissance days of the CF–104 era had been considerable. In total, there had been 76 "A" Category accidents during ten full years of operations, resulting in the loss of 23 lives. However, the CF–104 fleet had flown a prodigious 330,400 hours during the same period; a remarkable effort that would greatly eclipse the 246,700 additional flying hours flown during the fifteen years of the Conventional phase.

Above: *Typical of the incredible amount of detail that could be obtained with the CF-104's VICOM camera. This overhead view of the Paris Air Show was taken by 439er Bill McWilliams in 1975.*

- *photo by Nancy Johnson*

Different Strokes

By the Summer of 1972, 1 CAG was a completely Conventional Attack NATO asset, at least in name. For once, the new pilots arriving directly from the OTU had a distinct advantage over some of the Strike/Reconnaissance "old timers", since they had received a complete training course in the Conventional Attack discipline. Bill McWilliams flew the CF–104 in Europe from 1972 until 1976 with 439 Squadron, and his initial tongue-in-cheek impressions of the 1 CAG operation that first Conventional summer are rather revealing...

I got to Germany just after the two Strike squadrons, 421 and 441, had converted to Attack. 439 Squadron converted six months later. Strike pilots had one bomb and a time to drop it, and they spent hours calculating to the nearest second and yard. A joyless bunch, they cared not where they were nor what they saw. They were on time, period. Reconnaissance pilots flitted about like demented rabbits, always knew exactly where they were and recognized every dam, radar installation and missile site they saw. Both groups had flown single ship and were good at what they did. As the experienced squadron pilots, they trained the section leads, and those of us who were newly-arrived, although trained in Attack, were relegated to wingman status. There were times when biting one's tongue was best as these former loners tried to adapt to flying around with never fewer than three other aircraft...

Though the Starfighter had been very well suited for the low level, high speed, single penetrator Nuclear Strike role, the switch to the Conventional business highlighted a number of serious shortcomings. For one thing, the aircraft's range without pylon fuel tanks attached was a major limitation. During the Strike days, the weapon was carried on the centreline rack under the fuselage, which made available the single station under each wing to carry fuel; specifically, 1268 pounds of it in each pylon tank. However, if the wing pylon stations were used for fuel instead of Conventional ordnance, that would leave only the 2000 pound carrying capacity of the centreline rack for weapons carriage, and one could question the utility of going in harm's way at all with such a limited capability. Furthermore, as both a required offensive tool and a measure of self-protection in the Attack role, the aircraft was going to need a gun. Though the M–61 Vulcan 20 mm cannon selected for the '104 was unquestionably the finest weapon of its kind in the world, its installation would necessitate the removal of the extended range fuel cell in the nose, denying the Starfighter a further 750 pounds of gas.

Though the fuel limitations were perhaps the most serious problem, the aircraft's "shopping list" of necessary modifications for the Attack role was extensive. The Starfighter would require a whole new arsenal of suitable weapons, plus some form of an enhanced wing suspension system with which to carry them. Also, the sighting system of the '104 was optimized for Strike and needed significant improvement for Attack. Finally, the jet would require some electronic self-protection devices, and a coat of camouflage war paint.

One area that did not need improvement was the aircraft's superb low level handling characteristics, which were incomparable. Due to its exceptionally clean lines, it created very little form and parasitic drag. The high wing loading, although detrimental in a hard-turning air combat engagement, ensured an extremely stable flight at high speed "on the deck". In fact, the '104 cut through turbulence like the proverbial hot knife through butter. Bill McWilliams elaborates...

The tiny wings meant the '104 could be out-maneuvered by any aggressively flown Goodyear blimp, but did give it a strong suit in the low-level environment where fighters have had to live since the invention of surface-to-air missiles. It had "blow-their-doors-off" speed on the deck, and the small wing area allowed very high indicated airspeeds, even in turbulence that would wrench the wings off ordinary fighters. There are few fighters, even the new ones, able to catch a '104 at low

Above: *A CF-104 with a full war load of 5 BL-755 cluster bombs.*

altitude, and fewer still that can fly as fast in rough air.

Some thought loading a thoroughbred like the '104 with iron bombs was like delivering pizza in a Rolls–Royce - not economical but certainly classy. However flying low and fast was pure fun, especially in smooth air. In turbulence, speeds which would jar the fillings from your teeth in an airplane with real wings, were quite comfortable. Unless, of course, you looked at the tip tanks dancing around with a life of their own. The entire tail section also flopped and twisted as if attached with rubber bolts, but none of this frightening activity was transmitted to the cockpit and the nose stayed aimed where it was pointed.

Al Seitz describes the visceral and highly addictive sensation of hurtling a '104 over the treetops at very high speed...

Flight at very low heights can be among the most exhilarating of human experiences. Skimming treetops, getting right down into fields, seeing the startled faces of wingless earthlings, is a sensation little short of godliness. Double your speed and double your pleasure; it's a trip the likes of which cannot be chemically duplicated. Not without its price though, for it is as dangerous as exciting. A split second's careless inattention can result in a brush with unyielding earth, disintegrating airplane and aircrew.

*Very few vehicles fit more naturally into very high speed, very low level flying than the Starfighter. One of the more serious problems with this type of flying is turbulence. Its washboard effects can shatter a lightly loaded aircraft at speeds in excess of 400 knots. The thin-winged '104 eats up rough air with scarcely a burp... It is impossible to describe the sensation of speed that is yours when charging over the landscape at over 1000 feet per second. Directly below, if you dare look, is a simple blur. Objects half a mile from your path raced as rapidly as fence posts viewed from a racing automobile. Isolated trees appear on the horizon and pass under in seconds. They seem to duck at your approach. All, but **all**, your attention is riveted to the onrushing panorama ahead. The airplane seems to have a death wish; wanting to go ever lower and faster...*

While the '104 certainly felt aerodynamically very much at home in the high speed, low-level regime, the initial conventional weapons fit for the aircraft was somewhat less than optimum. In 1972, the Starfighter had only four types of conventional ordnance available; namely the BLU–1/B fire bomb (polite terminology for napalm), the CBU–2/B cluster bomb, the MK–4 2.75 inch Folding Fin Aircraft Rocket (FFAR) fired from the 19–tube LAU–3/A rocket launcher, and finally, the ubiquitous MK–82 500 pound General Purpose (GP) bomb. The BLU–1/B incendiary munition was specifically designed for external carriage and release from high-performance aircraft equipped with forced-ejection release systems. The CF–104 could carry three of these weapons; one on the centreline rack and one on each wing pylon. Napalm could be used effectively against combustible or partially combustible targets, or targets that could be damaged by intense heat. Targets falling into this category were parked aircraft, motor transport vehicles, exposed ammunition and supply depots, stationary armoured vehicles, enhardened radar and communications facilities, wooden rolling stock, exposed personnel and warehouses of combustible construction. The 100 US gallons of chemically-thickened gasoline was delivered from very low (down to 50 feet) and level deliveries and left a burn pattern approximately 100 feet wide by 270 feet long. An improved variant known as BLU–27/B was a standard BLU–1/B shell that had been welded at the seams and joints, then filled at a loading plant with a newer incendigel mix known as Napalm B. This new mix was very viscous; it looked and flowed like honey. The napalm family would remain in the Starfighter's conventional munitions inventory until 1981, and though its use tended to strike terror into the hearts of soldiers everywhere, its effects were more imagined than real. It was eventually eliminated for reasons of combat inefficiency and a general unsuitability of results on the modern battlefield. Nonetheless, the live drops were memorable, and many a CF–104 pilot has fond memories of trucking up to Pampa range in Belgium with a napalm cannister under each wing.

Next up in the munitions "bag of tricks" was CBU–2/B; a 19-tube dispenser of cluster weapons. Like napalm, this ordnance was delivered low and fast; between 500 and 600 knots fast, in level 1 "G" flight. The weapon consisted of the SUU–7B/A bomb dispenser and a load of 409 CBU–2 weapons, designed for use against soft-skinned targets and personnel. Only one of these bombs could be carried under each wing. Furthermore, it couldn't be carried on the centreline rack due to the possibility of aircraft damage when the bomblets were ejected. These individual bomblets were composed of a shell of 255 case-hardened ¼ – inch steel balls secured in a rigid shell, each of which possessed a cavity filled with RDX explosive. A tail, consisting of six vanes spring-loaded to the open position, gave the bomblet a high-drag flight profile after it left the dispenser. Armed slowly by a friction device after release to ensure safe separation from the host aircraft, this weapon could be rather devastating over a wide area if employed against tactically suitable targets.

The last free-fall ordnance in the CF–104's early Conventional inventory was the MK–82 500 pound GP bomb. This weapon, usually employed in the high-drag or "Snakeye" mode did yeoman service for the Starfighter during the Conventional phase of operations; albeit not without some initial teething troubles associated with arming wire configurations. The total weight of 560 pounds included 192 pounds of Tritonal explosive, and a retarding fin provided the weapon with a high-speed, low altitude bombing capability. It could be delivered either from level flight or a dive attack. NATO interoperability procedures would later be established, allowing the CF–104 a wartime capability of also carrying the MK–83 1000 pound bomb as well as the MK–84 2000 pound bomb within this GP bomb family.

The only forward-firing ordnance available during the early Conventional days was the 2.75 inch Folding Fin Aircraft Rocket (FFAR). Although it suffered from severe delivery limitations, it was still a potent air-to-ground weapon when employed properly with its many warhead variants and fusing options. It was adapted to operationally use high explosive anti-tank (HEAT), fragmentation (HE), white phosphorus, flechette or solid iron heads, depending on the job requirements. The rockets were fired from tubular launchers located under the wings, and were equipped with folding fins. Rockets **had** to be delivered from dive attacks and resulted in considerable exposure time to enemy defences for the attacking aircraft in a high-threat environment.

Air-to-ground weapons delivery tactics during the early days of Conventional operations were somewhat rudimentary and unimaginative. Most targets were attacked by elements of two aircraft (or multiples thereof) in which the element leader was responsible for navigating to the target and delivering ordnance within suitable release parameters. His trusty wingman was required to do little more than "hang on" in close formation and deliver weapons on his leader's commands in what was known as "welded wing" positioning. He was essentially along for the ride and lacked the challenge of individual target acquisition and attainment of the necessary attack parame-

ters, except in permissive and predictable scenarios such as Close Air Support.

Tactical formations for the Starfighter were designed to maximize lookout and survivability of the flight and to permit weapons employment with minimum exposure to enemy defences. No one particular formation could be employed as a panacea for all situations, and the formation would even change during the course of a mission to optimize survivability or weapons deliveries. One transiting formation for four-aircraft sections that stood the test of time was Low Level Battle Formation...

This formation allowed for a fair amount of maneuvering room within the standard references. The positions were purposefully designed this way to allow flexibility within the section to manoeuvre to optimize lookout, terrain masking, and positioning at turn points. ***All*** members of the formation were responsible for lookout. If attacking as a section of four from a level delivery, the formation would collapse into an Arrowhead Formation.

However, Arrowhead attack formation would not last long. Although it was very maneuverable, it was also highly vulnerable to attack due to a reduced lookout capability. Furthermore,

Above: *Bill Fuoco of 439 Squadron taxis back to the ramp on a wet afternoon at Baden-Soellingen after a trip to the weapons range. Circa 1976.*

- photo by Dave Jurkowski

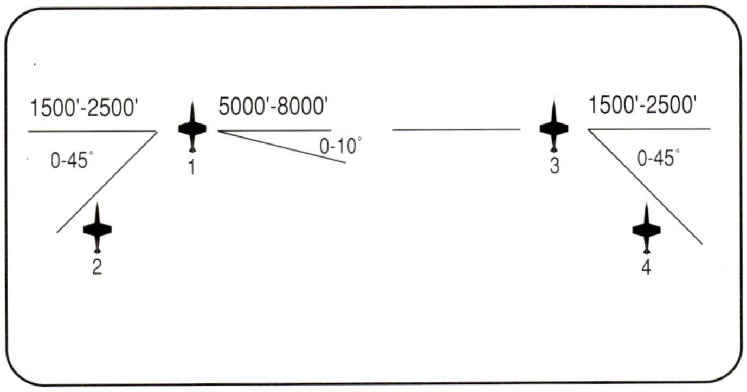

Low Level Battle Formation

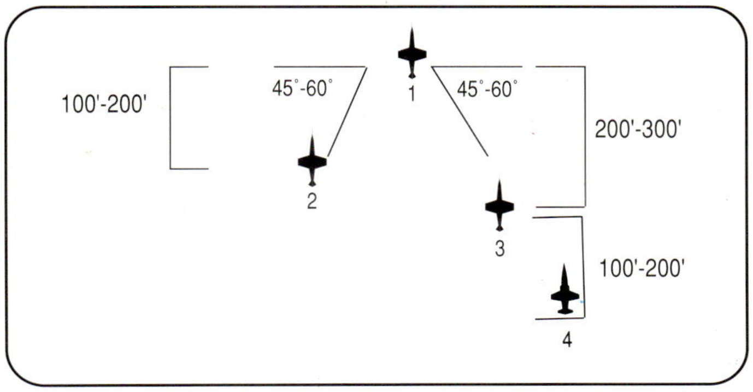

Arrowhead Formation

formation attacks other than in two-ship elements would eventually fall from favour.

If attacking from level flight conditions, the preferred tactic was a high speed, straight line fly-through from an easily recognizable Initial Point (IP). If a dive attack was planned, this would be accomplished either individually or in formation by a low level pop-up manoeuvre. In Central Europe, these deliveries were normally limited to a maximum of 10 degrees of dive as a concession to the frequently-low cloud ceilings in the region, and also to reduce exposure time to enemy defences. The run-in to a pop-up attack started at the IP and continued to the Pull-up Point (POP). Ideally, a good navigational feature would coincide with the POP, but when this was not available, the pull-up had to be initiated on timing from the IP. A successful pop-up attack required the pilot to manoeuvre his aircraft to a pre-planned weapons release point. Time was required to acquire the target, establish the aircraft in the correct delivery parameters and then put the sight on the target. The physical space required to satisfy this time requirement was known as the Minimum Attack Parameter (MAP) and was defined as "an imaginary circle around the target inside of which pre-planned dive parameters cannot be achieved". The POP was a position on the run-in track at which the climb to an attack profile apex altitude was initiated. Climb angles were normally the dive angle plus 10 degrees plus a short additional distance to allow for reaction time by the pilot. To fly this geometry properly, the pilot had to fly *exactly* to the POP, anticipate the pull-up, use 3 to 4 "Gs" to establish the climb, and

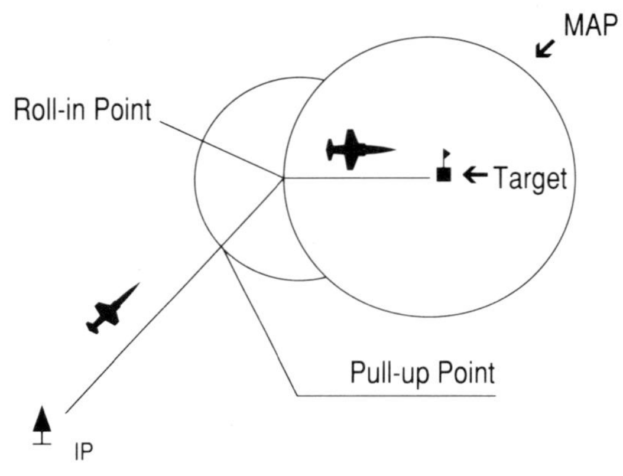

POP Geometry

then anticipate the roll-in to attack heading which would normally occur when the jet was at two-thirds of the apex altitude. Done properly, this POP geometry would result in the target appearing in the front windscreen on the attack roll-out. Done improperly, the target could be anywhere.

Eventually, a completely different concept of formation tactics, exploitable in both air-to-ground and air-to-air scenarios, would be adopted vigorously by the CF–104 community. This concept was known as Double Attack, and will be covered in depth later.

This is an appropriate place to delineate the ground attack tasks envisaged for the CF–104 with the advent of Conventional operations. The overall mission was still to trounce the Soviets and their cohorts so severely that cave dwelling would become an acceptable form of habitation for them, should they initiate hostilities. Nevertheless, deep Interdiction missions were out. The Starfighter could carry gas or bombs, but not both. Close Air Support (CAS) of friendly ground forces actively engaged with enemy ground forces was considered viable for the aircraft, though not ideal. The aircraft had a very wide turning radius at combat speeds for this type of operation and lacked sufficient volume of ordnance, an acceptable self-protection capability, and a sophisticated inertial navigation system for pin-point positioning under adverse and variable conditions. However, it was quite well suited to some Battlefield Air Interdiction (BAI) missions attacking an engaged enemy's rear echelons, and some short-range Interdiction and Offensive Counter Air (OCA) taskings... the so-called "one pass, haul ass" missions. These concessions to the aircraft's range limitations were qualified by the widespread feeling that a war in Central Europe would rapidly come to the Starfighters due to the advancing Red hordes, rather than the '104s having to go deep into the enemy's lairs.

However, the Starfighter possessed very limited carriage capability from its wing pylon stations, and a way was sought to augment the carrying capacity of the aircraft from these stations. This improvement was brought to fruition with the arrival of the Twin Stores Carrier (TSC) in 1973. Although the TSC heralded a major improvement in the carriage capabilities of the Starfighter, only the LAU–3/A rocket pods and the MK–82 bombs of the original Conventional ordnance types could be mated with this new suspension equipment. The fire bombs were too large in diameter to fit a brace of them on each carrier, and two CBUs exceeded the 1500 pound carriage limit of the wing pylon, to which the TSC was attached. Nonetheless, other ordnance was coming on line which could be carried in pairs on each TSC.

Purchased due to a perceived need for a broader battlefield capability in a cluster-type munition, the British-built BL–755 was introduced to 1 CAG operations in September 1973. This was a high-explosive cluster bomb in the 600 pound class that was designed to produce a high kill probability against a wide range of small targets on the battlefield. Owing to the nature of the individual bomblets, which operated on the shape charge principle, it had a very good armour-piercing capability with a secondary fragmentation effect. Each bomb was dropped as a unit, then functioned to release its 147 bomblets in an evenly distributed pattern. This weapon was designed for low altitude, high speed deliveries at up to 600 knots, in level flight or very shallow dive conditions. The individual bomblets, each weighing approximately 2.5 pounds, functioned on impact, and each bomblet had a high-explosive shaped charge for penetration of armour plating, as well as a fragmenting case which was very effective against personnel, non-armoured vehicles, and parked aircraft. The CF–104 could carry five of these weapons; two under each wing on TSCs, and one on the fuselage centreline. However, the cluster munitions story as it related to the CF–104 was not over... though the CBU–2B/A soldiered bravely on with the BL–755 in the munitions inventory until 1984, its carriage limits on the TSC, conservative post-combat cannister jettison limits, and generally limited weapons effects resulted in its replacement with the American-built MK–20 Rockeye II cluster bomb that year. This potent weapon would complement the BL–755 in the Conventional munitions inventory until Starfighter phase-out in 1986.

So much for gravity-fall type weapons, but what about forward firing ordnance improvements? Perhaps the greatest single point source of weapons joy to the CF–104 pilot, the M–61A1 six-barrelled 20 mm Vulcan cannon replaced the forward fuel bladders in 1974. This devastating weapon mated ideally with the Starfighter airframe, since due to its rock-solid stability at low level, the aircraft proved to be an excellent gun platform for an excellent gun. Aside from being deadly accurate, part of the magic of this weapon was its unearthly sound. Heard from the ground at a weapons range, the Vulcan produced a moaning roar and a sheet of flame from the muzzle that was a destructive statement in its own right. Even on controlled tests at home base by Maintenance, this weapon attracted attention, and a short burst sounded much like the world's largest metal door slamming shut. Bill McWilliams elaborates...

The 20 mm cannon soon became a tourist attraction, for witnessing a test firing at the gun butts was a mandatory exercise. Ground shots were limited to 18 rounds, three per barrel, as more would overheat the barrels without the cooling airflow of flight. As it was, the 18 rounds came out so fast that it sounded like a foghorn, and even with ear protection, visitors jumped...

This weapon could delivery 6000 rounds of high explosive or armour piercing shells per minute, but was geared down to a practical firing rate of 4000 rounds per minute in order to extend system life and prevent misfire. It's highly doubtful if even the most astute Starfighter pilots would have noticed the difference, so effective was this weapon in its tamed form.

Hardened targets were a particular problem for the Starfighter pilots of 1 CAG. Destruction of them presents unique problems of both munition design and delivery method. When considering the amount of effort this destruction requires, it is logical to conclude that the protection provided by hardening a target would not be wasted on something insignificant. The enemy wants to keep it safe, and therefore the fighter pilot wants to destroy it. The AGM–65 Maverick missile solved many of the design problems associated with hard target penetration, combining high terminal impact velocity (via rocket power) with an efficient shaped-charge warhead. The delivery method also presented certain advantages; among them, relative freedom from restrictive launch parameters, a large employment envelope, and a true "launch and leave" capability.

But the news wasn't all good, because with electro-optical guidance, contrast is required, and another element of defensive protection enters the equation... namely camouflage. Combined with prevailing weather conditions in Central Europe, combat employment of the Maverick was subject to certain limitations. Furthermore, the biggest limitation of Maverick to the CF–104 operation was that it was deemed unaffordable. Alternate methods for attacking hard targets would have to be explored, and the MK–4 rocket was the obvious first weapon to consider. However, a review of the geriatric MK–4 highlighted some severe limitations, including:

1. A lack of aerodynamic stability;
2. Unreliable functioning;
3. Severely degraded accuracy in shallow dive angles; and,
4. Insufficient penetrating power for target protective covers such as hardened aircraft shelters.

Therefore in 1971, the Canadian Forces stated a requirement for a new 2.75 inch rocket incorporating state-of-the-art technology in propellant and design. In response to this requirement, Defence Research Establishment Valcartier (DREV) developed the Canadian Rocket Vehicle–7 (CRV–7).

Though externally similar to most other 2.75 inch rockets, CRV–7 incorporated significant design improvements in propellant, igniter, nozzle, fins and warhead. These improvements gave the rocket a noteworthy increase in launch range and terminal impact velocity, an increase in stability, and a reduction in rocket dispersion, and mated these improvements for use with all existing 2.75 inch rocket warheads. Operationally, CRV–7 was fired from a 19–tube launcher similar in design and dimensions to the LAU–3/A. For training purposes, the rocket was mated with a 6-tube launcher designated the LAU–5002.

The superior performance of the CRV–7 was confirmed by an extensive program of ground and air launches. These tests confirmed a realistic doubling of the stand–off range which enhanced survivability against enemy ground defenses, as well as a greatly increased accuracy and a tighter impact pattern. Typical attack profiles for a two-aircraft CF–104 element in Double Attack formation were the Penis and Half-Penis deliveries; these monickers a direct result of the rather self explanatory flight profiles.

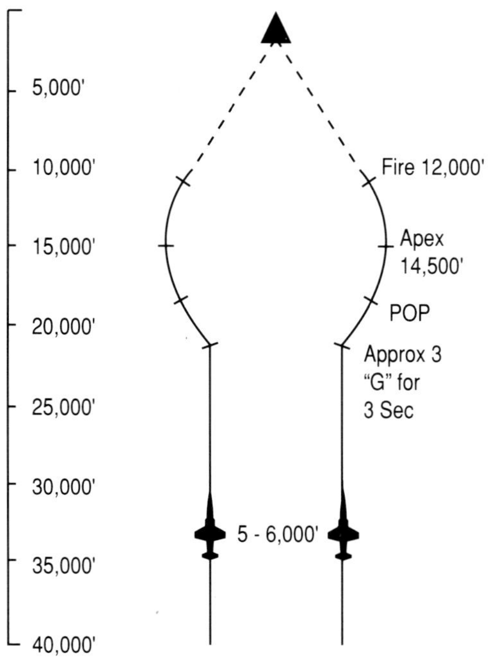

The Penis Delivery

For the Penis delivery, the Double Attack pair ingressed the target at 5000 - 6000 feet line abreast and "in the weeds". At approximately 22,000 feet range to the target (measured on a map), each aircraft did an outward turn through approximately 30 degrees, rolled out, then "popped" to apex at approximately 14,500 feet slant range from the target, and opened fire at 12,000 feet slant range. Both aircraft then performed a prebriefed escape manoeuvre to rejoin in Double Attack formation with mutual support as expeditiously as possible. The beauty of this attack profile was that it could be planned for whatever run-in airspeed and attack airspeed/dive angle was deemed appropriate. It also maintained Double Attack mutual support for a long time during the run-in-attack phase, and when executed correctly, it quickly regained it during the egress phase. Lastly, this attack profile employed CRV–7's enhanced stand–off capability to reduce exposure time to enemy defences.

Another derivative of this attack plan was the "Half Penis". During this profile, one of the fighters did a high speed level ingress on the target with whatever ordnance he deemed appropriate. The other fighter flew a staggered formation on his partner and performed the split and pop manoeuvres previously described, opening fire once the preceding fighter had passed over the target environs.

CF–104 pilots liked the CRV–7. John Bagshaw, who flew the '104 for many years both in 1 CAG and as an instructor at the OTU, flew with the weapon on a November 1977 Exercise Red Flag sortie against a Nevada desert training target complex...

The targets were specific points within an airfield complex. In one case, the target was two F–100 aircraft sitting on a runway lined up for takeoff... I selected a 5 degree attack, utilizing the extreme slant range of the CRV–7. Mission planning indicated a range of hills 1500 feet above target elevation with a vertical drop-off short of the target. Range from the base of the cliff to the target was about 14,000 feet. For this attack, I flew at 100 feet Above Ground Level (AGL) along the back side of the hill, pulled up over the hill still maintaining 100 feet AGL, and then rolled out with 5 degrees of dive, which positioned my aircraft at 13,000 feet slant range to the target.

A salvo of two rocket launchers (12 CRV–7s) was extremely impressive. Both aircraft were destroyed with ***inert*** *warheads.*

Formation tactics evolved considerably with the adoption of the Double Attack system in the early 1970s and its application to the air-to-ground as well as the air-to-air environment. Basically, Double Attack was two aircraft maneuvering in concert with each other for better visual and positional mutual support, maneuverability, greater fire power, kill efficiency, and flexibility. In the Dark Ages before Double Attack, if a two-ship tasking was accepted, it would generally mean a mission where the wingman was told to hang on, look out, and otherwise shut up! With Double Attack, element leaders still wanted their wingmen to hang on, look out and shut up, but they also saw a great potential in considering the element as two aircraft instead of as a single entity. In fact, Double Attack recognized the wingman as an almost equal partner with the leader. It allowed greater flexibility of motion and position while enroute, and if engaged by an enemy, the cell became two independent yet coordinated fighters. Obviously, this formation and maneuvering concept demanded more of the wingmen, and considerably more attack training was required to teach this system. Nonetheless, it was proven over time that with practice most inexperienced wingers were able to fulfill their half of the Double Attack contract. Though evolved as an air combat formation, Double Attack had definite applications at low altitude. The prerequisite for success was a higher experience level on the part of the pilots throughout the formation through increased exposure and training. Simply stated, the Lead needed to adopt all the responsibilities of Lead and a Two in a Battle formation, while the wingman adopted the responsibilities of a Three and a Four, including greatly increased navigational awareness and individual attack participation. While this basic formation might be temporarily collapsed during the final attack portion of a weapons delivery if a formation delivery was deemed appropriate, the idea was to revert to Double Attack for all its inherent advantages immediately upon target egress. The old "welded wing" formations, though still a useful part of the Starfighter pilot's "bag of tricks" depending on the requirement, were used much more sparingly after the advent of Double Attack.

Though the two-ship element was the heart of the Double Attack concept, additional elements could be added to the initial cell to form larger formations. Two very popular Double Attack multiple formations were called Card and Offset Card.

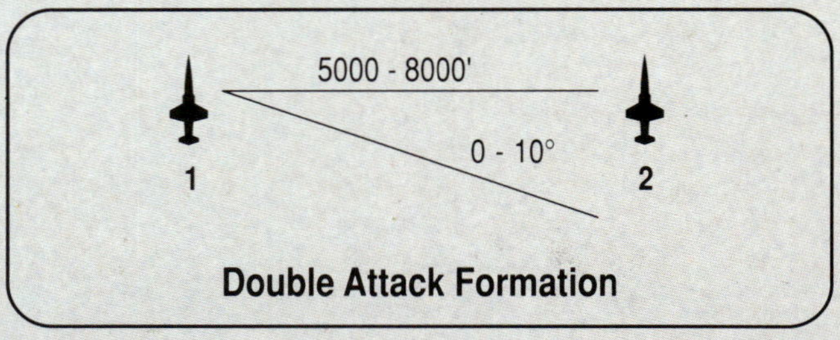

While we have already discussed the evolution of Double Attack and its application in CRV–7 rocket deliveries, the various types of new ordnance coupled with increased situational aware-

ness in the low level Attack environment spawned the adoption of other attack tactics as well. Along with the perennially-popular level fly-throughs and pop-up attacks, a new delivery method called the curvilinear attack was added to the CF–104 pilot's tactical repertoire. Essentially, curvilinear attacks were level attacks that ended with a hard turn onto the final attack heading from another ingress heading, allowing a few seconds of level flight tracking prior to weapons release.

The reason for designing this tactic was to present a more

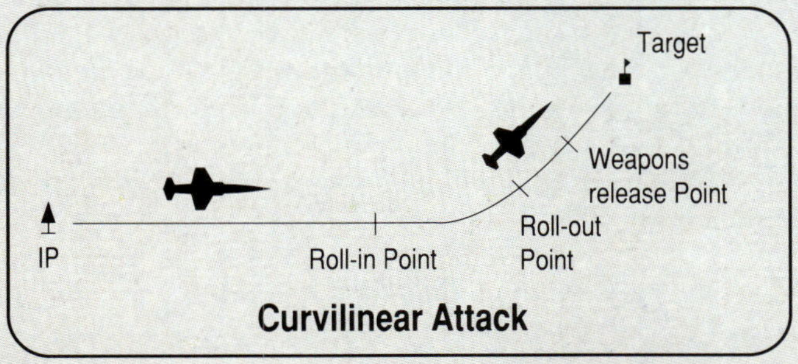

difficult target for ground fire during the very vulnerable time prior to weapons release. The parameters for using a curvilinear attack varied with airspeed and "G" (radius of turn), but it was critical to the success of the attack that the '104 pilot initiated the correct "G" load *exactly* at the roll-in point. Generally, these attacks, with notable exceptions, proved disappointing. Targets were easily missed due to lack of sufficient navigational features, incorrect "G" loading in the turns, difficulty in achieving proper release parameters, and "spitting out" the wingman during the roll-in, due to the intensity of the manoeuvre. It was also found that this jink onto the target sometimes **aided** ground defences in early acquisition of the attack aircraft, and compromised any element of surprise that may have otherwise been gained. Curvilinears were best suited for curving around terrain features when achieving surprise was not feasible. This could be done much further out from the target, to obtain a better attack heading when a level attack from the selected IP was not optimum.

Due to typically low cloud ceilings in Central Europe, a desire to provide minimum exposure time to enemy defences in this high-threat environment, and the dive angle delivery limitations of many of the CF–104's ordnance types, the 5 degree bombing attack became very popular. This manoeuvre was performed in the same manner as a popping delivery, with typical apex altitudes being 800 - 1000 feet AGL, typical release altitudes being 300 - 350 feet AGL, and a target tracking time of three to five seconds on attack heading roll-out. However, because of the need to lead the final roll-in when climbing through two-thirds of the apex altitude, and since this was a **very** small altitude difference for the low level ingress height above the terrain, the manoeuvre appeared continuously variable in three dimensions. No sooner did the Starfighter pilot aggressively establish his climb profile, than it was time to roll-in on attack heading, **simultaneously** converting his climb angle to the planned attack dive angle by roll-out... a sort of "curvipop", if you will. The beauty of this attack profile was that, due to the necessary attack geometry, it was commenced much closer in to the target area, thus narrowing the margin for error. Also, because of the continuous three-dimensional nature of the attack profile and the limited exposure time, the threat from enemy ground defences was somewhat reduced.

A very important factor to note with the CF–104's Conventional ordnance arsenal is that, almost without exception, actual overflight of the enemy target was required. While it is true that the CRV–7 rocket gave the CF–104 a very limited stand-off capability, there were no true "launch and leave" or "smart" weapons in the Canadian Starfighter munitions inventory. While some attempts were made to trial "toss" or lofting types of deliveries a considerable distance back from the targets, this delivery method was totally unsuitable due to the increased inaccuracies of the attack profiles, the limited damage capabilities of the weapons, and the pinpoint nature of most of the targets. Loft bombing, while interesting, would have to wait for a "smarter"

aircraft/ordnance combination.

Once the target had been successfully destroyed, the CF-104 pilot could now concentrate on a matter near-and-dear to his heart; namely, preserving his pink body for posterity. We have already discussed the need for mutually-supporting formations during the egress phase of an attack, but the arrival of this formation back at home base begged further concerns. It was a reasonable assumption on the part of 1 CAG pilots that if they were over on the other side of the lines attempting to ruin the enemy's day, chances were that the enemy would try to beat up on the home turf in a reciprocating manner. Therefore, it was felt that a returning formation should retain its tactical war-fighting integrity at combat speeds until the last possible moment before landing. From this logic trail evolved the Battle Break...

Now the Battle Break was, quite simply, a licence to fly low and to have fun. Of the several accepted ways to recover aircraft in Visual Flight Rules (VFR) conditions, this was the best deal for a fighter pilot. There was also considerable tactical justification, as this recovery was designed to get four aircraft on the ground with minimum exposure time at vulnerable circuit height and a minimum time at non-combat speeds. The four-ship team collapsed into a tight "finger" formation, with only a couple of hundred feet separation between individual members. This flight then scorched in at around 450 knots, 200 - 300 feet above ground and around 30 degrees off runway heading to a point just short of the runway. The formation then abruptly rolled to runway heading, then sequentially pulled up and established spacing downwind in the circuit for landing. The spacing between the aircraft was established by the timing and the intensity of the pull-up. Fighter pilots got to practice this tactic for its wartime applications. The *fun* part was just a fringe benefit. Though a common enough tactical recovery for some years, it would eventually be largely superceded by formation or single-ship straight-in approaches; the argument being that fratricide from nervous air defence forces on the home field was a strong likelihood in war. In peace, the reality was that the local natives were becoming progressively more restless, if not irate, over these high speed, low level run-ins as years went by. People like airshows, but apparently not every day of the week.

* * * * * *

In this day and age of sophisticated weapons systems, such as those on the CF–18 and the Panavia Tornado, all types of ordnance can be delivered with utterly reliable, practically ***boring*** accuracy with varying degrees of automation. The '104 was, until the last few years, very much a manual system where individual pilot skill determined the outcome of each and every bombing, rocketry, and gunnery event. Recent strides in weapons delivery technology are marvellous, a real aid to the fighter pilot; but we developed a tremendous sense of accomplishment in honing our skills on the Starfighter in manual release modes. We became ***very*** good, and very competitive. As we have already seen, Canadian '104 pilots did very well in international NATO bombing and gunnery competitions throughout the aircraft's operational life.

Typically, even our practice deliveries tended to be low and fast, allowing minimum exposure time. Delivery parameters usually varied from level flight to up to 10 degrees of dive, and delivery airspeeds from 450 to 550 plus knots - the faster the better. We used to have an elaborate betting system on practice range missions for quarters or Deutschmarks on the results of the different weapons events. For example, each bomb dropped or rocket fired within a given event, and the best overall strafe score with the gun would be worth a quarter to the winner from each of the losers. This is not to imply that our fighter pilots were a bunch of high stakes gamblers. Very little money actually changed hands when you consider a typical range mission would mean about six practice bombs dropped, three or four practice rockets fired, and several gun passes. Furthermore, it was very unusual for any one individual to "sweep" the competition. Each flight member usually had his own particular strengths on any given day. Nevertheless, rivalry was often fierce amongst the experienced, and I can remember days when three or four "bullseyes" or "shacks" (direct hits) from, say, ten events, were not good enough to get ahead financially. Stiff competition, when you consider that anything inside of 140 feet was a qualifying bomb by NATO standards. You had to be great, or there went the kid's lunch money.

* * * * * *

Hank Morris flew '104s with 421 Squadron in Baden-Soellingen from 1974 until 1977. In the mid-1970s, CF–104 pilots had garnered a reputation for making the extraordinary look routine in terms of overcoming less-than-ideal circumstances and still managing to get the job done. His story of a bombing mission to Siegenburg Range under difficult weather conditions epitomizes that fighting spirit...

*It was a Friday in February, 1977 and to finish the week in style, we had planned an eight-plane formation on to Siegenburg Range during a 20 minute range time slot. Each section of four would have ten minutes for six passes. To make it sporting (and tactically realistic), each section gave itself Bomb Impact Times (30 seconds into their respective range time). It was "teed-up" with the Range Control Officer at Siegenburg that the events would be a 500 knots curvilinear attack in pairs on both skip pits simultaneously, followed by individual passes on the skip pits, two 5 degree dive attacks, and two 200 foot level attacks. I led the first section and the squadron CO, LCol. Brian Smith, led the second. The weather was the usual haze; two-to-three miles flight visibility. Two minutes back approaching the check point, we switched to Siegenburg Range frequency. As we checked in, we overheard a flight of three American F–4 Phantoms from Spangdahlem being vectored towards the range. It appeared that they had transited at high level, then let down at Ingolstadt, and seemed unfamiliar with the range. It was obvious that they had been vectored around a few times trying to get lined up with the range itself. I can imagine the thoughts of the American pilots who had used up all of the 20 minutes of range time allocated to perform their training, and still had not found the range, when I came up on the frequency advising Siegenburg that eight CF–104s were two minutes back and had a Bomb Impact Time of 30 seconds into the period for the first run attack at 500 knots in formation. The silence from the F–4s was deafening, but it appeared that they were somewhat curious about this horde of '104s which was about to appear of out the murk and perform this series of events with eight aircraft. The F–4s asked to hold to the south while we proceeded with the exercise. It all went off as advertised with skip hits and qualifying scores to follow, and as my Number Four called off on his last pass, LCol. Smith and his wingman were pulling up into their first-run attack. The sequence was repeated with similar good results. As the second section disappeared into the murk, the leader of the F–4 section asked Siegenburg, somewhat in awe... "Who were those guys???" The reply; "Canadian '104s from Baden-Soellingen," then... "What are your intentions?" In a rather desultory tone, the reply from the American flight lead was, "**Clearance back to Spangdahlem**".*

A considerable amount of time has been spent dealing with the Starfighter in the Ground Attack role, which was its "bread and butter" *raison d'être* throughout the Conventional period. But what about exploitation of the aircraft's limited air-to-air capabilities?

Prior to the advent of the Double Attack system, Starfighter pilot trainees were taught to do things in the air-to-air arena that were unrealistic from both an aircraft performance capabilities point of view, and from a threat environment point of view. These unrealistic manoeuvres were also being taught from impractical formations. For example, Starfighter pilot trainees were being taught manoeuvres such as the slow-speed Scissors; a tactic guaranteed to herald the death knell of the Starfighter against any superior turning adversary, which was just about *everybody*. Not only did excessive, energy-depleting turns against an aerodynamically-more-efficient enemy make the CF–104 pilot vulnerable by "bringing the fight to the bandit's terms", it made him extremely predictable to other enemy aircraft who might be watching these energy depleting manoeuvres. They would have been more than happy to administer a quick *coup de grâce* to a Starfighter pilot who had been long on initiative but painfully short on judgement.

There is no doubt that a lot of the dubious maneuvering sequences taught initially to CF–104 pilot trainees stemmed from an honest desire to engage the enemy in a manner such as had been done during the Sabre days; but the Starfighter was not a Sabre, and the high threat environment personified by the vastly numerically-superior Soviet fighter forces changed matters as well.

Though a combat element would transit an area in near-line-abreast formation, it was felt until the early 1970s that the '104 wingman could not manoeuvre to maintain mutual support for his leader during an actual engagement. An early air combat tactics manual from the OTU is very revealing on this subject...

When the enemy is sighted and the attack is begun, or when under attack, the wingmen and the element leader will not be able to maintain their respective near-line-abreast positions. The initial turning will place the wingmen about 45 degrees back, and with the onset of maximum performance maneuvering, the wingman should fly in the maximum manoeuvre position, providing coverage for the leader. The maximum manoeuvre position is a 45 - 60 degree cone or "doughnut" about 1000 to 2500 feet back of the leader, and that position will be maintained by the wingmen throughout the engagement unless ordered otherwise by the leader. The element leader will manoeuvre his element as a separate unit but in direct support of the lead element.

When engaged, if the wingman positions himself outside the leader's 60 degree cone, he will be operating in his leader's "blind area" most of the time. The blind area is defined as "that area in the rear hemisphere which is out of the leader's field of view unless he strains to look" (a task he cannot perform while positioning for attack or tracking). This cone extends outward 30 degrees on either side of the leader's tail.

A better option would be to fly a 45 - 60 degree cone or "doughnut" which would ideally position the wingman 45 degrees from the leader's tail. The 45 degree position is unwieldy at 100 - 1500 feet slant range. At the 60 degree, 1500 foot position, the wingman's blind area overlaps that of the leader's so that the area dead astern of the leader from 2500 feet outward is not visible to either flight member.

If the planes of symmetry of both aircraft are rotated with the wingman on the inside of a turn, it is quite possible for an enemy to close to within gun range of the leader, without being seen by either member. The 1500 foot separation should therefore be extended to a distance of 2500 feet when the section is on the offensive.

It would not be possible for an enemy to close to within gun range without being seen if the wingman was flying on the 45 degree line with 2500 feet separation. In addition, the leader will be able to cover the wingman's lethal cone by only casual observation. Although #2 is primarily concerned with clearing the 6 o'clock area when the element is on the attack, the areas of responsibility change when they are under attack themselves. The wingman must continue to give range and clock information until the leader acknowledges a visual sighting. At that time the leader has the primary responsibility for clearing 6 o'clock and keeping the attacking element in sight. The wingman must now clear the forward hemisphere until the leader is again on the attack. Additionally he should move in closer to the leader (to 1000 feet) if the severity of the maneuvering will permit it. He must keep the leader informed of his range if he is forced into the leader's blind area or falls back.

The optimism expressed by this tactics manual regarding the wingman's ability to cover his leader from the Fighting Wing Position was, to put it charitably, unfounded. In reality, the wingman in this formation was essentially useless to his leader, except for serving as a potential shot absorber from other hostile forces. The CF–104 aerodynamically could simply not stay in a common, tight formation on an aggressively turning leader and simultaneously do a proper job of lookout and clearing his lead...

What, then, could be done to enhance the Starfighter's combat survivability in the always treacherous air-to-air combat environment? Fortunately for the CF–104 community, in the very early 1970s, the USAF was espousing the virtues of the Double Attack system, and this tactical concept of mutual support and more autonomous maneuvering by the wingman was adopted enthusiastically by the '104 world. This system, properly executed, reduced both defensive and offensive air combat to a series of initial moves which, if employed correctly, would

Above: *A most unusual cargo for a flatbed truck and for that matter, a most unusual way for a CF-104 to get around. This Starfighter is being transported back from the Northwest Industries plant at the Edmonton Industrial Airport to Nisku, the Edmonton International Airport for testing and shipment back to Germany after completing the DLIR process.*

defeat an attacking enemy or result in his destruction. There were several "Achilles heels" to this concept, though. The first was that it involved a considerable amount of judgement and expertise on the part of the wingman to manoeuvre aggressively in concert with his leader. The second was that, to be done properly, the concept required liberal use of the radios... a supposition that was very unlikely in the communications saturation, communications jamming environment of a Central European war scenario. Nevertheless, Double Attack embodied a *realistic* offensive and defensive air-to-air capability for the Starfighter and optimized its limited resources in this arena. The Double Attack pair was taught to maintain a very high energy level (i.e., in the '104, speed), maintain positions of mutual support, and resist the temptation to enter a protracted turning engagement with a superior turning enemy.

* * * * * *

In Air Combat Maneuvering, the aircraft displayed limited turning capability due to its high wing loading, but *great* acceleration. Only the F–105 and perhaps the F–111 were in a similar wing-loading league with the '104. Almost all the other fighter or fighter-bomber types we routinely practiced ACM with tended to have much lower wing loading. We would capitalize on the aircraft's aerodynamic properties with "hit and run" type tactics, not allowing ourselves to enter a hard turning engagement with a superior turning fighter. Although an occasional deviation from this norm by a highly experienced air combat pilot to capitalize on an adversary's mistakes was possible, in most cases, violations of the hit-and-run principle resulted in a severe drubbing for '104 pilots. "Turning and burning" was just not its forté. It took acres of airspace to turn the jet around at combat speeds and it's no wonder that ex-'104 pilots who now fly the redoubtable CF–18 Hornet have likened this worthy successor's close-in, hard-turning fighting capabilities to "a knife fight in a telephone booth". Still, the '104 could turn where we needed it to turn, down in the high-speed, low-level environment, and this was due to the better turning and engine performance in the denser air at lower altitudes. Few people realize that a "clean" '104 below 5000 feet Above Sea Level in full afterburner could *sustain* a seven "G" turn. Trouble was, in full burner, the pilot couldn't sustain it very long before he ran out of gas; fuel flows being *very* high at low level. A typical ACM mission might not last more than 30 - 40 minutes, of which perhaps only about 10 minutes actually involved combat. With less than 6000 pounds of fuel in a typical ACM configuration and a fuel flow rate probably eight or nine times that in pounds-per-hour (PPH) in afterburner, one does not have to be Albert Einstein to realize why fuel control was (and is) such an essential element of air combat.

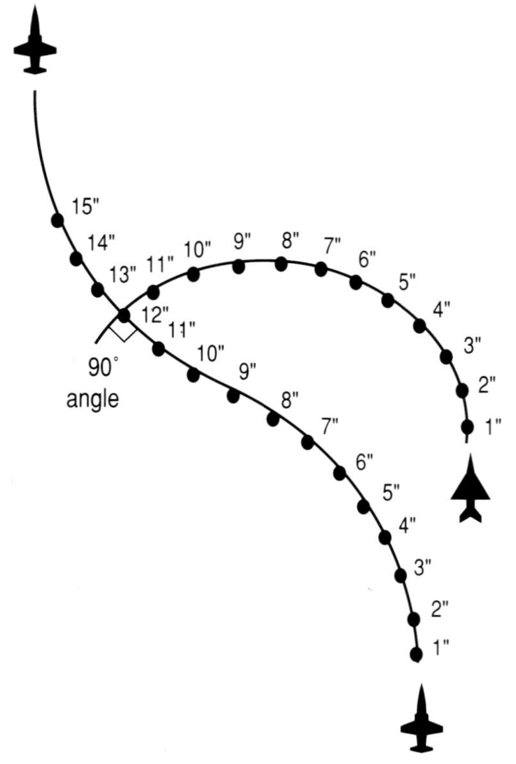

High Angle-Off Gunshot

* * * * * *

Defensively, scenarios were taught to defeat both missile and the closer gun attacks, primarily from the rear quarter, by enemy fighters. This was done purely for survival purposes. Offensively, CF–104 pilots were taught to close to heat-seeking missile parameters in an enemy's stern quarter for two reasons. First, and perhaps most importantly, it taught Starfighter pilots to visually recognize valid missile launch envelopes for such a time when they would possess an aircraft with air-to-air missiles. Secondly, because each "Fox-2" call (a simulated valid heat-seeking missile shot) was followed by an aggressive, high "G" missile defensive break by the defending aircraft, it allowed the CF–104 pilot to practice his one and only valid shot against a low wing-loaded enemy. This was the dreaded High Angle-Off gunshot...

Essentially, this tactic assumed a "worst case" scenario. That is, that the bandit saw the missile coming his way and aggressively maneuvered to defeat it. Should this not happen and the bandit were to disappear in the fireball of missile impact, so much the better. Also, should the missile miss and the attacker still remain unobserved, allowing him to close to a "guns tracking" firing solution on the bandit, ***again*** so much the better. But the real world dictated that the bandit would see the inbound missile and attempt to prolong his life. If both aircraft were at combat speed when the missile shot was detected at a range of, say, two nautical miles, the Starfighter pilot had about fifteen seconds to get a non-tracking, low Probability of Kill (PK) gun shot off against his adversary. This he did by aggressively pulling geometrical lead on the hard-turning bandit in his direction of turn (5 "Gs" for 5 seconds was an accepted rule of thumb) in an attempt to place the bandit in a position approximately 45 degrees off the Starfighter's nose. After that, the '104 pilot quickly rolled out, matched the plane of flight of his enemy, and anticipated the open fire point, which was one bullet-time-of-flight prior to when the bandit would cross the bullet stream. This was taught as a reference position of the enemy off the cockpit windscreen of the attacking fighter,[1] and the object was to have the bandit fly through the attacker's bullets and dissolve in a withering hail of cannon fire.

As an aside, since this manoeuvre essentially entailed a collision course by the attacker on the defender, and since the geometry of this shot was first taught to CF–104 student pilots from the relative safety of the two-seat CF–104D, it caused very high anxiety levels amongst the Starfighter instructor community. This was because, done properly, the attacker was "blind" or "belly-up" to the defender during the lead-pulling part of this manoeuvre. Acquiring the bandit visually immediately on roll-out or breaking off the engagement was absolutely necessary, as

[1] About 20 degrees removed from the gunsight reference.

otherwise the distinct possibility of a mid-air collision was only about ten seconds away. This realization raised snivelling to a rare art form on the part of the terrified instructor in the back seat, who could see much less than his pupil up front, and didn't know whether or not his student, during this intensely aggressive manoeuvre, was losing his perspective or situational awareness. This was commonly known as the student "having a helmet fire". Many is the CF–104 student pilot who has been treated to an earful of hyperventilation and unmanly blubbering from the rear seat during this part of the maneuvering sequence.

Naturally, matching the plane of the target's motion and anticipating the open-fire point were the other essential aspects of producing success on this attack. Done correctly, this manoeuvre would allow at least a 90 degree track crossing angle on the bandit, and once the firing point had been reached, the attacker had to execute an escape manoeuvre. This consisted of maximizing the track crossing angle on the attacked bandit (up to approximately 120 degrees) by aggressively turning *away* from him for several seconds, then unloading the aircraft to less than 1 "G" and accelerating straight ahead as fast as possible. Turning any more than to the 120 degree point was an unnecessary depletion of energy when the time could be more profitably spent accelerating away. This "hit and run" manoeuvre was always executed in this manner because the attacker had to assume the worst case, namely that:

1. he had missed;
2. he had really upset the bandit; and
3. that the bandit, bent on revenge, had reversed on the audacious attacker, and would attempt to cancel his life insurance policy.

When this manoeuvre was taught as a Double Attack tactic with two attackers, relatively simple initial moves allowed the wingman or "covering man" in the DA formation to close for a shot of his own on the bandit, while directing his former leader how to best escape or to reposition to provide mutual support on this *new* leader, depending on the bandit's action. This somewhat simplified scenario provides a graphic example of the fluid and changing nature of the leader/wingman roles within the Double Attack concept.

As more and more experience became commonplace in the Starfighter community with Double Attack tactics, and as the high threat multi-bandit environment that surely would occur in an air war in Central Europe was scrutinized, CF–104 tacticians acknowledged that Double Attack was not a panacea for all occasions. It was conceded that the formal contract between the two members of the Double Attack cell might break down for such reasons as loss of visual contact on the egress off a target, or the necessity for last-ditch defensive maneuvering by one of the team members, or simply an inability to maintain radio contact for communication with one's partner. However, it was stressed that the basic concepts always remained valid within the NATO Alliance, and ***mutual support of opportunity*** in the battle area with *any* friendly fighter was better than no mutual support at all, and going it alone. For this reason, the Double Attack mutual support principles were given the widest possible dissemination amongst the Air Forces of the Alliance.

There was another reason for teaching heat seeking missile parameters to the Starfighter pilots of 1 CAG. In 1972, it was decided that, when the Canadian Starfighters were formally brought on alert in times of tension, 441 Squadron would deploy to CFB Lahr and assume, along with its primary role of Ground Attack, a secondary role of Air Defence. Though it was clearly understood that the CF–104 could not be considered a potent air defence resource, once the fleet was retrofitted with the M–16 cannon in 1974–75, increased emphasis was placed on realistic aerial combat. Survival and success in the Multi-Bandit Environment was stressed as well as, how to capitalize on the fleeting potential for an offensive "kill" in what would surely be a target rich environment. There also appeared to be some potential to equip at least a portion of the CF–104 fleet with AIM–9 Sidewinder heat seeking missiles during wartime. 441 Squadron had been assigned a secondary responsibility to fly Combat Air Patrols (CAPs) in fixed patterns over the Schwabisch Alps, and on NATO Crested Eagle exercises, 441 would regularly man these areas for a fixed period. Along with the other Baden squadrons, they were also tasked to fly CAP missions in predetermined patterns over the Black Forest for base defence. It was decided to explore the possibility of Sidewinder carriage on the '104 mated to a catamaran which was in turn attached to the fuselage centreline bomb rack. Through trialing, it was determined that although the rack was suitable, the appropriate electrical connectors were all being used by retrofitted equipment such as the radar warning receiver. It was suggested that part of the CF–104 fleet could be modified with the appropriate wiring during a depot-level major inspection, but initial estimates determined that this would be cost-prohibitive. It would also have resulted in decreased operational flexibility by limiting the number of aircraft hulls that could be made available to 441 Squadron in wartime, since they would be the only outfit to get missile-equipped aircraft. Accordingly, and also because the end of the CF–104 program was looming ever nearer, the plan was

Above: *The complete conventional weapons suite of the CF-104 at retirement, including 20mm cannon, CRV-7 rockets, BL-755 and Rockeye cluster bombs, MK-82 GP bombs and practice weapons.*

scrapped, and 1 CAG Starfighters flew their CAP patterns with just the 20 mm cannon as armament.

Throughout the course of its operational career, the CF–104 was the beneficiary of numerous hardware updates and improvements, both to keep pace with the technological times and to improve its performance in the Conventional Attack arena. These changes were numerous over the years, and included replacement of the UHF radio and TACAN with improved versions, installation of a vastly improved servo altimeter, and the replacement of the original transponder with a 4096-code system. While these modifications significantly improved the avionics suite of the jet, three important electronic additions to the aircraft considerably enhanced its war-fighting capability over the years. These were the installation of the AN/ALR–501 Airborne Radar Warning Receiver (ARWR) in 1974, the replacement of the existing gunsight with the vastly improved Lead Computing Optical Sight System (LCOSS) at around the same time, and finally the replacement of the aircraft's original inertial navigation system with a state-of-the-art Litton LW–33 Nav/Attack system in 1979 - 1980.

The radar warning receiver added a few lumps and bumps to the Starfighter's sleek external lines; specifically, a "chin goiter" under the radome which housed the forward-sensing lobes of the system, and small rearward-sensing lobes on either side of the aft fuselage near the tailpipe. What it also added was a very significant self-protection capability from enemy radar threats. These were displayed through interpretation of a bank of lights and coded strobes on a small circular screen located prominently on the pilot's instrument panel. While it took some time to eliminate some spurious inputs to the system, the electronic wizards of 1 CAG Maintenance Squadron soon had the warning receiver working in top form. Considering its position in the evolutionary hierarchy of radar warning receivers, the 501 system functioned admirably, providing yeoman service to the CF–104 fleet for the remaining years of its operational life.

The AN/ASG–502 Lead Computing Optical Sight System (LCOSS) was designed primarily to predict accurate lead angles against maneuvering and non-maneuvering airborne targets. To achieve this, it had to be used in the air-to-air mode and provided with a radar lock-on to the target. An alternative to the use of radar was the depression of a throttle cage button, which slaved the sight to a position which predicted hits for firing at 1500 feet range and 150 feet per minute closure rate. This was useful because, if the opportunity presented itself, an unsuspecting bandit could be tracked with the gunsight without emitting detectable radar energy towards him. In the air-to-ground mode, the LCOSS reticle was manually depressed just like the old sight, **but** it was also roll-stabilized to give an accurate aiming reference for the delivery of air-to-ground weapons. In the event of some inertial navigation system failures which would affect the roll-stabilization feature of this mode, a backup manual mode identical to the old sight system was thoughtfully provided by the manufacturers. This sighting system proved to be incredibly accurate and reliable throughout the CF–104's remaining operational life, particularly after it was married to the Litton LW–33 replacement inertial navigation system.

The LN–3 inertial navigation set, the original aircraft system, was a very primitive variant. However, it was "the last word" at the time of its conception. During the 1970s, CF–104 pilots used to joke that the hamsters were getting tired out on the equipment's treadmill when it acted up, which was often. By the late 1970s, the failure rate of the LN–3 was incredibly high, the repair costs astronomical. A study revealed that the system could be completely replaced with a state-of-the-art inertial navigation unit of high capability and reliability for about the difference in forecast repair costs between the two systems throughout the '104's remaining operational life. And so it was that the CF–104 community obtained the excellent LW–33.

The LW–33CF inertial navigation system was a lightweight, self-contained inertial navigator that instantaneously and continuously supplied basic information on the aircraft's position, velocity and attitude during flight. It greatly assisted the pilot in flying the CF–104 on missions that might call for flight at low altitude utilizing deceptive turns enroute. The LW–33 solved the navigation problem and continuously supplied other avionic systems with precise heading, speed, altitude and position information. The navigation function of this new equipment was indeed superb. However, like any "all seeing, all dancing" system, there was a tendency to become "system lazy" and rely on it to the exclusion of basic common sense. System failures were indeed rare, but they could still happen; and just like in the old LN–3 days, one had to be vigilant.

The LW–33 was also tasked to automatically solve weapons release equations in a number of modes including, among others, Continuously Computed Release Point (CCRP) mode and Continuously Computed Impact Point (CCIP) mode. In CCRP mode, the aircraft was maneuvered to place the target, after visual sighting, under the gunsight aim point by the pilot. The pilot then depressed and held the weapon release enable ("pickle") button for continuous target designation. Weapons release occurred when the computed trajectory of the weapon intersected the target, and a pull-out tone was also generated to the pilot based on a practical safe ground avoidance by virtue of a 4 "G" pull-up within 2 seconds of command. The CCIP mode, normally simpler than CCRP, provided a continuous visual cue as to where the selected munition would impact relative to the target if released at any given point in time. As soon as the LCOSS "pipper" crossed the target, no matter what the release altitude, dive angle or airspeed, it was time to release the weapon. The CCRP function of the LW–33 was never fully exploited during the CF–104's remaining service years. Nonetheless, the weapons impact results in CCIP mode were very effective on occasions; although a problem lay in the fact that the system relied on barometric pressure inputs for target ranging, and that was only as accurate as the individual altimeter itself and the validity of the most current altimeter setting for the target. The LW–33's overall impact in weapon's release modes was to make a mediocre pilot (in terms of bombing skills) quite good, but the average 60 foot miss distance provided by the system didn't do much to improve the scores of the bombing "aces". However, to reiterate, the amount of improvement afforded in the navigational modes was nothing short of phenomenal, and the CF–104 pilots who were lucky enough to fly this system appreciated it immensely and placed a great deal of faith in it.

One operational improvement that should have been quite straightforward, but which was in fact quite evolutionary, was the quest to find a suitable coat of camouflage war paint for the CF–104. To regress momentarily, the Canadian Starfighters during the nuclear days were delivered with natural metal fuselages, white upper wings with huge national marking roundels, and pale green/grey underwing surfaces. The aircraft destined for Europe were delivered with horizontal stabilizers painted in the same manner as the wings; that is, white upper surfaces and pale green/grey under surfaces. The OTU aircraft at Cold Lake were given a coat of bright scarlet paint on the horizontal stabilizers. The rationale for these paint schemes was that during a nuclear exchange, the light colours would **reflect** rather than **absorb** nuclear energy, and thus increase the pilot's survivability chances. Furthermore, in the single penetrator role, the aircraft's only self-defence was its speed, and since *bona fide* Strike missions would not be flown with the same regularity as Conventional operations, camouflage was not as vital a tactical consideration. Nevertheless, it's a bit of a mystery as to why the Reconnaissance assets were not camouflaged, since their work was repetitive in nature. Perhaps this was due to the interchangeability of aircraft between roles, since the Reconnaissance aircraft were fully capable of performing the Strike role as well. At any rate, the aircraft maintained this high-visibility paint scheme until the role change in 1972. The rationale for the scarlet tail on the Cold Lake airplanes was a flight safety consideration. The bright tail was felt to be of good collision-avoidance value in the training environment, and also helped to highlight the jet when looking down on it from above, particularly with the vast, snow-covered wilderness of northern Canada in winter as a backdrop. Ironically enough, the red tail served another useful purpose in locating aircraft crash sites, as the tail section was often the only portion of a crashed Starfighter to survive ground impact relatively intact.

Starting in 1972, a solid coat of semi-gloss olive drab paint was phased into the European CF–104 fleet, but over the years this paint scheme was found to be still too bright to serve as effective camouflage. During the late 1970s, a considerable number of trials were done in quest of the optimum camouflage scheme for the CF–104s in Central Europe. An interim scheme of light grey and khaki was given serious consideration, but eventually ruled out as still being too bright. The final product, evolved in 1979, consisted of dark blue-grey and dark olive drab upper surfaces, and pale blue under surfaces. Also dating from 1979 was the adoption of low contrast national markings, brought about by the elimination of white from the wing and fuselage roundels, and the flag on the vertical stabilizer. The national markings had also been considerably reduced in size over the years as well. Naturally these paint changes were not all introduced fleet-wide overnight, and most of the final renditions were done at the Depot Level Inspection and Repair (DLIR) process, about which more will be mentioned later.

Along with the evolution of the overall paint schemes, individual organizations applied a plethora of distinctive unit markings to their jets over the years. During the Strike/Reconnaissance days, it was common to see the individual Wing crest painted on the air intakes or aircraft noses aft of the radome. The Aircraft Engineering and Test Establishment (AETE) at Cold Lake distinctively marked all their aircraft with a red "X" (for experimental) on the vertical stabilizer, and a number of other specialized markings used in the photographic analysis of various flight systems and weapons. The OTU for some time marked their aircraft during the later "bare metal" days with a distinctive red, white and black "Cold Lake" banner across the horizontal stabilizer, or painted a stylized "417" crest on the air intakes. Both 421 and 439 Squadrons in Europe carried several iterations of distinctive Indian head and tiger head markings respectively on their vertical stabilizers. 441 Squadron did not as a rule paint a distinctive squadron emblem on their aircraft, though several overall custom paint jobs on a representative squadron aircraft were flown over the years, and a narrow twelve-inch band of black and white checkers appeared in various places on the rudder from time to time.

Dave Jurkowski, who flew the '104 for many years both at 439 Squadron and then later at the OTU, had an experience where the distinctive yellow tiger's head was an unwelcome dead giveaway. Unit markings are only a source of pride when you want to strut your stuff; *not* when you would prefer to be invisible. At that time, they are a liability. Dave explains...

There have been many good one-liners transmitted on Guard frequency in Europe. I remember being embarrassed after having convinced myself that I (as a seasoned, Gordie DeJong trained, Central Region "Magellan") could never be uncertain of my position. But looking up one day at 560 knots and 500 feet AGL, I found to my incredible disbelief, a control tower and a runway not more than a mile on the nose! Galvanized by an explosion of adrenaline, I got down as low as I could (no one would see me, I panicked), stroked the burner (something to keep my hands busy; besides, I was too busy to wind my watch) arced around (below) the tower to where I could safely fly between the runway, taxiway, and plethora of exclamation marks over the German Air Force Transall transport awaiting takeoff (safely?... at almost 600 knots!?) and then disappeared into the (until recently) gentle morning mist. "Kaufbeuren Tower on Guard!" ... (Great! Now I knew which airfield it was, but how did it get there?)... Nice goink Tiger! Skip hit!!". Well, I guess certain things are placed in a young man's life to test the spirit and his navigation skills. Isn't it wonderful how you can re-boot life's learning curve in less than a minute!

Special events prompted some very unusual and colourful paint schemes as well. As has already been mentioned, 439 Squadron made a regular event of painting a unit "tiger bird" to serve as the squadron flagship for the annual NATO Tiger Meets, and this practice was often followed in varying degrees by other participating nations as well. This temporary modification was done with easily soluble paint, so that it could be removed after the particular event. The various weapons meets prompted individual attention to team aircraft over the years as well, and usually resulted in distinctive markings being applied to the air intake area, the vertical stabilizer, or the tip tanks.

If there were a prize for "most observable CF–104 on a continuing basis", 439 Squadron would have to win hands down for their annual Tiger Meet entry. However, the two other 1 CAG squadrons challenged the acknowledged masters of paint at their own game on several occasions. Firstly, 441 Squadron had applied distinctive rudder and numeric markings to a "metal" aircraft as far back as the sixties. Then, the Silver Foxes submitted a rather crude checkerboard scheme, which flew during August 1979. This particular paint job was somewhat carelessly conceived and applied, and really did nothing to emphasize the sleek lines of the '104. Next, 421 Squadron's Captain Bob Saunders designed a very pleasing scarlet-and-white motif in honour of the Squadron's 1981 visit to Maidstone, England to attend the dedication of a new 421 memorial at their wartime airfield near the town of Egerton. Finally, both the squadrons joined the Tigers in submitting distinctive schemes to honour the 30th anniversary of Baden-Soellingen as a Canadian base during 1983. Captain Terry Spraggs was responsible for designing the Red Indian's very attractive "arrow" rendition, while Captain Bob Johnson did equally fine work with the 441 entry. All three of these distinctive CF–104s, plus 421 Squadron's earlier variant, were the results of the superb craftsmanship of the 1 CAG Refinishing Shop, which was also responsible for the annual "tiger bird" iteration.

Across the seas, 417 Squadron felt obliged to mark the passing of the OTU into the history books with their beautiful red, white and blue scheme on 104 763 in July, 1983. The aircraft was actually flown into storage at Mountainview, Ontario in this state of dress.

Structurally, the CF–104 proved to be a very robust craft throughout its 25-year operational career. It had benefited from a wing reskinning program towards the end of its first decade of service, and in January 1979, the fleet started cycling through Northwest Industries in Edmonton, Alberta for a major Depot Level Inspection and Repair (DLIR) program.

In all, 78 CF–104s were extensively overhauled during this $17 million program, which lasted until April, 1982. While the Cold Lake airplanes were flown to Edmonton for the DLIR process, the European-based jets were stripped of engines, wings, landing gear, canopy and just about every other part that could reasonably be removed. Then, the skeletal aluminum carcass was loaded into the belly of a Pacific Western Airlines C–130 Hercules and flown to Northwest Industries. During the refurbishment, many, many systems were extensively rebuilt or completely replaced, culminating in a brand new coat of camouflage war paint. After the refurbished aircraft had been completely rebuilt, they were shipped through the city on a flatbed truck to Nisku, the Edmonton International Airport. While this procedure truly turned the heads of the locals, it caused considerably less consternation than taxing the aircraft there. Furthermore, most of the flatbed transportings were done in the wee small hours to minimize traffic disruption. At Nisku, the jets were put through a series of extensive flight tests by the Canadian Forces acceptance

Photo captions

1. *This very attractive paint scheme was applied to '763 to mark the closeout of the OTU at Cold Lake in 1983. '763 was flown into storage at Mountainview near Trenton still wearing this garb.*

2. *From top to bottom, the distinctively-painted unit aircraft of 441, 439 and 421 Squadrons thunder over the German landscape. These jets were specifically painted to help celebrate the 30th anniversary of Baden-Soellingen in 1983.*

3. *421's first red and white jet, affectionately known as "the coke can", overflies Central Dispersal at Baden-Soellingen with squadron commander LCol Fraser Holman at the controls. Circa 1981.*

test pilot, Captain Rob McGimpsey. Once the jets had satisfactorily completed these gruelling acceptance checks, they were disassembled and returned to Europe via Hercules transports again. The Canadian Forces were very happy with the results of this DLIR program, which stood them in good stead until the majority of the 50 selected to go to Turkey were given a final refurbishment by the MBB Corporation at Manching in West Germany during 1985 and early 1986.

Canadian Starfighter weapons teams represented the CF–104 community and the nation very nobly, during both the Strike and the Conventional years. In the 1970s, the annual nature of the Meet changed to a biennial gathering, and was hosted on a rotational basis by a different NATO nation each time. 1 CAG's first participation in a Conventional Meet occurred in 1974, having been too embroiled in the role change to participate in 1972. In fact, Baden-Soellingen played host to the 1974 Meet, and the Canadian Team did particularly well that year. Larry Crabb, the team leader, flew '104s with 421 Squadron from 1972 to 1975, and later commanded 441 Squadron from 1979 to 1981. Larry

remembers the 1974 happenings...

We formed our little team, including groundcrew, and commenced a work-up, mostly range work, navigation, timing, and tactical deliveries. Each nation was only allowed so many trips to Suippes, but we tried to get as much navigation in France as possible.

A number of interesting points came out of the work-up phase:

1. The groundcrew became our biggest asset. Their spirit was unbelievable! They fine-tuned each aircraft and they could fix anything in no time flat. The could scrounge everything, and turn an aircraft in seven to ten minutes. They also became the most dynamic team during the Meet.

2. Our clocks were terrible! Time was everything; yet we had the standard CF–104 instrument clock and the "Mickey Mouse" wrist watches. We had to calibrate each one, since points were lost if you were outside five seconds on target or at an equivalent target (EQ), and yet most of the watches were out by more than five to ten seconds in the 1.5 hours from Hack to target. Therefore, throughout the trip, you had to mentally adjust both your time-of-day, and the running time. We did not need the extra pressure!

3. We were unprepared with the cannon. Half-way through the work-up, John Glover went to Cold Lake to help accept the first CF–104 with the cannon. We really did not get much experience before the Meet. The loss of 750 pounds of fuel was also traumatic, since one tank had to be removed. The fixed iron sight was a joke, as the British and American F–4s had computing sights. I took our first gun to Suippes on a scab mission. As I was reaching minimum fuel, they fed me in between two French Mirages doing nuclear laydowns. I rolled in for a long burst with my heart racing with excitement. It was great to see the bullets going all over the pit and some hitting the target. Approaching the foul line, I obviously exceeded the rate kicker since I received a double kick. This produces lovely gun film as the target fills the screen on the second kicker. I was too low to bail out, and luckily I was able to pull it though! We found out later that the rate kicker was out of tolerance. This incident revived the age-old question of whether or not to have the kicker turned off on the range.

4. Practice makes perfect. Even with the old iron sight, we were able to get excellent bomb and rocket scores in situations where an error of one or two degrees of angle, a few knots of airspeed, or a few feet of altitude could provide disastrous results. Also, our "seat of the pants" navigation never failed us, whereas the more sophisticated American and British INS and computer systems caused mission failure when they were not working. We would plan missions, hitting three to four EQs, meet all times within five seconds, and do all of it on a 1:50,000 map covering a 200 mile leg... that's about twenty feet of map folded up in one hand!

And now on to the Meet itself. Following opening ceremonies, the missions were flown from May 27th to June 5th. 4ATAF teams (American, German, French and Canadian) worked out of Central Dispersal, while the 2ATAF teams worked out of South Dispersal. The French from Colmar with their Mirages were guests that year at the Meet. They were a "kick the tire, light the fire" group of fine pilots. They even got caught arming the guns within the dispersal. One pilot consistently butted out his cigarette on the nosewheel; and one was seen taxiing in with his helmet off, smoking a cigarette!

We only flew one or two missions a day for each of the four pilots. John Glover would attend all the mass briefings and so on, and organize our schedules and groundcrew activities. At a predetermined time, we would appear at Wing Ops for our mission. They gave us a TOT[1] *for the range, and the latitude and longitude of an EQ (including a picture). We rushed back to our planning area, pulled the maps, analyzed and planned the route; then calculated all the Time-of-Day back from the range, through the EQ, to a takeoff time. Forms were then submitted to the judges and clocks hacked. At this point, we had a nervous pee, talked with the groundcrew, got the spare aircraft started, and finally launched on the mission. Hopefully we could get on the runway when we needed it. We also had to remember the pages of rules on fouls, altitudes, airspeeds, "dos and don'ts" what to do in bad weather, and so on. The pressure was exhilarating, and once we were off the last target, we knew within ourselves how well we had performed for the team and Canada. Believe me, there was a lot of national pride at stake.*

Besides the individual range work, there were a number of tactical four-plane missions to be flown. A number of simulated targets were placed on an old abandoned range to the east of Suippes. It was an area covered with shrubs and fairly featureless terrain which made it quite difficult to navigate. As Lead of the four planes, I can still vividly remember the pressure of navigating, timing, and finally popping up for the tactical delivery, rolling in, and frantically searching for the elusive target through the haze. My mouth was so dry that I could spit dust, but my body was drenched in sweat. The manner in which one performed the manoeuvre really affected the timing (the time-of-fall of the bomb was even calculated) and the positioning in relation to the target. I always hoped that I would get a good bomb, since the smoke would then designate the target for my wingmen to attack.

Overall, Canada did very well. I was the top Attack pilot of the Meet. Our skill often overcame the lack of modern navigational systems, on-board computers, gun sights, and some skull-duggery from other teams (we were too naive then). It was always implied that the RAF turned the old phrase around to read, "It's not how you play the game; it's whether you win that matters". Enough said, except to say that the intense national competitive spirit and its implications led to the demise of the old format after the following two Meets; and also led to the introduction of the Tactical Air Meet (TAM) scenarios, which eliminated competition altogether.

In 1975, I was posted to 4ATAF Headquarters at Ramstein in the Attack Operations Division. I was the 4ATAF Officer of Primary Responsibility (OPR) and coordinator for the 1976 Tactical Weapons Meet at Twenthe Air Base in Holland. It was most enlightening to negotiate the rules, regulations, and scenarios with the Brits (who ran 2ATAF). They tried to make every rule, mission and event most compatible with the capabilities of their aircraft. Luckily, my experience in '74 enabled me to counter such moves and hopefully kept things fair. Allied Air Forces Central Europe (AAFCE) was finally evolving and taking its place as the superior Headquarters to 2ATAF and 4ATAF. They had the role of overseeing the Meet, providing judges and so on. Notwithstanding their best efforts to keep the competition at the ATAF level, it once again boiled down to national issues. They were not impressed with the intensity of the competition and the number of claims against the procedures, which in part were due to AAFCE's inexperience in running such a Meet.

Consequently, it was decided (by AAFCE) that the 1978 Meet would be called a Tactical Air Meet (TAM). It would downplay competition and try to develop integrated tactics, force packages, and employment concepts. Once again, I was 4ATAF OPR for the '78 TAM, and was proud of our efforts to meet the AAFCE objectives and integrate the 2ATAF and 4ATAF Air Forces. This has continued to evolve with a permanent school being set up at Jever, but I still feel that there were a number of positive aspects to the "winner take all" competitive side.

Having no intention of resting on the laurels gathered during the 1974 Meet, the 1976 team poured their hearts and souls into this second Conventional participation by CF–104 aircrews held at Twenthe, in the Netherlands. Team leader Jim McCullough flew Starfighters with 439 Squadron from 1973 until 1976, and vividly recalls the events of that particular Meet...

[1] Time on Target.

The ideal way to conclude a '104 tour in 1 CAG was to compete in a Tactical Weapons Meet (TWM). It was my good fortune to do just that prior to leaving 439 Squadron and returning to Canada. The 1976 TWM, held at Twenthe Air Base in Holland, consisted of four distinct segments for the Canadian participants. Specifically, these were the selection, the work-up training, the competition, and the politics and in-fighting that commenced once the competition began.

Under the rules of the competition, we were obliged to declare both a Primary and Secondary team. For each member of the Primary team, there was a named alternate who would assume the Primary team member's position should he, for any reason, be forced to drop out of the competition. We also had to select a group of technicians, which competition rules limited to fifty personnel, to maintain the five competition-declared aircraft. The technicians were under the superb guidance of Lieutenant Dwayne Lucas, and they proved to be an extremely talented and exuberant group. As usual, the armourers were the most colourful members of a very colourful group.

After the selection of the ground and aircrew members, there were two notable factors associated with the work-up phase that had to be addressed. Firstly, because the competition would be held in the 2ATAF area, we needed to gain experience in low-level navigation over both Holland and Belgium. Secondly, coincident with our work-up training was the introduction of the (then) new Canadian designed CRV–7 air-to-ground rocket.

The 2ATAF experience problem was solved by our good friends of the Belgian Air Force at Kleine Brogel, who invited us to spend two weeks flying from their Base, and gave us priority on range slots. Anyone with low-level experience in Europe will recognize how important this concentrated exposure to an unfamiliar area was in preparing for the competition. The CRV–7 Rockets arrived at Baden-Soellingen early in the work-up phase. Nobody on the team had ever fired a CRV–7 so we were into an "earn while you learn" situation. The first surprise we received was when we asked for the CRV–7 Ballistic Tables from which we could extract the correct settings for the gunsight. The response was, "What kind of tables?" After much discussion, it was decided that we had to start somewhere and the Armament Datum Line (ADL) reference point seemed about as good a place as any. Walt Pirie and I took the first eight CRV–7s to Siegenburg Range to try the ADL Theory. We ended up with five "shacks" and three fifteen-footers. We found that as long as there was no skid, the CRV–7 would go where it was pointed, and get there at a hell of a rate of knots.

After completing the two weeks at Kleine Brogel, we said farewell to the members of the back-up team: Dave Bashow, Jack Orr, and Bill Fuoco. We then proceeded with a concentrated flying phase at Baden-Soellingen that can only be described as a license to steal - we received outstanding support and were provided with everything one could wish for in the way of flying time, range periods and encouragement. Our principal supporters were Colonel Harvey Roddick and BGen. Jack Cadieux.

We deployed to Twenthe to commence the competition as part of the 4ATAF entry, which consisted of four teams. The two USAF teams from Bitburg and Spangdahlem both flew F–4s; the GAF team from Lechfeld, like ourselves, flew F–104s. The competition was to last two weeks, with a common Conventional weapon phase for the first week. During the second week, while the Lechfeld team and ourselves continued with Conventional weapon deliveries, the two USAF teams switched to night operations and Special weapon deliveries.

A typical competition trip consisted of aircraft operating singly or in formations of up to four aircraft in which a Bomb Impact Time (BIT) would be specified, and an Equivalent Target (EQ) would be identified, which the aircraft had to overfly enroute to the range. The EQ would be an insignificant bridge or similar structure which the aircraft had to pass over with a track error no greater than fifty yards either side of EQ boundaries and, for full timing points, no greater than plus-or-minus five seconds from the declared EQ time. After passing the EQ, the aircraft would proceed to the weapons range in use for that day for a first pass attack on the skip box, which constituted the Bomb Impact Time (BIT), followed by a ten degree dive bomb and rocket delivery from a tactical approach. The range exercise was concluded with a maximum of two strafing passes to expend 100 rounds of 20 mm ammunition.

I'm sure the foregoing sounds simple enough, and it is; however, just when you think things are going well on a TWM, politics set in and fair play and reason is cast to the wind. It was politics that tarnished the 1976 TWM and left a bad taste in many mouths. The problems associated with the 1976 TWM were of a single source origin from within the 2ATAF camp (thunder-flashes in the Barracks, borrowed maps to find violations) - Brits and fair play indeed!

Anyway, when the dust had settled after the last exercise was flown and all the politics were over with, 4ATAF emerged as the winner of the Conventional weapon delivery phase. The 1 CAG team of Bill Card, Walt Pirie, Roy Patterson, Hank Morris, and myself were the highest scoring national entry.

*I seem to have devoted a lot of space to the unsavory aspects of the 1976 TWM, and want to close with an event which we all felt provided a degree of retribution. When we lined the five '104s up on the runway for the flight back to Baden-Soellingen, there, very close to the runway edge, stood the entire RAF aircraft contingent... complete with champagne and glasses. We were offered a toast prior to departure, which we all agreed later reflected a touch of class. You just couldn't stay mad at people that responded in such a fashion. However, at the time, we all felt this was too good an opportunity to miss. Since we were operating what would have to qualify as one of the world's noisiest aircraft, multiple simultaneous engine run-ups seemed to be proper response to this God-given opportunity. I don't think we broke any champagne glasses; nonetheless, I am confident we left many sets of British ears loudly ringing... in fact, those particular ears may **still** be ringing!*

* * * * * *

As a member of the backup team that year, I have strong recollections of the intense work-up phase that preceded the Meet itself. As mentioned, some time prior to the event, the team deployed to Kleine Brogel airfield in Belgium, to get in some concentrated weapons delivery practice on Pampa Range, which lay just seven nautical miles to the south of the field. One fine morning, Walt Pirie, a primary team member from 439 Squadron, blasted off with myself on his right wing for a typical practice trip. This mission was doomed from the outset when Walt's nosewheel cocked 45 degrees off centre on the takeoff and stuck in that position. Consequently, the landing gear would not retract and, more to the point, there was serious concern as to what that cocked nosewheel would do to the aircraft on landing. We vigorously debated what could happen while we motored over the Belgian countryside at 260 knots with the landing gear down. The angle off centre of the nose gear was felt to be the critical factor. Because it was displaced so excessively, it was hard to tell whether the nosewheel steering would kick the wheel straight on touchdown or the wheel would become even more displaced, and possibly cause the jet to do a high speed ground loop. That in turn could have resulted in a blazing funeral pyre for one Walter Pirie. While the options were explored, the Squadron got the Canadair technical representative in Baden-Soellingen on the radio via telephone link. He *thought* the wheel would kick straight on landing but wasn't *sure*. "Thought..." ...swell.

Walt's options were rather straight forward. He could eject, or he could land and see what happened. Period. Walt opted for the landing; but instead of jettisoning the airplane, he was going to have to jettison the rockets, since it would never do to have them cooking off all over Kleine Brogel, should the worst occur. And so it was off to Pampa Range, to get rid of the rockets. Since we had no idea what the proper sight setting should be for a rocket pass at 260 knots (at least 200 knots slower than usual) with the landing gear down, Walt just took his best guess and salvoed the rockets in the general direction of the target. The range controller then casually mentioned that he thought all of the rockets had been fired, and we were cleared to return to Kleine Brogel. But you can't keep a good fighter pilot down... a lesser mortal would probably have been concerned as to whether or not he was going to turn himself into ashes depending on what happened to that nosewheel on landing. Not Walt. Ever the devoted weapons team member, he was more concerned with salvaging a decent weapons result, in *spite* of the circumstances; and that was evidenced by his classic remark to the range tower on departure, "By the way, Pampa... you got a score for me on that salvo pass?"

Incidentally, the nosewheel *did* kick straight on landing.

* * * * * *

Photos, clockwise from top: *1. Capt Bill Muncy rips by the Schloss Hohenzollern in this classic shot by Maj. Hank Morris in 1975. 2. Dave Jurkowski over the Ruhr's Eder dam on a low level mission. The Eder as well as the Moehne dams were breached by 617 Squadron Lancasters, the famous "Dambusters" on 17 May, 1943. Photo by Dave Bashow. 3. CF-104s of the Canadian team at the 1978 Tactical Air Meet, held at Wildenrath, Germany in 1978.*

Meanwhile, as mentioned, the Meet was becoming progressively more political in nature between the two ATAFs, and the mercenary attitude of some of the competitors was eroding the very fundamentals of professional excellence and good sportsmanship upon which the Meet had originally been founded. Slowly, inexorably, it was being driven towards a training and exercise type of event, with the competitive side being progressively reduced between the participating nations.

Rick Wall flew the '104 for nine consecutive years, both with 441 Squadron and later with 417 Squadron from 1974 until 1983. Rick recalls the '78 Meet, and the changing nature of that event...

In 1978, we had a week-long tactical phase followed by the competition. The team for that year was really two groups, a primary and a back-up. Keith MacDonald was our Team Chief assisted by Ian Struthers. The rest of the A Team consisted of myself, John Duncan and Marty Abbott. Bob Endicott, Clark Little and Cash Poulson rounded out the group - Cash led the drinking team.

The Meet, which was held at Wildenrath, was preceded by about two months of concentrated work-ups, mostly trips to the ranges we would be using in the competition. The CRV–7 rocket was new at the time and could be quite accurate. We were the first to use production versions of this rocket in Europe and I remember well our first trips to Siegenburg Range. We had both morning and afternoon range periods, and the guys that had been out in the morning had just destroyed the target which was a wooden "A frame" contraption. Well, they had just finished repairing the damage when we arrived for the afternoon period and proceeded to blow the target away with our rockets. The Range Officer, who had never before seen the CRV–7, blew his cool and accused us of using live ammunition and indicated that we were no longer welcome at his range.

The competitive phase, while an exciting time with lots of good flying, was also quite frustrating. We got along very well with most of the teams, particularly with the Germans and Americans, but the "win at all cost" attitude of one of the teams did much to ruin the Meet, and probably had a lot to do with the elimination of the competitive phase. I won't say which team it was, but they are an island nation and are sometimes referred to by a term that rhymes with "grits". The constant bickering was hard to take on the ground, but it even carried over to the air missions. I especially recall one sortie in which we were required to overfly a couple of targets enroute to a range. I was nearing one of the targets when I looked up and saw another aircraft (a Jaguar) coming head-on. I broke away to avoid a collision and then tried to get back on track, but it was too late and I knew I had missed the target. Later that day, we were told that one of the judges on the ground had observed the incident so it did not count as a missed target. Apparently, the "grits" decided to fly the route in reverse when returning to base and hadn't considered that there might be a conflict. There was much squabbling about scoring, and I suspect that this had something to do with the whole thing basically ending up in a tie.

We often forget about the groundcrews and their input, but what a super bunch of troops we had! They would work day and night, if necessary, to ensure that we had five serviceable aircraft - four and a spare. As a matter of fact, on the night that the tactical phase ended, the guys worked almost all night to paint the tails of our aircraft with distinctive Canadian markings. We wanted to keep the aircraft toned down as much as possible during the tactical phase, but we wanted everyone to see us in the competition. Imagine the surprise of the other teams when they arrived at the flight-line and saw our jazzed-up aircraft! this is not to say that it was all work and no play - au contraire. As a matter of fact, our guys won a trophy for contributing the most to the spirit of the Meet - sort of a Miss Congeniality Award.

Though there was still somewhat of a competitive side to the 1980 Meet held at Ramstein and the Canadian team acquitted itself well, 1980 would be the last year of true competition between the nations and the ATAFs. Also, the name had changed in 1978 from Tactical Weapons Meet to the more innocuous sounding Tactical Air Meet, or TAM for short. Pierre Rochefort flew '104s with both 421 and 441 Squadrons in Baden-Soellingen from 1981 until 1985. He participated in TAM '82 as a team member, and he has very strong feelings about the devolution of the competitive side of the Meet...

Up until 1982, the Allied Air Forces Central Europe's Tactical Air Meet had been a regular competition between the fighter units of its two Allied Tactical Air Forces. Claiming flight safety, 2ATAF had been pressuring everybody into making it a non-competitive event. Having been instrumental in the winning of the last three TAMs for 4ATAF, we, the Canadians, were naturally against that. In fact, our representative at the pre-event meeting had let it be known that we probably would not participate unless TAM remained a competition. To no avail, the doves won; and we went anyway.

When the smallest team of the Air Meet landed at Jever, West Germany, we were hardly noticed. Indeed, with six pilots, thirty-one ground support personnel, and five aircraft, we sort of disappeared within the confines of the airfield. Only for a while though. When our weapons convoy arrived, the whole base was in turmoil. As a standard load on the planned weapons range missions, we were each to carry six CRV–7 rockets, six practice bombs, and 350 rounds of 20 mm ammunition. The air meet's directing staff was busy trying to find a rule to prevent us from carrying all these weapons. They couldn't. We were "flying high". Although it wasn't an official competition, it became apparent that the Brits wanted to play, and we were going to go along with it. The Falklands War was going on, and that electrified the atmosphere even more. 1 CAG led the first mission. Typically, our team captain assigned a young pilot as the flight lead. More whispering from other nations' aircrew as this fuzzy-bearded Canuck stands up to give the mission briefing. All went well until he nearly ran out of fuel trying to make good his assigned Time on Target...with his flaps still in the takeoff position. The team captain took over and, except for us, nobody ever found out what had happened. The boss did a lot of preaching that night.

As one would suspect, it was not all war and no play. The biggest social event of TAM '82, except for the appearance of Miss Penthouse '82, was the nightly Canadian-style barbecue; beer and steak. Lots of both. The Brits returned the favour by "Harvey-Wallbanging"[1] us. We just had to be better, so at the final social event, while the Dutch sprayed their squadron logo on everybody's backside, we showed up in flying suits, formal mess kit shirt, cummerbund and bow tie. That did it. It did even more when we flew back home in this attire.

The last mission of TAM '82 was a firepower demonstration... first mistake. Unrestricted...second mistake. We showed up at the weapons range on time - naturally - and proceeded to each salvo (from a 13,000 foot range), six rockets followed by a three-second burst of ammunition and the dropping of our six bombs on target. We impressed. The Danes threatened to bill the Canadian government for the destruction of ground targets which they had just acquired for the Meet, but they enjoyed the demonstration.

All in all, TAM '82 was great. We were small, but we were good. Damn good. And anybody that said differently quickly found out how wrong he was. His chest hurt for the next two days. In retrospect, it's a good thing TAM '82 was not a competitive event; although we probably would have won anyway..

---

[1] A potent alcholic concoction

Starfighter

In the sky suspended on wings of eagles
Aloft above far-reaching cloud
Turned golden by the rays of sunset
Enclosed in the heavens peaceful shroud.
As sentinals of our nations freedom
Through the solitude of the central blue
We hurtled with the sound of thunder
Descendants of the famous "Few".
May the lines we etch across the sky
Be bold, and straight, and true
And may we never forget in age
That such was the path we knew.

Jon Williams, 1973

Slipping the Surly Bonds

After the standard external checks of the aircraft, which wasn't much of a walk around in the case of the CF–104 considering the extremely small wing area, the pilot shoehorned his way into what could charitably be called a roomy work space. Roomy perhaps in comparison to a telephone booth, but hardly a Boeing 747 flight deck. From this point on, the jet became a unique entity, parting company with any other aircraft that the pilot had previously flown. The first impression that he got was one of being a long, long way out in front of the machine. The second impression was that the cockpit had been thoughtfully engineered; not to the extent of today's latest generation aircraft, but at least with some attention paid to ergonomics. The engine instruments were arranged in two neat vertical rows on the right hand side of the front panel, and most other dials, switches, and pieces of equipment were logically grouped by function. The placement of the various warning lights was an improvement also. Most fighters of the day looked like the warning lights had been thrown at the instrument panel by Johnny Appleseed. Not so the '104. Here they were organized into a compact, neat, rectangular visual display called an annunciator panel, just beside the pilot's right knee on an instrument sub-panel. Furthermore, these tidy rows of lights were actually *words*, such as *"Fuel Level Low"* and *"Canopy Unlocked"*, as opposed to the standard "cherry" light of the past. In order to draw your attention to this panel, any light that had cause to illuminate would also cause an amber rectangular *"Master Caution"* light to come on dead centre on the front panel. In addition, along with providing aural tones, this light would not extinguish until it had been hand-reset by the pilot. There were various additional warning lights placed throughout the cockpit that merited more pilot attention than those included on the annunciator panel. Those that spring most readily to mind were the fire warning lights...

Lockheed designers had squeezed not only one, but *two* large rectangular red lights with the word "FIRE" emblazoned upon them into the confines of the compact front panel. Since there was only one engine, and the front panel was less than three feet wide, they were completely redundant; and I feel I can speak for the entire '104 pilot community when I say that the illumination of either one was more than enough to get your attention. This opinion has been borne out by the hapless few who have actually seen the system "in anger". I have been told that those lights become as large as two lengths of two-by-fours; impossible

Above: *An eye-pleasing but tactically useless 6 ship echelon left formation, staged as a PR shot in 1979.*

to miss under any conditions short of a coma.

But it was only after an external power source had been applied to the Starfighter that it became truly alive. Bill McWilliams recalls some of the wonderful sensations garnered during start and taxiing...

The canopy had to be left open for start, and the air in the cockpit crackled and moved. Even at idle, the engine had a definite presence. A nudge of power - but not more than 80% RPM - moved you from the line. More than 80% moved the inlet guide vanes, set up a howl like a wounded moose, and caused three things to happen: the aircraft moved in a satisfactory fashion for a super young pilot; chocks and ladders moved smartly in the opposite direction; and the boss' eyes rolled heavenward as he reached for the phone to call servicing for the name of the pilot. The engine was a tattletale...

Taxiing was like sitting at the pointed end of a spear. Cockpit mirrors were installed for pilot morale; they confirmed that there were indeed semblances of wings, just long enough to keep the tip tanks from bumping into the fuselage. The nosewheel steering button on the stick became a UHF transmit switch when the weight was off the left main wheel. Many a tower controller was treated to the anxious breathing of a landing pilot whose left wing was being held up by a crosswind, thereby keeping the weight off the left wheel, and the nosewheel steering, now desperately needed, wouldn't engage. The solution in a left crosswind was to stuff the stick hard to the left and compress the oleo to let the wheel know it was on the ground.

The engine run-up was a comedy routine. First, you advanced the throttle slowly to Military power, to the accompaniment of much noise and smoke, and the pitot tube nearly stabbing the runway as the nose oleo collapsed. Then, slow power reduction for a while to check the exhaust nozzle, and a "chop' to idle. Now, just as spectators thought you were coming to your senses and giving up, you slammed the throttle back to full Military. Doing that in a T–33 melted the turbine blades and fried the tailpipe. In the '104 it was supposed to prove that the engine wouldn't compressor stall, which it never did on this check anyway. The J–79 engine was a comfort to pilots. It was able to swallow substantial bolts or birds - if the latter were not sitting on a very large branch - without a tremor. It was as reliable as the "Get a haircut" lecture from the new C.O. ...

Takeoff was child's play. Nosewheel steering was engaged and the afterburner was plugged in, which gave a smooth, positive light in seven stages. The stick was simply held in the neutral position until approximately 20 - 25 knots below the computed takeoff speed, when back pressure was applied. From then on, flight was (usually) inevitable. Throttle response was truly awesome. Unlike some other jet aircraft, fuel control units metered JP–4 to engine and afterburner such that the pilot never had to worry about over-temping the engine; the net result being that one could bang the throttle around as desired. A real stop-go lever. Also, unlike today's high bypass engines, spool-up time was very rapid; the resulting thrust changes instantaneous. The power was always there when needed, and this was a tremendous advantage when flying close formation, and also for making rapid corrections to airspeed in any phase of flight where this was required, such as in the landing pattern or when dropping bombs, where speed accuracy is vital. Often, today's bypass engines produce significant delays from throttle movement to engine response, a condition that requires some forethought to compensate for on the part of the pilot. This was certainly not a problem with the '104.

I personally had the unusual experience of flying the jet in both temperature extremes, starting with three years as an instructor (after a long tour in Germany) in Cold Lake, Canada, where we had square tires and -40°F weather for weeks on end in winter. We used to joke that we had eleven months of winter and one month of bad skiing, but it wasn't far from the truth. The good news was the remarkable effect that the cold air had on jet engines. The acceleration on takeoff had to be experienced to be believed. It was guaranteed to "roll your socks down", or, as it has been occasionally rather graphically described, "peel a foreskin back". One of the parallel runways at Cold Lake is over 12,000 feet long, and on an afterburner takeoff on a -40°F day in a "clean" (no external stores) aircraft, the pilot could have 450 knots on the clock by the end of the runway. If one hesitated with landing gear retraction even a second after nosewheel rotation, a landing gear overspeed was the inevitable result.

In marked contrast to this experience were memories of operations in the Arizona desert as an exchange instructor at the USAF/GAF Fighter Weapons School. Over the years, I suppose I have flown just about every configuration the '104 has to offer, but as an antithesis to the clean jet in wintertime Cold Lake, the dart-tow ship in summertime Phoenix springs to mind. This consisted of two wing tip tanks, a wing pylon tank and the dart rig itself, a cumbersome target device that looked like a huge foil paper airplane that was reeled out in flight from under the left wing. On a 140°F runway temperature day, the takeoff roll was spectacular, and certain to make a devout Christian out of even the most practiced atheist. One can joke about "gravel sniffers in the nose" to sense nosewheel rotation time; this situation really called for it. It is important to note that tire fail speed was 239 knots, and at that temperature and configuration, takeoff speed was around 235 knots. The jet ended up clawing her way into the air, waging a personal war with Sir Isaac Newton for every inch of altitude gained. It was always a near thing and happiness was staggering away into the heavy summer desert air with the gear safely tucked up and the runway behind you. All this for the dubious privilege of letting someone shoot at you...

Landing was always an impressive, though usually straightforward, event. The approach speeds were fast by anybody's standards, but one got used to the speed just like anything else. Normal landing configuration was with LAND (full) flap selected, and a long, flat final approach was flown at 175 – 180 knots with touchdown at 155 – 160 knots minimum. To these basic speeds were added extra knots for any fuel over 1000 pounds, crosswinds, gusty winds, external stores, mother, wife, kids, family dog, etc. In short, it was not at all unusual to add 20 knots to the basic speeds. Boundary Layer Control (BLC) was added to the razor wings to lower landing approach and touchdown speeds with LAND flap selected. Because this BLC was only effective down to about 82% engine RPM, the aircraft was unusual in that it was routinely landed with power on. When instructing, we threatened dire consequences to the novice who pulled the power to idle prior to touchdown, since this would result in an abrupt loss of both BLC and lift, usually on one wing before the other, and at best, a bone-jarring arrival on the runway. In reality, as long as the pilot smoothly and slowly reduced power to idle, there was no controllability problem.

Landing patterns could also be flown with TAKEOFF (half) flap configuration at slightly higher approach speeds than LAND flap, but BLC rolloff was not a factor to worry about. A flapless landing, however, was both an emergency and a memorable experience, especially at night. Final approach/touchdown minimum speeds were 230/195 knots respectively, plus additives. Starfighter pilots flew a long flat final approach going like a scalded cat and feeling like they were continuously on the ragged edge of disaster. Descent rate was around 800 feet per minute, and the approach tended to be flown on a combination of both airspeed and angle-of-attack (AOA) indications. In fact, there was a caution in the Pilot's Notes that sternly warned at no time to allow the rate of descent on a flapless approach to exceed 2000 feet per minute, as recovery could require more than 400 feet of altitude.

In all cases, the aircraft was landed with crab on, and the pilot just kicked it straight with nosewheel steering on the post-landing roll. As can well be imagined, increased stopping power was highly desirable and provision was made for this with a big 16–foot diameter drag chute and an excellent anti-skid braking system. If these didn't work, or if we had a takeoff emergency or a slippery runway, we had an arrester hook mounted under the aft fuselage that snagged a cable at the end of the runway. And if that didn't work, well then it really wasn't our day. We almost never attempted aerodynamic braking. After all, how efficiently can you aerodynamically brake a pencil?

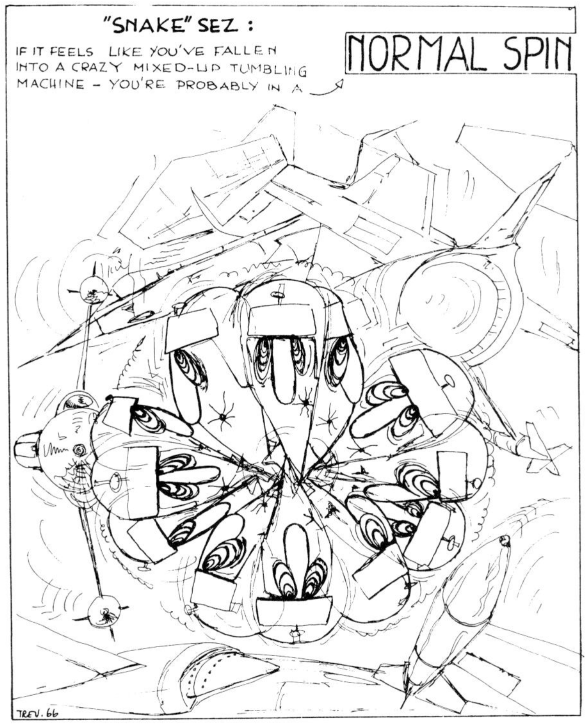

Stalls and spins were another flight area approached with great caution. Due to the aerodynamics of the high "T" tail, the aircraft was prone to a phenomenon known as pitch-up at high AOAs. Beyond a certain point, this pitch-up was uncontrollable, and resulted in severe gyration (or even structural failure) of the aircraft and a large loss in altitude before recovery to level flight. It was possible to develop stall angles of attack very readily and rapidly during abrupt manoeuvres, even though relatively small amounts of stabilizer were used. In supersonic flight, the usual stall warnings were inadequate to prevent excessive AOA, and an Automatic Pitch Control (APC) was therefore provided which initiated corrective action at the proper time to prevent reaching an AOA high enough to cause pitch-up under any operating condition. These warnings took the form of a stick shaker and a kicker, which abruptly kicked the stick forward. It was, in effect, both a built-in buffet warning and an artificial stall that occurred ahead of the aerodynamic stall. Stalls were never practiced to completion; recovery action was initiated at either shaker or kicker action, depending on configuration, and stalls were never practiced below 25,000 feet AGL. In fact, a preferred pilot option to the practicing of stalls was the practicing of slow flight. Bill McWilliams explains...

We did slow flight (160 to 170 knots, depending on weight) at 30,000 feet in the landing configuration. With full flap, 16th stage engine air was blown over the flap trailing edge, delaying flap stall. This air shut off when power was reduced below 85% RPM. This always resulted in one flap stalling before the other - take your pick - and the fastest uncommanded half roll you ever wanted to see. As instructed, I pulled off the power and saw the Alberta landscape appear in the top of the canopy and start to get a lot closer real fast. The reason for starting the affair at such high altitude was apparent. So was the practice that wise '104 instructors had of locking their left hand behind the throttle to prevent the student from going to idle power before the main wheels were on the ground.

Spins were violent, gut-wrenching manoeuvres and intentional spinning was prohibited. A friend of mine had a wild ride one day when one of the main landing gear doors accidently deployed in supersonic flight during air combat practice. Although he executed a brilliant recovery, the thrill factor was so high that it was several minutes before he was capable of coherent speech. Even when he *did* speak, he sounded as if he had been sucking helium for some time. Thus, though he had done some terrific aviating and probably saved an aircraft, he failed élan rather badly.

Kevin Vaillant is one of the few '104 pilots to take the Starfighter's ultimate "wild ride", but even *he* will admit that an upright spin is a somewhat drastic step to take in a CF–104 as a last-ditch guns defence manoeuvre...

On the morning of May 5, 1983, Captain Doug Erlandson and I prepared to take on Captain James Kelly and his wingman, Captain Bob Wade in an Air Combat mission. After a quick briefing and private discussions concerning tactics, we took to the skies over Cold Lake, Alberta in pursuit of the opposing team. The weather was ideal for air fighting, with a 3000 foot ceiling topped at 12,000 feet MSL.[1]

After a quick engagement with no positive results, I found myself at 20,000 feet MSL, about 3000 feet above James Kelly. As usual, James was impossible to sneak up on and pulled hard into me. Our wingmen were busy with each other, so we were in a One-versus-One situation. In an attempt to salvage the advantage, I commenced a Barrel Roll to maintain my position. I felt confident because I had sufficient energy to manoeuvre (20,000 feet, .92 Mach). As I continued the roll, I unloaded the back pressure to prevent the nose from dropping. The aircraft then shook violently, to the degree that I was unable to maintain a grip on the control column or throttle. I held my hands against the canopy to prevent my head from hitting it as I continued through a flight profile which is difficult to describe.[2] *No doubt James was gaining the advantage while this was happening. After approximately three seconds, the aircraft stabilized in a nose-high left hand spin. Anti-spin control inputs had no effect and it appeared impossible to lower the nose and regain control. The altimeter was unwinding rapidly through 15,000 feet, and the airspeed was zero as I heard James and Bob call for me to abandon the aircraft. For several reasons (most of which are stupid when I look back on them) I did not eject, and remember thinking that there must be something I could do. My mind recalled a conversation with our American Exchange Officer at the bar and I immediately deployed the drag chute, normally used on landing. The nose immediately dropped to 80 degrees nose down; the altimeter was winding through 12,000 feet as I entered cloud. I lit the afterburner, jettisoned the drag chute, and waited for the airspeed to climb. I was through 8000 feet with only 320 knots when I felt I could wait no longer. I lowered half-flap and pulled to "stick shaker" as the nose slowly rose on the attitude indicator. I broke out of cloud at 3000 feet above ground, 45 degrees nose down, with 420 knots on the clock. I was able to recover with almost 800 feet to spare, and immediately climbed above cloud to re-enter the fight. I was sure that James Kelly had been unable to take a shot at me...*

---

1 Altitude above Mean Sea Level.
2 The violent head-battering characteristic of a Starfighter upright spin has sometimes been referred to as "painting the canopy", since helmet paint was usually deposited liberally on the inside of the plexiglass canopy during this charming sequence!

For all the violence of the upright spin, an even more insidious variant of the manoeuvre was the flat spin. Though deceptively smooth, in an aft centre of gravity situation, recovery from this condition was essentially impossible, unless the nose of the aircraft could somehow be forced down. Dave Ghyselincks flew '104s with 441 Squadron from 1980 until 1983. On April 30, 1982, Dave flew a Fighter Weapons Instructor Course air combat training mission against a CF–5 from 419 Squadron in one of the Cold Lake ACM ranges. That trip would leave a lasting impression on him. The exercise had proceeded normally through two engagements; in fact, Dave and 104732 had put on a respectable performance against the more agile CF–5, managing to keep all his tail feathers intact while also taking some gun camera film to boot. It was only after a decision was made to have a third engagement that things started to go very wrong. Dave elaborates...

We knocked off the second engagement near the floor of the area, which was set at 12,000 feet, and started a climb south-bound. When the fuel was checked, I still had 200 pounds of it to play with, and the CF–5 was well above his minimum fuel state. I decided to start a final engagement, knowing that I would only have time for a couple of turns without using any afterburner, before "bugging out".[1] *We set up near the boundary of the area closest to the base, heading just west of North at 17,000 feet. Tony*[2] *called ready, line-abreast on my right. To preclude getting further from the runways, I called for the turn-in with slightly less altitude and speed than optimum.*

I made a flat hard right turn at full dry[3] *power and reversed as soon as my nose was pointing about five degrees to the right of the CF–5. Tony did a hard left in a slight climb, but his rate of turn was less than mine. When he crossed to my left and over 1000 feet above me, he was just starting to reverse, and I was in a hard left turn, flaps down, with about 30 degrees lead on him. Passing through a northerly heading, I checked my fuel, and decided to separate by first threatening the F–5 and then continuing the left turn until the TACAN needle was on the nose. The CF–5 was now at about my left ten o'clock in a hard climbing turn to the right. I reversed again, pulled my nose up to his elevation, and started a slow right turn which would put me in a position that could look like a tracking solution. I could see the CF–5 would run away from me as I had bled off most of my airspeed by this time, but that's just what I wanted him to do. The couple of seconds it would take for him to figure out that I was slow would be enough for me to separate to the edge of the area, using my altitude for propulsion.*

When the CF–5 passed through my twelve o'clock, I completely unloaded the aircraft, and gradually put on full left aileron. The roll response was very sloppy, so I fed in some left rudder. I wanted to see some land as, for the last few seconds in the climbing right turn, I had had nothing but the other aircraft to refer to on a blue sky background. Sure enough, I saw a lake I recognized to be an edge of the area reference point, at my left nine o'clock for about ten miles. I could also see that I was in a steep climb of around 50 degrees of pitch.

I wanted to get away from the F–5 and dive toward that lake, so I maintained full left aileron and fed in full left rudder while remaining unloaded to get the nose to drop; but now it seemed like the aircraft was absolutely refusing to roll. In the next moment, the lake I had my eyes on disappeared below the canopy railing and towards the rear; and it did so in a blur. Excuse me? Out of habit, I whipped my head around to the right, as the lake would have to reappear over there...right? By now I had centered the controls, and sure enough the world showed up on the right; but it was going by pretty fast. I knew the aircraft was out of control, in an upright spin, and called Tony to "knock it off"[4]*, telling him about the spin. The power went to idle, the stick forward and right, and the left foot pushed hard. Before the trim motor could run its course*

full down, the yaw rate stabilized.

The nose was up slightly, maybe two or three degrees, the wings were dead level, and the horizon was going around at a pretty good clip. I told Tony and Joe[5] *what was happening, and they had a visual on me; I could not see them, and could not care what they did. The engine kept idling away through all this, quite content. The controls did not seem to have any effect. The altimeter went below fifteen thousand feet in 500 foot swings. I told the others that my actions were not helping and that I would probably have to jump. I knew only seconds were left, and there was just no time to deploy the drag chute.*[6] *I gave it another try by centering the controls and then slamming them back to their full deflection to see if the aircraft attitude would change. After I had counted to five, not one iota of difference in the nose position or the rate of rotation could be detected. I was being pushed slightly forward in the straps, but certainly no more than on drag chute deployment during a normal landing.*

I tightened the straps; the decision was made. There was no rush to eject, but the aircraft was lost. I untied the tape recorder from my right thigh as I figured it was probably not designed for ejection, and I threw it in front of my left foot. By now, both Tony and Joe were taking turns on the radio telling me to bail out; this was fairly annoying because I had already decided to jump. I figured they knew something I didn't.

Without replying on the radio, I put my head back and pulled the

[1] A combat egress from an engagement, with no intentions of returning to the fray.
[2] Tony Hearst, the FWIC student in the front seat of the CF-5D.
[3] Same as Military power, or full power without afterburning.

- photo by Bill Johnson

ring. I could see the canopy bow go by, and the very next instant I was dangling in the chute, feeling silly but relieved. My knees hurt, and when I looked down I was mesmerized by the CF–104 between my feet , directly below me, spinning quietly upright in the crisp cold air. Without a parachute, I would have fallen right onto it. Soon I was drifting away with the wind, and I took a look at my knees. They appeared ugly, but going through the torn bloody flight suit I could feel with my gloved hand that all the parts were still there. I tried some bending, and they worked fine.

I saw the CF–5 circling me and waved to show that all was well. Unfortunately, the radio was in the seat pack and not on the Mae West. I looked over and saw the CF–104 about a mile away and approaching the ground. Boy, this is a long ride down… I tried to guess where I was heading. It would be either scrub woods, or possibly a small pond; the seat pack jettison decision would have to wait. By now my aircraft had disappeared, and I remember seeing a small plume of smoke where it had obviously hit. Pretty soon I spotted a small clearing ahead and tried to guide the chute towards it. Yanking on the risers worked, but I hit the bottom of a tree on the far side of the hole. I had my radio out of the seat pack and was opening the first-aid kit when I heard the chopper. I called him once and was hoisted out a minute later. Being fortuitously in the area, the pilot had managed, with a great deal of help from Joe and Tony, to spot my chute before I hit the ground.

When we got to the Base, I found out that during my adventure, two pilots had died on the runway in a CF–5 while overshooting from a practice flapless landing. I felt much sillier about my accident, and sad about the deaths. While I sat in the hospital, I tried to comprehend what had gone wrong.

I always flew with my APC and stick shaker engaged, even on the firing range. The only time I ever turned the pitch control system off was for prolonged flight below 250 feet AGL, and only when it had been declared standard procedure. I reasoned that the paddle switch located on the stick (and which we always tested before flight) would be available to suppress the system if it malfunctioned. I never ***did*** *experience a malfunction. During this flight, the shaker operated a couple of times during the earlier engagements, and I respected the signal; indeed I was depending on the shaker to allow me to fly the aircraft close to its limits. Perhaps I had come to rely too much on this cue to keep me out of trouble.*

Prior to entering the flat spin I have described, the shaker (and of course, the "kicker") never twitched. I can only postulate that I flew the aircraft smoothly into a climbing attitude, which resulted in the airspeed bleeding off to below taxi speed without unduly alarming the pitch control system. Even with the stick completely forward at this point, the adverse yaw generated by full aileron deflection overpowered the rudder's marginal effectiveness and initiated the spin. Had I been aware of the precarious situation I was in, I should think I would have left all

[4] The standard radio call to cease an air combat training sequence.
[5] Joe Molnar, the Instructor Pilot in the rear seat of the CF-5D.
[6] Which might, possibly, have been able to force the nose of the aircraft below the horizon, and into a recoverable spin mode.

flying controls neutral and waited for the completion of the ballistic trajectory.

The spin entry was very smooth, almost imperceptible... no gyrations, and no oscillations around the roll axis. The picture I remember from "Snake's" books is accurate: you could hold a brimming full glass and never spill a drop. Once the spin had started, I reacted quickly on the controls and throttle, but never did raise the flaps from **takeoff** *to* **up** *- it just felt wrong to do so at low speed, I guess. Spin recovery was not something one practiced, even in the simulator.*

The accident investigation revealed that the speed brakes were out when the aircraft hit the ground. I could not explain this as I had no recollection of extending them. It was discovered that I hit my knees on the bottom of the instrument panel on ejection because I had "sewered"[1] in my seat. I am sure that this was a result of the ballistic inertia reel being located between my shoulder blades and pulling with great force to bring the back of my neck down.

Another revelation from the investigation was that the absolutely "clean" aircraft configuration with only 1700 pounds of fuel and, more importantly, an empty cannon ammunition bin, resulted in an aft centre of gravity which made the spin irrecoverable. Spin entry would also have been near impossible without this aft C–of–G condition.

Just a few days earlier, during the same FWI course, one of the instructors had a frightening experience in a clean CF–104 at altitude. He encountered a momentary loss of control at high speed and zero "G" when roll-coupling produced a departure in the yaw axis, followed by a series of violent gyrations around all axes and culminating in a low speed dive recovery. The pilot literally painted the inside of this canopy with his white helmet.

104732 was a good aircraft; she was one of the few LW–33 birds on 417 Squadron and a poor choice to write off. FWIC '82 became an expensive course...a few weeks after my accident, during an air-to-ground range mission, Kerry Cranfield was forced to "jettison his airframe" when a broken afterburner fuel line caused a massive engine fire.

Because of the jet's rather awesome out-of-control characteristics, pilots generally developed a phobia about flying slow in it **at all**. During latter-day service at the Fighter Weapons School, we instructors would routinely demonstrate a confidence zoom to zero airspeed. Actually, it was perfectly safe under pre-ordained conditions of centre of gravity and fuel weight. The trick was in recovering gently, using a very conservative maximum reading on the APC gauge, and rolling the aircraft towards the nearest horizon. Ailerons were very effective well past the stall. In reality, if the pilot were just to take his hands off the controls in the vertical stall condition, the aircraft generally knew what it wanted to do better than he did, and would usually recover to a recognizable flight attitude from which a full recovery could be easily made. This would not want to be done low to the ground though. Altitude losses in out-of-control situations in the '104 were formidable. For example, ejection was a checklist procedure if recovery was not completed by 15,000 feet AGL.

Every CF–104 pilot has a particularly soft spot in his heart reserved for remembrance of his first Starfighter flight, for that's when all the magic began. Almost without exception, the '104 student felt more than just a little bit behind the aircraft this first time, and Al Seitz was no exception...

After a month of preparation, strapping in, starting and taxiing were almost anti-climatic. Pre-takeoff checks just like the simulator... Now a firm grip on stick and throttle, and let's do it! On the brakes, throttle to full military power - 100% RPM, all vital gauges in the green, and release brakes. The Starfighter starts a sprightly roll forward, but as the throttle goes outboard and full forward, it sags as the jet exhaust nozzle opens wide. Then - Wham! That conglomeration of metal and people trembles with energy as a white-hot fire ignites in its tailpipe. Inertia protests and I am slammed back into my seat as the bird leaps forward. There are five engine gauges you are expected to check before reaching the line-speed marker, a distance-to-go indicator two thousand feet ahead. This is where a pre-computed airspeed must be showing, or the takeoff aborted.

The cockpit is a blur, and I've missed the marker. I hear the voice from the back..."Line speed OK. Rotate now. Gear up. GEAR UP!" My, he's impatient. "OK, flaps up and watch your attitude. Pull the nose up. Look at your Mach!" Christ, I can't see over the nose now. I missed the line speed, and the 170 knot rotation, and the 190 knot liftoff, and almost the 260 knot gear speed. And now he's yakking about the Mach! Where in hell's that ASI? There! We're just supersonic going up through 12,000 feet. I pull the nose up to what appears vertical before the Mach Meter bleeds back subsonic.

The voice again, "Remember, we want to level off at 35,000. You want to start lowering the nose about 3000 feet early." By the time I find the altimeter again and react we are through forty grand. The Man takes over long enough to pull the throttle out of burner, and level off. Had I entertained thoughts of flying this bomb without benefit of dual instruction?

But soon familiarity made the speeds very manageable, and the aircraft's behavior predictable. However, another early thrill for the budding Starfighter pilot was the Mach 2 run, done on about his second or third solo flight. It was easy to get overly excited and forget things during this event due both to the relative inexperience of the pilot in the aircraft, and the understandable exhiliaration of going twice the speed of sound. One eventual luminary in the Starfighter pilot community got the airplane up to Mach 1.3 but couldn't understand why it was accelerating so slowly, until he realized that his takeoff flaps were still down! Seeing this, he *raised* them at that speed (speed limit for retraction was Mach .85) and continued on to Mach 2!! Talk about blind faith in the structural integrity of the jet...

Larry Crabb recalls the big day that was his Mach 2 run...

While undergoing conversion training at Cold Lake, each student had a Mach 2 mission in a clean bird. The day I did mine in February 1972, atmospheric conditions were excellent and I was able to reach Mach 2.04 in a shallow climb. I was fascinated to see the DME unwinding at about 22 miles a minute and the "SLOW" light flashing as the inlets heated to 121°C. I pulled her out of burner to idle, raised the nose and watched as the RPM still remained at 100%. It was a euphoric feeling as this beautiful bird soared upward like a big dart being hurled through the air. All of a sudden, I was shocked back to reality as I passed through 60,000 feet, realizing that the engine could "blow-out" with the resultant loss of pressurization. This would bring instant death since my blood would have boiled. I instantly rolled her on her back and quickly pulled her down. It was a long, quiet trip back to base as I reflected on my stupidity and swore to double my efforts to always treat this beautiful beast with the utmost respect and to be ever cautious! Needless to say, I did not talk about my experience.

* * * * * *

Because the flying weather in Central Europe - the most common home of '104 operations - can be particularly grim, the aircraft had to be optimized for instrument flying. Although navigation aids consisted merely of the inertial navigation system, TACAN and, to a certain extent, the ground mapping radar, the instrumentation itself was first class. Even though it didn't have a Horizontal Situation indicator (merely a bearing pointer

[1] Slid underneath the lap strap.

and Distance Measuring Equipment), the attitude indicator in the Canadian version made up for it. It was an enormous five-inch sphere, grey over black with the compass headings etched in the sphere itself. It really spoiled pilots on Ground Controlled Approaches to minimums in particularly rotten weather. The Rhine Valley was especially bad in winter, with a half-mile flight visibility being routine. Needless to say, at final approach speeds in excess of 180 knots, one's flying had to be precise and accurate.

The F–15A radar (not to be confused with the F–15 Eagle) had both air-to-air and air-to-ground modes. Although the air-to-air mode was extremely primitive by today's standards, it was still a useful tool in the hands of a skilled operator. However, the air-to-ground radar was really first class. Raw (as opposed to processed) radar returns were provided, so one had to become good at interpretation; but once this was mastered, one could navigate (and even bomb) off it with a very high degree of accuracy. Unlike synthetically-processed radar returns, which can look like a photograph, the F–15A radar in a ground-mapping mode was only straightforward when flying over large lakes, coastlines, or large, distinctive cultural centres such as cities. At other times, such as flying over mountainous terrain, one had to take such items as the radar's line of sight and subsequent effect on the scope presentation into account. Good radar navigation in the CF–104 was quite an art form.

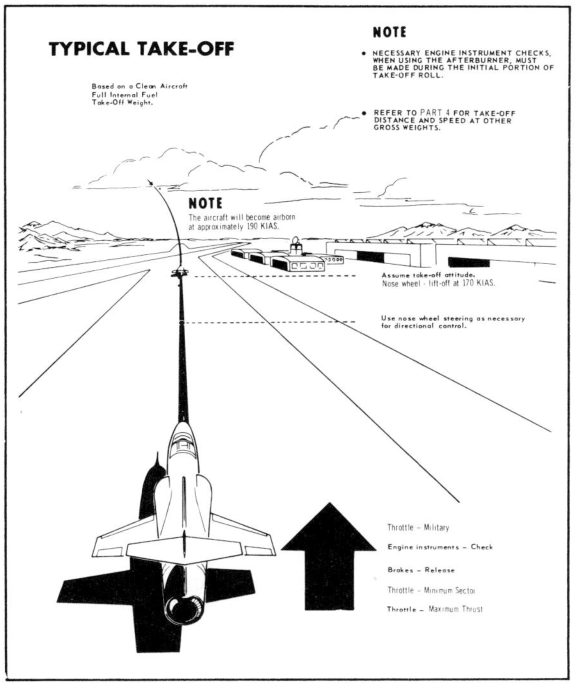

Night flying was downright pleasant in the '104, with good cockpit lighting and excellent visibility. Our version had completely red cockpit lighting, and I remember being bitten by that once on a night low-level radar navigation route. I had marked some reference lines on my map in red ink, and soon found out that the net effect of red lines under red lighting was invisible lines.

Night formation was a rather dicey business on a dark night since there was no phosphorescent strip lighting and the external lights that *were* available were very limited. They consisted of white, amber, red and green lenses, strategically located on the sides of the fuselage, and either on the wing tips or on the tip tanks. The trick was to arrange all these lights into some predetermined geometrical pattern when nothing else was available. Night formation takeoffs and landings were not normally a problem though. On takeoff, the rose glow of the aircraft afterburner provided a great deal of reflected light, although it sure could get dark in a hurry when afterburner was deselected. In a landing configuration, the lead aircraft's landing lights tended to bathe his machine in enough light to provide easy reference to normal daytime formation cues. An afterburner takeoff at night was a treat to the eyes. The rose glow of the afterburner plume, which extended 30 - 40 feet behind the aircraft was evenly interspersed with white shock diamonds of hot gases.

Noise was a part of the unique personality of the '104. It made distinctive sounds that manifested themselves on engine run-up and in the overhead break. On run-up, the 15,800 pound thrust General Electric J–79 engine made an unearthly shriek that was dubbed "the moose call" because it sounded exactly like a moose in rutting season, and became the cause for nervous banter during the moose breeding season in northern Alberta where we were based. Perhaps even more distinctive was the unique, supernatural moaning sound, like the wail of a wounded banshee, made by the '104 in the overhead break for landing. Sometimes it's a pity to let science get in the way of romanticism. Unfortunately, both the moose call on engine run-up and the moaning in the overhead break had technical explanations. The "moose" was due to a rapid repositioning of the engine inlet guide vanes; and the "moaning", I am told, was due to disturbed airflow over the engine air bypass flaps. But to those of us who flew her and lived around her, this was just more '104 magic.

The '104 was a relatively sophisticated aircraft in its heyday. However, as pilots we used to marvel at the seemingly incongruous effect activation of a given button or knob would have on a supposedly unrelated system in the aircraft. Examples of this are legion, but one that comes to mind was running up engine power from idle to retract a stuck windshield rain remover! There were so many of these quirks and foibles that '104 students became just a little gullible to say the least, and from this situation was born the legendary "Order of the Thruster Thumpers".

Now the '104 had explosive canopy jettison thrusters, rather phallic in appearance, mounted on each side of the canopy sill, just about abeam the pilot's head. These thrusters would explosively blow the canopy clear of the aircraft in an emergency, or as part of the ejection sequence. The '104 also had a warning-lights-and-horns test switch that illuminated all advisory, caution and warning lights in the cockpit, while making appropriate noises. The switch was replicated in the rear seat instructor's position of the two-seat trainer, and activation of this test function was a standard part of the pre-start check. Preying on student vulnerabilities, one instructor very early in the program thought he would have some fun with his charge by reviewing the various idiosyncrasies of the aircraft, and then suggesting that if the warning lights would not go out when the test switch was released, pounding either one's fist or another blunt object vigorously on the thruster would remedy the errant lights. In reality, the instructor simply held down his own test switch in the rear seat, and did not release it when the student released his in the front until a suitable display of strenuous physical activity had been elicited. The hardest part of this whole operation was keeping a straight face. Our groundcrew were wonderful and often reinforced the myth by either helping with the pounding, or offering a substitute item such as a screwdriver to take the stress off the Starfighter student's poor tired fist. We didn't manage to get everybody, but there were some memorable achievements, including general officers. Once an instructor found that he "had a live one", this foible was judiciously reinforced by other instructors throughout the course, just to increase credibility. At the end of the course, the most deserving souls were awarded a trophy with a "nice having you" caption, inducted into the "Order of the Thruster

Thumpers", and sworn to secrecy for all time.

Another idiosyncrasy of the aircraft created one of my fondest memories of the '104. There were just too many "T" and "D" shaped handles in the cockpit to efficiently activate various systems such as rudder pedals, canopy jettison, emergency hydraulics, the drag chute, and a number of other items; and a lot of them looked uncomfortably alike. Back in the sixties, one worthy attempted to adjust the rudder pedals while on the ground by using the canopy jettison handle with *spectacular* results, especially when viewed through the rather startled eyes of the groundcrew in attendance.

During September 1975, our squadron deployed for two weeks to Kleine Brogel, Belgium, while our runway in Baden, Germany was being resurfaced. One day, I was leading a four-ship flight on a nearby bombing range and had a very senior squadron officer as my Number Two. I had already finished my post-start systems checks and was waiting for the rest of my flight to check in, when I glanced over at my Number Two just in time to see the drag chute door on the belly of the aircraft pop open and the chute come streaming out! The next thing I heard was a meek little voice coming from Two (who didn't think I could see him) saying that he was having "a small problem" and would have to abort. Later investigation on my part with the groundcrew revealed that this rather absent-minded senior had been adjusting his rudder pedals with the drag chute handle. To make matters worse, our hero reputedly attempted to hush this minor embarrassment by offering the groundcrew a case of the finest Belgian beer if they would keep a lid on the event. Being both enterprising and honourable chaps, they agreed, took the beer, and then because the story was just too juicy to suppress, promptly blabbed it all over Western Europe. The fall from grace in the hero trade can be swift and brutal.

Another famous quirk of the Starfighter was the CF–104D's proneness towards having a stuck microphone, usually with highly embarrassing results for the crew. It was a relatively common occurrence, but not common enough to imbue the pilots with caution. I was personally victimized by this quirk one day while flying in Europe with a squadron buddy, Brian Bainbridge...

It's been said that that a good airplane, good company, and good flying weather really bring out the little boy in a fighter pilot; something that is never far below the surface. This particular spring day was a fine one for a low level navigation route and we were in great spirits. As we scorched over the German countryside, we were joking, laughing, singing songs, and generally being very silly. We were also, unbeknownst to us, on continuous radio transmit from the time of takeoff! Although we must have sounded foolish, it wasn't nearly as foolish as we felt when we thought of the marvellous song-and-dance routine we had just provided everyone on Baden-Soellingen tower frequency for at least five minutes.

Nevertheless, if Brian and I felt a little sheepish, we were a long, long way from winning the prize. *That* honour was reserved for one of the CF–104 students at Cold Lake during the late seventies. During the mission in question, Cold Lake tower was being manned by an all-female crew. The student, in the front seat of a dual, had cleared the active runway after landing and checked in with ground control for clearance back to the 417 Squadron ramp. That clearance was provided by a very attractive ground controller with a very appealing voice. At this point, our student, who had just landed, took off again... only this time on a verbal flight of fancy, unwittingly telling his very captive audience in extremely explicit terms just what he would like to do with her in a sexual sense. He was candid, he was inspired, but most of all, he was *live*. Such were the risks of the CF–104D...

* * * * * *

Over the service life of the Starfighter, several myths developed concerning the aircraft's reputation, and it is time to set the record straight. It should also be clearly understood that these myths were all foisted upon an uninformed world public by the media, and did not originate with the Starfighter operational community.

The first myth that needs to topple is that one needed to be Superman to fly the '104. While the aircraft itself, and particularly its role and operating environment, demanded a very high skill level of '104 pilots, the concept of *superhuman* skills being required to do this is, of course, absolute rubbish. It *is* true that the aircraft, while basically very predictable, trustworthy, and delightful to fly - *as long as it was handled within clearly defined limits,* - made extreme demands on pilot ability; and definitely required either prior tactical experience or a very capable *ab initio* student to fly it in an operational milieu. This was due to the role, the single-seat crew concept where the pilot had to perform all the aircrew tasks, the high-density European air traffic environment, and the extremely poor and unpredictable weather conditions which prevailed. The pilot demands probably reached their peak during the days of the Conventional Attack role, due to the host of attack options available and the greater diversification required in bombing skills and low level tactical navigation. Also, after the establishment of the Fighter Weapons Instructor Course (FWIC), CF–104 pilots spent a considerable amount of time honing air combat and air gunnery skills in an aircraft not ideally suited to those activities, and which demanded excellence if one was to achieve credible results. Interestingly enough, in the late seventies and early eighties, when the pilot work load demands were probably at their zenith, the accident rate had actually dropped off when

Above: *Maj Dan Dempsey of 441 Squadron gets ready to climb aboard with a welcome assist from a technician. Baden-Soellingen 1985.*

compared to the early years of CF–104 operations. This, I think, speaks very highly for the professionalism of the pilots, the excellence of the training system, and the degree of comfort that operating within a mature program brings.

While some transport pilots may bemoan the demands placed upon them by a host of different departures and approaches, a Starfighter pilot did all these things **on his way to and from work,** where the **real** business of being a fighter pilot began... on the bombing range, in the air combat maneuvering area, entering the tactical low level navigation structure, and so on. Add to this the fact that, more often than not, he was doing it in formation and alone in the aircraft, without other crew members to share the workload, and you get a reasonable impression of the demands of the job. There was no apprenticeship type of progress for individual performance demands on the pilot within the aircraft; no logical progression over time from the right seat to the left seat. The CF–104 pilot was a qualified aircraft captain from the time he "hit the ground running" in Europe, and only his combat effectiveness and his ability to lead others in the air were honed through an apprenticeship process. But superhuman qualities? Definitely not. This is yet another example of inappropriate press hype that in all fairness may have been fuelled by a relative handful of '104 pilots back in the early days of the program, who probably started believing their own press clippings. Here are a few of the more blatant examples of journalistic overstatement prevalent at the time that fuelled the Superman image...

"If the Red Menace ever decides to become more than just a menace, the Forces of Freedom can be comforted in the knowledge that (pilot's name) is on our side."

"That night in the Officers' Mess, they raised their glasses to the Ace of Aces, the Best in the West, the Top Gun."

"(pilot's name) was a hired gun, and in that soft summer of 1974, Canada's superstar in the deadliest of games - defending freedom."

To the vast majority of Starfighter pilots, the overstatement by the press of '104 pilot qualifications was a source of continuous amusement, as Bill McWilliams mentions tongue-in-cheek...

Most of us enjoyed the notoriety, at least a little, and felt squarer of jaw and steelier of eye. Only supermen could fly such a killer airplane; it said so right in the Elk Pasture Times Weekly...

However, as long as one obeyed the rules that the jet clearly established, and was completely prepared for the worst eventualities, such as an engine failure at any given moment, the aircraft posed no special problems. Jim Robinson of Houston, Texas acquired CF–104 104633 from the Norwegian government a few years ago as military surplus, and flies the jet on a regular basis as part of a display organization known as the Combat Jets Flying Museum. Jim makes some very interesting observations on flying the jet in a non-tactical environment, particularly since he has never been a military aviator. Nonetheless, Jim is a highly seasoned corporate pilot with extensive jet experience, including flight time in the Museum's older operational types, such as the T–33A jet trainer and their Canadair F–86 Sabre...

Taming the Beast?

"It is the most dangerous, insidious airplane that I have ever flown, having many coffin corners that you can get yourself into without natural warnings...and leaving yourself no place to go!"

- Veteran Starfighter pilot

This quote was taken from the introduction of a Squadron/Signal Publications book entitled ***"F–104 Starfighter in Action"****.*

I sat dejectedly and a little embarrassed as an ex-Starfighter driver told me that as a pilot I was still wet behind the ears. He went on to say that even though I had a long way to go he just might some day be able to teach me the extra special pilot techniques required to fly an F–104. This barrage of belittlement began to sound like a broken record during the months I searched to no avail for someone to teach me to fly the Starfighter. I began to think they might just be right, that there really is some demoniacal disposition about this aircraft that only those with astronaut or test pilot backgrounds can learn to master.

Along the way doubters were saying that I would be dead within six months. These unbelievers stated that I had no business in an F–104 and why wouldn't I just stick to what I had. They went on to say that a man such as myself with just average piloting skills and abilities could never tame a beast like the Starfighter.

I have heard things like this all my life and I have never paid much attention to them. From experience I have found that if one wants something bad enough, with lots of work and effort, one can accomplish anything one sets out to do.

I feel the man was correct when he described me as an average pilot. I don't possess any bigger than life aviating skills; I am merely a competent, safe pilot. However, I am living proof that you don't have to be ten feet tall and bullet proof to fly an F–104 Starfighter. I have always maintained that anyone with the right amount of hard work and good training can fly anything they want. This statement I am sure will draw much criticism from all those individuals whose egos are tied tightly to the type of flying they do. It is a detriment to these folk's self-esteem to think that some "average pilot" can come along and fly something that is meant only for supermen. This is not to take away from the hard work and perseverance that got these gentlemen where they are today; however, they should be admired for their competence and achievements as mortals, not as Gods. There are many in aviation who would have you believe that it is only by "mirrors and magic" that an aircraft gets from point A to point B. Those who proliferate this myth do so because it is a boost to their self-esteem. If the general public knew that most possess the skills to fly an aircraft and that with hard work and determination they could, those "mirrors and magic" types just might have to come down off their pedestals. These are harsh words, I know. A good friend of mine once said that to be a good pilot one has to have an ego. I feel my friend is right, with one caveat. The ego must be in control by the individual in the face of reason.

I finally did find someone to teach me to fly the Starfighter and he did it in fourteen hours. This is not a tribute to my piloting skills, but instead to his skills as an instructor. The '104 in the beginning was difficult to fly. It didn't behave at all like anything I had ever flown. However, as the lessons went on, the skills needed to control the aircraft were patiently and expertly imparted, and low and behold, I learned to fly the jet. There is nothing magical about this aircraft; it doesn't wait like a coiled snake to kill you if you make one wrong move. It is unforgiving, true, but well within the "average pilot's" ability to master if he will just pay attention to his reasoning faculties. "Crawl, walk, run," as another good friend always says.

Interesting words from Jim; words that I hope will go a long way in dispelling the Superman myth.

But there is considerably more to *tactical* fighter flying than making small houses big and big houses small; and comparing the degree of difficulty of flying a '104 in a structured, non-tactical venue with operations in a dynamic, tactical environment is rather like comparing apples and oranges. One must be very careful not to generalize based on a limited experience base. Nonetheless, Jim's comments, in terms of basic aircraft handling demands, certainly have merit. The Starfighter was not an outrageously difficult aircraft to fly, but was an extremely demanding instrument of war.

At any rate, when all was working properly, the airplane did outstanding work in the low-level high-speed environment. When it didn't, you had to think fast, since the '104 had the glide ratio of an anvil strapped to a manhole cover. A friend of mine is the source of one of my favourite '104 stories. He was motoring along at low level one day in the Moselle area of Germany when he suffered a catastrophic bird strike that totalled the engine, necessitating an immediate ejection from the doomed machine. Apparently every warning light and horn in the cockpit came on. His statement to the accident Board of Inquiry is a classic:

"I looked inside the cockpit, saw all those pretty lights and just knew I'd won a hundred free video games, but didn't think I'd hang around to play them."

Al Seitz's comments reflect the feelings of the entire CF–104 operational community regarding the need to act promptly and decisively in the event of critical emergencies low to the ground...

It is perhaps a mixed blessing that the characteristics of an ailing CF–104 make for easy decisions. It has been said that if this bird flames out, it lands straight ahead, regardless of current position or altitude. In truth, it has an engine-out glide ratio of three-to-one, or half a mile forward for every 1000 feet of altitude. It takes a minimum of 12,000 feet (15,000 feet is a more realistic figure) to complete one 360 degree gliding turn. With its minimum glide speed at 245 knots, the idea of bellying it into the nearest pasture just isn't on. First impact would result in a ball of fire. To make it to a runway, you must have your flameout pretty close to home, and fate is rarely that cooperative. So if that engine quits, give it back to the taxpayers and walk home.

Many aircraft have been christened with nicknames over the years by those who work with them, and the CF–104 was no exception. Some liked to call it the "Zipper", the "Zip", or the "Silver Sliver". We would occasionally refer to it in jest as the "Aluminum Death Tube", "The Lawn Dart" or the "Flying Phallus", but more often than not, we would just call it the "'104" or by its given name, the "Starfighter". Somehow it seemed so appropriate - an elegant name for an elegant aircraft. The jet just couldn't conjure up a derisive name from those who flew her. Other airplanes got "Thud", "Hog", and "Aardvark"; not so the '104. I *never* heard anyone in the pilot community call it "the missile with the man in it". That was pure press hype. Perhaps more to the point, I *never* heard a pilot call it " the Widowmaker", and I don't know a self-respecting '104 pilot who would. This is because none of us who flew her blamed the jet for the relatively high accident rate incurred during the '104's operational life, especially during the early transition days. I will have more to say on this topic later, but for the most part, the demanding role of the CF–104 in NATO operations was the main reason for the elevated accident rate, not the aircraft itself.

Sam Firth, who was a part of the CF–104 program virtually from the outset, recalls the origins of this most unfortunate and undeserved nickname...

The poor reputation of the '104 stemmed from the Luftwaffe in the early '60s. Principally, there are two reasons... the first one is that the '104 was designed as a straight-line Mach 2 interceptor, and nothing else. It wasn't designed to rat around at low level with nuclear bombs on it, or Vicom Cameras. It wasn't designed to hang iron bombs on it or for air-to-ground purposes, and while it had a capability for dog fighting, you don't dog fight in the classic sense with a straight-line Mach 2 aircraft. Nonetheless, NATO purchased it because it was the cheapest buy for the numbers that you gained.

Almost straight away, the Luftwaffe began to lose a large number of '104 aircraft, and to kill pilots in the process. The second reason for losses was due to the fact that the Luftwaffe was still recuperating from WW II, and the gap between '45 and '56 when they had no air force. They began with some Canadian F86s in 1956, plus a Canadian Detachment up in Oldenburg, and very soon they had moved on to the '104. The sophistication of that aircraft was just too much both for their aircrew training program, and equally, if not more so, for their technical training program. The upshot of it all was that pilots who were improperly trained were flying an aircraft which was not as well maintained as it should have been; and that is putting it about as mildly as I can.

With the large number of losses, the German popular press began to pick up on it, and chastised the German Government for purchasing the aircraft. Some prominent magazines took up a cudgel in order to embarrass the government. The resulting political ramifications resulted in the downfall of the Chief of the German Air Staff, General Podinski and the elevation to power of General Johannes Steinhoff, quite a well-known German aviator from WW II. General Steinhoff brought in an

- photo by Bill Johnson

old WW II crony named Major-General Hrabak to take over the German '104 program to correct it where needed, and to reduce the accidents in order to get the press off the West German Government's backs.

At this time, I was Senior Officer Flight Safety at #1 Air Division Headquarters in Metz working for Group Captain Mussels, a pretty tough taskmaster. The Germans consulted the Canadians, due to our better accident record, in order to find out how and why we did things the way we did. They then adopted many of our maintenance practices and flying training techniques, and as a result, their accident rate dropped.

Notwithstanding, the moniker of Widowmaker remained; and it is unfortunate because every time Canada lost a '104 or two, and there was no other news deemed worthy, our own press would trot out the appellation of Widowmaker, along with what we should be doing about it. Once, I remember watching the national media make complete asses of themselves in calling down the '104, even to the point of interviewing a "Think Tank Expert" from Washington who called the aircraft "unstable", if you can believe that...the CF–104 being the most stable aircraft that I have ever flown. I have never heard a single person who flew, maintained, controlled or guarded that aircraft of any air force (and that includes the Luftwaffe) call it the Widowmaker. I get a little upset even now when I think of how badly that aircraft was maligned and most undeservedly.

But though the German media did their best to malign the Starfighter, the air-minded German public loved the aircraft, and loved to see it on display. Since so many NATO nations including Germany flew the '104, I think the aircraft became a symbol of the Alliance to the German nation. However, the adverse publicity during the high accident rate period of its career was extensive enough to inspire the Teutonic sense of humor. They joked that if you wanted to own a '104, just buy an acre of land anywhere in Germany. Sooner or later...

Nevertheless, if ever an aircraft had acquired an unwarranted moniker, it was the Starfighter. In all, there were 110 "A" Category CF–104 accidents throughout the aircraft's 25 year operational career, and these accidents resulted in 37 pilot fatalities. What one needs to study is a breakdown of aircraft losses during each year of operations.

Starfighter Accident Breakdown

Year	AC losses	Air Accident Rate/10,000 hrs	Hours Flown (Approximate)
1961	1	-	77
1962	3	6.32	7,900
1963	9	3.66	21,800
1964	9	2.60	34,600
1965	12	5.18	38,600
1966	5	2.09	43,000
1967	8	2.39	46,100
1968	8	2.44	45,200
1969	9	3.17	44,200
1970	7	2.09	28,800
1971	5	4.96	20,200
1972	-	2.09	19,100
1973	5	3.09	19,400
1974	5	4.77	18,900
1975	2	1.63	18,400
1976	1	1.48	20,200
1977	3	2.13	18,700
1978	3	1.58	19,000
1979	1	1.58	19,000
1980	3	2.76	18,100
1981	3	2.56	19,500
1982	5	3.63	19,300
1983	4	2.42	16,500
1984	2	1.63	12,300
1985	-	-	8,300

Perhaps the key statistic here is the accident rate per 10,000 hours of flying time. Although the annual aircraft losses were significantly higher during the earlier years of the program, it must be remembered that significantly more airframe hours were being flown at that time, prior to the down-sizing of the Air Division. The early loss rate gave cause for concern, and these accidents have already been discussed in considerable detail. The cause factors were numerous, but tended to centre around aircraft systems "teething troubles" (which were all ironed out as the program matured), and inappropriate behavior by the pilots (which unfortunately never went completely away). Part of the earlier problems centred around the insistence by authority of almost banning young, highly capable "pipeline" pilots from program entry. Time and later experience proved that the pipeliners, properly trained, were *at least* the match of their seasoned pilot brethren in handling the Starfighter in the dynamic low-level environment. This was largely due to the fact that things happened very rapidly in the '104, and the rapid reflexes of youth, combined with a lack of ingrained bad flying habits transferred to a very different weapons system, paid great dividends when pilots were confronted with adverse flight situations. In reviewing all the CF–104 crashes for this book, I was truly startled to note how few of the fatalities were directly attributable to aircraft system malfunctions. In fact, of the 37 aircrew fatalities, only four were cases where it could be said with absolute certainty that the failure of aircraft systems was directly responsible for the loss of pilot life. Interestingly enough, three of the fatalities were due in one form or another to the emergency egress. One pilot was hit by the seat on ejection, another parachuted into the crash fireball, and a third experienced a seat malfunction, though the ejection sequence had been left too late at any rate. A number also perished simply from ejecting outside the envelope of the escape system. Of the four deaths directly attributable to the aircraft, only two were similar; namely, unexplained control malfunctions at low altitude. *All* of the other fatalities were a result of some form of pilot inattention. Of the 110 "A" Category accidents, 21 were due to Foreign Object Damage (of which 14 were directly attributable to birdstrikes), 14 were due to in-flight engine failures, 6 were directly caused by faulty maintenance, and 9 were lost in mid-air collisions. A full 32 struck the ground for one reason or another while flying at low level, usually under adverse or deteriorating weather conditions.

Bill Turnbull reflects on the accident cause factors during his tenure as a CF–104 pilot, and comments on some of the lesser-known technical malfunctions that the aircraft experienced...

During the late sixties, fatal flying accidents happened with almost monotonous regularity. We were authorized 36,000 flying hours annually for the Air Division's 108 aircraft. Our write-off rate was around 2:10,000 hours, or about six or seven aircraft per year. Some half of these accidents were fatal. During my four years in Europe, there were twelve funerals. I attended three of those, and that was three too many.

Of the four 1 Wing pilots killed while I was at Lahr, one hit a house in Belgium on a perfectly clear day, one hit the crest of a hill in a snow shower, another cut a swath through some trees in marginal weather and never came back up, and the fourth clipped a ridge, once again on a clear day. The good weather accidents occurred just after passing a target, which led the Board of Inquiry to speculate that the pilots had been looking back at the targets and had inadvertently allowed their aircraft to descend. The others occurred on target run-ins.

To illustrate what came to be termed "press-on-itis", I can still visualize a particular rail line search on one of those hazy days when the ceiling was officially unlimited but the forward visibility into sun was effectively nil. To judge by his radio calls, the pilot ahead seemed to be doing OK. Not to be outdone, I found myself flying ever lower to maintain visual contact with the ground ***until I suddenly had the sensation of flying through a railway station, that is, I looked out to the side and saw people standing on the platform****. Being afraid of hitting wires, I broke off, wondering why I had persisted so long.*

I almost met the same fate as a squadron mate and neighbour while running at a target obscured by a local snow shower. The ground rose slowly and the snow hid the highest point. Visibility to one side was better than straight ahead, and the dimly perceivable horizon there conveyed a false sense of height. All I knew was that the rooftops were very close when the visibility, which had been bad, suddenly dropped to zero. Knowing that there was higher ground ahead, I initiated an afterburner pull-up to escape. Had I been attempting that run-in a few minutes later, when the edge of the squall had moved closer to the highest point of land, I might well have hit the high ground before I had time to react. I suspect that is what happened to my friend.

I have always carried a certain guilt from that accident because I did not broadcast the difficulty I experienced reaching the target. The pilot ahead of me on the mission had called clear, and I assumed there was some way to get at it. It was while I was preoccupied with trying to find an alternate avenue of approach, that the fellow behind me began his fatal run-in. Whether a radio call would have deterred him from following is hard to say.

As a result of this accident, the Wing charged the first pilot on a training wave with some "responsibility" for those who followed. He was to rule on the safety of any portion of the route. By this simple device, it was hoped to break the "alone and unafraid" or competitive mentality which might lead to pressing on in bad weather.

I don't know that competition with one's peers was the motivator in the accidents which plagued all three Wings. I came to believe it was competition between one's self and an imaginary standard; part of the "macho" self-image which went with the trade, and which was characteristic of contemporary male society. To admit fear was a sign of weakness. Since no one else would confess to sometimes being afraid, you thought you were the only one. It was all unspoken. There was never any explicit pressure to push your luck.

Low level operations are inherently dangerous, and situations could arise in the most innocent circumstances. One nice clear morning, I was descending into a deep, vertically-walled valley in the French Jura mountains. Unbeknownst to me, and not marked on the map, was a high-voltage power line which stretched from one ridge to the other. The supporting pylons were hidden by trees. While spherical metal markers were suspended on the wires, these were only visible if seen against a sky background. Certainly, they were invisible from my descending vantage point. When still some 800 - 1000 feet above the valley floor, I was alerted by my peripheral vision to something above the aircraft. Glancing up, I saw the metal spheres and wires flashing past the canopy, close enough that I instinctively ducked behind the instrument panel. Not knowing how many wires there were, my first fear was losing my head, the second losing the stabilizer. Neither happened, but it was sheer luck that the aircraft passed perhaps 20 feet below the lowest wires.

These incidents and accidents are only mentioned to disprove any notion that the F–104 deserved its nickname of "widowmaker". The aircraft was unforgiving, but most of the fatal accidents with which I am familiar were more attributable to the combination of people and roles than to the aircraft itself.

In recent years, aircraft crashes in Europe have claimed lives on the ground. We were lucky in that none of our accidents did so, although some came close. When a 441 aircraft hit the ridgepole of a Belgian house, it flew on for a few hundred meters before exploding. The engine continued straight ahead, skipping across the fields until it bounced up through the window of a neighbouring house and came to rest beside the dining room table. The family, who had just sat down in an adjoining room for morning tea, were unhurt.

Most crippling technical malfunctions resulted in successful ejections, although some of those were very close calls. One exception occurred at 4 Wing when a CF–104 rolled inverted on short final, giving the pilot no chance to bail out. A very persistent Board determined that the aircraft's control spool valves exhibited microscopic scoring from hydraulic fuel contamination. These valves were slotted, pencil-like rods which received control inputs from the pilot and ported 3000 psi hydraulic fluid to the control surface actuators. If they began to seize due to scoring, uncommanded control surface and control column movements were the result. It turned out that these valves had been accorded a 1000-hour life by the manufacturer, but we had removed the life limit. There were none in the supply chain, and it was going to take over a year to acquire and progressively replace all of the valves in the fleet. Incredibly, someone asked, "Should we tell the pilots?". The pilots were indeed told and, over the next year or so, a few aborted their missions and brought home aircraft which seemed to have developed a mind of their own. That was the only period in my experience during which the aircraft was really suspect, and it was not

Above: *Truly ready for safe sex, Capt Gerry Bayles is the acme of sartorial splendor as he proceeds to his aircraft modelling the complete NBCW ensemble. 21 January, 1986.*

comforting to fly at low level with controls whose condition was uncertain. I felt that almost any malfunction ***except*** *a control failure was manageable at low altitude.*

The structural integrity of our aircraft may also have been a bit uncertain, at one time, but that was less widely known. The GAF lost an aircraft, which had logged less than 1000 hours, at Luke Air Force Base when one of its wings came off during a weapon delivery. A special inspection revealed a handful of others with cracked wing fittings. Lockheed had ***lifed*** *this part at 3000 hours, but the investigators determined that the lifetime was based on a strike mission profile requiring only one 4 "G" pull per flight hour. Some of our aircraft at Cold Lake had reached 2500 hours, and every corner in the bombing pattern required 4 "Gs". Therefore, it came as no surprise to me when one of the Cold Lake aircraft came apart after passing through the wash of another at supersonic speed. The pilot survived the bailout only to be castigated by the Board of Inquiry, but I always felt they missed the real cause. My feeling in those years was that our Boards, comprised as they were of amateur investigators, were unlikely to find technical flaws in a complex aircraft, and almost invariably fell back on constructing "pilot error" scenarios.*

They may well have been correct in most cases, but that would have been pure chance. The CF-104 had no flight data recorder. Most accidents totally destroyed the aircraft. It would have been very difficult, even for experts, to find technical cause factors. Therefore, statements like "The Board was unable to find evidence of any technical failure" were gratuitous.

One of the enduring no-nos in the flying business is premature release of information concerning fatal accidents. On one occasion, the Canadian Forces' Network (CFN) tersely announced in mid-afternoon that a Lahr aircraft had crashed, killing the pilot. Late in the day, I was tasked to photograph the crash site. Unaware of the CFN announcement, I never thought to call home. I fact, I can't recall whether I even had a telephone at the time...very few Canadians did in those days. In any event, mine was the last mission of the day, and I was unusually late getting home. My poor wife was nearly hysterical when I walked through the door. She had heard the radio report and feared it was I who had been killed. That scene may well have been repeated in many other homes.

Nevertheless, aircrew and their families were not the only members of the Starfighter community that were deeply affected by aircraft losses. Blaine Feltmate served as Line Servicing Officer for 421 Squadron during 1977 and 1978; then as Avionics Officer with 1 CAG Maintenance Squadron from 1978 until 1980. However, it was his duties with the Crash Recovery Team that truly reinforced the grimmer nature of the business to him...

Being the second ever engineering Lieutenant posted to 1 CAG, there were many things that left impressions about the time I served in Baden, both with 421 Squadron and with the Maintenance Squadron. The one thing which always stands out is the people - their professionalism, motivation, and sense of purpose. The other thing which stood out, sometimes far enough to trip over, were the egos of a few of the "old-time" fighter pilots. Their "work hard", and especially "play hard", attitude provided memorable entertainment at many a TGIF. Because of the small size of this closed community, friendships developed quickly and naturally among all the military personnel. It was this fact that made my secondary duty as "Crash Recovery Officer" particularly difficult.

Statistically, I believe we averaged about one aircraft loss per year in Europe. Although no one wished to reinforce that statistic, one could always sense a feeling of apprehension and tension when that statistical time was exceeded. In over half of the aircraft accidents to which I responded, the aircrew initiated successful ejections; the remaining did not. Responding to the fatal accidents was the hardest thing I did in Europe. One accident involving a pilot whom I knew well, remains vivid to this day...

The day was clear, except for that light haze that seems to cover Germany for ninety percent of the year. From the top of the ridge, I looked down into a shallow valley; I could see a bridge in the distance.

Above: *A CF-104 on landing rollout. Note the extended speed brakes and the canopy, which is just in the process of being opened.*

That was the target. Below me, no more than 10 or 15 feet from the top of the ridge, a bit of the shrubbery had been disturbed and a few feet of the Rhine soil had been pushed aside. Nothing in this picture portrayed the devastation that lay in the fields beyond the ridge.

The pilot had been doing an attack on a bridge in the valley. Unfortunately, he mistook a second bridge nearby as the intended objective. In the final phase of the attack he recognized his mistake, acquired the correct bridge, and pressed on with an extended low level attack. Due to this change in the attack profile, he became a victim of the surrounding terrain as he tried to climb to safety out of the valley which was imperceptibly closing in around him. The gun film taken from the aircraft confirmed these details. The film also showed how the aircraft's "kicker" tried to prevent the aircraft from stalling as its pilot fought to climb the CF–104 out of the trap the valley had now become.

The CF–104 hit the ground with its underbelly, near the top of the ridge. The aircraft remained intact momentarily as it became a projectile, being hurtled above the fields beyond the ridge. Then, with a massive explosion, the aircraft began to disintegrate, strewing its parts over a five-square-mile area. The forward section of the fuselage miraculously remained intact and continued like a large bullet for an additional half-mile, until it hit the tree line of the forest surrounding the fields. After hitting the ridge, all of these events happened in a matter of a few seconds; ejection was impossible. The pilot was found dead in his seat in the cockpit, which rested in the trees about a mile from the initial impact point on the ridge. Several days later, a helicopter search finally located the large turbine section of the engine, an additional two and one-half miles past where the pilot was found.

When I first went to Europe I was invited, as was customary, to a dinner in France with 421 Squadron, where I was introduced to the Squadron members. Three and one-half years later, when I left Baden, I was the only person leaving Europe ***alive*** *of the four officers who sat together on that first welcoming evening at the "Garlic Pit". This had to leave an impression. The impression, however, was tempered by the knowledge that flying the CF–104 in Europe, at high speeds and low level, had inherent risks. The aircraft was mechanically sound and well-maintained, but was very unforgiving of mistakes in the low level flying environment. Everyone understood this, none better than the pilots themselves. After every accident, I made it a point to take a backseat ride; I'm not quite sure why - maybe to reaffirm my faith in the aircraft and in those who flew them.*

For those interested in statistics, of the approximately 750 pilots who were trained to fly the CF–104, the numbers meant that each trained pilot had about a 15% chance of being involved in an "A" Category accident, and about a 5% chance of "coming home in a box". This is a very commendable record, when spread over an operating life of 25 years in the highly-demanding low level role, often in atrocious weather and without the benefit of a second crew member or a second engine, which undoubtedly would have resulted in considerably fewer aircraft accidents. It is also worthy of note that in the late seventies and early eighties, when CF–104 pilots were at their absolute busiest in the Attack role, the accident rate was for the most part very low. The Canadian performance record is in fact very good when compared to that of other NATO allies operating in a similar environment. Furthermore, CF–104 losses compare very favourably with those of its predecessor, the F–86 Sabre. During just *twelve years* of operational flying, there were 282 "A" Category Sabre accidents, of which 112 were fatal. Additionally, these accidents occurred in a much more simplistic aircraft and in a much less demanding, single-faceted, high-level environment. Yet has anyone heard the Sabre referred to as "the Widowmaker"? I think not...

I have frequently heard it asked if, with all the socializing

Below: *The front instrument panel and the left and right side panels, as the aircraft was equipped in the early seventies.*

Home Fires Burning

While the bulk of the CF–104's operational flying took place in Central Europe, a significant amount of aerial activity also took place at #6 Strike and Operational Training Unit (6 ST/R OTU) and the Central Experimental and Proving Establishment (CEPE). Both these units, subsequently renamed 417 Operational Training Squadron (417 OTS) and the Aerospace Engineering and Test Establishment (AETE), were absolutely essential ingredients to the overall success of the Canadian Starfighter program, and both strongly deserve the recognition already given to their European contemporaries.

6 ST/R OTU served as "the cradle" for all aspiring CF–104 pilots, but prior to arrival at this unit, all Canadian pilots transitioning to the Starfighter before 1969 underwent low level navigation and weapons delivery training for three months at the Sabre Transition Unit (STU) in Chatham, New Brunswick. Bill Turnbull remembers his days at the STU, as seen through the eager eyes of a "pipeliner"...

Naturally, we were all terribly excited about flying the legendary F–86, although the unit was only equipped with Mk–5s. Their "hard" leading edges and de-rated Orenda engines rendered these particular versions of the aircraft somewhat less than exciting. Nevertheless, the first mission, which was also one's first solo (a dual version of the Sabre was never built), generated a unique kind of excitement.

The syllabus comprised only two kinds of missions - low level navigation and weapons deliveries at Tracadie Range. Most of the former were chased missions. For the latter, a rail-type bomb rack carrying several Mk–106 smoke bombs was mounted under one wing.

The STU was kind of a crazy place where risk-taking seemed to be the norm. Minimum altitudes were dictated by foliage heights, and marginal weather was not an impediment to low flying. In fact, I don't recall any particular instruction on what to do if deteriorating weather was encountered enroute. Low level routes were not deconflicted, and some ran in opposite directions using the same waypoints. Needless to say, there were occasions where pairs of Sabres met head–on while rounding a bend in some river valley. I don't know to what extent this cavalier approach influenced our thinking, perhaps setting some of us up for the accidents which were to follow in Europe.

Ken Thorneycroft recalls his STU experiences from the vantage point of returning home to see an old friend, and the subsequent comfort that familiarity brings...

In May of 1962, I found myself receiving refresher training in the T–33 at Gimli, Manitoba in preparation for the Sabre Transition Course scheduled for later that year at Chatham. At Gimli, the nucleus of what was designated to become 434 (ST/A) Squadron had gathered; some one dozen "old timers", most of whom had previous tours on Sabres, although there were a couple of "clunk" drivers thrown in for good measure. After about four weeks and some 20 to 25 hours of refresher flying, we dispersed for a little leave prior to joining forces again at Chatham in July.

We all arrived safely and settled in for the Sabre Course. It promised to be great fun because, following transition (or refresher) to the Sabre 5, practically all our flying was scheduled to take place in the low level environment. We also met up with the "Senior" course, nominally the nucleus of 427 (ST/A) Squadron. It was headed up by Squadron Leader R. G. (Bob) Middlemiss, with Squadron Leader O. B.

Above: *Truly a "Douglas Racer" and probably the world's fastest DC-3, "Pinocchio" and its two clones, "Dolly's Folly" and "Woody Woodpecker" provided every. CF-104 pilot with a sedate introduction to radar navigation.*

Philp as his #2. Course One was also made up of ex-Sabre and CF–100 drivers. (In those days, Transport weenies and lesser breeds need not apply!) Course activities proceeded apace, and we found ourselves spending a lot of time in Ground School learning all about strip maps. This was new stuff for most, if not all of us, and we weren't sure it was going to be all that it was cracked up to be. Timed turns and flying to turning points and targets with a time tolerance of plus-or-minus 10 seconds was going to be a challenge. It marked the first time any of us had seen the new 1:500,000 topographical maps, and I must say that we were generally very impressed with them. In any event, we went through hundreds of them in our "cut-and-paste" activities. The strip map developed into a super navigation tool for a pilot working in a cramped cockpit. It did take some time to utilize them effectively, but that is why we were at Chatham. As I recall, the enroute speeds were in the 300 knots regime with dash speeds into the target at about 360 knots, which provided an interesting ride in a Sword on a hot day over lumpy terrain. However, as we gained experience, the flying heights came down to that allowed (never lower!), and we even started to anticipate check points before they appeared rather than navigating by looking where we had been, which was the case for the first few trips. As the course progressed, we started dropping MK–106 practice bombs (Jam Cans) on tactical targets in the Tracadie range. This proved to be a lot of fun and even with the rudimentary bombing equipment in the Sword - eyeballs and a pair of timers - the scores soon became quite reasonable. It was great to be back in the Sabre... a super aircraft in every respect with no major vices, although some of us had a little trouble with the hard wing on the Mk–5. On one trip, a member of our gang pulled a bit too tight on final, stalled, and thumped in short of the runway. A bent bird and injured pride were the immediate results. The subsequent ribbing from all and sundry was a little harder to handle for our intrepid birdman.

Most of the course members were married types who had gotten away from the joys and sorrows of barrack and Mess life. Everyone tried to return to the days of their youth and the Mess (bar) became a very merry place. It took a little time for us to appreciate there was a time for work and a time for play, but once that fact was recognized, things became slightly more serene and on the rails.

Before leaving Chatham, our group wanted to leave a memento for the Mess. Our sparkplug (and sometime adjutant) Flight-Lieutenant Hugh Rose thought it would be great to present the Mess with a bell, inasmuch as we were going to be "Bluenosers". He managed to talk Canadian Pacific into donating a locomotive bell which had seen service on a CPR mountain locomotive. It was a truly tremendous piece of kit which weighed in at over 300 pounds, and it produced a most satisfactory "clang" that would waken the dead. We engraved our names on this beautiful gift and overwhelmed the Base Commander by our generosity when we made the presentation! It's hard to believe, but the bell was subsequently liberated from the Officers' Mess (with some trouble, I expect). It was eventually recovered, and to the best of my knowledge is still residing in the lower bar at CFB Chatham.

One final point. During our last days at Chatham (the 427 gang was on course in Cold Lake), we learned that there was a slip in the training program. Course #1 would form the nucleus of 427 and 434 destined for Zweibrucken, and Course #2 (ours) would now become the nucleus of 444 to be based at Baden-Soellingen. Even though we had given Chatham the "Bell" as potential Bluenosers, I think all of us thought the new Squadron and locale were going to be just fine. What better motto could a Strike/Attack Squadron possibly have than 444's "Strike Swift, Strike Sure".

6 ST/R OTU had actually formed in October 1961 under the able command of Wing Commander Ken Lett, who would eventually rise to the rank of Lieutenant General in the Canadian Forces. The initial cadre of staff who had been trained in the USA found their first few weeks exceptionally busy, even though they had not as yet received any aircraft. As has already been mentioned, the syllabus for the OTU needed to be developed, lesson plans for the extensive ground school written, and the initial instructors had to take the complete ground school course themselves. The OTU received its first aircraft (CF–104D 12635) on January 16, 1962 and then started receiving jets on a regular basis from two separate sources. All the duals were manufactured by Lockheed at their Palmdale plant, while the single seaters were all assembled by Canadair at Cartierville. The duals were flown to Cold Lake from California by OTU staffers, thus providing a welcome break from the frantic preparations for the students at the OTU. Lieutenant General (Retired) Lett recalls those early days of CF–104 operations at Cold Lake...

That first year was "memorable". We had a staff who were attempting to learn concurrently with the students. The latter were without marital attachments for six months, some for the first time in years. The instructors attempted to be good hosts, while keeping the home fires burning in the "married patch". It was a hectic period with flying scheduled seven days per week for the first fifteen months.

We ferried in excess of one hundred aircraft as Cold Lake became a staging area for Canadair's output. As a result, we had seventy to eighty '104s holding down our ramp and eventually we ferried about thirty back to Canadair for overseas shipment. To say the least, we were travellers. It seems to me that I was either in Palmdale, Cartierville, St. Hubert (home of Air Defence Command) or Ottawa continuously.

The first three weeks of the 24–week CF–104 course were spent in "the schoolhouse", learning all the technical and handling details necessary to fly the jet. During this period, radar and inertial navigation practice was conducted aboard the three hybrid Dakotas... "Pinocchio", and its two contemporaries, "Dolly's Folly" and Woody Woodpecker". Of this trio, "Woody Woodpecker" unfortunately crashed in 1963, killing all three crew members aboard.

The official 417 Squadron History describes a breakdown of the rest of the Starfighter syllabus...

From the fourth to the eighteenth weeks, the instruction days were split, with half a day being spent in the classroom and the other half on the flight line. The ground school continued with navigation and radar systems operation, weapons delivery theory and intelligence. On the flight line, four CF–104D trips were given prior to solo, followed by several solo handling missions which gave the pilots the experience and confidence necessary before entering the next phases of their training - formation and instrument flying.

After he had received his instrument rating and three or four formation trips, the course member was ready to fly tactical formation to and from the controlled bombing range. Radar bombing and navigation combined with visual bombing and navigation were the real meat of the course and provided a great amount of friendly competition amongst the students. The Starfighter is probably the best low-level, high-speed aircraft in the world, and the trainee gained much confidence in himself and the aircraft during this phase of training. By the time he graduated from 6 ST/R OTU, the CF–104 pilot had completed 90 hours of CF–104 flying, 32 hours of T–33 instrument proficiency flying, and 200 hours of study in ground school.

Ralph Annis was a member of the very first CF–104 student course, and has vivid recollections of those hectic days; in particular the innovative inertial nav system...

Our first introduction to the inertial navigation system (LN3) and ground map radar vaulted us into a new high tech environment, making training on the new weapons system a thoroughly enjoyable and exciting period. Northern Alberta proved to be an excellent training area for using our radar because of the many large and easily identifiable lakes. Without them we probably would have been eternally lost, since radar prediction was relatively unknown at that time. The bombing range with its 10–mile cut through the forest saw thousands of passes made by screaming machines as low as 50 feet above the ground, practicing low altitude drogue deliveries. Each aircraft carried six small practice bombs with a smoke charge that marked your hit (or miss). With four aircraft using the range at one time and four more entering as you were leaving, it was always a busy place. It's too bad some of our environmentalists couldn't have been with us to watch moose browsing unconcernedly along the run-in line in the midst of thunderous noise.

During our stay in Cold Lake, our course changed from a single squadron to two squadrons, with Wing Commander O. B. Philp joining Bob Middlemiss as the first two Squadron Commanders for the Air Division in Europe. We flew hard at Cold Lake, but our time there was marred by the fatal accident to Jake Mulhall. That night, we all agreed that Jake would never want us to grieve, so the entire Officers' Mess erupted in a farewell party to a fine officer and pilot. I think that was the night that the "Ant Master" called "Dead Ants" while I was standing on the bar, and because I had farther to fling my body than any of the others in the Mess, I got nailed as the new "Ant Master". It was an expensive evening.

Ken Thorneycroft, who was now to become CO of 444 Squadron and lead Baden-Soellingen into the Starfighter era, recalls his impressions of the student syllabus and life at Cold Lake at the time...

Following a bit of leave and a long journey across Canada, our gang took up residence as the "junior course" at #6 Strike/Recce Operational Training Unit located at CFB Cold Lake, Alberta. We soon got settled in, checked out the Mess, and eventually found our way down to the flight line. The CO was Wing Commander K.C. (Kennie) Lett and Squadron Leader Bill Paisley, his deputy. The most vivid memory I have of that first trip to the hangar line was the impressive line-up of CF–104s. Were there really more than 90 birds? My "guesstimate" may be out by a fair margin but there sure was a lot of aluminum sitting on that flight line. The only problem was that of that vast array of hardware, only a very few aircraft were serviceable at any given time. As I recall, the average day would start with hardly more than eight or nine aircraft ready to fly. The aircraft was just coming into service, deliveries were still taking place, spares were in short supply, and the technicians were still groping with the mysteries of this new breed. The most common fault was associated with the Inertial Nav System (LN–3) and many, many ground aborts could be laid at the doorstep of this new-fangled piece of equipment. LN–3 problems were closely followed by problems of afterburner light–off at the start of the takeoff roll. Once again, many ground aborts were caused by failure of the afterburner to light.

In any event, as "newies" at the OTU, we didn't have to worry about the '104 for quite some time as we had a lot to accomplish before taking to the air. First on the program was a three-week course at the Field Technical Training Unit. Here we were exposed to all the systems utilized in the '104 and it was unquestionably a very useful start to our course. The FTTU was followed by full-time attendance at Ground School where in addition to more "cut and paste" strip map action, we attempted to get "genned up" on all the pilot-operated systems in the Starfighter, with a lot of emphasis on the LN–3 Nav System and the NASAAR ground mapping radar.

At last we started to do a bit of flying, first of all in the trusty T–33 followed by a new wrinkle, ... flights in converted Dakotas - converted in that they were fitted with a '104 nose cone and equipped with the LN–3 and the NASAAR radar. It was great fun motoring around the countryside at 120 knots using the Nav system and radar to make our way from point to point. We thought we had it aced in short order - little did we realize that the difference between flight at 120 knots and flight at 420 knots plus was going to be extremely interesting. Incidentally, the addition of the '104 nose to the old Gooney Bird enhanced its performance - it turned out another 5 knots at cruise power. (However, I'm not certain it enhanced the outward appearance of the venerable Dakota!)

The day finally arrived when we were to get our first crack at flying the '104. My first trip was November 24, and after a long and desperately cold walk around, my instructor (Flight-Lieutenant Williamson) finally permitted me to escape to the relative warmth of the cockpit where I immediately found that I was all thumbs - it seemed to take forever to get strapped in and spurs engaged! And the checklist, which I thought I had completely wired, departed my numbed brain. But with a lot of help from the backseater, the checks were finally completed and we were ready to go. From the first time I opened the throttle and pulled away from the line, the '104 was a winner in my books. Good solid nosewheel steering, good visibility, and heat in the cockpit on the ground to boot. Super!

The ugly rush down the runway on takeoff was exhilarating. (When the afterburner lit, you might as well release the brakes 'cause you were going to move regardless!) I don't remember checking the line speed, but I do remember that we did an afterburner climb and it sure was something to look behind you at 30,000 feet and see the airport almost directly below. Air work on the first trip involved a run to Mach 1.3, approaches to the stall (stick shaker only) PFLs,[1] circuits and approaches (flapless, takeoff and land). The higher speeds in the circuit and on the approach seemed very comfortable, and the '104's landing gear capability to absorb the landing shock

Above: *Completely oblivious to a very wet fate a nannosecond away, Capt Bruce Reid is about to receive the traditional "dunking" after passing the coveted 1000 flying hour plateau in the Starfighter. Capt Harv Wregget is "doing the honours" while squadron CO LCol Larry Best bars the door. Bruce would later perish in the Nevada desert during an Exercise Red Flag mission in February, 1979. So long, chum.*

- DND photo by Cpl Cecile Lagasse

[1] Practice Forced Landings.

was sure great for the ego. The one remaining surprise on trip #1 was the pleasant shock of the chute as it was deployed. Great trip.

Two more dual trips were the order of the day and we were then turned solo - feeling very comfortable in the aircraft by that time. The following half dozen missions were devoted to conversion training and formation. This was followed by an intensive period of visual bombing trips at the Canoe Lake range and preliminary low level cross country exercises leading into the Combat Profile Mission phase of the course. Complementing the visual bombing and the visual CPMs were radar bombing missions and radar CPMs. The ground/water contrast in the Cold Lake area made radar navigation relatively straight forward once the course members became accustomed to the speeds used, i.e., 420 knots and 450 knots enroute with dash speeds to tactical targets of 540 knots.

Somewhere along the way we entered the night flying phase, and most drivers found the aircraft a joy to fly at night. Towards the end of the course, the trips became more complex, and finally culminated with a "graduation" mission involving a four-tank '104 carrying a 2000 pound "shape" practice nuclear weapon, similar in size and weight to the live ones the Squadrons would be equipped with later on in Europe. Our course graduated in April 1963 with about 90 hours in the '104 flown on some 70 missions, and everyone departed for leave in order to get ready for the trip to Germany.

Several other "odds and ends" have remained in my memory regarding my student days at 6 ST/R OTU...

Our course instituted the ritual of a weekly "dining in". Great for morale and a lot of fun. Fortunate, too, that we "enjoyed" a large percentage of bad weather days following these weekly bashes.

It was about this time that we invented "Cobra Venom" which became the Squadron drink. 1–1/2 ounces of Cointreau, 1–1/2 ounces of Benedictine, and 1–1/2 ounces of Drambuie were loaded into three individual pony glasses. At the signal from the official "timer", the lucky drinker had a total of 12 seconds to consume this delightful concoction. (4 seconds max per pony: ergo 3 x 4 = 444.) It wasn't long before the guys tried to set a record, and I believe one chap eventually got the time down to 3.8 seconds - timing measured from the point the first glass touched the lips until the last one left the lips. We found from experience that a pair of Cobra Venoms per session was the maximum anyone could "safely" handle!

The Base Commander at one point grounded all three courses in residence at Cold Lake because a barrack inspection revealed minor damage which had somehow occurred following a "social" evening at the Mess. In fact, he was so incensed that he threatened to cease training all people on course unless the culprits owned up. The three "COs designate" went to see him later and reached an "accommodation" which got us back into the air and damage to the barrack block repaired.

Finally, the pilots of 444 gathered in Trenton about mid-May, complete with wives and families, and launched for Europe; compliments of 437 Squadron Yukon aircraft. We landed at Marville, and after an overnight stop we were bussed to 4 Wing. The next few days were devoted to getting settled into PMQs and checking out our new Squadron quarters situated in the South dispersal at 4 Wing.

Bill Turnbull's experiences on course at Cold Lake were not nominally different from anyone else's, but they serve to reaffirm the Air Force policy of the time to train all CF–104 pilots in the Strike role, irregardless of their ultimate employment...

In those days, we were all trained as Strike pilots. There was no recce training conducted at Cold Lake. Once again, the major emphasis was on low level navigation but now radar navigation was added. Training missions were flown "under the bag" in the rear seat of the dual at a nominal 500 ft. AGL. Hand flying, manipulating the radar and trying to correlate its return with a standard map kept the pilot very busy indeed.

The instructor's job was to keep us from running into the ground. On one mission during a sunny early spring day, my instructor was unusually quiet for the longest time. Suddenly, over the intercom came the sounds of snuffling and snorting, followed by the exclamation; "Oh my God. I fell asleep!" We figured he'd been asleep for at least 15 minutes.

To teach us radar interpretation, a C–47 Dakota was modified to carry the CF–104 radar in its nose and several radar consoles in the cabin. The grafting of a CF–104 nose cone to the Dakota's led to its being dubbed "Pinnochio". The Dakota would fly around a low level route while several of us struggled to make some sense out of the radar images, always under the stern gaze of one of the staff Navigators.

Day and night radar deliveries were also taught. Surprisingly, these could be almost as accurate as visual deliveries. In fact, the only impediments to the accuracy were the measurement uncertainties of radar cursor width and sweep time.

Although "flexible response" had been proposed as a strategy some 10 years earlier, it was yet to be officially embraced by NATO. Consequently, only nuclear weapon delivery modes were included in the syllabus. These were the level delivery from 2000 - 3000 ft. AGL, the 50 ft. AGL laydown delivery (visual only) and the low altitude drogued delivery or LADD manoeuvre.

The last involved a Mach .85 run-in at 50 ft. (visual) or 500 - 1000 ft. (radar) followed by a 3.5 "G" pull-up to a 35 degree pitch angle. During the run-in, a pair of timers were started as the aircraft passed some selected reference point. At the end of the run-in time, a tone signalled the pilot to initiate the pull-up. Weapon release occurred when the second timer ran out. After weapon release, the pilot performed an inverted escape manoeuvre in full afterburner to weapon burst height. The idea was to dash away at supersonic speeds since the weapon blast wave travelled at the speed of sound. Of course, the prompt radiation could not be outrun. Escaping at burst height was intended to place as much of the aircraft's mass between the source and the pilot as possible.

Many of the low level navigation missions, ended with a weapon drop somewhere in the Cold Lake range. The last CPMs of the course were conducted near maximum gross takeoff weight with four fuel tanks and a 2000 pound "Shape" - a concrete filled replica of a typical nuclear weapon. With daytime temperatures now in the 85° F range and Cold Lake's elevation, this ran us pretty close to the maximum tire speed at rotation. Our formerly nimble airplanes were now terrible handling things which didn't want to fly below about 450 knots.

Shape drops were always chased because occasionally the Shape drogue chutes wouldn't deploy. If the chute didn't work, when you rolled inverted during the escape manoeuvre, you'd find the Shape just outside the canopy, flying in close formation with you; so the chase pilot's function was to call the chute.

All of the course graduates were destined for Europe. All had been trained for the Strike role, and all held Cosmic–Z clearances. Our postings were unknown until the end of the course. Of my group, I was the only one sent to a recce squadron - 441, then located at 1 Wing, Marville, France. Frankly, I was pleased for I never felt comfortable with the notion of personally delivering a 1 megaton nuclear weapon.

In later years, the decision would be made during the first half of the course as to who would receive reconnaissance training. Instead of the nuclear weapons syllabus given to the potential Strike pilots, the recce candidates were given special training in their future role. This entailed study of tactical photographic equipment and techniques, mission planning, and learning all the essential elements of information required for the various types of tactical targets to be encountered in Europe, along with flying visual recce missions against a variety of representative

targets.

Early "teething troubles" *did* seriously affect the serviceability of the jet at the outset of operations though, and were enough to inspire cynicism in some quarters. John McKee was an airframe technician at Cold Lake in the earliest days of the CF–104 program, then later at 3 Wing in Zweibrucken. He notes that '104 servicing problems all started with a rather ill-thought-out cold weather trial by CEPE of the aircraft, late in 1961...

CEPE had received the first '104 in Cold Lake for trials in the winter of 1961 with average temperatures at -35° F that lasted into the early spring. They decided after a few short weeks that it wasn't cold enough, so they went to Churchill for further trials. It was warmer there by ten degrees, -25° F! It tells you something of the mentality of the day! Running up and down the runway and burning out brakes that first year was making us wonder just what we were getting!

In 1961, some techs were sent to the States for the first of the '104 courses. Transistors were just coming into vogue at that time, so the electronic and communications techs had to relearn theories pertaining to transistor circuitry. It was quite a change from tube technology!

The '104 aircraft courses for all tradesmen were fully booked starting in January of 1962. That was when I took the airframe course.

Within weeks we started working on the first of the '104s; duals numbers 632, 633, 634 and 637. It soon became apparent that we had bought "pigs in a poke". The heat and vent system wound up becoming one massive problem that from the first day would keep these aircraft grounded instead of in the air. Fifty man hours on the ground for one hour in the air was proving that the cost effectiveness was atrocious. Furthermore, fibreglass ducting was blowing up in the electronics bay. It should have been heavy-walled aluminum or even steel ducting. It wasn't that this was occurring occasionally, it was all the time! Our supply system couldn't keep enough of this ducting in stock.

Another bad problem that was always ongoing was air entrapment in the hydraulics of the #1 and #2 flight control systems. The pilots' complaint would be of a vibrating aileron or elevator and rudder control surface. More often than not, we would spend half a day bleeding the hydraulic system to get maybe two hours flying time, only to repeat this procedure if not every day, at least every third day.

Because the landing shock load on this aircraft was in excess of 50,000 pounds, what was called a liquid spring was used for damping purposes. It was charged with a silicon oil to 1100 pounds "plus". This unit was an absolute nightmare! It was ALWAYS being replaced. If you looked at the strut it would leak. If you glared at it, those bloody seals would blow, and you would have silicon oil all over the tires and brakes!

From the airframe point of view, this aircraft was, is, and always will be a flying disaster... a garbage bucket with an engine in it.

Above: *In this unusual photograph taken near Cold Lake, '789 and a 434 Squadron CF-5 are formating on a privately owned Hawker Sea Fury.*

Very strong words from John, and lasting impressions that were not generally held by the Starfighter maintenance community. However, John's impressions of that period are indicative of the concern felt by the maintainers for the long term health of the aircraft, and the ability to "put rubber on the ramp". In the fullness of time though, as systems experience increased and innovative maintenance procedures were adopted, the serviceability rate improved dramatically.

Life for the RCAF servicemen and their families at Cold Lake during this time-frame was not exactly the gracious living being enjoyed by their confrères in the Air Division. The official 417 Squadron History explains...

In the early 1960s, when 6 ST/R OTU was formed, the description of RCAF Station Cold Lake as "semi-isolated" had real meaning. To get to Cold Lake from Edmonton required an all-day ride on one of the slowest passenger trains in North America, or a bone-jarring 185 mile drive over what was wishfully described as a gravel road. Once in Cold Lake, the majority of personnel lived in barracks if single, or in one of the 1055 married quarters. Along with the married quarters, the Service had built three schools, two chapels, a 40-bed hospital, a small shopping area, and a recreation centre complete with a movie theatre.

To fill the off-duty time for the 7000 people on the base, approximately one-third of whom were servicemen, eleven team sports, fourteen individual sports, and sixteen groups and clubs were available. The surrounding area abounded with fish and game for those who were inclined to fish and hunt. Despite the emphasis on sports and clubs, 1600 babies were born at the Cold Lake Hospital between 1954 and 1964; a birth rate higher than that in Calcutta.

Part of the rationale for the remote location of the base at Cold Lake was to cause a minimum amount of disruption to Canadian citizens, while simultaneously maximizing training benefits. However, the Starfighter community there soon found out that, contrary to expectations, the CF–104 produced a very loyal and supportive following amongst a majority of the northern Alberta residents. Dan Rooks, a civilian who lived near the training area explains...

My experience with the Starfighter was that of a civilian who lived along one of the low level training routes frequently used by 417 Squadron out of Cold Lake. I had at that time lived about 60 miles south of CFB Cold Lake near the town of Marwayne. This was farming and ranching country and although we had become used to jet traffic in the area it had, up to the early sixties, been in the form of CF–100s practicing intercepts.

This had not prepared us for the arrival of the Starfighter. The Canuck had been almost gentlemanly in its actions at fairly high altitude. It didn't make too much noise and you could usually see them coming from some distance off. The Starfighter made no such allowances. One moment you could be walking across a quiet field or pasture and the next, with no warning, there was a '104 about 500 feet over your head travelling hell bent for election. The noise was something else. It was loud... it was great! If ever a noise was beautiful, it had to be that of a Starfighter flying on the deck. We loved it!

Contrary to what some would like you to believe, we never suffered any ill effects from the low level flying. Neither did the domestic or wild animals, and this was in an area with a high concentration of low level flying over a period of many years. The aircraft were great to watch and we all looked forward to seeing them in the skies over our community.

Throughout the mid-sixties, the heavy training schedule continued, and although the CF–104 program was reaching maturity, the syllabus was continually adjusted and refined as threat intelligence assessments were modified and appropriate tactics evolved. Public relations work continued, and in the centennial year of 1967, crowds at airshows across the country thrilled to a display of low and fast precision flying by Flight-Lieutenant René Serrao in a Starfighter. In a special tribute to Canadian fighter aviation, René teamed up with Flight-Lieutenant Jake Miller in a CF–101 Voodoo for the season, performing a beautiful precision aerial ballet at many airshows throughout Canada.

On February 28th, 1968, the RCAF ceased to exist, the Canadian Armed Forces were born, and on March 11th, 6 ST/R OTU was officially renamed 417 Strike/Reconnaissance Operational Training Squadron (417 6 ST/R OTS). In November of that year, the STU at Chatham closed its doors upon retirement of the venerable and much-loved Sabre. Low-level indoctrination training was henceforth to be carried out in the newly-purchased CF–5 Freedom Fighter at CFB Cold Lake. However, introduction of the new jet took longer than anticipated, and one group of aspiring CF–104 pilots received transitional training in the WT–33 at Rivers, Manitoba. Nonetheless, by April 1969, a resurrected 434 "Bluenose" Squadron was up and running in the fighter pilot training business with their brand new CF–5 aircraft. Almost immediately, a friendly rivalry started between the CF–5 and CF–104 squadrons, and this included some rather derisive remarks about the other communities' "mounts". Popular CF–5 name calling of the day included "the 72/72nd-scale model fighter", "just like a fighter, only smaller", and the ever-popular war cry, "eat 'em alive in the CF–5".

Throughout 1970, the expertise in both Strike and Reconnaissance was maintained on Squadron, while simultaneously, a great deal of work was being generated to develop tactics for the upcoming Conventional role. Also, dating from March 1971, air combat maneuvering was included as part of the Conventional conversion package, along with air-to-ground weapons and tactics. In the spring of that year, the OTU underwent yet another name change, to 417 Tactical Fighter (Operational Training) Squadron. 417's peacetime roles were also reviewed, and eventually evolved as follows:

1. to train CF–104 pilots to a Limited Combat Ready (LCR) status for duties with 1 CAG;
2. to provide proficiency training in air combat maneuvering, weapons, and ultra-low level navigation as required for 1 CAG pilots;
3. to augment 1 CAG squadrons and have all 417 Squadron instructor pilots renew their Combat Ready status on a annual basis; and
4. to train selected 1 CAG Combat Ready pilots to the level of Fighter Weapons Instructor through a highly-specialized "postgraduate" training course.

The peacetime training sojourn each year to Europe was actually done in response to a wartime role, since in the event of hostilities, the majority of 417's instructor pilots were to be war task assigned to the Air Group. The OTU instructors jealously guarded and greatly welcomed this annual requirement, since it allowed them to fly and "swap lies" with 1 CAG pilots for a couple of weeks each year, along with supporting the local economy by actioning Mother's shopping list at the Base Exchange, and recharging the "garlic batteries" through gracious dining across the Rhine in France.

Two other wartime roles were envisaged for 417, of which one was logical and understandable. That was, quite naturally enough, to continue to train LCR Starfighter pilots for the Air Group. The other war role was to augment existing air defence forces in the defence of North America against the manned bomber threat. This was real "Audie Murphy" tasking, since the '104 had no air-to-air missiles and, until 1974, no gun either. For some time prior to acceptance of the M–61 Vulcan 20 mm cannon, in the infancy (and unrealistic) days of CF–104 Air Combat Tactics, CF–104 pilot trainees were actually taught the dreaded ram tactic... The idea here was to approach the bomber co-heading from directly below, then commence a vertical pullup, neatly clipping off the enemy's horizontal stabilizer with a wing (!?) and then completing a successful ejection to live and fight another day. Hmmmmmm. Fortunately, the coming of the cannon obviated the need to pursue this nonsensical tactic, and the 417 instructors none-too-reluctantly "handed in their Samurai swords" on the issue.

Along with having a colourful and talented series of American and British exchange pilots on operational duties with the overseas Starfighter squadrons throughout the era, 417 Squadron was blessed with the talents of many fine exchange officers as well. Over the years of the program, the OTU was ably augmented by numerous American and British pilots, along with one each from Australia and the Federal Republic of Germany. Mike McCarthy was one of the American "jewels in the crown" from 1972 until 1974. This combat seasoned fighter pilot brought a great breadth of experience and maturity to the training establishment... not to mention an enduring Caesar Salad recipe that contained enough garlic to ward off a whole Wing of vampires! Mike recalls his Canadian experiences, and his time in the CF–104, with great fondness...

Like a lot of people, I don't always recognize major events in my life as they're happening. Such was the case with the CF–104. When I first saw it, sitting on the ramp at Eglin AFB in Florida that summer day in 1963, I had no idea it would play such a major role in my life. My Air Force nurse wife, who I had not even met yet, would leave the Air Force because of it. My daughter would be born in Edmonton because of the 'Zipper", her Godfather none other than the World's Oldest Fighter Pilot, Bill Ross... who I also hadn't met at that point. Thanks to the "Aluminum Death Tube", I would have the privilege of flying in a monster 36-ship flyby for Prince Philip... one of the more memorable events of my flying career. It would also determine the path of my career in the USAF to a considerable extent.

But that was all to come. On that summer day in 1963, I had stopped at Eglin AFB during a cross country flight, and the CF–104 was apparently there for testing of some sort at the Proving Ground. Why do I remember it 27 years later? Simply because it had absolutely no markings on it, save for a very small RCAF stencil somewhere on the fuselage. It looked like it had just come out of the factory, which it probably did... a piece of polished aluminum that looked like it was going a thousand miles an hour just sitting on the ground! Although the F–104 had been around the USAF inventory for some time, this was the first Canadian "Zipper" that I had ever seen. I remember remarking to my friend George McKenna, that "I'd give anything to fly that airplane". I don't know if I ever got to fly that particular airplane, but a decade later, my dream came true. I had assignment as an Exchange Officer at Cold Lake, Alberta and I was going to fly the fabulous CF–104...I was the envy of all my friends, and life could not have been sweeter!

The summer of 1972 was a time of transition for me in more ways than one. I was a 31 year old USAF Captain, flying F–4Es as an Instructor Pilot in the Replacement/Training unit at Homestead AFB, outside of Maimi. I'd been there since 1969, when I returned to the States after flying 124 missions from Ubon, Thailand during the Southeast Asian war. By then, I'd met my lovely wife alluded to above, and she was the proud new owner of a fighter pilot...me! Linda was also a Captain, and was assigned as a nurse at the base hospital. During the spring, I'd seen an announcement saying that an exchange pilot was urgently needed for a tour at Cold Lake. I had always wanted an exchange assignment, and wasted no time in making the necessary calls to the personnel people. The Luck of the Irish prevailed, and a few months later I had the assignment... but there was a catch. Since there was no position available for Linda at Cold Lake; she would have to leave the Air Force in order for me to take the assignment. Obviously, she chose to separate, and it was probably a decision that she would have made at some point anyway, since the Air Force wouldn't allow pregnant women to remain on active duty. Nonetheless, it was a difficult choice for her...one that I did not fully grasp at the time. At any rate, my new civilian wife and I packed everything into a Porshe 914 that July and headed North. The "Canadian Experience" was about to begin!

When we arrived at Cold Lake, new runways were under construction, so I actually ended up checking out in the airplane at Namao, in Edmonton. 417 Squadron was deployed there for a good portion of the summer, which was not too bad, since it was only 180 miles away. However, I'll never forget my first night! We stayed in the Grand

Photo by Bill Johnson

Centre Hotel, which even now seems like something out of an old John Wayne movie... brass beds, and bar fights going on downstairs at all hours. Since our quarters weren't ready yet anyway, we made a quick decision to spend the checkout phase in Edmonton. For the next few weeks, we ended up at the Greenbriar Hotel in downtown Edmonton, and I would go out to CFB Namao every day to fly.

I had never flown any version of the '104 before, and most of my time had been spent in the various versions of the F–4 Phantom, and in Training Command. Fortunately, the CF–104 had basically the same engine as the Phantom, so that part was pretty easy to master. I was teamed up with Ray Dunsdon for my first few rides, and off we went! What do I remember about it, and what were the differences? For starters, the feeling of acceleration was much greater in the '104 than in the F–4. The Phantom was much heavier, and consequently more sluggish on takeoff roll. In the Lockheed/Canadair Special, when you lit the burner, you knew something was going to happen! Since you sat much closer to the ground, you definitely felt like you were riding the world's fastest tricycle. With a takeoff speed of 219 knots fully loaded, you probably were! The heavier stick forces soon became instantly apparent. The CF–104 was an incredibly stable airplane, mostly because of its extremely high wing loading ("what wing?" the skeptics would ask). Wherever you put the airplane, it would stay there until you moved it. Not so the F–4. It had a very sensitive flight control system, and while you eventually got used to it, it was never fully satisfactory. Even looking in the cockpit to check fuel while in formation would cause you to bobble... very difficult to trim up in formation. This led directly to my next observation about the CF–104. Since it had a "T-Tail", the airplane was susceptible to pitch up. At very high angles of attack, the wings would blank out the airflow over the high tail, which meant that the lift from the tail was no longer balancing out the lift from the wings. Thus, the aircraft would pitch up and go out of control. Since it required all the air in hyperspace, and then some, to recover, this was not a good thing. To protect those not attuned to this sort of thing, Lockheed installed a stick shaker which would shake the stick to tell you that your aggressive maneuvering was about to get you in a lot of trouble....it was a gentle hint to "lighten up". If you were slow of brain, and long on courage (a bad combination!) and continued to pull on the pole, it would eventually kick forward with a force of 50 pounds. Now this is healthy, and would definitely get your attention. If you still kept pulling, you would indeed experience the dreaded pitch up. Pulling too abruptly would also cause you to go right past the normal angle of attack warnings faster than you could say, "Kelly Johnson"; so the kind citizens at Lockheed also rigged the stick shaker system to activate if you pulled on the stick too suddenly. Since I was used to rapidly moving the stick in the F–4, where it didn't have the same effect, I was doing the same thing in the '104... and encountering almost constant rate shaker. I remember checking out an F–104A pilot in the F–4 at Homestead. He couldn't seem to get the beast settled down, and was overcontrolling the first few rides. Now I was having the opposite problem. It took a few minutes to convince Ray that I wasn't spastic. Once you got used to it, it was a much better control system. This was very noticeable at low altitudes and high speed. Whereas the F–4 was rather goosey at 500 plus knots close to the ground (the manual even recommended locking the shoulder harness to prevent getting into a pilot induced oscillation, for gods sake!), the '104 was rock solid. Pushing the power up just meant you had to retrim.

My checkout did require that I learn a new language. I found that the Canadian Air Force used a mixture of USAF and RAF English. On my first pattern, the tower asked me if I was going to overshoot? Since I was on final, and lined up right down the centerline of the runway, I said, "No". In USAFese, an overshoot means you didn't turn enough to get lined up with the runway, and might have to go around. In

Canadian parlance, it meant "was I going around." "Reheat (after burner), undercart (landing gear), Mess (Officer's club), and pissed (drunk) posed similar problems until I mastered my new environment. I even learned the Canadian all purpose word - "eh?"

Time passed quickly, and my checkout continued back at Cold Lake. Some other impressions during those first few months are still vivid even now, many years later. The CF–104 was a perfect example of form following function. Everything about the airplane was there for a purpose, and the design was extremely efficient. The cockpit mirrored this concept, and you could reach everything easily without contortions. All the instruments were very close to the pilot, and well laid out. Even changing the radio at night in weather formation was simple, since it was right in front of you on the instrument panel. Trying to accomplish this same simple task in an F–4 was enough to make a grown fighter pilot cry! In many respects, the "Zipper" was years ahead of its time, even in the early 1970s. Perhaps the best illustration was going Mach 2, or twice the speed of sound. You just took off in afterburner, and left it on, climbed at 450 knots until you got to .9 Mach, then climbed at that airspeed (indicated airspeed varies with altitude, so it's easier to fly a constant Mach number... saves computing airspeeds in your head). When you reached the tropopause, around 36,000 feet, you just leveled off, still leaving the afterburner going. Going supersonic was no big deal. The only way you knew it had occurred was a slight change in cabin pressure and the instruments jiggled for a second. I could usually sense it in my ears without looking at the gauges. All the while the bird was very stable... nothing like Chuck Yeager's X–1 in "The Right Stuff". The acceleration increased around 1.4 Mach, and the dial just kept on inching up the Machmeter. When you got around 1.8, the airplane started to yaw a bit, but not bad. Finally, at Mach 2.0 or 2.1, you would get a little light that started flashing "SLOW" in red. This meant that the compressor inlet temperature was getting too hot from the friction of all the air passing over it and you had to slow down. Coming out of burner at that point was like hitting a wall... you really slowed down rapidly. However, what knocked my socks down was the fact that the airplane was still accelerating, even when the "SLOW" light came on. To top it off, you still had plenty of fuel left to fly for another 45 minutes! Doing this same stunt in the F–4 was a major test of your knowledge of physics. You had to fly a complicated profile where you climbed, then unloaded until you hit a certain Mach number, climbed at that airspeed, unloaded again until you hit a higher Mach number, and then climbed until you hit Mach 2. You usually hit it in a climb, headed for the moon. When you finally got there, you pulled out of burner, rolled over, and started looking for a place to land because you were getting pretty short of fuel. I think I topped out at 50,000 feet or so the first time I tried it. Here I was at Cold Lake, in an airplane built well before the Phantom that did it effortlessly...amazing! That's what I mean about it being years ahead of its time.

Now I probably sound like I'm bashing the F–4, but I'm really not. "Double Ugly" got me through many combat missions during our Great Patriotic War, and I will always have a soft spot for it deep down in my pancreas. It could also turn reasonably well, given the performance standards of the day. This I quickly found was something Kelly Johnson's little hot rod could **not** do. Over the top manoeuvres, like loops, were truly a test of one's manhood, especially for the uninitiated. A real thrill ride the first couple of times, and high aviation adventure. You'd rocket down to 10,000 feet or so, and pick up 450 knots in burner, or 550 in military power, and then start the pull heavenward. By the time you had the nose pointing straight up, you put the flaps to the "takeoff" position. This fooled the airplane into thinking it had a wing. You'd finally stagger over the top somewhere near Neptune with about

Above: Engine run up on a cold winter's night at CFB Cold Lake.

*150 knots. On a good day, this might be 24,000 feet... a mere three miles of sky! Now the next part **really** surprised me. At full power, and low airspeed, the engine had enough torque to actually turn the airplane around its vertical axis. Here you are on your back, trying to maintain a straight path, and the nose is actually yawing! You had to use rudder and aileron to keep it straight. I'd never experienced that before. Now you started the downhill slide, and hopefully remembered to pull the flaps back up as you went through 450 knots on the way down. A variation of this was the 450 knot military power loop...strictly for closet masochists with a latent death wish. Getting over the top, with any semblance of airspeed required correct technique on the pull. Too much, and you bled off the airspeed, still headed straight up. Too little, and the same thing happened, but it took longer. Nice way to learn about the stick shaker system. Actually, it wasn't all that bad...but it did get your attention the first few times. As you may have deduced, a turning fight with another lightly loaded airplane was not the CF–104's forté. Best to separate and come into the fight with more of an advantage. But then, it was never designed to do that. Originally conceived as a point interceptor, it found a niche as a low altitude Strike fighter, especially in the German and Canadian versions. All things considered, it was simply a great airplane to fly, and truly one of the classic fighter aircraft. Given its incredible performance, it was actually a very easy airplane to fly. It even floated on landing, which really came as a surprise.*

As summer turned into fall and then finally into winter, I learned why Cold Lake had the adjective in front of the noun. Every pilot should have the opportunity to take off at Cold Lake in a clean CF–104, when the outside air temperature is -50°. The first time I did it, I couldn't believe it! I could only run the engine up to about 80 percent before the tires started slipping on the pavement. I pushed the power up for takeoff, quickly checked the instruments, and lit the burner. Now things really started to happen! I got airborne in what seemed to be about three feet, and pulled the gear up as quickly as I could so the gear limit speed of 260 knots wouldn't be exceeded. Cold Lake had a runway length of 12,000 feet, and by the time I passed over the end of it, I was at warp speed. That takeoff, and coming back into the pattern as #4 in a formation leaving contrails all throughout the pattern, are memories that I'll never forget. Certainly different than flying in the tropical climes that I was used to. In fact, during the really cold times, you could follow an entire dogfighting episode by just looking at the contrails which visually depicted the entire battle, from the surface to however high you went.

After my initial checkout in the airplane, I started flying with students, and life settled into a normal routine. I was very impressed with the calibre of pilots I flew with, both the students that came through 417 Squadron, and the instructors and operational pilots that I encountered. We were also a rather international outfit since the unit had two other exchange officers; Merv Paine of the RAF and Dave Leach of the RAAF. Merv somewhat rattled the Canadian Customs officials once when he and I returned from a cross country trip to the States in two of the single seaters. When asked, "How many on board, and what nationality?", he startled them by saying, "One Brit and one Yank, in two Canadian airplanes!" Merv was full of little tricks like that. In a previous life, Dave Leach, the Australian, and myself both flew at Ubon Royal Thai Air Base in Thailand. He in the Avon Sabre, which was very similar to the Canadian Mk–6 Sabre, and myself in F–4Ds. We didn't really know each other at that time, but made up for that at Cold Lake.

But back to my impressions of Canadians...I found them somewhat of a combination between the USAF and the RAF. I was very impressed with how the Canadians gave the pilot credit for having some common sense. Even a young pilot was given broad guidelines, and the system had much more flexibility than what I was used to. When I returned to the USAF, I found it difficult to return to the more structured environment. I attributed part of their attitude to the fact that Canada had a relatively small force, and that they were very selective about to whom they gave pilots' wings. They had very few weak sisters. Most of the pilots I ran into were more concerned about being professional pilots, and weren't consumed by "careerism". Perhaps for this reason, they tended not to take themselves so seriously, which I found refreshing. They all seemed to take great pleasure in being the best they could in their jobs and found fulfillment in that. They did not appear to be constantly looking for the next rung on the ladder as so many of my USAF peers seemed to be. The fighter force was of such a size that most of the pilots knew all the other fighter pilots and their capabilities. I especially admired the way they were given credit for being able to figure things out for themselves...micromanagement was a rare thing. Unification had been in force for several years, but was not enthusiastically embraced by the pilots that I knew. They still preferred their separate identity, which indeed is what they went back to a few years later. Probably as a group, they were the best collection of pilots that I came across. I don't say that because I'm writing this piece...they honestly were. Their low level capability, especially in Europe, was absolutely fantastic. A most noteworthy group of aviators.

A few other memories stand out. The flyby for Prince Philip took place at Baden in the spring of 1973 when all three squadrons received their colors for being in service for 25 years. I was over in Europe for the annual rotation of pilots between Cold Lake and Baden, and was fortunate to be in the flyby. Getting 36 airplanes in the sky at once, and joining up in a show formation is no small undertaking. It's very much a "crack the whip" affair for those furthest from the leader. A minor movement by the lead is magnified several times over by the time the last pilot in the formation makes it. We practiced it for two weeks, and it was just a lot of fun flying. In the USAF, that sort of thing is frowned upon, so you can see my fascination with the whole effort. I still have a picture of the 36 ship Diamond of Diamonds, and it brings back a fond memory every time I look at it.

I also had the opportunity to test the first Radar Homing and Warning gear that went into the CF–104. In my misspent youth, I angered enough North Vietnamese to the point that they fired a considerable number of Surface to Air Missiles (SAMs) and Flak at myself and my friends. The area around Hanoi was especially terrible, and so consequently I had seen a lot of real life radar warning indications, and knew what it was supposed to look like. Al DeQuetteville was the detachment commander for some testing at Eglin AFB where they had some real SAM–2 and other Soviet radars that we could fly against. My job was to see if it really worked as advertised. Unfortunately, it didn't the first few times. The manufacturer kept trying to convince everyone that what we were seeing was normal, but it most certainly was not. Al stuck to his guns, and eventually it got fixed, but it took a lot of head scratching before it was resolved. Engineers would have you believe otherwise, but electronic warfare is still a lot of black magic, and things don't always work the way they should. In this case, it was caused by a lot of radio frequency reflections bounding around inside the antennae housing that picked up the signal. It took a bit of redesign, and some stuffing of styrofoam to absorb reflected signals, but eventually the problem was solved.

I always remember the experience, because when I returned from that five week trip to the States at 2:00 a.m., the Fair Linda informed me that I was soon to become a father! Thus, three months before I ended my tour at Cold Lake, my Canadian, Erin, was born after a wild ride on a Dakota to the hospital at Edmonton. A perfect ending to a perfect experience.

So there you have it! I have often remarked that the two years I was associated with the CF–104 were the happiest of my life. It was a rare blend of new experiences, a different perspective that I acquired, and the sheer fun of flying one of the world's truly classic airplanes that made it so memorable. At the time I saw the first CF–104 in the early sixties, I had no idea that all this was in store for me. Today, I pass by a Luftwaffe F–104G daily that's parked on the lawn near my office at Luke AFB, Arizona. It never fails to elicit a memory similar to those I've described above. A remarkable airplane (or aerodyne, as Ed Rozdeba used to say) and a remarkable experience. To paraphrase Ernest Hemingway, "It was good and true."

By 1973, 417 Squadron was training about 24 pilots per year on four separate courses for 1 CAG. Also in that year, the Squadron checked out three Norwegian fighter pilots in the aircraft, so that they might form their own Operational Training Squadron. This was done in the wake of a 22 aircraft sale to Norway that year on stocks that were viewed as surplus to needs. (A similar sale of CF–104s to Denmark had occurred two years earlier). As no one envisaged that the CF–104 would remain in service until 1986, inevitably there would be times downstream of these sales that the Canadian Starfighter community would rue the day they parted with their "surplus" jets. Also in the summer of 1973, the first Fighter Weapons Instructor Course (FWIC) since the Sabre era was planned and run by the OTU. Its stated aim was to provide weapons and tactics expertise on the squadrons overseas, and a limited number of these courses were also obtained out-of-country, at the USAF/GAF Fighter Weapons School at Luke Air Force Base in Phoenix, Arizona. From 1976 onwards, the Canadian FWIC was run jointly by 417 Squadron and 419 Squadron, the CF–5 training community of the time; 434 Squadron having moved to Chatham and left the fighter pilot training business behind.

The summer of 1974 marked the first Dissimilar Air Combat Training (DACT) exchange visit, at which time 417 hosted Naval Fighter Squadron VF–201 from Dallas, Texas in their F–8 Crusaders to an event that would become a tradition. This first exchange, known as STARCRUS '74, provided invaluable training in a role where current Canadian operational expertise was sadly lacking. The objectives of the DACT exercise were as follows:

1. to enhance pilot knowledge and proficiency through dissimilar fighter-versus-fighter engagements;
2. to expose pilots of both squadrons to the latest and most viable Air Combat Maneuvering concepts of the other;
3. to provide a realistic training program for the resident Fighter Weapons Instructors Course; and
4. to validate the air-to-air tactics employed by both squadrons.

Over the years, a long and enduring friendship evolved between "Navy Dallas" and 417, which continued after VF–201 transitioned to the two-place F–4 Phantom in 1977. The professionalism of the post-engagement debriefs improved considerably over the years as well, as things evolved from who could rant and rave the loudest, to the advent of the instrumented Air Combat Maneuvering Range and the placement of Airborne Instrumentation System (AIS) pods on the CF–104. Thus, emerging technology took the "cheat" out of ACM, and the proof was there for all to see in the post-flight evaluation of the mission tapes. The STARCRUS, and the later STARPHAN series of DACT exchanges were also augmented by exchanges with several other American fighter units, including VF–154 and VF–301 from Miramar Naval Air Station, San Diego, California.

- photo by Nancy Johnson

Along with a considerable number and variety of formal instructional duties, 417 "staffers" occasionally performed a number of other diverse flying activities, such as ferrying various dignitaries to CFB Cold Lake for sundry purposes. Ray Dunsdon vividly recalls one such event, when he and Al French were tasked to bring the legendary Lockheed F–104 test pilots Glen "Snake" Reaves and Tony LeVier from the Palmdale facility to Cold Lake for the ten-year CF–104 reunion in 1972. Ray would probably have been more appreciative of Snake's flying skills had he not been so preoccupied with viewing his life flashing in front of his eyes...

Al French and I flew two duals to Palmdale, and brought back Snake Reaves and Tony LeVier. Tony hadn't flown a CF–104 for over seven years; Snake only flew to put on his five-minute demo. At any rate, Snake and Tony did all the flying on the way back to Cold Lake. The formation takeoffs, etc. were terrifying, and when we arrived at Cold Lake, Tony and Al landed. I advised Snake that he was cleared to do his show. He started the display 20 feet above the end of the runway, 420 knots, 10–20 degrees nose up, and then performed an 8-point roll. I was sure we were dead, but I couldn't bail out inverted that low. He completed a perfect 8-point roll and levelled out at 420 knots, 20 feet above the runway. As the time was close to 6:00 p.m., most people had moved to the Mess. I pointed out its location and Snake flew by at about 20 feet. I was happily waving at friends on the front balcony when he started a series of snap rolls; about four, I think. Then for his landing, he was into stick shaker all the way around final turn, pulled the 'chute 20 feet in the air, landed and turned off the runway in less than 1000 feet, as smooth as silk!

During the mid- and late-seventies, 417 Squadron proudly demonstrated the Starfighter to the public whenever possible. A three-aircraft formation team, known successively as the Deadeye Zips, then the Alberta Arrows, regaled audiences across the nation with their precision manoeuvres from 1976 until 1982. Additionally, many other individual airshows and flypasts were performed by Squadron members over the years, in support of numerous celebrations and community events.

The Starfighter was certainly an airshow crowd pleaser. However, there was a bit more to being a summer display pilot in the Zipper than the public could ever imagine. Laurie Hawn, one of 417's stellar Instructor Pilots of the era, recalls...

No Sir, we never went below 300 feet

Well, after watching all the fun that Ron Doyle, John Bagshaw and Dave Burroughs had flying airshows in 1976, I decided that the Deadeye Zips were for me. The 1977 version of this supersonic trio was to include John Bagshaw as Lead, myself as Two, and Dave Bligh as Three. Like garlic-breath, we couldn't get rid of Burroughs entirely, and he was to figure prominently in one of our more spectacular feets. I used the word "feets" intentionally, because that's what we stuck in our mouths more than once.

After a warmup at Meadow Lake in April, we got down to some serious practice trying to perfect what, for us, were a couple of unique moves. These included coordinated dirty-clean 360 degree turns, with the clean aircraft doing two of them at 6 to 7 "Gs" around the dirty aircraft doing one with gear land flap hanging. We were inspired by the Blue Angels doing clean/dirty loops in their Skyhawks, but decided that it would be easier in the '104 if we turned the manoeuvre on its side. We also tried hard at doing a mirror pass with Lead and Two in canopy-to-canopy knife-edge passes. It wasn't too bad except when each guy tried to correct to the other, and then we looked like a mirror pass of two windshield wipers. With three aircraft, the intent was to keep someone in front of the crowd all the time... well, most of the time... alright, occasionally. After a few other passes, we'd finish off with opposing high speeders and a rejoin to a bomb-burst head-on to the showline. Part of the year we were allowed to be aerobatic, and we'd include rolling manoeuvres and a roll-under break. We decided that it was dumb to alternate aerobatic and non-aerobatic shows, so we took a little fighter pilot licence as to where and when we did the aero shows. I'm not sure why we didn't get fired once or twice.

Did I mention Burroughs? On April 28th, we were to take four aircraft to Comox to put on a show for the Royal Roads graduation parade. Showing a distinct lack of judgement, we asked Burroughs to be Number Four. Due to aircraft availability problems, we proceeded to Comox in dribs and drabs. Baggy went first so that he could do a quick recce trip down to Roads. Then all went well until, on the way back to Comox, he espied one of Her Majesty's Canadian Boats cruising the coast. Ever the benevolent one, Baggy decided to brighten the poor fishheads' lives with a touch of the sound of freedom. Make that several touches, with a sledgehammer. As he pulled off from his last pass, he realized that they were really getting into the spirit of the whole thing by setting off smoke charges for his reciprocal enjoyment. The fact that he was partaking of their live-fire exercise only became clear on return to base when he was met by an adoring Base Operations Officer (BOpsO) who had just gotten off the phone with one of Her Majesty's Senior Canadian Boat People. No sense of humor, those fishheads.

We didn't stop there. Burroughs and I were next to depart Cold Lake and, unbeknownst to us at the time, we would nearly top Baggy's

Above: *An unusual front quarter view of AETE's '704 near Cold Lake, 1983.*

stunt in spectacular fashion. We had filed off just in time to make it to Comox before the airfield closed for a practice by the Snowbirds. Enroute at altitude, Burroughs had an inadvertent kicker and lost the hydraulic generator. He turned off the Automatic Pitch Control, but didn't say anything to me. Why be a wimp? As we approached Comox, we had just enough time for one low pass. Not knowing about his previous problem, I put Burroughs in line astern and lined up on the ramp. Ahead lay the line of Snowbirds with engines running, and Baggy now in Cat Beaulieu's[1] other seat. Beyond the 'Birds was a line of 409 Squadron Voodoos, and several 407 Squadron Arguses. We approached at a stately 540 knots...or so, and a couple of hundred feet...or so. "Take that, you dog-whistles," I say as we scream overhead with burners cooking. "Very impressive," comes the very sarcastic voice of Gord Wallis, who is Snowbird Lead. "Just jealous," I think to myself. Then Tower comes up and says, "Zip Two, are you OK?" "Hey, what's going on back there? I'm Lead; I have a right to know." I look down at the shadow and, to my shock, I see only one aircraft silhouette. "Burroughs, check in; are you OK?" Burroughs finally comes up, a little shaken, rejoins and we proceed to initial and land. To back up, just as we approached the Snowbirds, Burroughs either got into my jetwash or had the kicker fire. Afterwards, Baggy said that if we could harness that pitch rate, we wouldn't have to take crap from any of those F–5 pukes anymore. He said that one second we were in line astern; the next he was looking at Burroughs' top planform; the next he was looking at the bottom planform, and then at the top again. Baggy still doesn't know how he missed me. Anyway, this little act caught the 'Birds just as Lead had called the brake release for taxi. Baggy said it was the greatest bomb-burst he had ever seen, even if it was only in two dimensions! There were Tutors scattered everywhere. Burroughs, in the meantime, was riding out the gawdamnedest Pilot Induced Oscillation he had ever seen, when everything went black. He could faintly hear voices around him and came to the immediate conclusion that he was, in fact, dead. Not a totally unjustified conclusion, really. After a few more seconds, the voices persisted and Dave realized that they were talking through his nose. So he took his helmet off, rotated it 90 degrees, put it back on, and did up the chinstrap. Whereupon, we proceeded to land and be met by the same adoring BOpsO.

We're not done yet. That night in the back bar, we're reliving the day's adventures with a couple of Golden Throat Charmers (the beer, not the Snowbirds). There's a bunch of other troops around, when in walks the Minister of National Defence, Barney Danson. Geez, I didn't realize we were in that much trouble! No sweat. Barney's on a visit to the coast and has wandered away from the Base Commander's reception in search of some real company. He is soon on a first name basis with everyone there. About thirty minutes later, a panicky, distraught, and subsequently livid Colonel Mortimer comes charging into the back bar looking for his lost Minister. Accusing us of contributing to the delinquency of a Minister of the Crown, he led Barney away, at the latter's protest.

Not done yet. The next day we're set to do the thing at Roads. Remember Roads? We do, and it's blessedly uneventful until we return to base. In one of his more lucid moments the night before, Baggy has promised Terry Hallett that we'll do a flyby over his house. Well, Terry's house is in the middle of Courtenay. But Baggy is a man of his word, and we did the deed, much to Terry's delight and his neighbours' not-so-delight. For good measure, we also do a pass over the Mess, as it's now past bar-time. What we forget here, of course, is that the Base Hospital is right across the road. Anyway, to make a long story short, our season is off to a great start. Colonel Mortimer calls Pete DeSmedt to disinvite the Deadeye Zips to the Comox Airshow later in the year, and requests that we never darken his doorway again.

Above: *Converting jet fuel into noise, the Alberta Arrows climb for altitude during an airshow rehearsal over northern Alberta, 20 May, 1977. Lead, John Bagshaw; Left wing, Dave Bligh; Right wing, Laurie Hawn.*

- DND photo by Vic Johnson

A couple more shows follow in Portage and Alsask. Just before Moose Jaw, we find out that for the Cold Lake Airshow, we are to be renamed the Alberta Arrows. It seems that someone wanted a CF–5 aerobatic team for this show, but 419 Squadron couldn't make it happen. What a name! But at least we'd be allowed to do some aeros. Moose Jaw was good, and then we had one week to become aerobatic. We used the excuse to generate a couple of practices each day, and felt ready to go. I don't think the Red Arrows were threatened, but three Aluminum Death Tubes going the speed of heat pushed by three screaming J–79s managed to get a few folk's attention.

The next weekend it was back to non-aerobatics again, and we were off to Minot for their airshow, which had been called Northern Neighbours Day (remember that name). With the exception of four '106s and four T–38s flying by once each at Flight Level Nosebleed, the entire show was Canadian.

Many of the social events were organized by Al Pietch, a veteran of many years on the airshow circuit. His airfield, Pietch Patch, is only a few miles south of Minot, and made an excellent place for altimeter checks. Except for Bligh forgetting his flaps on one turning pass and violating the show line by a mere mile, the flying went very well. The parties, on the other hand, were exceptional. Between Al Pietch's beer truck, a receptive O'Club, and a rowdy bunch of Canucks, we managed

[1] An ex-Starfighter pilot, but at the time of the story, one of the Snowbirds.

to make our mark. The Base Commander seemed genuinely interested in how we could keep up the pace. We assured him that it was just a matter of practice and opined that, perhaps next year, he should consider inviting the Mexican Air Force and calling it Southern Neighbours Day. He allowed as how that idea might have some merit.

Comox next. With a Change of Command parade, we were back on the list of invitees. As mentioned, we had decided that switching back and forth between show types was a pain in the ass. Our boss, Pete DeSmedt was there doing a Board of Inquiry on a Snowbird prang, so we thought we'd try the unauthorized aero show on him. What we forgot to do, however, was give the aero script to John Glover, who had offered to do the commentary. John would announce a "dirty" pass, and someone would come by in a slow roll; or a four point roll instead of the announced level 360 degree turn. After a couple of passes John caught on, and instead of announcing what we were about to do, he would comment on what we had just done. After the show, we waited for the axe to fall from the Boss, but all he said was "nice show" and bought us a beer. Licence to steal...

Abbotsford was the final show, and what a great place to finish off. With the weather and the displays, it's got to be the best airshow in the world. It sure brought our summer of great flying and fun to a fitting climax. The average trip that summer was .7 hours, and a lot of log book pages were filled with not much total time. The Zipper was a great airshow airplane, and I don't think I have ever had more fun out of a summer's flying.

One of the true joys of being an instructor pilot at 417 was the occasional opportunity to take an "enthusiastic amateur" flying. Since there were many CF–104Ds on Squadron strength, and "the pit" or rear seat was often superfluous to needs when an instructor was flying the aircraft solo, we used every opportunity possible to provide many service members with a taste of the Starfighter in action. Doug Keall was an armament technician at 417 Squadron in the late 1970s, and in 1 CAG until the CF–104 close-out and beyond. Along with being a Starfighter fan *par excellence*, Doug is an accomplished aviation artist who has often used the CF–104 as his subject. Doug's enthusiasm for the jet is patently obvious in this recollection of two training flights made with 417 Squadron instructors back in 1977...

It's a short enjoyable walk to the servicing shack where the pilot stands at the counter and asks for the book on the airplane like it was a hamburger. I stand behind him listening to the ignorant comments from the groundcrew and trying to figure out how to put a pair of turquoise ear defenders on my head with one hand.

The smoke is so thick it hurts my eyes, and the smell of grease pencils and that horrible coffee is almost too much. Out onto the flight line, walking that funny walk that you have to do wearing that parachute, and always the tinkling and jangling. From the back all the airplanes look the same, but I'm looking for one that has 639 painted on it, so inevitably you have to change direction halfway out there because you can finally make out the numbers on the airplanes, and you started out the wrong way. It always looks like you are lost. A great way to start a trip in a Starfighter.

Other sounds start to drown out my tinkling and jangling; things like the weird sound of the mules and start units, refuelling bowser farts, two-way radios blaring, the chirp chirp of another jet landing, practice bombs being cranked up on racks.

I finally find the airplane with 639 painted on it. There is a large air hose laying under it, and a thick rubber electrical hose plugged in causing the navigation lights to flash. Stepping into the heel piece of each spur and bending down to strap it on. Clop, clop, clop, clop.

Snapping in the two top ends of my chute, the two bottom ends go down through the loop between my legs and back up snapping into the same "box" with a satisfying metallic click. Rotate the box, tighten up the chute, and stand there hunched up like an idiot while the ground crew take their time rolling up the "remove before flight" streamers on the canopy jettison safety pins.

Finally, you take the first of six short steps up the ladder, leaving the ground. Left leg in over the sill and stand on the seat, bring the other leg in and step down into the wells, grabbing the canopy rail for balance and feeling with the spurs on your heels for the steel balls; snap...that's one...fumble fumble snap... that's two; sit down and tighten up the chute some more, then clip the survival seat pack to the parachute on both sides... clip clip... and seat pack lanyard to the right shoulder of the chute harness. Next grab the lap belts, lengthen them a bit, pull the nylon tab on the chute auto release arming cable, and slide the key into the key slot on the right lap belt.

Hopefully there is a guy on the ladder who hands you the shoulder harness from behind, one on each side, and you fit the oversized loops on the oversized bar on the left lap belt. Fasten lap belts together and lock centre; tighten lap belt, both sides evenly and as tight as you can get it.

Now to reach down and lock the entire harness and tighten the shoulder harness; keep in mind this is all being done within about a minute. And I'm not completely strapped in yet!

Again hopefully, the groundcrew has taken the helmet out of the blue helmet bag and rested it on the glare shield in front of me.

I'm removing the turquoise ear defenders and handing them to the guy standing on the ladder; then quickly reaching for the helmet to get it on over my ears because of the noise. Helmet is on but hair sticking out; shooing it back under (where I'll sweat more), and putting on gloves, reaching back with your right hand, it meets the green rubber oxygen hose that the guy on the ladder shoves out somewhere from behind the seat. Match it with the end of hose coming from your loose mask; next emergency oxygen bottle in your chute is plugged into the same hose. Snap two flimsy plastic leads of the intercom cord together... HUMMMM...instant hot mike; explosion of his breathing, snap, snap, UHF preset channel. Snap to ATIS.

This Cold Lake ATC Information Bravo; Cold Lake weather two thousand scattered three thousand overcast; visibility four; haze; temperature five Celsius dewpoint one six, wind zero two zero at ten, altimeter two niner niner six; arrivals and departures on three zero left and right; inform Cold Lake ATC on initial contact you have received Information Bravo... This is Cold Lake Information Bravo; Cold Lake weather two thousand *click... the breathing again.*

"All set back there?" "Yes, Sir." "Okay." We wind her up. I look out of the cockpit in front. He's got his right arm extended first finger out and makes a winding sign to the start crew, high pressure turbine air thrusts its way into the guts of our huge J–79 engine and the needle on our RPM gauge climbs. One finger for each 10% RPM until just before 40% he makes the gloved "throat cut" motion across his neck. The sound is winding up as well, but still I can hear the breathing. The noise is deeper now and a very noticeable vibration, and with the hum of electronics in my ears, his exhaled breath becomes a whistle. Then the CSU is shut off and winds down rapidly as the groundcrew fold up the huge awkward heavy hoses.

As she winds up to sixty percent, he starts into the checklist:

Okay
RPM's steady
Hydraulics good
Nozzle good
Fuel flow good
Gyros steady
Tacan off STBY
IFF squawking

UHF Channel One
And speed brakes
Out...In...
Two controls
Watch your knees (my stick yards out...)
Forward, back, side, side
Back to neutral check
And indicators good
Land ...land
Barber Poles good
Four Takeoff flaps
and APC. *(Both of us staring at the Auto Pitch Control Gauge)*

As the ground crew tweaks the left blade, the stick between my legs violently shakes, gauge climbs to four and back down. Stick shaker good. Right blade tweaked and APC to five, and the violent forward thrust of the stick between my legs, good...

Channel One preset
Cold Lake Tower - Deadeye One Eight on the ramp...
Deadeye 18 cleared to taxi; time 0813.

Trims good. Inlet Temp, RPM, hydraulics good. Oil at 42 psi...good. Nozzles good - Temps good...fuel flow and quantity good ...seat pin out. *"Yours, Doug?" "Out." "Good." Ready to roll ...throttle jumps ahead slightly; we are moving. We take a bit of a lurching nose dive as he checks brakes, power...manual... and the pedals move as the nose swings. Needle going left, ball going right. Compass heading good. "Check your strap in, I'll check mine." Visors...chin strap...mask...oxygen normal. Normal test. Box is... Locked. Lanyard, lap belt, seat pack, spurs and seat pin is out. Brake, and both hands on sill.*

Two weapons techs stop us, and disappear under us doing a "last chance" inspection, pulling safety pins. Thumbs up...eat pin is out. We're rolling. More throttle. Canopy down. Locked. Three hooks and light out, and we taxi to the hammerhead of Three Zero Right. From Cold Lake Tower: "Deadeye One Eight, taxi into position and hold." Lining up with the centre of the runway... Brakes... ***Deadeye One Eight cleared for takeoff.*** *"All set back there?" "Yep!" "Okay." Brakes good. Oil pressure 42... good. Off the brakes. WHAM; afterburner. Just like a kick in the ass. Airspeed winding up 70... 80... 90 knots... rotate.*

The whole world of the edges of the runway is a perspective blur. Runway lights trying to tear your eyes from the RPM gauge. **BEEEBEEEBEEEBEEEB THUD THUD.** *Gear up, airspeed still winding up. Climbing out over the threshold.*

He starts to hum, but the hum comes out jagged in spurts as his voice box is bodily shaken...but he's used to this... he thinks it sounds like a lullaby soothing nerves ...he's right. We bank 30 degrees to heading One Five Zero. She's a bbitt bbumpy today. Still climbing to two thousand feet, heading west and looking for smoke in the sky.

"Okay Doug, you have control." (I have control?) Then my mind started to react...I have control! Gingerly, with my gloved right hand grasping the stick, I didn't know what to do; lost ,and miles behind this machine.

Not familiar with the seemingly hundreds of dials, switches, and gauges in front of me, it took time to find the ones I needed and read what they had to tell me; and time is what you don't have. "You have control," I said. "I have control," he replied with as much of a shrug as the harnesses would allow. I explained I wasn't quite up to all this yet. So he took over, thundering along at five hundred forty knots and two thousand feet.

We climbed out to about ten thousand to get a bigger picture. It took less than one minute. Just yard up on the stick, roll her over the top (inverted) then look around and roll out as you dive....but what happened was this! Eleven o'clock high, five miles... a '104; into a couple of "G" with a grunt we rolled inside... throttle jump... into a rolling scissors...showing our belly to him, maintaining 2 "G" in the turn... roll out 30 degrees and look.... back on 2 "G". Okayy, NOW we rolled out..."TAKATAKATAKA!!!" Just like a little kid! "GOTCHA!" Loud screaming metallic. We were alongside about 1/2 second, long enough to see. "Did you see who it was?", crushing under 4 "G"s. "Yes,

Above: *Doug Keall's cartoon jokingly suggests that OTU pilots may have occasionally been prepared to live with some minor servicing defects in order to allow the aircraft to remain serviceable for another flight.*

- courtesy of Doug Keall

I did," (gritting teeth)..."was Cotner." I still don't know if he saw us or not. He would never admit it, and rightly so. I hardly feel the 2 "G" now...on my first trip we got a kill! Yahoo!

The rest of the trip, we dropped down to a thousand feet in the slightly bumpy air; bouncing...tip tanks flexing the seven foot, steel wings. Constantly, the sound of his breathing; inhaling and exhaling coming through. My eyes drifted down...clock still ticking and headings tumbling back to stabilize. All the little arrows vibrating (from what I can tell with my rattling eyeballs)... DME is winding back slowly, altimeter varying slightly with the bigger air pockets, the smells...

Of the disinfectant on the clammy green rubber mask, my own sweat, the "cockpit" smell that I love so much, and the occasional fart (very important if you don't want your stomach to blow up)... get used to it.

So this is the feeling...the routine world of Chuck Yeager and Ivan Kinchloe... the clammy green rubber mask, your own breath echoing around in your head, the vibrations and that beautiful sun glinting off the canopy, and of the ...wandering mind jolted by a voice.

Click Click.

***417 OPS Deadeye One Eight** ...waiting*

Deadeye One Eight go ahead, Harv...

Is Keith flying now?

Ahhh, yes he is.

Thank you. We will be in green in about six minutes.

Click Click.

Tower Deadeye One Eight initial left...Deadeye One Eight Tower initial left...traffic F–5 on final two miles.

Ah, got him and ...This will be a full stop. One Eight full stop roger.

*Watching sideways down as the F–5 lands. Roll... compass swings 180 degrees; stopping at 300, we roll out and the runway is huge, swallowing us up. Heavy thudding sound, nose rotating down, heavy vibrations even to the bones ...shock, forward against the straps (he pulled the drag chute handle). "Seat pin can go in now, Doug." We pull off to one side. On the brakes. Nose lurching, sort of a quick "S" turn, and drop the chute on the side of the taxiway. (I finally get my pin in.) "Pin in okay". He opens his canopy, I reach over and unlatch, explosion of engine roar and cool air blast. We were on the ground already! Instantly finding out how wet my backside is from sweating, in the 40 knot winds of taxi. Instantly giving in to the temptation to rest both elbows on the sill, also instantly realizing how uncomfortable this is while still strapped in! Unlocking the shoulder straps from the lap belt produces another temptation...to flip those grey straps back over your shoulders. The way you've seen it done so often. I guess this action is unique to the C–2 seat, but it becomes a routine and enjoyable part of '104 flights. It's a semi-satisfying feeling... **living** through another flight long enough to be back on the ground rolling on three wheels.*

Three months and seven days later ... I forced myself up early,

Inset at left: *104 790 heads for the stratosphere on an air combat training sortie in 1975.*

donned my newly acquired flying suit and drove to another part of the field to chase down a particular pilot who had been rather civil in conversation with a mere armourer. I found him... we almost had a midair on the stairwell!

"Hi, aren't you the guy from Moose Jaw?" "No, but I was... (thinking)... I haven't flown with you yet." "What are you doing today?" "I'm just checking that out." Up the stairs two at a time. "Yeah. Ok. Ahh...what would you like to do?"

He's joking... what would I like to do? In a Starfighter with a chauffeur...a fighter jock with 2000 hours? 'Well...ahh...could we buzz my home town?" "North Battleford...isn't that too far?" he asks with a grin. "No," I said, "it's on Route 2." He looked... "Ok, why not?" We strapped in... some total stranger helping me. It was cold out... all strapped in. I looked around... a slightly different cockpit! (Oh my God, are they all different?)

Thinking back on our takeoff that morning, I was consciously aware of the contrails coming off our tips, T-tail and actual fuselage. This was a rush I was slow to forget! Heading to the southwest following the Beaver River ... over a few miles in a few seconds.

Suddenly I realized where we were approaching and already past... Chocin, Jackfish Lake!... between the highway and the lake (no need to navigate for awhile) and with a 7000 foot minimum altitude imposed, a nice 2 "G" bank over North Battleford. As we rolled out, I remembered that I was flying Bligh Airlines...he had been one of the Zips the year before. Switch to hot mike. "Can you show me some of those airshow type rolls...?"

The violence took me by surprise. CRASH! My helmet with my head inside against the canopy and my shoulder against the sill as the world spun... stopped...CRASH! Rocking back into my seat now upside down... CRASH! Why is this airplane beating me up? Rocking back into my seat... it must be 1 "G" all the way round... CRASH! Wings level.

*My heart beat coming back from six/eight time! Wow! Maybe I can relax...no? Oh well, I guess I did ask for the rolls! A nice sharp eight pointer not as violent as the four point. We pick up a reference lake and dig the map out of the knee pocket. Bombing along, I instantly sank into the welcome routine exhale, inhale, exhale, inhale ... in jerks and spurts through the wheezing clammy mask. Now I know. The Starfighter **does** have one of the highest roll rates.*

"Well, where are we now?" he asks as we dig out those route maps again. Study the shape of the lakes... climb... go inverted over the top..."there it is". Cranked over into a 4 "G". "Where? Oh yeah, Ok,

Photo above: *104 705 during AETE's 1974 BL-755 cluster bomb trials. The dramatic blue and white paint scheme on the weapons was designed to make for easier photographic tracking after release from the aircraft.*

Inset at right: *Sunrise on the California Desert. 417 Squadron frequently assisted the USAF Test Pilots School at Edwards AFB by allowing some of their students to fly some very specific flight test profiles from the front seat. An experienced OTU instructor pilot always "babysat" from the back seat...*

there," as he lowers the nose in a dive; we are pointing right at the lake and we're supposed to be doing 450 knots. A quick glance round the dials in front of me, looking for airspeed. There. It says 520. Out go the speed brakes (or as he likes to call them, the boards). We settle into the routine of navigation for a while. It is a comforting thing to do I find, as I get used to it. To travel this fast and know exactly where you are every second. It's very bbummmpy now. It only took a few seconds to slow down and flip the boards back in with his thumb. Exactly at 450!

I start to relax and enjoy things, but find when I do I'm hopelessly behind what is happening. Our breathing is still whistling irregularly in spurts. I'm constantly trying to build up saliva in my dry mouth to have something to swallow when the time comes.

The 4 "G" has loosened my mask a bit, so I'm cranking it on a little tighter with the little wheel beside my nose (realizing I would have liked to shave a little closer). My whole face has a thin clammy film of sweat.

Looking ahead now over my instrument panel, I see the back of his helmet as it disappears dipping forward. Probably digging something from the knee or calf pocket of his flying suit, I'm guessing. "Oh shit," he says. His head pops back upright and the stick jumps back between my knees. I start to feel the vise-like grip of "G" building up and instantly tense up in response, staying ahead of the rush of blood to my feet. I was about to ask him what was up when the throttle jumped forward, violent and ghostlike. "What's up?" (I guess we are!) In afterburner now, watching exhaust nozzle temp climb, altimeter winding up...using up that saved saliva, now swallowing it...ears grinding and popping. "Oh yeah, Doug...how are you back there? I almost forgot this is an airtest for pressurization...How're your ears?"

A very important question which would now be asked every few seconds. In less than a minute we were at 30,000 feet. Throttle back, out of afterburner, a little negative "G" over the top, level off, check differential pressure...it was lagging but coming up slowly. The Master Caution light came on, and half a second later the low fuel warning light came on. From this height, a TACAN lock-on to the base and a gentle nudge of the stick forward was reassuring. I still don't know if we could have glided back, but it didn't matter as it turned out we had plenty of fuel.

Well, six hundred pounds or so... gear down, flaps down. Anyway, landing was smooth and fast and uneventful. The tires always very rough feeling at first, and sounding very loud. Straining very hard forward against the straps as the chute popped.

Nose following the nosewheel behind us into a swerve onto the high-speed cutoff. Release the drag chute and pull the oversized lever on the canopy catch for the blast of cold wind and noise...rolling, taxiing over the gaps in the tarmac slabs. That same satisfied feeling and shit-eating grin came over me. The '104 is quite a lady, and I feel like I've just been laid.

Though the Cold Lake training area offered a high degree of realism in a host of tactical ways, the Canadian fighter community was always thirsting for experience in the most realistic combat training scenarios. For this reason, starting in 1977, Canadian Starfighter pilots deployed to Nellis Air Force Base in the Nevada desert to participate in the well-known Red Flag training exercise. Laurie Hawn flew Starfighters in Europe with 441 Squadron, and as an instructor at 417 Squadron from 1971 until 1978. He graphically describes what it was like to participate in one of these renowned exercises with a CF–104...

"Felon Two has a three-ringer at 6 o'clock!"

"Roger, Felons burners go!"

"OK, it's a pair of Fishbeds; keep extending!"

"They've broken off; come out of burner and check the Thuds at right, 2 o'clock high!"

"We're clear-SAM! SAM! left, 10 o'clock, take it down and pop some chaff!"

It's off us; lead has contact-pickle, pickle - NOW; burners go!"

"Your six is clear, let's get out of here!"

The Migs and the SAMs aren't real, but the radio calls and the pumping adrenaline are very real. For four weeks in 1977, '78 and '81, pilots from Canada and West Germany flying 417 Squadron CF–104 aircraft engaged in "combat" where the only element missing was the actual physical agony of getting shot down by anti-aircraft guns, surface-to-air missiles, or enemy aircraft. All seven tactical fighter squadrons of the CAF have been represented at Red Flag at Nellis AFB, Las Vegas, Nevada in what is the most realistic and valuable training exercise available.

Red Flag is an exercise run continuously since late 1975 by the Tactical Air Command of the United States Air Force. Among the many lessons relearned in Southeast Asia was the definite requirement for a training area where aircrew could learn and practice the skills that would enhance their chances of survival in actual combat. Historically, most aircrews have been shot down in their first ten missions - one mistake was all that separated them from a fiery death. The aim of Red Flag is to allow the crews to fly those first few missions, make the mistakes, and get "shot down". What is paramount is learning why you got shot down and what you can do about it next time.

Flying from Nellis, the exercise is conducted in the Nellis Tactical Range north of Las Vegas and the Fort Irwin Exercise Area to the southwest. Within these ranges are targets such as airfields, SAM sites, armoured convoys, industrial complexes, rail yards, tunnels, and troops. Also on the ground are a myriad of realistic enemy threat simulators operated by specialists whose job it is to "destroy" the Blue Force Capitalist Aggressors (Good Guys). Overhead the sky is dotted with Migs in the form of F5Es, F4 Phantoms, F15A Eagles, and F16s, who comprise the Red Force Pinkos (Bad Guys). To defend freedom and Mom's apple pie and strike a blow to the heart of the DRPCBs,[1] a balanced force of 100 aircraft from 25 units of the US Air Force, US Navy, US Army, US Marine Corps, Air National Guard, Air Reserve, RAF, and Canadian Forces are mustered. Blue Force aircraft types have included CF–104s, CF–5s, AV–8A Harriers, Buccaneers, F–100 Super Sabres, A–7 Corsairs, FB–111 Aardvarks, B–52 Stratofortresses, RF/F4 Phantoms, F–105 Thuds, A–10 Wart Hogs, 0–2s, EC–121s, C–130 Hercules, C–141 Starlifters, F–15 Eagles, and F–16s.

Mission types vary widely and encompass the entire spectrum of possible combat assignments for a tactical fighter. Let's follow a typical four-plane mission. Approximately two hours of planning are needed to decide on the type of attack to be carried out. This depends largely on the type of target and the surrounding terrain. The route of flight is planned in detail to minimize the effect of the enemy defences. This is best accomplished by planning to keep something solid, like mountains, between your aircraft and the radars to escape detection for as long as possible.

Once the planning is complete, a detailed briefing is conducted by the leader to ensure that all members in the section are fully aware of all the details of their responsibilities in the upcoming mission. Knowing just your own mission is not enough, however. With many other sections in the same area and times-on-target minutes apart, it is imperative that section leads get together to deconflict their routes. Relying on the "Big Sky Principle" could easily result in meeting a B–52 head-on in a mountain pass, with the attendant soiled shorts. In addition, many missions are flown with the direct support of F–105 Wild Weasel or RF–4 Reconnaissance crews. To work successfully together, it is necessary to ensure that we know each other's procedures and capabilities.

Planning and briefing complete, the fighters are manned to begin the not-inconsiderable task of trying to get airborne on time. At any time

[1] Dirty Rotten Pinko Commie Bastards.

there are over 250 fighters on the ramp at Nellis. When about half of them are trying to get airborne at the same time, the problem is much like getting out of a stadium parking lot after a football game. But the tower control is very good, and despite the Federal "Ah-the-war-can-wait" Agency, everyone can get airborne on the right day.

Once the frustration of getting airborne and out to the range is over, the war is on. Before entering the range, the section changes to strike frequency and descends to an operational altitude and airspeed. The normal plan is to get lower than a snake's belly and so fast that your hair is on fire. In layman's terms, this translates to 100 feet above ground and up to 600 knots. Radio silence is strived for, especially since an airborne EC–121 was practicing communications jamming most of the time anyway. The first section of the range is free from ground threats, but is the domain of the "Migs" with their ground-controlled intercept radar. Other than the F–15 with its Star Wars radar, the adversaries have very limited success against the CF–104. The CF–104 is difficult to spot because of its size, low altitude, and speed capability.

Flying over the type of terrain in the Nellis range is a new experience for Canadians as few of us have flown in a desert and mountain environment before. One minute you're climbing in full afterburner to clear a 5000-foot peak in your path, and the next you're making a rapid descent back to the desert on the other side of the ridge. Careful route study is essential, as is undivided attention to the task at hand.

Getting close to the target area, the SAM and AAA threats become a factor in addition to the Migs. Due to our tactics, very few CF–104s are claimed by these threats. Approaching the target, the section either splits for separate run-ins or closes up to concentrate the bombs on target, and as each pilot reaches his pre-planned attack parameters, he squeezes the pickle button to unleash his ordnance. Practice ordnance is carried on most missions, but several sorties have been flown with live 500-pounders and the Canadian-developed CRV–7 rocket. The CRV–7, Canada's "secret weapon", is something new to the Americans, and its long-range capabilities create a lot of interest. Where possible, bombs are scored by airborne umpires in RF–4 Phantoms.

Once the ordnance is on target, the section fights its way out of the range at low altitude and high airspeed. The last task is to get back on the ground at Nellis along with all the other strike aircraft and adversaries, who all seem to be out of gas at the same time.

At the end of each four-plane mission, a Red Flag debriefer sits down with the flight and conducts a thorough analysis of all aspects of the sortie with the emphasis on lessons learned. At 1500 each day, a mass debriefing is held, and each section lead is given the opportunity to "show and tell" what his flight did right or wrong, and what they learned from the mission. A fighter pilot being closely akin to a fisherman when it comes to telling the truth, this is sometimes a very traumatic experience. As all debriefs are video-taped and all fighter pilots love an audience, there is also no lack of aspiring Bob Hopes in the group. Red Force (Migs) and White Force (surface threats) also debrief, and lists are displayed showing which Good Guys were shot, when, where, and by whom. Whimpering and open weeping are discouraged. By the time the mass debriefing is over at around 1700 it is time to plan the next morning's mission.

After the first two weeks, aircrew and most of the groundcrew are rotated and fresh blood brought in. In this manner, 417 Squadron trains up to seven squadron members and seven pilots from Germany over the month period. The only difference during the second half of the exercise is the inclusion of a package of close air support missions run in support of the US Army in the Fort Irwin Exercise Area. This includes working with air and ground forward air controllers and an airborne command and control centre operating in a C–130 Hercules.

One of the more interesting days often included in an exercise period is when the Blue Force CF–104s get to be Red Force for a day. On one occasion we wreaked havoc among a strike force from the US Navy. It was with vindictive delight that the Canadian Mig force tallied up their kills. One "Mission Impossible" scenario was MAC[1] Escort wherein it was the task of Blue Force to escort seventeen C–141 Starlifters and C–130 Hercules loaded with equipment and 1500 troops through the enemy defences to their drop zone at Fort Irwin. It's a lot like trying to hide an 800-pound gorilla in the ladie's powder room.

From purely an operational effectiveness standpoint, Red Flag is a very gratifying experience. The success rate of CF–104 missions compared favourably with the remainder of Blue Force. Relying on our small size and speed, our fighter crews are consistently able to penetrate, attack, and escape relatively unscathed using tactics which have withstood the test of time, and many Maple Flag exercises. On most days the enemy do not even see a maple leaf.

The professional and enthusiastic approach of all the Red Flag staff over the years has provided an invaluable opportunity to evaluate our tactics and training in a controlled but very realistic environment.

Which leads us into a description of the Canadian-unique Flag exercise, known naturally enough as Maple Flag...

Red Flag is remarkable for its air-to-ground and air-to-air tactical realism. However, for all the state-of-the-art range facilities and the excellent weather of this desert location, Nellis AFB itself suffers the enormous handicap of being situated at the epicentre of the Las Vegas Control Area. The resultant Air Traffic Control delays when launching and recovering whole fleets of exercise aircraft severely limits the amount of valuable mission time over the ranges. The 417 Squadron History explains how the "northern alternative" came into being...

When the Canadians were at Nellis for an exercise in the autumn of 1977, Red Flag's creator, General Robert I. Dixon, USAF, Commander of Tactical Air Command, outlined this problem to his old RCAF comrade and fellow Spitfire pilot Lieutenant General William K. Carr, head of Canada's Air Command. The idea of Cold Lake was put

Above: *An unusual five-plane Vic formation with a tipped CF-104D leading four "clean" single-seaters, 1976.*

[1] Military Airlift Command.

forward and a trial exercise was scheduled from April 22 to May 20, 1978. The 4000 square mile range at Cold Lake, covering an area the size of Lebanon, with uncluttered airspace and a more than adequate air base nearby not only satisfied the problems mentioned, but have offered tremendous potential for future use by other countries.

With other NATO nations now seeking the Red Flag standard of training, the U.S. faces a real problem of just where to do it. The already crowded base at Nellis is shared by a number of sensitive agencies who don't take kindly to any influx of foreigners. The location of Nellis AFB and the Red Flag ranges in desert terrain is less than ideal, and it was thought likely to be of more benefit for NATO training to be held in an area that at least resembles the European homelands of the member nations. The Cold Lake ranges are covered with lakes, trees and hills, which provide all the ingredients for realistic target concealment that would correspond to conditions in Europe.

A number of Canadian squadrons rotated through the various Maple Flag exercises run during the CF-104 era. 417 Squadron, as a resident of Cold Lake, was called in on each and every one of them to add an element of class to the proceedings. 1978 marked the inauguration of the first joint USAF/CF Maple Flag exercise, which depended heavily on American technical support. The exercise was of two weeks duration, with the second week being a repeat of the first following a swap-out of crews; and it was held twice annually, in May and in October. 417 Squadron participated in its final Maple Flag (MF11) in May 1983. This popular exercise was almost identical to Red Flag, with the essential difference being the more European-like terrain and weather. Also, one did not have to cycle through the Nellis standard ten control frequencies just to accomplish the mission. 417 Squadron traditionally dedicated two aircraft, complete with Airborne Radar Warning Receiver (ARWR), camouflage, and towards the end, the new LW-33 navigation/attack system to this exercise. In all, over 80 CF-104 pilots participated in Maple Flag during the Starfighter era. On a lighter note, as well as displaying its normal high standard of operational prowess during these exercises, 417 Squadron won the coveted Maple Flag Crud Trophy no less than five times.

* * * * * *

The often fickle winter weather at Cold Lake had ways of turning on the resident aviators. Since the Base's primary function was student fighter pilot training, we OTU instructors tended to have our lives run by the Almighty Student Progress Board, with its neat little pigeon holes of requirements and eventual "Xs". We also annually hosted several special courses, including FWIC, and these pilots got a Progress Board as well.

I remember the first week of February, 1977 as being characterized by day after day after day of forecast freezing rain; that dreaded weather phenomenon that pilots probably respect above all others. We were hosting a 1 CAG Continuation Course, and checking out some of the Combat Ready pilots in a new form of defensive air combat known as Low level Defensive Maneuvering (LLDM). Since these tactics were flown supersonic and at ultra low level (only a few hundred feet above the trees), the first training mission was dual with an instructor babysitting from "the pit" of a CF-104D. I had been scheduled to fly with Brian Bainbridge (B^2) of 439 Squadron again (somebody should probably have legislated against this daring duo going flying together, based on previous experience). Friday morning of the week in question dawned and, based on four consecutive days of forecast freezing rain which had never materialized, we had not "turned a wheel" all week. Naturally, the Almighty Board was conspicuously devoid of "Xs", and everybody was beginning to question the weather forecaster's ancestry. That morning, the forecast was a repeat of the same old thing, with no improvement expected until late in the weekend, indicating the flying week would be a complete bust and we would really be behind the power curve by Monday morning. And that's when the Boss rolled his eyes heavenward and made a command decision... "Screw it," he said. "That damned forecaster has been wrong all week. It's not gonna rain, and besides... even the Basic Course are doing ACM. The missions are short. Launch the fleet!"

Well, no points for guessing what happened next... Not only did 417 Squadron launch every available aircraft, but the CF-5 community over at 419 Squadron, seeing the bustle of activity over on our line and thinking that we knew something that they didn't, did likewise. Brian and I were first off on this

Above: *AETE's CF-104D does a loop near the base at Cold Lake, 1983.*

single-ship mission against an imaginary bandit; and since this trip profile consumed fuel at a horrendous rate, we were down to landing fuel weight and back at the Base, mission accomplished, a scant 45 minutes later. However, in the short time that we were away, Cold Lake ATC had issued a weather warning that freezing rain had indeed arrived (about fifteen minutes after our takeoff) and had ordered all airborne aircraft to divert to Edmonton, about 130 nautical miles away. Since we had spent our airborne time at very low level and at some distance from the Base, we had not received the message. The first time that we heard the bad news was when we checked in with Tower, quite close to the field. By then, it was an academic issue. Without the gas to go anywhere, we were going to have to land at Cold Lake… one way or another.

It seemed that we were not the only ones in a bind. In all, about ten jets had launched, of which six successfully diverted to Edmonton. That left four of us who would become the card-carrying members of what was later referred to as the Cold Lake Bonspiel.

In the short time that we had been airborne, Mother Nature had turned the Base's long parallel runways into two huge curling rinks. Brian made a normal landing from the front seat and basically had the jet slowed to taxi speeds within 3000 feet on a 12,000 foot runway. However that's when the ***real*** fun began. We quickly found that the runway surface was so slick that we could neither stop completely, nor turn off the runway. We then spent the next 7000 feet of runway going at about five knots, deciding whether or not to drop the arrestor hook and engage the barrier cable. Believe me, at five knots, it took a long time! We finally decided *not* to engage the barrier, since that would close the runway and there were other aircraft to recover. Instead, we would taxi over the cable leaving ***that*** option open to someone else, make one last attempt to clear the runway; and if that didn't work, flameout the engine and get the trusty groundcrew to tow us back to the ramp. Well, it ***didn't*** work, and we ***did*** flameout the engine about 800 feet from the end of the runway, after informing the Squadron of our problem. As we were waiting for the tow crew to arrive, we noticed a CF–5 about to land on our runway. Being extremely reluctant to jump down to the exceptionally slippery tarmac, we convinced ourselves that the CF–5 driver, realizing our plight, would certainly engage the barrier, putting us out of reach. From a rather smug and amused viewpoint, we watched this troop repeating our passage down the runway, more erratic if anything. However, our smugness changed to outright horror when he ***didn't*** take the barrier, and furthermore, was completely out of control and pointed at our pink bodies!

"B^2, I think we best be getting out of here!"

"Roger **that**!!"

In a blur and a heartbeat, we leapt from the aircraft, almost

Above: *Five F-4's of VF-201 "Navy Dallas" led by their skipper, Commander Jon Jordan, join three 417 Squadron CF-104s over the 417 Squadron ramp while on an autumn 1977 visit. The Starfighter pilots are: Lead, Laurie Hawn; Left wing, Ted Lee; Right wing, Dave Bashow.*

breaking our respective necks, and quickly scrabbled away from the '104 as fast as our wobbly legs could carry us. As it turned out, the CF–5 missed our jet by 20 feet and ended up tail-first in a snowbank just behind us. I'll say this though... that CF–5 pilot certainly had panache. At the very point that he was just passing our aircraft, he was completely turned around 180 degrees to his heading on landing, still travelling in the **landing direction,** but with his nose pointed towards the approach end of the runway. He was obviously just along for the ride and, making the best of a bad situation, he extended his hands in front of him, palms up, and gave the finest Gallic shrug I have ever seen. It had Brian and I in stitches!

We were really fortunate as a fighter community on this one. I think that the worst damage was a broken light on the outer runway that a CF–5 totalled on its way to the boondocks.

* * * * * *

The 1980s ushered in some rather lean times for 417 Squadron in terms of aircraft resources, and the community occasionally cast baleful glances backward in time at the wisdom of selling 44 Starfighters to the Danes and the Norwegians back in the early seventies. An increased number of students on the Basic Courses in 1980, combined with five aircraft being out of the system on DLIR at any given time, necessitated a considerable amount of creative scheduling, including flying on weekends. However, the job got done, and 417 found the resources to participate in FWIC and one of the two Maple Flags held that year.

Harald Riedel was an experienced German Air Force fighter pilot who served with distinction as a "POW" squadron instructor from 1979 until the close-out in 1983. An avid outdoorsman, Harald and his family fell in love with the Great White North and willingly requested a fourth-year extension to his exchange tour at Cold Lake, just to spend additional time in Canada savouring the wilderness and the unrestricted flying. However on June 24, 1980, Harald and Rick Wall, flying together in 104651 on an FWIC support mission, lost an argument with a rather large bird at low level, and were forced to do a "nylon letdown", thereby getting a chance to get a little closer to nature than they had bargained for. Rick elaborates...

The mission was one of the big Fighter Weapons School gaggles, where we had half the aircraft on the base attacking a target and the other half defending it. I was supposed to be leading a 4-plane section of bombers. Actually, we also had a bunch of U.S. Navy folks involved with E2C Hawkeyes, F–4s, A–4s, etc; so it was quite a big deal. Of course, after all the planning and briefing was done, we found out that my section was down to two duals. Hauptmann Harald Riedel, our German Exchange Officer, was supposed to be my #4 and was now without an aircraft, so he decided to jump into my back seat. John Laidler took the other dual and flew on our wing. Our target was a communications site near Fort McMurray, and for the first twenty minutes or so everything was great. We hadn't been bounced, and were on time and on track, of course. As a matter of fact, I had just told Harald that the only way we could get closer to track would be to get lower, when all hell broke loose. I looked up from my map, and right in front of us were what appeared to be three or four of those big white pelicans that hang around up in that area. It was really too late to do anything, and before I knew it, one of them went by the right side of the cockpit and another by the left. I think we took the left one in the engine because I could feel the impact. I pulled up and looked at the gauges and there it was... your classic compressor stall - 70% RPM and 700 degrees EGT! A simulator instructor would have been proud. Things really got interesting then. I remember calling to John Laidler that we might have to get out, and to stay with us. I was hollering at Harald and he was hollering at me. John was talking to us, and then the Navy Hawkeye got in on it. Joe Molnar, who was the student leading this whole thing, was trying to find out what was going on. It got kind of confusing, so we sort of tuned everything out. I was trying to get the thing re–lit, but had absolutely no control over the engine; I couldn't even shut it down. The throttle was binding and didn't seem to be hooked to anything. We had zoomed to about 2000 feet, and were on the back-side headed down when I told Harald we would have to go. I think he had already decided that because he said he was ready. I told Harald to eject and away he went. I waited a bit and then pulled the D ring. They told us later that Harald went at about 400 feet, and I got out at about 275 feet AGL...much too late. The good part is that I am scared of heights and didn't have much time in the chute to worry about it. I recall the loud bang when the seat fired, and then tumbling. Finally, when the parachute opened and I dared to open my eyes, I saw the wreckage and the trees coming up at me. Just that quickly my chute caught the tops of some trees and I stopped, about a foot off the ground.

The time on the ground, about two hours, went by quite fast. After my heart rate dropped below 200, I finally opened my seat pack and took out the radio. There were several airplanes orbiting overhead and I felt better being able to talk to someone. The terrain was muskeg, and I sank to my ankles when walking around. Two other things bothered me. The black flies were murder, and I started worrying about bears. Ultimately, I solved the problems by sitting in my dinghy -the only dry place - and wearing that silly looking hat with the mosquito netting. I also had the axe in my hand, to fend off the bears. I'm sure it was quite a sight. I finally got through to Harald on the radio. He was complaining about his wet feet, so I told him to get into his dinghy, and he did the same thing. The chopper finally arrived to take us back to base. I had always hoped to finish my career without having been in a helicopter, but there was no other way out.

The Flight Surgeon that was assigned to me was a young doctor, which was a mixed blessing. He was really disturbed when I admitted to having several cigarettes while waiting to be picked up. This was going to screw up the test results, something that was really not of great concern to me at the time. When they finally let me talk to Harald, I found out that he had a sore back but otherwise was OK. Later in the day, after all the tests were done, the only thing on my mind was getting out of the hospital and having the world's largest glass of scotch. The CO of the hospital came by on his evening rounds, and in spite of my pleas, stated that the rules were that I had to stay overnight, and to just get used to it. About a half hour later, my young Flight Surgeon came by; and I pointed out to him that I was perfectly fit and there was really no reason for me to stay any longer. About two seconds after he sort of agreed, I was gone. Harald tried the same tactic later, but because of his sore back he had to stay.

1981 witnessed the introduction of both a system and a mode of training into the CF–104 syllabus which greatly enhanced the effectiveness and the wartime survivability of the Canadian Starfighter pilot. The system was the high-tech LW–33 inertial navigator; the training mode was the introduction of air-to-air gunnery into the Basic Course syllabus. Course 72 was the first to be exposed to the finer intricacies of shooting at a 6' x 30' cloth target being towed by the venerable T–33, though the FWIC students had been doing it for some time. CF–104 pilots in Europe would later establish a regular gun firing camp at Leeuwarden in the Netherlands, blazing merrily away at targets towed either by T–33s or RNLAF F–16s.

The aircraft resource "crunch" was somewhat painful in 1981 as well, and though 417 was still able to support FWIC, two

Maple Flags, and the last CF–104 Red Flag deployment, an airshow team could not be fielded that year. The 417 Squadron History notes how the OTU coped with the aircraft shortages at this time...

The Basic Course syllabus by 1981 had been extended slightly by two weeks, to allow for larger courses and dwindling resources. In this manner, 417 could annually train 24 Basic students, several refresher pilots, the FWIC, as well as support Maple Flag, Red Flag, and the occasional exchange for DACT training. This was predicated on a unit establishment of ten singles and ten duals from an available total of 25 CF–104s. The squadron looked forward to a slight easing of the resource strain in 1982, once DLIR was completed.

1982 was the last *full* year of CF–104 operations by 417. It was a busy year, which included a DACT deployment to Miramar Naval Air Station, San Diego, as well as participation in Maple Flag IX and FWIC'82. The aircraft resource situation was a little better in 1982; better that is until the FWIC students got their hands on the jets...This Course *really* cut a swath through 417's fleet and two jets were destroyed; one from a flight departure during air combat, and the other from an afterburner fire. The good news was that both pilots ejected safely. Nevertheless, 417 managed to field a display team in 1982, and Captains Keith Robbins and Dave Owen had a truly superior show, dazzling audiences across the continent as only Starfighters in motion can.

The first months of 1983 were hectic indeed, with graduation of the last Basic Course (#75), participation in Maple Flag, and the running of a six-student FWIC Course. This course was twice the normal size, but had to provide enough expertise in 1 CAG to last until the Group's conversion to the CF–18 was complete in 1986. The OTU's activities culminated with the presentation of the Air Standard in June, followed by Squadron shutdown on the First of July. Since its inception in 1962, the OTU had graduated in excess of 750 students and provided many specialized and refresher courses along the way, flying almost 138,500 hours in the process. The OTU had soldiered on through 21 years of producing first-rate fighter pilots on Canada's most sophisticated aircraft, leaving an extremely proud legacy in the wake of its departure.

But 417 Squadron was not completely out of business yet. A number of the Squadron aircraft were flown into long-term storage and further disposition at Mountainview, Ontario. It was also decided that the eleven 417 aircraft that had been through the DLIR process were to be transferred to 1 CAG to augment the Group's dwindling fleet of CF–104s.

The options for the transfer to Europe were transport by Hercules, or simply to fly the five duals and six singles across in a leapfrog operation, and this had never been done before in the CF–104. Initially nicknamed by an unknown staff officer as "Operation Sheer Lunacy", the flyover plan was supported by Col. Sam Firth, the Air Command Deputy Chief of Staff Operations, who "sold it up the chain" to NDHQ. The route taken was to be from Cold Lake to Winnipeg, Trenton, Goose Bay, Sondrestrom, Keflavik, Leuchars, and finally Baden-Soellingen.

The fearless leader nominated for the flyover was Major Lawrence Sianchuk; the last Squadron Operations officer (SOPSO) of 417 Squadron. What follows is his personal diary of this historic trip...

OPERATION STARLEAP

Dead Eye Blacks

Lead Maj. Lawrence Sianchuk
2 Capt. Bob Wade/ Capt. Terry Cosgrove
3 Capt. Phil Murphy
4 Maj. Wally Peirson/ Capt. Guy Dutil

Dead Eye Blues

Lead Maj. John Laidler
2 Capt. Dan Bouchard/ Capt. Kevin Vaillant
3 Capt. Keith Robbins
4. Maj. Dud Larson/ Capt. Tom Lawson

Dead Eye Golds

Lead Maj. Stan Jones
2 Hptm. Harald Riedel/ Col. Sam Firth
3 Capt. Rick Gelinas

- 2 Hercules carrying maintenance support and acting as "Duck Butts".
- Total of 65 aircrew and groundcrew participating.

Day 1 - Saturday July 3, 1983

Col. Firth arrived early in the morning by T–33 from Winnipeg. Departure of the fighters was scheduled for 0900 local. One Hercules launched early so that groundcrew would be in position for a quick turnaround in Winnipeg. Gold Two was left on ramp with a hydraulic problem but was airborne about an hour late. After takeoff all aircraft stayed below the 1000 foot AGL ceiling for a final pass over the 417 ramp.

Started at 9000 feet, but stepped down to 7000 feet to try to remain VFR. We saw downtown Saskatoon, but then hit solid cloud about 50 miles east. Four plane IFR all the way to Langruth, with Winnipeg forecast to be clear. Blacks set up for straight-in approaches in pairs on Runway 18. Just before landing, a wall of water moved across the field from the south. Subsequent sections landed singly because of the heavy rain.

CBC was waiting for interview, but Black Lead was too involved in flight planning for the next leg which was the most fuel critical of the

Above: *104 731 banks steeply over the Cold Lake Military Flying Area, 1983.*

trip. Blue Lead took on the press in an interview that lasted about 45 minutes.

After a meal at the Mess, the formations started up in the torrential rain. Ankle-deep water stood in some places on the ramp. Since fuel was critical, Black Lead requested Runway 36 for takeoff, but was cleared for the two mile taxi to 18, even though the winds were calm. The combination of tanked aircraft, 25° C temperature, and heavy rain made for long takeoff rolls and slow rate-of-climb south over the city. By the time Gold Lead called for taxi, ATC had reconsidered, and cleared the remainder for a Runway 36 departure to avoid more noise complaints.

Enroute, everyone was stuck in the cloud all the way to Thunder Bay at FL 270. Just east of the Lakehead, the duals started to be concerned about fuel remaining compared to distance to go. Black Two was especially concerned, since his tip tanks would not feed until he had only 2800 lbs. of internal fuel remaining. He later reluctantly wrote up the aircraft as unserviceable for fuel feed in Trenton.

Day 2 - Sunday July 4, 1983

Black Two's aircraft was test run and fuel feed still proved unreliable. The Captain was not impressed with the Squadron Engineering Officer at this point. However, the decision was to leave the aircraft behind. It looked like our luck was running out already as the remaining fighters launched for Goose Bay in another bout of heavy rain. Our spirits were lifted as we arrived at Goose Bay in fine weather with two kegs of German beer waiting. Meanwhile, back at Trenton our maintainers showed their usual ingenuity by lifting the needed fuel "gizmo" from one of the other CF–104s recently flown to Trenton for disposal. Black Two and the remaining Hercules missed the beer, but landed in time for the arctic char later in the evening.

Day 3 - Monday July 5, 1983

The weather at Sondrestrom wasn't good enough to qualify for the Aircom directed destination limits. Decision was made to slide one day. ATC arranged to delay the altitude reservation by 24 hours. Everyone enjoyed a day of taking in the various tourist attractions that Goose and the nearby area had to offer.

Day 4 - Tuesday July 6, 1983

Goose was hot and muggy. Sondrestrom was suitable, and so was Keflavik. After some deliberation, it was decided to try to get back on schedule with a two-leg day. Accommodation in Keflavik would be a problem if we delayed.

After what seemed like hours in the 30° C heat during start and taxi, all eleven aircraft were airborne. Once again we were in the cloud at FL270 until about 200 miles from the Greenland coast. The Herc confirmed the weather was good at the half-way point, so our Section descended early for some pictures of the Starfighter against some very rugged terrain. The VFR overhead pattern proved interesting, 2000 feet AGL over the runway was about 300 feet above the rocky cliffs on downwind. After landing, the groundcrew on the Duck Butt Herc confirmed that all the fighters were "green" on turnaround. There was no need for the second Herc to land, so a quick radio call on company frequencies had them overfly Sondrestrom to take their position as Duck Butt for the next leg.

Above: *104 704 head-on just after takeoff at Cold Lake. The photo was taken from AETE's Tutor and its special, rear facing camera.*

A call to our Exchange Officer in Keflavik gave us an expert opinion on the weather: "The last report was 1800 broken and 15 miles vis; I've been here two years and it's never been better than this!" Things were going too smoothly until Three's parachute got soaked in JP–4 during refuelling. All the spares were on the airborne Duck Butt, so one of the backseaters took over for the Keflavik leg and Blue Three travelled by Herc.

The three Sections lined up for takeoff in sequence on Runway 28. Gold Three had a small problem getting his canopy closed, but a quick check by our alert groundcrew revealed a Pentax strap hanging over the side.

The takeoff was in the opposite direction to the destination, so a burner climb out of the Fjord allowed for a left turn to the easterly course without much delay. We leveled at FL270 in "severe clear" Greenland summer weather over the two mile high ice cap. The mountains, glaciers, and lakes of the east coast soon came into view... this was definitely the most spectacular scenery of the trip. The plan was working perfectly. The Duck Butt crossed the coast just as the first section caught up. The weather was so good that a photo pass on the Herc was suggested. Cameras were readied and distances to go to the turn point were exchanged. Only after the matching of distances with "no tally" did someone figure out that the Herc's turnpoint was 60 miles south of ours.

The weather was still good at Keflavik and we had lots of fuel, so Lead elected to let down early for a visual approach. The weather was not quite as shiny as predicted, but the radar had no trouble picking up the point of land where the runway was supposed to be. The combination of the low sun angle and a runway which blended well with the volcanic countryside caused Black Lead to fly through for an "orientation pass" [1]. In thirty minutes, everyone was down; Operation Starleap was back on schedule with the tricky legs behind. The next day we would even have alternates.

Time for a little relaxation, and at dinner in the Officers' Club, we were introduced to one of the local F–4 Squadrons. The 57th FIS was saying good-bye to some of the boys who were going "Stateside" the next day. As usual, the Canucks adapted quickly to the situation.

Day 5 - Wednesday July 7, 1983

It was clear as a bell in Ireland, and Leuchars, Scotland was fair with a solid alternate. We filed the same ICAO flight plans as usual and started engines on the first four fighters at 1100 local. When Blacks called for clearance, ATC did not have one forthcoming. A call to 57th FIS OPS indicated a problem with our route, which cut briefly through Belfast airspace about 200 miles north of Ireland. Realizing it would not be resolved from the cockpit, Black Lead elected to shut down and top up the jets. By the time we had walked to Base Operations, our friendly Herc captain had sorted out the problem. The flight plans did not have the required 15 minute separation between sections. Finally the fighters were all airborne, one and one-half hours late.

On letdown to Leuchars, we hit European weather again, and the forward inflight visibility was very poor. Black Lead set up for a right

Above: *AETE's 104 895 salvoes rockets at the Primrose Lake Evaluation Range, March 1974. The aircraft was lost due to a gun malfunction in flight on March 19, 1974. The pilot ejected safely.*

[1] Hmmmmm.

hand overhead pitch, which turned out to be to the left. It was too late for an echelon change, so the Dead Eyes pitched in reverse order, just as though we always did it that way.

Day 6 - Thursday July 8, 1983

The weather was IFR at Leuchars, but fair at Baden. One dual launched early to get our German exchange pilot home early so he could do some administration after his three-year tour. Later, the remainder launched for an uneventful trip to Baden over much more familiar terrain. For many of our pilots, it was their last trip in the Starfighter.

On arrival in the Rhine Valley, Blacks did a short tour over the Schwarzwald to burn off fuel before calling for landing. As the lay of the land was not totally familiar to the formations, Black Lead did another "orientation pass" from the west over south dispersal... 417 Squadron's last pass. Blues and Golds pitched out shortly after Blacks.

As we taxied into south dispersal, the fire trucks were waiting to wash the salt off each bird in turn. The Base Commander and a few of our old friends were standing by with a welcome cold German beer. The "aging CF–104s" had performed admirably; 77 sorties without a major unserviceability.

However, this last leg of the long crossing was a little more eventful than Lawrence Sianchuk's cryptic diary notes would have us believe. John Laidler explains...

We were happy to doff our immersion suits for this leg after having worn them since Goose. Before the flight, Kevin Vaillant had asked me if he could borrow my small Nikon AF to take some pictures on the last leg, but I said no, if he wanted any taken to give a shout, and I would oblige him. I thought no more of it until somewhere over the North Sea I felt this "presence" beside me, looked left, and was presented with this humongous moon from the back seat of Dan Bouchard's airplane (I knew he had the front seat on that hop). I was laughing so hard, I could hardly say "close it up" to take the shots. My autopilot made it easy for me, however.

Kevin later said it took him five minutes to get everything down, while retaining only his boots, helmet, and oxygen mask.

417 Squadron was not the only Canadian military unit on the North American side of the Atlantic to fly the CF–104 with distinction throughout the Starfighter era. The other was the Central Experimental and Proving Establishment (CEPE); later renamed the Aerospace Engineering and Test Establishment (AETE) in May, 1967. From 1959, when a test team performed a preliminary service evaluation of the F–104C, until 1983, when AETE's last Starfighter was ferried to Trenton, this unit was extensively involved with the flight testing and downstream evaluation of the CF–104. During those 25 years, 171 project reports and numerous other less comprehensive reports were issued detailing the test work conducted by AETE on the Starfighter, and these papers provide a history of the aircraft, its modifications, improvements and problems. CEPE test pilots participated in the Category I Flight Test Program and the contractor demonstration flights completed in 1962 at the Palmdale facility. They also conducted the Category II Flight Test Program at CEPE Uplands and at the Cold Lake Detachment. This second program included weapons systems evaluations, the AN/APG–502 radar evaluation, extensive aircraft performance evaluation and validations, photo-reconnaissance system testing, and cold weather trials. CEPE also established a detachment at Canadair that performed production aircraft acceptance flights and, after European deployment, established a detachment at Scottish Aviation in Prestwick, Scotland, which performed acceptance flights following periodic overhaul and modification programs. Mark Fairley was a Canadian Forces Acceptance Test Pilot at Prestwick from 1971 until 1977; remaining so long in Scotland that he practically became an institution there. Mark shares some of his recollections of this excellent, though little-known facet of CF–104 operations...

While CF–104 operations within the RCAF/Canadian Forces did not begin until 1961, the Prestwick story probably commenced in 1956 when Scottish Aviation Limited (SAL) was awarded their initial Canadian DND contract to overhaul a select number of CF–100 aircraft. This liaison proved to be an obvious lead-in to what turned out to be a long-term relationship between SAL and the Canadian Forces, as this relatively small yet obviously capable company was to retain this contract throughout the first sixteen years of CF–104 operations in Europe. During this time frame, the vast majority of the major programs at Scottish centered around the on-going requirement to provide a timely and effective overhaul or update of aircraft structure and systems, thereby maintaining the technical integrity and capabilities of the CF–104 fleet in general.

The Canadian Forces also had a strong role to play in this venture, for while the contractor was tasked to provide the necessary technical expertise, the associated responsibilities of quality control, logistic and administrative support, flight test and ferry, and overall program management had to be provided by on-site RCAF/Canadian Forces personnel. To this end, two Canadian military detachments were formed. On the technical side, #5 CFTSD (Canadian Forces Technical Services Detachment) came into being, and with a continuous manpower of 9 - 12 personnel, was tasked to provide all aspects of technical, logistic and administrative support, along with a workable and effective Quality Assurance program. Additionally, as Flight Test Authority for the RCAF/Canadian Forces, CEPE was called upon the form a second detachment to meet the obvious flight testing commitment and the associated movement of aircraft to and from their primary locations in Europe.

The initial programs at Prestwick were for the most part noticeably active, for along with the on-going requirement for structural and system maintenance, a number of aircraft "trials" were set up in an attempt to validate or improve current aircraft systems. One of these trials focused upon the performance of the aircraft radar, and tragically, during one of the test flights, the CEPE test pilot, Flight-Lieutenant Ian McKnight lost his life. This subsequently proved to be the only accident of such magnitude during the entire sixteen years of CF–104 operations at Prestwick Airport. It must be sadly noted, however, that a further three pilots who were originally involved in the CF–104 test programs at Prestwick were to lose their lives in aircraft accidents in later years. Briefly, these pilots were:

1. *Capt. Jack Lumsden - killed while flight testing a CT–114 "Tutor" aircraft out of Canadair, Ltd., Montreal in 1966;*
2. *S/L Norm Ronaasen - killed during Canadair "Challenger" test operations in the Mojave Desert, California in 1980;*
3. *Col "Ned" Henderson - killed in a CF T–33 mishap in Nova Scotia in May of 1982.*

It was my good fortune to know the latter two of these gentlemen as close friends, as indeed they were to many. As such, they will always be remembered.

In the early 1970s, CF–104 operations at Prestwick took an interesting turn as the Canadian Government decided to sell 44 aircraft abroad; 22 to Norway and a similar number to Denmark. The Danish Government elected to purchase their aircraft on an "as is, where is" basis, in view of which the required technical and flying support was of a somewhat limited nature. The Norwegian program was to be much more extensive however, and as the Royal Norwegian Air Force (RNoAF) preferred not to provide on-site technical support, Canadian Forces personnel were invited to meet this task, including the flight test and ferry commitment. It is interesting to note that upon completion of the initial RNoAF program in 1974, all 22 aircraft (now converted to Norwegian specifications) were again returned to Prestwick for further modification and update. The formula for this second contract was to be similar to the first, and although Canadian Forces personnel were to retain the technical and flight testing responsibilities, RNoAF pilots now trained on type would provide assistance with the ferry commitment to and from the designated bases in Norway. In summary, the two Norwegian contracts, coupled with the Danish program, collectively covered a period of some 54 months, commencing in early 1972 and terminating in mid 1976. Needless to say, this was indeed a very interesting era at SAL, with the ferry trips to Northern Norway an enviable highlight in all respects.

It should be pointed out that the Scandinavian contracts outlined above ran in concert with the previously programmed Canadian repair schemes, a circumstance which created a relatively heavy, albeit welcome, "in-house" workload for all concerned. However, upon completion of these programs in 1976, these circumstances changed drastically, to the extent that by mid 1977, all the contracted repair, overhaul or conversion programs of a major nature had been completed. This situation notwithstanding, it must be remembered that at this particular time, plans for Canada's New Fighter Aircraft (NFA) were well beyond the talk or rumour stage; and understandably perhaps, the future of Canada's aging Starfighters was placed under close scrutiny, particularly on the financial side of the scale. In view of these circumstances, (and undoubtedly a number of others of which I am not cognizant), the only CF–104 contract functioning at Prestwick from mid 1977 to late 1978 was one of a minor nature for exterior painting.

In 1979, the decision was taken to dedicate a reduced number of CF–104s to a final overhaul/update program, so that Canada's operational commitments overseas would not be jeopardized pending the arrival of the New Fighter Aircraft. On this occasion however, Scottish Aviation did not win the contract, and accordingly, Canadian Starfighter operations at Prestwick Airport, Ayrshire, Scotland were terminated in their entirety. "CFB Prestwick" had closed.

If there was one determining factor governing CF–104 operations from Prestwick Airport, it had to be the weather, primarily due to the fact that while Prestwick International possessed high calibre approach and landing aids for commercial traffic, they did not marry up, most regrettably, to the particular equipment carried in Canadian F–104s. Moreover, CF–104 aircraft conducted their business utilizing UHF radio frequencies, of which Prestwick Tower and Approach Control possessed but two, (and frequently monitored but one!). If you add to this equation one antiquated and apparently rather temperamental ground approach radar, you have all of the necessary ingredients for some really exciting moments in the aviation game. Having now set the stage and most of the players, I shall proceed without further delay with the primary reason behind this rather lengthy preamble, for which I extend my apologies.

During a routine "home trip" from CFB Baden, as per normal circumstance I inquired through channels as to the current status of the Prestwick weather, still being some 45 minutes to the southeast. In pilots' jargon, the reply came back as "scattered cloud and all the 9's" (U.K. terminology) or, as we often called it, "clear and a million" or CAVOK. Any or all of these terms are always music to a pilot's ears. Approximately 90 miles out, I commenced my descent over the Solway (Firth) and shortly thereafter entered a solid layer of cloud. This was not by any means abnormal however, and giving it no more thought than it deserved, I busied myself retuning my somewhat temperamental onboard radar, striving to pick up a workable "paint" on Ailsa Craig, a huge bowl-like rock jutting out of the Firth of Clyde some 26 miles to the southeast of Prestwick Airport. (Ailsa Craig was one of the mandatory check points for CF–104 operations at Prestwick, and was often fondly referred to as our primary navigational aid, along with, on occasion, the Safeway parking lot in the small village of Prestwick itself!). Continuing my descent, I finally picked out Ailsa at a radar range of about 14 to 16 miles, (not good), and now at my assigned altitude of 5000 feet, homed in on this forlorn rock which had ushered me safely homeward on so many occasions. Overhead Ailsa, and now chatting amiably with Prestwick Tower, I turned towards the northeast and received clearance to continue my descent to the airport, which seemed to be appropriate and completely in order in view of the previously acquired weather sequence. At this point I found that I was experiencing a little difficulty finding those "clear and a million" conditions, and upon further descent to 700 feet over the Firth of Clyde the warning bells finally started to clang, due I'm sure to at least some degree of complacency on my part. Further discreet inquiry into the weather situation produced a reply something like "brief rain showers in the local area producing reduced visibilities". This was not particularly good news, as due to a somewhat modest fuel state, I was now committed to an approach and landing at Prestwick Airport. To this end, and speaking in what I hoped to be my

- photo by Bill Johnson

most professional tone, I asked radar for confirmation of the fact that I was indeed over the Firth of Clyde, bearing in mind that as previously noted, the performance of the on-board radar was just a shade marginal. Back came the reply from Prestwick. "Musket 90," (my call sign) "we're not allowed to do that." (I must confess that I really pondered over this strange reply, but was to find out subsequently that this restriction had something to do with local Air Traffic procedures and the somewhat limited abilities of the ground approach radar.) After a brief pause I countered with, "Well, could you give me a hint then?" There

CF–104 ACCEPTANCE TEST PILOTS
SCOTTISH AVIATION LTD. (1961 - 1978)

AETE Pilots	
F/L Ian McKnight	1961 - 1965
S/L Norm Ronaasen	1963 - 1966
F/L Frank Gilland	1964 - 1966
F/L Jack Lumsden	1964 - 1965
F/L (Capt.) Hector MacGregor	1966 - 1968
S/L (Maj.) Clive Loubser	1968 - 1969
F/L (Maj.) Ned Henderson	1969
Capt. Mark Fairley	1971 - 1977
Capt. Laurie Illingworth	1977 - 1978
I CAG Detachment Pilots	
Capt. Ron Tomcheck	1969 - 1970
Capt. Willie Floyd	1969 - 1971

was a stony silence for a further few seconds, followed immediately with some hearty laughter and the words, "Musket 90, you're doing just fine. Give us a call on the ground please." Seconds later I popped into bright sunshine and landed without further incident, possessing, I might add, a much healthier respect for the climatic irregularities of Southwestern Scotland.

In my opinion, CF-104 armament systems and associated equipment were quite well designed and for the most part, seemed to function as advertised in our handy "how to fly" manuals. This fact was clearly demonstrated one day as I was preparing to depart on a routine airtest. Aircraft post start and taxi checks complete, I had moved the aircraft ahead into the designated "pin-pulling" area, and while the armament

technician conducted his stray voltage checks, casually viewed the currently vacant runway and general airport scene directly in front of me; a very relaxing, repetitive, and on occasion, rather mundane circumstance which unknown to me, was soon to change. On CF–104 aircraft, the tip tank jettison sequence was virtually "fool" or "Murphy" proof, for the system was designed in such a way that if one tip tank blew, inadvertently or otherwise, the other one followed automatically "sans delay". I can personally vouch that this is indeed the case, for my reverie was rudely interrupted by a single terrific explosion, and I instantly

Above, Operation Starleap: ***Back row*** - *Col. Sam Firth, Maj. Stan Jones, Capt Bob Wade, Capt Terry Cosgrove, Maj (USAF) Dud Larsen.* ***Middle row*** - *Maj. Wally Peirson, Capt Dan Bouchard, Capt Keith Robbins, Capt Guy Dutil, Capt Kevin Vaillant, Capt Rick Gelinas.* ***Front row*** - *Hauptmann Harald Riedel, Capt Phil Murphy, Maj. John Laidler, Maj. Lawrence Sianchuk, Capt Tom Lawson.*

Below: *My, what an unusual helmet... 104 642, piloted by Dan Bouchard closes up for John Laidler's camera during Operation Starleap. The bum in the back is Kevin Vaillant.*

- photo by John Laidler

found myself sitting amidst a rather massive fireball which was a real attention getter. I can remember glancing back toward the outer right wing area where I knew the armament technician had been, and feeling tremendous relief at seeing him scramble clear, hands over both ears in obvious pain and shock. Instinctively moving the throttle forward, I noted that the aircraft seemed to be responding normally, but with the live runway in front of me I felt somewhat compelled to contact the tower prior to entering the runway area. Moving ahead slowly, I transmitted something like, "Prestwick, I seem to be having a small problem here - permission to take the live." Immediately, back came the "super-cool" reply, "Musket 90, I can see that - you're cleared onto the live runway."

Remarkably, this incident produced only minimal damage to the aircraft, and more importantly to the personnel involved, although all of us returned to our duties somewhat shaken and chastened by the event. Needless to say, the remainder of the daily flying program was cancelled!

My third and final anecdote concerns one of my predecessors at Scottish Aviation, the late Norm Ronaasen, a fine gentleman in all respects, close friend, and of surprise to no one, I'm sure, the "pilot's pilot".

Once again, this story centers upon "Ailsa Craig", that hunk of granite at the top of the Irish Sea, and its single inhabitant, a resident lighthousekeeper. Passing overhead on virtually a daily basis, it appears that Norm came to feel a little sorry for this "keeper of the light" and his apparently lonely existence, and decided that perhaps he should make some effort to do something about it. To this end, in view of the fact that the Festive Season was quickly approaching, Norm wrote and forwarded a greeting card extending his festive wishes, and suggesting that perhaps he could pay him and Ailsa a visit in the not-too-distant future. Although all of these things eventually came to pass, it was the simple way that he addressed his greeting card that provided us with a small, yet appropriate laugh. The envelope simply read:

Lighthousekeeper,
Ailsa Craig,
Ayrshire, Scotland.

Some neat guy that fellow Ronaasen, and I'm certain that chances are more than reasonable that this seemingly small gesture provided a large ray of sunshine into an obviously lonely existence, vocation and circumstance.

Over the years, AETE also evaluated modifications to existing aircraft systems as well as new systems. Notable projects included work on the arrestor equipment, stick shaker, canopy jettison and escape system, engine emergency nozzle closure system, various fuel system modifications, electroluminescent light strips, and a chemical defence system for Starfighter pilots, to name but a few.

As a special Centennial project, it was AETE that assembled the test team and prepared 104700 for the attempt on the world altitude record in December, 1967. Throughout the total service life of the CF–104, AETE was responsible for ensuring that the aircraft provided to the various squadrons were equipped and entirely capable of performing their assigned roles effectively, efficiently, and safely. It was entirely fitting that on October 17, 1983, AETE was the last CF–104 unit in Canada to officially fly the Starfighter when 104646 was delivered into storage by them at Mountainview.

- Photo by Bill Johnson

CF-104 '842 sporting both the VICOM photo reconnaissance pod and the Red Ensign flag. This aircraft was transferred to Turkey in 1986.

104 650 was a Cold Lake aircraft until transferred to Baden-Soellingen in 1983 during Operation Starleap. It was also transferred to Turkey in 1986.

104 785 in the olive camouflage scheme representative of the early-to-late seventies. This 441 Squadron aircraft is now a pedestal monument at CFB Baden Soellingen.

104 893 in the tri-color camouflage scheme, complete with low visibility national markings, in which the CF-104 fleet ended its Canadian service career. Tranferred to Turkey, 1986.

104 763 went out in a blaze of color, as the flagship for 417 squadron during the OTU close-out ceremonies in 1983. Presently in storage at Mountainview, Ontario.

104 756 was one of many "Tiger birds" used annually by 439 Squadron in Europe. Transferred to Turkey, 1986.

104 880 in the striking second iteration of an overall "Checkerbird" scheme. Presently used as an Aircraft Battle Damage Repair (ABDR) instructional airframe at Baden-Soellingen.

104 805 in its dramatic red and white finish for the 1983 Base festivities, at Baden-Soellingen. Fondly referred to as "The Toothbrush", this aircraft is presently used for ABDR at Baden-Soellingen.

Side Profiles by Ron E. Lowry

Passing the Torch

It's not over, until it's over,
*But **when** it's over, it's **really** over.*
- Yogi Berra

Though the CF–104 would soldier on bravely in Central Europe throughout the first half of the eighties, the fast approaching service introduction of the CF–18 Hornet meant that the Starfighter was living on borrowed time. Furthermore, some of the older generation CF–104 pilots were definitely going to have to overcome a technological mind-set against the new equipment and new ways of doing business that this equipment permitted. Tom Lawson, who flew '104s with 421 Squadron from 1981 until 1985, found this exemplified by the skepticism with which the older hands greeted the introduction of the LW–33 navigation system. He also comments on the feelings of the Starfighter community in Europe as the lady approached her retirement…

The Starfighter in the '80s

When we got to Germany, in the late fall of '81, it was a good time to be a rookie on squadron. The fact that I didn't realize this serves testament to the abilities of the senior guys to heap traditional abuse on the "wingies". You see, the new guys were coming off the Cold Lake OTU with a pretty good working knowledge of a modern inertial navigation and weapons system, the LW–33. Our structured tutelage, provided by "Tex" Findley, provided us with a leg up. The older guys, confused and threatened by an electronic black box that gave rookies skills that had previously taken years to hone, were trying to piece together what had been given to them during the foggy ground-training lectures. Secretly, they laboured in the cockpit before each flight, scrambling to develop a relationship with the cold digital display. They would painstakingly load turnpoints and target data, and select confusing modes of delivery, but back at the squadron they'd harangue the Lieutenants…

"What happens when the system shuts down in mid-flight, friend? What do you do when the needle points north, when you know you want to go east? What do you do then? Give command of the section to your wingman and hope his box is working? No way. I'll keep my map thanks, and I'll be there when it counts! You hang onto my wing, watch my six o'clock, and shut up. If you find any extra time, you can spend it trying to get your computer to work!"

A year later, it was obvious to everyone that the system was never meant to replace the map. What it did do was give the pilot something accurate and reliable to crosscheck his navigating with, and lower the chances of complacency errors. Further, through bands of low-lying fog and following the confusion of a "furball"[1], it patiently pointed at the next turnpoint, accurate to half a mile; and that magic bug let you know what speed you'd need to get back on time. A serviceable LW–33

[1] One of the many slang words used to describe an air combat engagement.

virtually guaranteed flawless navigation and target times, and the dreaded system aborts were almost unheard of. They happened, and they threw flight Leads into a cold sweat... but they were rare. A glance at the accident records shows that the 1980s were good to the Starfighter community. There were damaged engines and low-level ejections, but incidents of collision with "strato-granite" were confined to another era. The new navigation system played a big part in the safety record we set in the '80s. There were other contributing factors.

After 417 Squadron shut down during the summer of 1983 and the shiniest of the Canadian-based '104s did a "Hog Hop" across the North Atlantic, the squadrons in Baden-Soellingen were jet-rich. As the Starfighter era came to a close, the thing the Commanding Officers most feared was the onset of a "flying club" atmosphere. There was nothing to fear, really. The pilot pipeline had shut down, and with that came the realization that there would be no more rookies to upgrade. By 1985, nearly every pilot on each squadron had achieved section-leader status. No longer did the scheduler have to juggle names in search of the ever-elusive perfect program. With this increase in the experience level of the average Soellingen pilot came an expansion of what was expected out of a mission. The standard three-target mission was replaced by a five-target circus, planned strategically around the range at Siegenburg. Anything more than marginal VFR weather would find sections of Red Indians, Tigers, and Foxes racing by the range. Standard entry points were a thing of the past. Every pilot knew every entry to the range, and even a three minute break between scheduled German or American range times would be filled with diving attacks by marvelously accurate Canadians. The fact that the skies over Germany seemed always to hold at least a section of Canadian jets bore witness to the unflagging enthusiasm of the hungry fighter pilots.

With the improved flight experience of the pilots came a blossoming of the corporate knowledge held by the groundcrew. The days were gone when the new private would have to read his five-finger check off the fingers of his leather gloves. Hiccoughs in the preflight routine, such as generators falling off line or computers overheating, were met with a barrage of technical quick-fix wizardry. Years earlier, maintenance had devised a system where a van-load of technical specialists would be ever-present in the dispersal. A call to squadron ops would be answered by this "snags" vehicle, and an abort could often be avoided. By the mid 1980s, the groundcrew waiting in this van were 1 CAG's version of the Maytag repairmen. The average line groundcrew had built up a couple of years on the jet, and his competence became more expected than appreciated.

Around the time of the annual NATO Tactical Evaluation, however, this competence was viewed by more than squadron pilots...and it was recorded. Excellent ratings became the trademark of the squadrons at Soellingen in the '80s. Under concentrated scrutiny, working for days in the close, pressurized quarters provided by the bunkers, the advantages of experience were borne out. There was little chatter on the operational frequencies, colour film proved the high success rate of the missions, and section briefings made such use of SOPS that they were unintelligible to the outsider. Throughout the bunker, evaluators would find pilots concentrating on the high-speed target portion of their maps. We were good and we knew it, and the evaluators could see it.

Tom Lawson wasn't the only person who noticed the tremendous professionalism of the CF–104 communities in the 1980s, as Dave McIntosh explains...

I was Base Commander at Baden from 1983 until 1985. What really impressed me during this time-frame was the fact that the groundcrew were able to keep up the serviceability rate. Not only were they keeping an old, old airplane in the air, they were, in the majority of

cases, working out of shops and hangars that were being completely renovated for the CF–18 program. In many cases, supervisors and key personnel had been taken out of the '104 program and sent on CF–18 technical courses. The groundcrew did outstanding work during this period.

During the spring of 1984, members of the Air Group received a taste of things to come when a small detachment of CF–18s from 410 "Cougar" Squadron, the Hornet OTU, deployed from Cold Lake to Baden-Soellingen in an exercise known as Rhine Hornet. As if to graphically underline the many innovative features and superior combat capabilities of the Hornet, the CF–18s made the Atlantic crossing nonstop with air-to-air refuelling, in stark contrast to the "island hopping" route of the Starleap Starfighters, accomplished just the year before. Although Rhine Hornet provided the air force with an opportunity to strut the new jet a little in the old neighbourhood on a good-will tour, it was also planned for the very practical need to validate some of the aircraft's impressive systems, and to confirm the jet's compatibility with the existing Baden and Lahr infrastructures. Two specific examples were extensive airborne camouflage trials of the Hornet, flown in formation with Starfighters under a variety of different weather and terrain background conditions, and a "try it on for size" trial of the CF–18 with existing Hardened Aircraft Shelters (HAS) at the two bases. In both cases, the trials were a resounding success. The drab air superiority grey of the Hornet appeared to be the best compromise for a myriad of conditions, and the Hornet fit - although sometimes without a great deal of room to spare - into all the existing shelters.

Laurie Hawn was one of the "founding fathers" of the Hornet OTU, and would eventually rise to command 416 Squadron at Cold Lake in 1989. He has acquired a wealth of experience in the CF–18, just as he had over the years in the CF–104, and is ideally suited to compare his two favourite aircraft. Though the

Below: *The final practice for the final CF104 flypast... 441 Squadron over the Black Forest, 24 February 1986.*

technological superiority of the Hornet is unquestionable, the reader will notice that the Starfighter has earned a warm place in Laurie's heart forever; an abiding feeling with all who flew this wonderful aircraft. Since English is "Hawnski's" second language, the following brief glossary is provided...

Washing machine	-CF–101 Voodoo
Baby jet	-CF–5
Mattel driver	-CF–5 pilot
AOI	-Aircraft Operating Instructions
Yellow gear	-external ground start equipment
APU	-Auxiliary Power Unit
High gain	-the ultra-sensitive mode of CF–18 nosewheelsteering
PIO	-Pilot Induced Oscillation
Corner Velocity	-the minimum speed where a pilot can physically pull the maximum "G" structurally allowable for any given aircraft

Trading Spurs & Stainless Steel for Leg Garters and Plastic

Anyone who flew the CF–104 considers it a highlight of his career. If you lost your fighter virginity on it, as the saying goes, it will always be your first true love. I felt that way about the Starfighter and always will, especially because it bugs the hell out of old "washing machine" and Mattel drivers, as well as the young guys. The only thing they've peeled back is their covers. Nevertheless, after about 11 years and 1700 hours of full-time and part-time flying in Kelly Johnson's masterwork, I was eager to try something new.

Having been lucky enough to get in on the ground floor of the New Fighter Aircraft Program, I was cunning enough to write myself into the initial cadre of Hornet drivers. Someone believed my snivels anyway, because, on 01 November, 1982, I was strapping in for the first

Below, inset: *The sign of things to come... Capt John MacNeil leads 2 CF-18s around southern Germany in May, 1984 during Exercise Rhine Hornet.*

training trip on the reformed (and reformed) 410 Squadron. Having had an abbreviated (to say the least) AOI course and about seven hours in the F–18 simulator in St. Louis, I was ready to dazzle the trusting Pete Pilcher of McAir in the back seat. My last trip on the '104 had been only three days before, so I was eager to see if we had really made progress worth all that money.

The first thought that strikes you as you walk out is - "What have I forgotten, and how come I can walk upright and not sound like a cowboy? Oh yeah, no parachute and no spurs. God, I miss those spurs already; what about my identity?" Your first impression as you approach the Hornet after the Zipper is "Geez it's big". You can't just walk up, stand on your tiptoes and look into the cockpit. When you do your walkaround, you don't have to practice the duckwalk to have a look at the undercarriage. The latter, by the way, looks like it would be more suited to support a B–52 than a fighter - "even Gillespie couldn't do a hard landing in this puppy". You'd have to be Kareem Abdul Jabbar to hit your forehead on the leading edge of the wing; and then it would only bruise instead of cutting like a scalpel. Two things strike you as you reach the blunt end. First, the thing's all tail; but, since fighter pilots never get enough, that's okay. Each horizontal stab is about as big as a '104 wing - "This baby's gonna TURN!". And the tailhook - no wonder they have a convention every year in its honour! That thing is definitely designed to peel it the other way.

Up the built-in ladder (nice touch) you go to a cockpit whose small size belies the overall dimensions of the jet. It's no bigger that the '104. Strap-in is a pain in the toosh. Four leg restraints and there's no macho way of slipping them on like cooly clicking your heels into the Lockheed C–2 seat. After the customary maritime lanyard, comes the "simplified" (?) combined harness. It's very comfortable once it's all done up, but not nearly as quick as the old harness. The oxygen hookup is one connection to the regulator mounted on the harness with no bailout bottle hose (since added) - "hmmm, not sure I like this". Comms are connected at the same location. "There, all set. Hey, what's this extra hose? Oh yeah, my G–suit; I still think these are for sissies." I'll learn to regret that statement.

Pre-start check - "Guess I'd better follow the checklist", although Pete is getting impatient and telling me that a quick left-to-right like every other jet will do. He's right, of course. Round the switches you go until you get to the fire warning light test. "Who's that bitching at me [1]? At least they could have made her sound sexy." Check's complete and a quick look outside to find the start cart to signal the windup. "Oh yeah, no yellow gear. Why, this means I can really go to some neat places on cross-countries." After firing up the internal APU, you go for the start switches and find only one with a left/right position for the respective engine. I could never figure out why they put two start switches in a single engine airplane like the '104, anyway; I always hit them both. Post-start checks take about as long as in the '104, once you get the hang of it, even though there are a few more things to check. And just like the '104, after a few trips you wind up waiting for the INS to finish doing whatever it was that Tex Findlay told you INSs are supposed to do.

Chocks away and off you go, holding the nose wheel steering button. "God, this thing is sensitive!" "Hey, this is great, I can taxi and wave to the adoring crowd with both hands." Pre-takeoff checks cover the same sort of stuff, except that there's a whole lot more aluminum, er...composites, moving when you cycle the stick. "How do all those flappy things talk to each other?" Taxi past 419 Squadron on the way to 31 Left, trying to look cool and nonchalant. "It's a good thing this canopy sill comes a bit above waist level."

"Cougar 13, cleared takeoff." "Rojah." No fancy, sky-blackening runups here; just release brakes and go to mil. Another straight push on both throttles and you're into burner with nice smooth lights like the '104. The jet is clean-clean and wants to get airborne long before you're used to with the Aluminum Death Tube (101 and baby-jet drivers are not allowed to use that term). After about 1000 feet and 100 knots, you start to rotate and, at around 1500 feet and 140 knots, it just feels right and you smoothly slip the surlies. "A HUNDRED AND FORTY...I'M GOING TO DIE!" Snickering (or is it whimpering?) from the back seat as you clean it up and climb away quickly with an ever-so-gentle, but very unmanly, pitch PIO. You can hit about the same speed at the end of the runway as you could in the '104. But, if you want to water your eyes, just keep rotating at about 150 knots until you can look back through the twin tails passing 10,000 feet and see the end of the runway.

Rate of climb is exceptional in mil power as you level off at forty-plus in about five minutes and forty miles. I guess that's what having all that wing does for you. "Man, the visibility out of this thing is something else. I can turn around and look right up my own... back seater. Okay, impress me jet; how fast will you really go." Into burner with no hesitation and very smooth lights. Just like the trusty J–79, the F–404 engines seem unstallable as you progressively try burner lights at slower airspeed and higher altitude. The burners light nicely at less than 150 knots and well above the CFP 100 legal limit of 48,000 feet. You can bring tears to the eyes of the most hardbitten CF–5 driver the way the throttles can be cycled without complaint. Of course, that's old hat for those of us who were used to real engines in real airplanes. From slow speed the acceleration is positively erotic, but as you approach the mach, the proud Starfighter on your wing has had enough of the upstart. The needle-nosed sliver grows bigger in your mirror and, at about 1.2, you're suddenly staring up the flaming... ah, tailpipe as it quickly becomes the proverbial dot. As the Zipper driver is coming out of burner to keep it under mach 2, you're struggling to get past 1.6 on your way to the most I've ever seen of a little over 1.8. "Oh well, I guess that's why Fighter God invented mach 4 missiles."

"Okay, so I can't outrun you; get back here and fight like a man!" Even the most diehard '104 driver must admit that the airplane was not meant to turn, except perhaps against a "washing machine". The expression "to bank as if to turn" was coined with the '104 and '101 in mind. The Hornet, on the other hand, is probably the most awesome air-fighter in the world today. The electronic flight controls and massive control surfaces make for extraordinary response and ease of maneuvering. Who knows, the way Glasnost is going, maybe we'll see the Fulcrum at Maple Flag and be able to make a direct comparison. Sustained 7 G turns are **de rigeur**, *loops can be started at less than 250 knots and a split–S takes as little as 2500 feet. "Follow me through that from 3000 AGL, you DRPCB!" Where the '104 had a corner speed of about 510 knots at 7.33 G, the Hornet can pull its 7.5 G at a shade over 300 knots. "Okay, so I'm a sissy, but you're not getting that GD G–suit back."*

Any guy who flew the '104 in Europe knows that Alpha is just a spot on the ground on the way to Siegenburg. Alpha is also a new word in the Hornet driver's lexicon which describes what really sets the airplane apart. Where the '104 would pitch up about about 22 degrees angle of attack (alpha), the CF–18 alpha warning tone does not even come on until 35 degrees. Even then it's only to tell you that you're not getting the most efficient performance out of the jet and not that you have reached incipient death. "What's that Pete? You want me to what? STALL AND SPIN IT?! ARE YOU CRAZY?? These things are expensive?!" After a demo, you give it a try and find that as you run out of flying speed at 80 - 90 knots (no, I didn't drop a 1), you can settle into a nice controllable 50 - 60 degree AOA hangup, keep pulling and watch the AOA pass 90 degrees (the readout goes to 99.0) or kick it into the prettiest little low yaw rate spin you ever saw. To do the latter, you need to hold full aft stick, full pro-spin aileron, full pro-spin rudder and have one throttle at idle and the pro-spin throttle at full mil. To recover, just

[1] "Bitchin' Betty"; the voice warning and advisory system installed in the CF–18.

take your hands and feet off and it stops instantly. With a lot of the initial cadre being old high T–tail drivers, this was pretty neat stuff and we argued that it was not really out of control because it was so easy to recover. We all enjoyed showing this off until D'Ville was forced to decree that it was indeed a spin and that it qualified as a prohibited manoeuvre according to the AOIs. Where the '104 dictum was "Depart and Die", departures in the Hornet are not uncommon and come in handy, if unintentionally, as a last ditch manoeuvre. Roll rate is not as fast as the '104 but is more than adequate and can still rattle your head off the canopy. Now that the Zipper has finally slowed down so we can catch up, we'll show him what "turn and burn" really means.

All Starfighter pilots know that real men fly at fifty feet; so let's take her down and shake up the birds. The airplane accelerates at low level much like the '104 and will go up to the mach easily in mil power… if you're clean. Load it up and it's not quite as pretty. Nothing will ever be as smooth as the '104 going like the hobs of Hell on the deck, and that certainly includes the CF–18. The automatically compensating stab cannot entirely overcome the effects of low wing loading and you can be in for a bumpy ride, especially if it's windy. What's disconcerting is not so much the vertical bumps but the airplane seems to wiggle its hips as well as giving a lot of little side-to-side bumps.

"Okay, let's try out some of the goodies." The INS is the same platform as the LW–33 of the '104 and as accurate. There are a lot more features available, however, and like in the latter days of the '104, it's easy for a guy to become an INS-cripple. The displays are cosmic and give you more information than even the sharpest old Zipper driver can process. The neatest thing about the system is the radar. While the basic picture for air-to-ground mapping is not as good as the '104, the expand features allow you to break out buildings, runways, hydro towers and even run–in lights. For air-to-air the radar really excels; I think I can count the number of lock-ons I ever had with the '104 on one hand. There's no hiding from this baby. Fred Kenny would have a hard time with this jet, as you need all ten fingers and a couple of toes to operate all the switch-mongery on the stick and throttles. It takes a little while but the piccolo playing starts to become second nature.

"Damn, is it time to go back already?" As we pop the boards to head down, there is a slight pitch-up but nothing like the '104. We'll do a radar first and check out this Head–Up Display instrument flying. It's nice but can be disorientating with the right background. Smooth and easy to fly in the pattern, the Hornet's gear speed is a little lower than the '104's at 250 knots. With the gear comes full flap (and we're talking

Below: *104 735 on a winter's day behind the barbed wire at Baden.*

a lot of flap). The approach speed will make a '104 driver's life flash before his eyes as the on-speed angle of attack matches around 130 knots. Even T–bird drivers are asking us to keep our speed up. "What are you whining about now, Pilcher? I'm not too shallow; this is how real fighter pilots are supposed to approach the runway. Okay, I'll get it back up to the Navy glidepath of 3.5 degrees" As I put the velocity vector just past the button, Pete reminds me to keep the power on, but starts to whine again when I start to flare. "You want me to fly it on like this? That's going to hurt!" As the wheels arrive at the ground, the jolt is one that even the most ham-fisted guy on his first '104 trip at 417 would have a hard time matching. Pete assures me that that's the way it's done; something about letting the airplane know we've arrived. We certainly have! You can grease the Hornet on just like the '104 but you can get a squirrely landing rollout if the flight controls still think that you're airborne. It's power up as you hit and instantly you leap back into the air. "Now that's a TOUCH and go!" Now it's once around the pattern and back to initial. As you roll into the break at 300 knots, it's hard not to pull 4 or 5 G; the aircraft feels like it's on the rails. The only bummer is that there's no J–79 howl to make CF–5 guys look longingly skyward. As you roll out downwind and find the runway you think, "Geez, this is gonna take a half roll and pull through." But as you coast around the corner at an eye-wateringly slow 140 to 150, you realize that this is the easiest aircraft to fly in the world. One more concrete-pounding touch-and-go and we pull into a closed pattern. "Now this is what the airplane was designed for - shit-hot closed patterns. We'll really be able to impress those civvies on cross-countries now."

Time's up and, as we roll out, I try out the anti-skid brakes. "No wonder they didn't bother with a drag-chute." There are a few more after landing checks than the '104 as you "ask" the airplane via the built-in test display and flight control display how it feels. "Just fine, thank you, Master."

Back in the line again, I try unsuccessfully to act nonchalant after amassing a total of 1.1 hours of CF–18 time. I can't get the smile off my face but, at the same time, I feel a little guilty. I have deserted my ever-faithful Starfighter mistress for a younger and stronger (but definitely not prettier) sweetheart. In one flight, she has captivated me and swept me off my feet. (Okay, so I'm easy.)

I will go back a year later for one last trip in the front seat and once more set my hair on fire in front of a fire-breathing J–79. The differences in performance and systems are even more dramatic to me then, as I step back two generations in fighter technology. I realize that we have definitely made the right choice with the CF–18. I am also grateful to the '104 for having brought me through unscathed over the years and there is a lump in my throat as I kick out of my spurs for the last time. I could not have lost my virginity to a more lovely lady. "Well, gotta run now, ma'am. We've got some Eagle-drivers visiting 410 and some asses to kick. The Sabre-days are back."

Dave Jurkowski accumulated a similar amount of '104 experience to Laurie Hawn over the years, and as Base Commander, CFB Cold Lake, has also had occasion to fly the CF–18. While also acknowledging the technological superiority of the Hornet, Dave carries a deep affection for the Starfighter, and cites a graphic example of how native fighter pilot skill and cunning, coupled with knowing your mount, can often triumph over high technology and false assumptions; even in a theoretically obsolete aircraft...

The CF–104 was a classic. To quote a German F–4 Phantom driver, "Ze F–4 is a war machine. Ze Starfighter - now dot is ein airplane!!" Sure, it couldn't carry wall-to-wall Snakeyes, but it could go just about as far as the CF–18 at low level with the same number of bombs (5), but do it at much greater speeds. Speed? Well, not many other fighters could keep up at low altitude. I still maintain that the only reason the '104 had such short, stubby wings was to have somewhere to put the ailerons! Survivability? Because of our speed, size and lower level operations, no Canadian "Zipper driver" was ever "shot down" by either air or ground threats in the three Red Flag Exercises in which we participated. In fact, to prove the point, Captain Laurie Hawn and I (on his wing) let it be known that, at a specific time-of-day and from a specific heading, a specific SAM site up in Tonopah Range would have the opportunity to be the first to shoot down a CF–104. We rounded the southern corner of the Kawich Mountain Range and overflew the site as advertised on the last day of the exercise. Except, to give them a fair chance, we flew in close formation at 285 knots, gear and flaps down, lights on! They missed us! However, we had yet another last laugh. Thinking we were two Harriers, two Marine F–4s (opposite direction) considered us to be no threat. Hawnski called gear, flaps and burners, and within two minutes, we "shot down" both F–4s.

All good things must eventually come to an end, and the CF–104 program was no exception. A transition plan for the Air Group was established, with the 1 CAG squadrons to re-equip in the following order: 439 Squadron, 421 Squadron, and lastly 441 Squadron. The Tigers were indeed the first to go on November 30, 1984, vacating their home in South Dispersal so that it could be made ready for a reconstituted 439 Squadron, complete with Hornets, the following summer. However, unexpected vertical stabilizer fatigue problems with the CF–18, coupled with unusually harsh flying weather at Cold Lake during the winter of 1984/1985, and a temporary shortage of spare parts required some creative readjustment of the overall CF–18 implementation schedule. This resulted in the already-formed 409 "Nighthawk" Squadron being moved to 1 CAG in April 1985, in 439's original reactivation slot. The decision was also made at that time to keep 441 Squadron in Canada and re-role it into NORAD operations out of CFB Cold Lake. In this manner, the 439/421/441 Squadron fifteen year monopoly of Canadian fighter operations in Europe ended.

In order to ease the burden of the new squadrons in transitioning to operations in the Central Region, each new CF–18 squadron arriving in 1 CAG was "twinned" with an existing CF–104 squadron during their work-up period to combat readiness. In general, this program worked quite well, and during the last year of CF–104 operations in Europe, it was not at all unusual to see "mixed bag" formations of Starfighters and Hornets thundering over the German countryside as they went about their transitional business. However, there was no doubt in the remaining Starfighter pilot's minds that the end of a marvellous era was slowly, inexorably approaching, and Tom Lawson captures the mood of the European CF–104 community at that time...

There was a feeling of urgency amongst the pilots as 1986 drew close. Those who needed flying time to pass the 1000–hour point became the top priority on the daily schedule. Others jockeyed for position on one-way flights to Turkey. The keen edge was disappearing. Years earlier, as the F–18 squadrons opened up operations in Cold Lake, we knew our days were numbered. But there was a feeling that the Starfighter could never really be replaced. This could be put down to a self-induced blindness and a love for the aircraft and squadron camaraderie. In fact, the '104 couldn't outfight a jet left in Germany, except for the odd German '104 out of Furstenfeldbruck. Though pretty, our jets were old. Rarely would a jet-log be signed out that showed less than 5000 hours. Inverted or negative–G manoeuvres would bring up flies out of the basement that had probably been airborne back when our COs were air cadets. Canada had skipped a generation of fighter technology, and it was time to make up the difference. However, when 409 Squadron showed up in Europe and we were tasked with passing along our vast experience, there was a short time when we could fool ourselves. Every instructor could afford himself the feeling, based on experience rather than skill, that his pupil could never been as good as himself. It seemed clear that these electronic wizards could never achieve our mastery of the European skies, but soon it was equally clear that the baton had been passed.

409 Squadron was declared Combat Ready in June, and all too soon it was 421 Squadron's turn to disband; an event which followed closely on the heels of the arrival of the reconstituted 439 Squadron at Baden-Soellingen. Thus on October 31, 1985, the Red Indians ceased Starfighter operations and closed the books on an extremely proud record that they had blazed across Europe during the CF–104 era. Gary Hook flew '104s with the Squadron from 1982 until 1985 and his article of the time in Der Kanadier, the Baden-Soellingen newspaper, records the mood of the moment and reflects on the perceived shortness of a fighter tour in Europe...

421 Squadron stands down CF–104 operations

Since November 1963, the distinctive howl of the '104's J–79 has filled the local airways. After 22 years of this ubiquitous sound of freedom, everyone has come to accept it being as common as the Schwarzwald to the east, or the interminable winter fog. However, in four short months, the Baden skies will no longer host the music of the venerable Starfighter.

Today, October 30th, marks the second step towards cessation of CF–104 operations by 1 CAG. 421 Red Indian Tactical Fighter Squadron will stand-down until June of 1986, when LCol. Ed McGillivray will return with seventeen other pilots and a full complement of CF–18s. They will re-form 421 in Europe with the Hornet and begin a new chapter in the Squadron's 43 year history. The third and final step in ending CF–104 operations will occur next February when 441 Squadron flies the last operational mission.

The Red Indians have had a long and distinguished career here in CFB Baden and have represented the Canadian Forces in Europe with pride and professionalism. They have established ties with 341 Squadron of the Luftwaffe based at Memmingen, and have built close friendships with many of its pilots. Also, through a series of fortunate coincidences, the Indians have redeveloped a strong friendship with a seemingly obscure organization in the United Kingdom, called 127 Wing. However, this Wing was very significant to the Squadron as it included 421 for a time under its command in England during the Second World War. As participants in the NATO exchange program, friendships and professional interchanges took place with pilots from Italy, Denmark, Britain, Spain and Holland, to name a few. Yes, the familiar red indian head and crossed tomahawks are recognized throughout NATO.

Squadron life is a unique experience here in Europe. To quote the vernacular, "one is living in the fast lane". Reflecting back to that sleepy-eyed arrival at 5 AMU, it seems like an eternity ago that we were pushing for a little elbow space as the throngs from the Boeing fought for position at the baggage pick-up. Then, relief is at hand when your sponsor tracks you down and leads you around for those first few confusing days. Ausfahrt, umleitung, ID card to get on base, funny looking trucks replacing the familiar sixteen wheelers, roads that never seem to run straight, and so many other invasions of what formerly constituted familiarity are the norm. The first few weeks never seem to end but then you realize that you have been a year in Europe and you haven't even visited Strasbourg! Where does the time go?

We settle into a routine of "mass hysteria". There is always a little panic to get to Met briefing on time. The weather changes, the schedule is shuffled, the range is closed, the CO wants that memo "yesterday", housing says your landlord needs 100 Deutschmarks more for the electricity, ops says they want you for your power-on ten minutes ago, and then, poof! Nirvanah! You are now seated in the "real office", the one with that trusty grey and black ball called the attitude indicator, all those straps; that snug feeling of the '104 cockpit that spells home. The throttle goes up for the second time, the burner lights; one kick, then the second. At 140 knots the line marker speeds by, the centreline is a ribbon of white, the nose eases up, and then that familiar lift of the seat as the jet becomes airborne. All is behind you now for a brief time; the memos, the landlords, the cancellations. However, the trip ends, the hassles re-emerge, and life goes on. Now it is two years in Europe and maybe next weekend we'll go visit Strasbourg.

Then, there goes the wonderful doorbell at 0400 hours. At first you think it is a bad dream but reality creeps in and you are greeted with that dreaded word... Snowball!! The grogginess clears as you speed off to work, whoops, back to the house for your pass, then off again. The world turns into a giant green bunny reunion as everyone suits up. The planning begins, the air attacks come and go, a gobbled-down sandwich as new taskings arrive, out the door with enough equipment for three people as you half run, half stumble to the HAS. Then, the mission is completed and the cycle rejuvenates itself. The hours fly by until those words of joy emanate from the loudspeakers, "Exercise 8599 is Endex at this time". Three years in Europe now and everyone keeps telling me about that cathedral. Tomorrow I'll go to Strasbourg; that's final.

Wherever the time has gone these last few years, it has now run out for those on 421 Squadron. Some pilots will stay on the '104 as members of 441 Squadron, some will return to Canada, and some will switch to desk jobs within the Air Group. Whatever the task lying around the corner, a special time has ended for the Red Indians. A squadron is a unique family; everyone goes through so much together. When it all ends, a certain part of the individuals involved ends as well. The memories of the good times and the not-so-good times meld to form an overall feeling, rather than a recollection of individual events. That feeling is a special one that words cannot describe, and as 421 Squadron stands down CF–104 operations today, it is at its peak.

With 421 Squadron gone, that left just 441 Squadron as a

Above: *This dramatic gun camera film was taken by Larry Crabb at Decimomannu in February, 1981. Range is less than 1,000 feet and the target was pulling 7 "Gs" at the time! Note the tip vortices peeling back from the wingtips.*

- photo by Larry Crabb

CF–104 presence at Baden, and its life as a Starfighter unit would shortly terminate as well. But in the last few months, the ultimate fate of the 1 CAG Starfighter fleet had to be finalized. Eric Thurston, the last CO of 421 Squadron describes the colourful transfer of the remaining operational CF–104s to Turkey…

The End of a magic era

On the 20th of January, 1986, at CFB Baden-Soellingen, the Commander of Air Command, Major-General L. A. Ashley, and Major-General O. Dincer of the Turkish Air Force General Staff signed a working document. It was accepted as the basis of an agreement between Canada and Turkey for the transfer of CF–104 aircraft and the associated material from the Canadian Armed Forces to the Turkish Air Force.

Early the next morning, six CF–104s launched from CFB Baden-Soellingen for their final home at Turkish Air Force Base Diyarbakir in eastern Turkey. Thus began a series of CF–104 ferry missions, cargo flights and sea voyages that, during the next few months, resulted in the transfer to Turkey of 44 serviceable CF–104s (39 singles and 5 duals), six non-flyable CF–104s, and tons of equipment.

When the Memorandum of Understanding was finalized, the program was titled "The Military Assistance Program for the Transfer of CF–104 Aircraft and the Provision of Logistics Support to the Turkish Air Force"; but for ease of administration, identification, annotation of documents and, to avoid repeated tongue injury, the code name "Taurus Maple II" was selected. Taurus Maple II was the second of the Turkish-Canadian Taurus Maple military assistance programs. The first, still in existence, was established in 1980 for the support of T–33 aircraft and other aerospace equipment manufactured in Canada and owned by Turkey.

From an operational point of view, the groundwork for Taurus Maple II had already started in November of 1985 with my appointment as the CF–104 Transfer OPI, responsible for the execution of the ferry missions and the coordination of the transfer of the vast amount of CF–104 spares and support material. Early in December, a meeting with Turkish officers was held at Turkish Air Force Headquarters in Ankara, and upon my return to Baden the real work began. Over the Christmas and New Year's holiday periods, the proposed ferry routings, the flight plans, the flight logs and overflight clearances through France, Italy, Greece and Turkey were developed; although throughout the transfer period, in order to reconfirm the flexibility of air power, many modifications were introduced.

Because of fuel considerations, the chosen routing consisted of three legs: firstly, CFB Baden-Soellingen to Italian Air Force Base Gioia del Colle, an F–104S base about 20 miles inland from the Gulf of Taranto; secondly, Gioia del Colle to Turkish Air Force Base Bandirma, another F–104 base located on the northern shore of the Sea of Marmara, southwest of Istanbul; and finally, Bandirma to Diyarbakir, located in eastern Turkey overlooking the banks of the Tigris River, approximately 75 miles north of the Syrian border.

The aircraft were configured with both tip and pylon tanks, and consequently enroute altitudes ranged between 26,000 and 29,000 feet and speeds between .83 and .85 Mach, especially on the long first leg to Gioia del Colle. Fortunately, because of the accuracy and reliability of the Litton LW–33 inertial navigation system, the routings were not constrained to airways with only TACAN waypoints. Additionally,

Photo: *Last of the last… 441 Squadron in April 1985. At front - LCol K.R. Betts, Maj W. Peirson; center - MCpl Maillet, MCpl Hupe, Cpl Perry, Maj MacNeil, Maj Doyle; rear - Sgt Pieroway, Capt Bayles, Capt Burt, Capt Sullivan, Capt Squires, Maj Savard, Capt Knowles, Capt Richmond, Capt Kovach, Capt Anderson, Capt Holmes.*

1. *Journey's end... This CF104 is about to touch down at CFB Baden-Soellingen.*

- photo by Christian Nachbauer

3. *The last ferry crew outside their hotel in Gioia on morning of their departure for Turkey. L-R back – Marc Ouellet, Walt Pirie, Dave Huddleston, Mike Spooner, Rob Godwin, Don Squires, Judge Wenham. L-R front – Eric Thurston, Wally Niemi.*

2. *This dramatic shot was taken from the Number 3 position in a 4-ship formation immediately prior to take off. Numbers 1 and 2 are scant seconds into their take off roll. Note the gunsight reticle, which shows that the pilots combat check list is complete.*

- photo by Gary Hook

because of the preprogramming ability of the system, all possible routing variations and emergency airfields were pre-loaded for each of the three legs. You old LN3 CF–104 jocks will appreciate how helpful that was, especially when trying to fly military routing through France on a busy commercial day. Of course, that only applied to the single; ferry flights in the dual were still a test of navigational and fuel-conservation skills, especially the Baden to Gioia leg and the final leg to Diyarbakir over the Turkish highlands east of Ankara.[1]

In order to enter the French military routing, the departure from Baden's Runway 22 consisted of an afterburner (AB) climb to 17,000 feet to avoid Upper Red 11 airway running between Strasbourg and Stuttgart, then a normal military power climb to overhead Bremgarten before crossing into France at Colmar. Because air traffic control coordination in the Rhine Valley was excellent, the AB departures not only minimized fuel consumption, but also eased the transition to the French military air traffic control system.

Typically, the first leg to Gioia was approximately a two hour "plus" flight. For the first ferry mission, the Italian routing followed the west coast south of Rome, and then an easterly turn towards Gioia. Subsequently, the routing was changed to cross the Italian mainland further north, overhead Pisa to the east coast, then a southerly turn towards Gioia. This routing, although no shorter, was easier from a traffic point of view, and it also made for an easier procedural descent and approach into Gioia. Since terminal radar was not available there, clearance was normally requested for a random TACAN to avoid the 90 nautical mile, fuel-consuming arc approach to Runway 32.

The second leg from Gioia to Bandirma followed a routing from Brindisi into Greek airspace on a south-easterly track to the islands of Milos, then a north-easterly turn to enter Turkish airspace south of Izmir before proceeding north to Bandirma. There was no doubt that on the first ferry mission the Turks were waiting for us to arrive. Overhead Izmir, I requested further clearance from Istanbul Control on the common enroute frequency, and promptly received three separate clearances: one from Istanbul Control, one from Izmir, and a third from Bandirma. Unfortunately, all were slightly different, so a few miles were chewed up sorting that out; however, the good intentions were appreciated.

The third and final leg from Bandirma to Diyarbakir (the shortest at approximately 600 nautical miles) was typically flown at 13,000 feet under IFR control at the request of Turkish authorities. Nevertheless, because the ground elevation was generally high throughout the trip, the sightseeing was outstanding. Approaching Diyarbakir, IFR was cancelled, weather permitting, and 15 to 20 minutes of superb low level flying was carried out between Diyarbakir and the Turkish/Syrian border over barren lava fields and sparsely located villages, scattering sheep herds.

Depending on the departure time at Baden, overnight stays were either in Gioia or Bandirma. Early launches refuelled quickly in Gioia and pressed on to Bandirma for an overnight of tremendous Turkish hospitality, while late launches stopped at Gioia and then continued to Diyarbakir the following day.

The unsung heroes of the entire operation were the maintenance, supply, and transportation personnel of CFB Baden-Soellingen. For the CF–104 transfer technicians, under the direction of the DCO, Major Peter Gartenburg, it meant maintaining the CF–104s at peak condition, cataloguing the myriad of spare parts and support material, providing turnaround crews at Gioia for each ferry mission, and providing specialist teams to assist Turkish maintenance staffs in both Baden and Diyarbakir, while at the same time introducing the CF–18 into operation at the Air Group. Supply and transportation personnel were inundated with spare parts and support material emanating from both the maintenance squadron and local supply depots, all of which had to be packaged, temporarily stored, and then loaded for transfer to Turkey via Turkish transport flights from either Baden or Lahr, or by sea transportation to Istanbul for those items either too heavy or bulky for aircraft. Additionally, supply personnel travelled to Diyarbakir to help that base's supply personnel unravel the spare parts and support material nightmare when it arrived in Diyarbakir.

The turnaround and repair crews prepositioned at Gioia were outstanding. Like any other Canadian deployment or exchange, by the time the aircraft arrived, all requirements had been organized - food, fuel, flight planning, transportation, even courtesy visits to the Base Commander and, if necessary, minor repairs. However, any repair became a time-critical problem because of the finite time limits for entry into Greek airspace. It is certainly a credit to those groundcrews that not one aircraft was turned back from Greek airspace because of an elapsed entry clearance time.

Of the 44 CF–104s flown to Diyarbakir, eighteen singles and two duals underwent periodic inspection at the Messerschmitt-Boelkow-Blohm (MBB) aircraft facility in Manching, West Germany. The remainder went "as is", in terms of time remaining before periodic inspection. Normally, when an aircraft was ready for the first test flight, the test pilot was flown to Ingolstadt by T–33. Once the aircraft had passed the Mach 2 run, pylon tanks were uploaded and if the remainder of the test card was successful, the aircraft was recovered at Baden. Otherwise, all major test flight unserviceabilities were repaired at MBB. During the duration of the periodic inspection program, Major Gord Hatch, Captain "Judge" Wenham and Captain Wally Niemi conducted all the test flights.

Besides test pilot duties, Wally prepared the flight logs for the routes, calculated the times, fuel and altitude requirements and also instructed Turkish pilots both in Baden and Diyarbakir on the difference between their F–104s and the CF–104, especially the Litton LW–33 inertial navigation and bombing computer. During that time, I really got to know Wally, his quiet sense of humour, his dedication to any task that he was assigned, and his loyalty to his friends, his compatriots and the Air Force; and consequently, his death while flying a CF–18 at Cold Lake was not only a very personal loss for me, but as always, an unwelcome realization of my own mortality.

The six non-flyable CF–104s were shipped from Baden to the MBB plant and were flown to Turkey via Turkish C–130 aircraft starting in late April of 1986. Of these six, CF–104s '737 and '787 were eventually put back into flying condition by the Turks to replace three CF–104s ('795, '866 and '839) which were destroyed in flying accidents in Turkey during 1987 and 1988.

Fortunately for me, during the rather hectic four-month period from January to May, I had the capable assistance of and advice from Major Mike Spooner; when he was not busy sorting out the Base Operation Officer's in-basket, which on a normal day was similar to the Toronto land-fill problem - or so I have been told. Mike was also responsible for selecting the pilots for the ferry missions between January and May; a real juggling operation considering the 30-day currency requirements and the fact that CF–104 operations officially ceased at the end of February. After the ferry missions were completed and I had been posted back to Canada to a staff position in Air Plans, Mike coordinated the final transfer of the remaining spares and support material.

The ferry missions took place with various numbers and combinations of singles and duals, mostly as a function of the production of the periodic inspections by MBB. For each mission, consisting of a series of two to three aircraft per flight, the preselected aircraft, normally including two spares, were flown twice at Baden to confirm systems reliability, especially fuel feed. Of course, the best laid plans, etc, etc, etc... For example, on the occasion of the last ferry mission, I had reserved for

[1] The CF–104Ds were never modified with the LW–33 system.

myself the honour of the last departure of a Canadian CF–104 from Baden, ending over 24 years of continuous service in Europe; however, approximately ten minutes after I had started my aircraft and anticipating the glory of that last take-off, I heard Mike Spooner's radio call as he limped back to Baden because his pylon tanks would not feed - a likely story! Consequently, Mike holds the record of flying the last Canadian CF–104 from Baden.

Like any other military flying operation, weather was a major factor. On at least two occasions, departure from Baden had to be delayed because of poor weather at Gioia. In fact, weather limits at Gioia were established higher than normal IFR limits because of the fuel situation normally experienced overhead Gioia, coupled with the fact that the flight-planned alternate of Brindisi, Italy had limited facilities for CF–104s, and maintenance crews were situated at Gioia with no transportation to get to Brindisi. Of course, as soon as weather delay was experienced, overflight clearances were no longer valid, and consequently there were many panic phone calls to the Canadian Forces Attaché (CFA) offices in both Rome, for the Italian and Greek overflight clearances, and in Ankara, for Turkish overflight clearance. Considering the sometimes marginal communication systems available, it was a miracle that longer delays were not common. However, the entire ferry operation was marked by a very cooperative effort on the part of all the nations involved, and is testimony to the good will of all the NATO members.

Communications and planning were made much easier because of the Canadian officers located in Turkey. Colonel Conn Platz, CFA Turkey, was the inside man with the Turkish General Staff in Ankara, and provided the necessary link with our program partners on almost a daily basis. Major Cumhur (Jim) Ilcan, a Turk by birth and a Canadian Forces officer by choice, was posted to Diyarbakir as the Taurus Maple II liaison officer, and provided excellent coordination and translation services. During the entire operation, Jim tried unsuccessfully to convince all the ferry pilots that Raki, the Turkish national alcoholic beverage, was the elixir of life. Most of us found, however, that it clouded one's mental ability as much as it clouded the water with which it was normally mixed.

For everyone involved in the ferry operation, it was a golden opportunity to experience wonderful Turkish hospitality, and to see a beautiful part of the world that many can only dream about. The Turkish Air Force personnel were remarkable hosts, and the Turkish people were extremely friendly. The country was beautiful to fly over, from the idyllic shores of the Mediterranean, over the interior steppes and mountains to the high plains area of Diyarbakir. On every ferry operation, with the exception of the first, the aircrews returned to Baden via an overnight stay in Istanbul, at either the Istanbul Hilton or at the stately Turkish Officers' Mess, both strategically located overlooking the Bosphorus. Thus for a short period of time, fighter pilots lived like transport pilots do for their entire flying career. After flying commercial to Frankfurt, the crews were picked up by military bus for the final return to Baden, sometimes arriving at the Baden Mess on Friday night just in time to play catch-up with the beer-call crowd.

Obviously, there are many war stories and tales of daring-do that will require telling over the years - the first arrival in Diyarbakir, the fastest aircraft painters in the world, the Turkish baths of Bursa (the ancient capital of Turkey), the labyrinth of bazaars in Istanbul, the gold-toothed rug merchant of Diyarbakir, communication failures in Greek and Turkish airspace, lost or forgotten passports, military escorts (Uzis included) through the streets of Diyarbakir, Topkapi Palace, Turkish tea and coffee, arrival gifts from excellent hosts, pistachios and wine, and many more. But the telling of those tales is best left to the 37 aircrew and countless groundcrew (preferably over a cold beer in the back bar at Baden at the next '104 reunion) who made the operation such a tremendous experience.

In retrospect, the operation was an unqualified success, and from a personal point of view, one of the most rewarding periods of my flying career. As those early months of 1986 quickly passed and summer rapidly approached, there was a gnawing realization that flying the CF–104 would soon be over forever. After 18 years and 2688 hours on this unique machine, I kept thinking how much I would like to do it all over again. Unfortunately, it did come to an end on May 6, 1986 in CF–104786 at Turkish Air Force Base Diyarbakir, when I landed the last Canadian CF–104. As I taxied in, I thought about those great 18 years - many friends made, unfortunately some friends lost, the common bond engendered by an operational commitment in a foreign country, and the unique, remarkable experience of flying the '104. As the mighty J–79 finally and reluctantly yet so characteristically whined to a stop, there was no doubt that a magic era had ended.

The CF–104 Starfighter will always be a lot of different things to a lot of different people, and those people will choose to remember her in a lot of different ways. Perhaps one of the more unusual methods is that of Al Stephenson, who flew the jet during her twilight years. Al has elected to immortalize the '104 in song, sung to the tune of the Beatles' "When I'm 64"...

So Long '104

Now that you're older, losing your wings, in a month or so,
We will still be sending you to Siegenburg Range,
Pampa, Suippes, they're all much the same.
Firing our rockets, dropping our bombs, Bullseye that's the score.
Glad to have met ya, we'll never forget ya, CF–104.

I remember the first day at 417, strapped into your seat,
Plugging in the burner, oh what a kick,
One hundred eighty, pull on the stick.
Pointing you skyward, flying Mach 2, who could ask for more?
Glad to have met ya, we'll never forget ya, CF–104.

Above: *The last farewell... 441 Squadron says goodbye at Baden-Soellingen 26 February 1986.*

- photo by Mic Mayr

We all love you still! Plastic, split-tail, 'lectric jets
Just don't have that thrill.

We have flown you in Europe for twenty-two years, now it's time to go.
Spending time in Marville, Grostenquin, and Lahr,
Drinking beer in Zweibrucken's bar.
Farewell dear Soellingen, adieu my old friend, like I've said before
Glad to have met ya, we'll never forget ya,
SO LONG ONE "O" FOUR!

All too soon after 421's stand-down in October, it was the last week of February, 1986, and with the standing-down of 441 Squadron, time to bid a final farewell to the Starfighter. Gary Hook recalls this solemn event...

It was a typical February day in the Rhine Valley that cold, damp Saturday. The skies enshrouded the valley with its blanket of grey hugging the hills of the Schwarzwald, embracing all of us with its European winter gloom. The inimitable howl of the J–79s came out of Central Dispersal as 441 Squadron started their engines; a routine procedure that had graced our valley home for some 24 years but was now being done for the last time. Yes, the CF–104 would fly again, but today marked the last time that they would conduct an operational 1 Canadian Air Group tasking.

Lieutenant-Colonel Adamson taxied out of Centre with his flock of twelve in close tow. Those of us who had done this for years watched with detached disbelief. It seemed that the CF–104 had always been here, and yet we were watching it for the last time. A winter chill was in the bones that blustery day, but the real chill came from watching our beloved jet make the final trip to the active runway.

As we waited for that final flypast, it was not a festive party mood as one might have imagined. The resident "'104 Mafia" had swelled it's ranks for this historic weekend, and '104 pilots from across Canada had dusted off their spurs and come back to Germany to witness the closing ceremonies. A great party was in the making, the ingredients were all there, but yet we were gathered outside in a very sombre mood. No doubt those who had flown this great aircraft, those who had laboured over it to keep it flying, or those who had supported it were all ensconced in their

Above: *Color Birds graveyard. This photo was taken in Baden's South Dispersal in 1986. All three of these aircraft, painted for the 1983 celebrations, were eventually used for aircraft battle damage repair practice.*

individual thoughts.

I was standing out on the taxiway with several other '104 drivers. We were looking back and forth, north and south, trying to be the first to spot the approaching formation. We finally picked up the distinctive exhaust trails to the south. The twelve-ship was coming at us, but for the longest time, they did not appear to move. The exhaust trails hung in the damp haze of the valley; without sound, without movement. The formation passed overhead, not fast, not low, but with the grace and strength that only the '104 could project. They came out of the haze, backlit by a hazy winter sun, leaving an indelible image on the mind. However, the moment I remember most was after the overhead break; the final aircraft touching down. Watching that graceful lady slow down, dip her nose as the drag chute deployed, was indeed special. There was no talking, no joking around; just a quiet, knowing group watching every move that wonderful aircraft made as she waltzed down Runway 04 at Baden for the last time.

This wonderful aircraft had served Canada and the NATO Alliance nobly for nearly a quarter of a century. It witnessed Canadian military aviation progress from an early post-war technology through several generations of fighter development as a bridge to the present day. It is perhaps only fitting that the CF–104 Commerative History published specifically for the Close Out Ceremonies in 1986 should have the final say on the end of this unforgettable era...

All those personnel involved with the CF–104 Starfighter through the years share a common place in aviation history. Time has already entrenched the Starfighter as a classic aircraft. From its days as an all-weather Strike bomber through the Conventional tactics of the 70's and 80's, the CF–104 remained a solid performer. During deployments to Decimomannu, Tactical Air Meets, annual NATO squadron exchanges and NATO Tactical Evaluations, CF–104 crews were respected for their professionalism and operational standards. It was for this spirit of the CF–104 era that man and machine will be remembered long after the smoky silhouette and the sound of the J–79 engine are gone from the skies of Central Europe.

- Per Ardua ad Astra

Thanks for the memories, Kelly Johnson...

Below: *This Jim Baxter cartoon underscores the emotional nature of the Starfighter stand-down.*

- courtesy of Jim Baxter

Below: The robust Starfighter landing gear didn't often let the pilot down like this

Alle Kunst ist umsonst wenn ein Engel in das Zündloch prunst...
All skill is in vain if an angel pisses in the flintlock of your musket.

- Field Marshal Gebhard L. von Blücher

This brilliant, charismatic and earthy Prussian warrior, who combined with the Duke of Wellington to defeat Napoleon Bonaparte at Waterloo in 1815, was certainly a fatalist. He intimates that in spite of the best laid plans, fate may intervene to deal an unkind blow for which there is no preparation. However, there were numerous CF–104 pilots who were well and truly "along for the ride" on occasion and yet managed to salvage the

Some Close Calls

situation by smart flying, prompt and decisive action, good luck, or most frequently, a combination of all three. Due to the very nature of the business, a lot of these close brushes with disaster were the result of spectacular ejections under equally spectacular conditions. Here are a few examples...

In May 1967, Mac McGregor had been seconded from 430 Squadron at Zweibrucken to Lahr for temporary airtesting duties. Though his story was briefly mentioned earlier in this book, it is well worth recounting in the detail of his own words...

I was sent from Zweibrucken on the weekend of 20–21 May 1967 to assist 1 Wing with some maintenance test flying in preparation for their participation in their first ATAF exercise from their new home. The move of the Wing from Marville was only partially completed, and air traffic and emergency services had not as yet been assumed by the

RCAF from the French Air Force.

My first flight was scheduled for Sunday morning in CF–104 '748, configured with a recce camera pod, tip tanks, and full fuel load. Visibility was 5 miles, with scattered cloud, temperature 15° C, wind light and about 30 degrees off Runway 21 heading. Takeoff distance was computed at 4164 feet, and the aircraft came unstuck at 205 knots. I selected gear up, and at that point my plan for the day started to come unglued. As reconstructed by the Board of Inquiry, events went something like this...

Takeoff to engine malfunction	1.8 seconds
Decision and reaction	2.0 seconds
Seat delay after actuation	1.0 seconds
Ejection to aircraft impact	1.9 seconds

A grand total of 6.7 seconds flight time for an airborne distance of 2393 feet.

My own personal glide ratio was apparently better than that of the '104, and I landed on the runway some 560 feet or so beyond the aircraft impact point. The aircraft snagged the chain barrier some 700 feet from its touchdown point at an estimated 170–190 knots, dragged the barrier some 230 feet, and then continued on for an additional 1645 feet.

When '748 lost all enthusiasm for continuing with this particular mission, I soon decided to dissolve our partnership. The canopy jettisoned on request, and the ride up the rails was quite gentle, with the exception that this was one of the few occasions where I had neglected to fasten my chinstrap, and the airblast very rudely removed helmet and mask. Height achieved during ejection was estimated to be about 150 feet over the runway, having been modified by a sink rate at the time of initiation, and no doubt influenced by the 50 lbs. or so by which I surpassed the other dummy - the one on which figures for seat performance were based.

The aircraft impact ruptured the fuel tanks and the vaporizing fuel ignited. From my vantage point, the view of the runway was totally obscured by a seething mass of flame, and I am told that first and second degree burns to my face probably occurred while I was still in the seat. The flames subsided rapidly however, and only a small portion of my chute was burned as I proceeded back to the concrete. My arrival was firm and completely lacking in grace.

There was at the time, and perhaps there still is, a detailed and comprehensive form entitled "Report on Injuries or Death Therefrom" which was required to be completed under such circumstances. It was to be prepared by the medical representative on the Board, in this case, Dr. Lyall Howlett. Since it was not concerned in this instance with the "Death Therefrom" portion, I was consulted extensively. As a result, my activities for some indeterminate time preceding, during, and following the event are a matter of record. Included in that record is my dinner menu for Saturday evening (I missed it), what I had for breakfast Sunday (a sticky bun and a cup of coffee), how many hours sleep, etc. Also included is my emotional response to the incident, classified by Lyall, as I recall, as one of "pessimistic startle". This means that I couldn't believe that something like this was happening to a nice fellow like me. I didn't really expect that my chute would have time to open; and when it did open, I expected it to burn, with subsequent grievous bodily harm to be occasioned by either the flame or the sudden stop. But I should have kept the faith, since my burns were minor. I also had a slight nick on my chin from having my mask pulled over my head, and I limped for a week or so from bending a knee around an emergency seat pack that accompanied me to the deck. I spent the next week or two, while I waited for the burns to heal enough for me to redon an oxygen mask, doing things any grateful repentant sinner would do: noticing grass growing, flowers blooming, birds singing, increasing my flying insurance, and gradually slipping back into my usual slothful ways.

Since Lahr had not yet settled into any normal routine and the normal administrative support staff was not in position, I spent a great deal of time with the members of the Board of Inquiry as they pursued their deliberations. In fact, I typed a large part of the proceedings of their Board for them. The cause of the compressor stall was the ingestion of a small metallic object, which had escaped detection as it lay in the area of the engine by-pass doors waiting to be sucked into the engine when the gear cycled. While it was regrettable that the accident happened, I was particularly impressed with the number of airmen who had looked for FOD (Foreign Object Damage) as they worked about the aircraft, and had done FOD inspections at times and in areas where their duties did not dictate that they should. The whole affair only strengthened my conviction that we had the finest airmen in the world.

The performance of French Air Force personnel was outstanding. The tower controller saw flames more or less envelop the '104, heard the detonation, and had hit the crash alarm before the aircraft hit the runway. They duty crash crew arrived at the burning wreckage within two minutes and penetrated the flames, thinking that I was in the cockpit. Fire fighters from the main fire hall arrived at the same time as the duty crash crew which had been positioned at the base of the tower. In all, sixteen firefighters manning four vehicles participated, and the fire was completely extinguished within four minutes of the alarm. Now I ask you - where else could one get service like that at 0930 on a tranquil Sunday morning?

Mac McGregor was not the only CF–104 pilot to have an extremely close brush with death. Rob Porter, who flew '104s with 441 Squadron from 1978 to 1982, had a harrowing experience on August 27, 1980 at Terschelling Range, an island practice bombing range off the coast of Holland. Porter and other Silver Foxes were on a summer deployment to Soesterberg, Holland, and enjoying the usual rigors of summer deployments in friendly places. Also, being within twenty minutes flying time of the North Sea bombing ranges was giving them an opportunity to practice their weapons deliveries in a new and exciting environment. Rob Porter had no idea when he took off from Soesterberg that warm August morning just *how* exciting it was going to get. Gary La Croix, a member of the flight that day who would later go on to test the CF–104 at AETE, picks up the story from here...

Our Squadron Commander, Lieutenant-Colonel Larry Crabb was leading the mission. I was flying the Number Two position with Major Rob Porter ("Herr Porteus") acting as Number Three on an element lead upgrade, and Captain Luc Trepanier brought up the rear as Number Four.

The initial part of the mission was routine; out to the range and into the first few weapons drops. The only anomaly was that Number Three was getting "no drop" calls from the Range Controller.

However, things definitely took a rapid turn on one of the later passes. We were in the standard canned "box pattern", executing 5 degree, 350 foot releases at 510 knots. I had just come "off hot" and was about three-quarters of the way around the cross-wind leg when Number Three called "in hot", for yet another attempt to get a bomb off. If you can imagine, I am now in a left climbing turn, through about 1500 feet, looking over my left shoulder, down at the target area. The next thing I heard was a transmission from the Range Controller to the effect of, "Three, I'm sorry to say you still have no bomb release, but there are pieces falling off your airplane."[1]

Well, it felt really strange as I grasped the magnitude of what had just been said. My good friend Rob was hurtling himself at the ground, "at the speed of heat", and someone was telling him his airplane was becoming unglued. At this point, time quite literally seemed to slow down, as I witnessed the ensuing events.

I moved my centre of vision to a point about two miles upwind of the target. My slant range to this area was about three miles. What

[1] In fact, the complete left leading edge flap was separating from the wing.

seemed like tiny splashes started appearing on the water over a range of several thousand feet. These were rapidly followed by one large splash; all of this occurring in less than two seconds real time. The next thing I saw was a bright white streak of light, and I thought to myself, "why is Rob firing a rocket now?" Within milliseconds, my brain snapped to the reality of his ejection seat firing. It seemed that almost simultaneously a huge splash erupted from the water and Rob's chute blossomed, only to disappear almost immediately.

The whole sequence probably occurred within four seconds, and Rob's time in the chute seemed like less than a second. At that point I was convinced that there was no way he could have survived.

Not having witnessed the above events, Number Four was calling for Number Three to check in, as we went into a high orbit over the range. I radioed, "Four, I don't think Three will respond." Meanwhile, the Range Controller could be heard giving precise directions to a rescue helicopter. Within minutes, the chopper was overhead Rob and was initiating a hoist recovery. We later found out that the chopper had to drop Rob back in the water, since he was still attached to his parachute, now filled with several tons of water. I don't know how he did it, but with a badly dislocated shoulder and other injuries, Rob apparently managed to extricate himself from the chute harness and grab the rescue sling for a second, successful hoist. These rescue details were not revealed to us until later. In the meantime, our three-ship returned to base, with outward stoicism, but inwardly quivering at the prospect of having just lost one of our cherished comrades.

The story, of course, had a happy ending, and Rob Porter, after a brief recuperative period, would live to fight another day. Inside the doomed Starfighter, Rob had been desperately fighting for his life. Out of control and inverted, he knew that safe ejection parameters were out of the question. In a last-ditch effort, Rob deliberately introduced aileron into the direction of this uncommanded left roll, and got the aircraft righted just enough to eject sideways, at no more than 100 feet over the cold North Sea. His remarkable presence of mind in that split second without question saved his hide. Rob would go on to complete a distinguished operational tour on Starfighters, but he would never again live his life quite to the full extent that he had in those few intense seconds over Terschelling Range.

Garry "Sky" King was another troop who had an extremely close call in a Starfighter. He flew CF–104s with both 441 Squadron and 439 Squadron from 1965 until 1971 and on July 21, 1967, he was on exchange with his squadron at Karup, Denmark. Garry recalls the subsequent events...

The Day I Met Jonathan Livingston Seagull

I was on a routine reconnaissance patrol mission over the Baltic Sea looking for East Bloc shipping coming out of the Baltic Straits and into the Kattegat when the incident occurred. Specifically, I was returning to the base approximately two miles off the Danish coast, at 300 feet above the water when I ingested a seagull into the left intake of the Starfighter. I saw the bird in front of me flapping its wings wildly, but I had absolutely no time to react. It ricocheted off the radome into the left intake where it knocked off a couple of impeller blades and started a massive FOD compressor stall in the J–79. When I heard the noise of the engine disintegrating behind me, I zoomed and attempted a relight. The relight was unsuccessful, and by this time I'd lost all my excess airspeed and was proceeding down the other side of my apexed flight profile. Wrongly, I decided to try another relight - to no avail. I then made the decision to eject. I pulled the ejection handle and waited for what seemed to be an eternity before the canopy blew away and I was ejected into the airstream.

I felt myself tumbling forward, felt the butt snapper push my seat away, and then after about three forward somersaults the parachute opened. I knew I was very near the water because I could feel it close to me, so I immediately reached down beside my right hip to pull my survival handle. It wasn't there, and before I had a chance to figure out what had happened to it, I was in the water. Total time from deployment to the water entry was approximately three seconds.

I immediately became a passenger on a frightening ride as the wind-propelled parachute dragged me at a fair rate of knots across and through the waves. Since I was still puzzled by the loss, or the supposed loss of my life support equipment in my seat pack, and because I was not in a very good sea tow position, I released myself from the parachute. This was a mistake of course, because I had not inflated my Mae West. I immediately sank, swam to the surface, treaded water, and attempted to inflate this piece of kit. The activation toggle was missing and I immediately sank below the surface of the water again. I struggled to the surface, took off my helmet and reached down again to activate the Mae West. This sequence was repeated several times and I was becoming puzzled and slightly panicky because I was unable to find the toggle to inflate it. I swam and treaded water above and below the surface for about five minutes until finally, being almost out of energy, I decided to let myself sink and concentrate on finding the elusive toggle. I took a deep breath, relaxed, and sank below the surface. Immediately, I grabbed the bottom of my Mae West, folded it up towards me so I could have a good look, opened the flap and discovered the toggle stuck underneath the CO_2 actuator. I dislodged the toggle and gave it a yank. The Mae West inflated, and I floated thankfully to the surface. Almost immediately after I hit the surface, for some unknown reason, I punched my stop watch.

At the top of the sea swell I could see a thin strip of land - the Danish coast. At the bottom of the swell, I was surrounded by waves. I was content for the time being to tread water, but could feel that the sea was quite cold. Directly above me, I noticed a lone seagull orbiting;

Above: *Usually, the pieces weren't this big... The remains of 104 631 are returned to CFB Cold Lake in November, 1974.*

obviously I had just killed his mate, or her mate. The seagull was to stay with me throughout my time in the water.

I took off my boots and spurs and removed all the extra accoutrements out of my flying jacket and the leg pockets of my flying suit. Although the Mae West was inflated, there was a ring of bubbles around the oral inflation valve which bothered me. Since I was so relieved to have a Mae West that was keeping me afloat, I was reluctant to push my luck and try the oral inflation valve. After a few minutes of treading water, I decided that because of the very low ejection altitude I could not expect to be rescued immediately, so I started dog-paddling toward Denmark. What seemed to be a long time later, I suddenly felt a very choppy motion on the water, looked directly over my head and saw a Danish Sea King helicopter. A paramedic was lowered on a winch down to the water; he landed right behind me and I grabbed onto his arm. He put a safety harness around me and we were hoisted together up to the helicopter. As I was put on the stretcher in the helicopter, I noticed my stop watch - it read 25 minutes. We then proceeded to Aalborg where I was admitted to the military hospital.

Interesting Footnotes:

1. The quick rescue was attributed to a 14-year-old Danish boy who saw the accident while playing on the beach on the Danish coast. He ran to the nearest telephone and phoned the coast guard - not his mother, but the coast guard. As it happened, there was a Sea King helicopter conducting training off the east coast of Denmark and they were diverted to my area.

2. This boy reported seeing an aircraft explode and crash; he did not see a parachute through the entire sequence. Other people on the beach saw the same accident and jumped in their boat to come and rescue me. Unfortunately, the quill shaft of their outboard motor broke just as they were getting started, and it took them a half hour to replace it. They were en route to me when the helicopter appeared.

3. Incredibly, the pilot of the Sea King helicopter was an old friend who was on the same Wings course in Canada with me three years prior. His name was Captain Ova Stalle. Once I was in the back of the helicopter, he asked the crewman in the back what country I was from and when told I was a Canadian, which was obvious from the Canada flashes on my shoulders, he said, "What's his name?" (Having trained in Canada, he knew we wore name tags on our flying suits.) When the name Sky King went forward, I could hear a commotion in the cockpit and suddenly appearing over me on the stretcher was my old friend, Ova Stalle. I hadn't seen him since graduation parade.

4. Upon arrival in Aalborg, I was immediately taken to the base hospital where I was immersed in very cold water in a bathtub, and it was there that the Base Flight Safety Officer conducted his initial investigation. Apparently I was in the early stages of hypothermia and it took a long time - an hour and a half - for my body temperature to get back to normal.

5. Ova Stalle offered to fly me back to Karup. On arrival, the entire Canadian detachment plus what seemed to be the entire base was out to greet me. They all lined up and I, quite emotionally, shook hands with approximately 500 people. I was originally listed as missing and presumed dead, and therefore I was now being looked at by everybody as a man that literally had returned from the dead.

6. After examining the Canadian sea survival equipment, the Danish authorities admitted later that they would not permit their Danish pilots to fly over water with our equipment. As a result of the accident, several UCRs (Unsatisfactory Condition Reports) went into the Canadian system to improve the lot of the Canadian pilot when flying over water. The mystery of the missing seat survival pack and the fact that I could not locate the release handle when I reached for it on ejection were subjects of intense debate during the conduct of the Board of Inquiry. The Board accused me of not having my seat fasteners tight, which I denied. Virtually everything was recovered from the sea including the survival seat pack with the fasteners pulled tight! In fact, the seat pack had slipped up, and was lodged in the small of my back when I checked for the release handle. Needless to say, a UCR subsequently was submitted for the seat fasteners.

7. When I asked Ova Stalle how he had found me so quickly, he said he just went to the east coast and started looking. I was right in the centre of an oil slick; obviously my dog-paddling was not too effective.

8. The sensation of flying through the air remains very vivid, and the noise sensation particularly so. The extremely high turbulent wind noise changed dramatically to total calm and quiet when the chute opened, except for the sounds of the waves and foam very close to me. I landed right on top of the aircraft which had crashed into the sea just seconds prior to my entry, and I splashed into the foam patch caused by the crash of the aircraft into the sea.

9. After I had shaken everyone's hand on the tarmac at Karup, I was taken to the bar in the Mess where an extensive debriefing took place into the small hours of the morning.

Fortunately for the Canadian Starfighter fleet, not all close calls ended in ejections. Pierre Rochefort had two very memorable "high anxiety level" experiences, the first of which occurred while he was still under training at Cold Lake...

I remember the date well; it was December 18, 1980. I was flying some sort of Basic Fighter Manoeuvers (BFM) trip with an Instructor Pilot (IP) in my back seat, against another IP flying a single seat aircraft.

To set the stage, it must be said that in BFM I was, at best, an average trainee. Up to that point, I had believed that extensions at 0 "G" were quite unnatural and uncomfortable. However, having been "caught up with" on many instances during egresses, I was determined not to let it happen much more. During "bar talk", a seemingly-knowledgeable IP had mentioned that in order to be able to look better for "bogeys" from his cockpit, he never strapped into his ejection seat too tightly. Since we were wearing bulky winter flying gear at that time, this certainly seemed to be the sensible thing to do.

So on that very cool December morning, I did not strap into the aircraft very tightly as I took off for a BFM training session. After performing a third half-hearted extension from a simulated dogfight, I could sense that it was not to the IP's liking. Cash had a way of teaching which definitely left an impression on you. It could be good or bad... but you remembered the lesson. Anyway, on the fourth extension, Cash rightly elected to demonstrate the proper extension technique with a little "physical" coaching. He thrust the stick forward and put the aircraft into a steep dive at minus one "G". As I was loosely strapped in, this had the effect of flipping me and the seat pack attached to my behind out of the ejection seat. As Cash relaxed the pressure somewhat, he unknowingly wedged me back into my seat sideways. To compound my (soon to be our) predicament, the top of my helmet had gotten stuck on bolts sticking out of the canopy front quarter panels. If that was not enough, my sternum was also resting on top of the control stick, permitting the dive to continue at 0 "G".

Feeling the pressure on the stick, Cash probably figured out that I had finally understood what a proper extension manoeuvre was and had volunteered to continue the egress. In fact, I was so far up against the cockpit instruments and canopy that I could not even talk. Fortunately, we were on "hot mike" and as Cash casually mentioned that we were flying through the "soft" deck[1] at "Mach Crit" and that I could "knock it off", I gargled something to the effect that I was stuck and unable to control anything, thank you.

Cash instantly realized the problem we were having and started pulling out of the dive... against my thoracic cage, which later proved to be quite painful. I managed to reposition into my seat during the recovery and, following a well-deserved session of verbal abuse, flew the

[1] 10,000 feet above the ground.

aircraft back to base.

Although seemingly a benign incident at first, we had come close. We had flown through the "hard" deck[1] *in a dive at 770 knots Equivalent Airspeed (KEAS), which was twenty knots above the maximum allowable airspeed. The groundcrew had never experienced the return of an oversped '104 and they hardly knew what to do with it. Cash, had he elected to eject from the aircraft, would have done so above the maximum safe ejection speed, thus rendering his chances for a successful ejection slim. So it is a good thing for both of us that he stayed and overpowered the weight of my torso against the stick. Needless to say, following the debriefing from this trip, it was Miller time!*

If you see post-1980 pictures of Canadian '104 cockpits, have a close look at the top of the front quarter panels. Where you would normally see a series of bolts protruding about one eights of an inch, there is a semi-circular bar covering the end of these bolts. It is called the Roche mod. No other dummy ever stuck his head in there after I did.

Roche's second bad scare in a '104 took place in Europe a short time later, and involved the triggering of the Automatic Pitch Control stick "kicker" on a recovery from a bomb delivery. This device, which was meant to assist the pilot in recovering from an aerodynamic stall at altitude, caused a lot of premature greying of hairs when it was triggered either inadvertently or through ham-fistedness close to the ground...

It was in the spring of 1981. I had just completed Combat Ready (CR) training at my new squadron and had passed my Tactical Evaluation without a hitch. So, with less than three months in Europe, in one of the most demanding flying environments in the world, I was eagerly anticipating an early upgrade to Element Lead. Not so fast, kiddo! First, you have got to scare yourself and survive.

There were two other Frenchmen on my squadron. I befriended them almost immediately and we nearly always flew together. They called us the French Connection. With the odd Anglo, preferably as good as we were, we formed a pretty efficient team. One day, this foursome was scheduled for an air-to-ground range mission at Siegenburg Range, just North of Munich, West Germany. The weather at homeplate was absolutely terrible, but the lead elected to brief, start, taxi, arm and wait for takeoff limits. Sure enough, the Anglo aborted on start and there were no spares. The four-ship instantly became the French Connection.

Takeoff limits did come up and we took off in a vic formation. We penetrated cloud almost immediately and I did not see anything other than my lead's wing tip tank and fuselage roundel for some twenty-five minutes. After rather excitedly switching radio frequencies, I realized to my amazement that we were actually cleared "hot" on the range. Later, I was to find out that it was normal procedure for Range Safety Officers (RSOs) to let Canadians on the range, even in poor weather conditions. Our whining was just too much for them to handle!

The two Leads with whom I was flying had obviously done this before. My voice must have given up the slight concern I felt, as the designated formation Lead reassured me: "Roche, make sure you stick to the pattern and don't miss the base call." Easier said than done. There was low-lying fog all over the range, except for the target area. The ceiling was no more than seven hundred feet and the visibility around three kilometers. Considering that we were dropping lay-down bombs at around four hundred feet and at a speed of six hundred miles per hour, it was going to be sporty indeed.

The first couple of passes went well... for the other guys. While I was threatening the wildlife in the nearby forest with wild and misdirected bombs, they were getting direct and near-direct hits on the target. I was getting very frustrated. After all, wasn't I part of the French Connection too? So I started to pay more attention to what they were doing rather than what I was doing. The rest was a classic near-disaster for me.

On one of the bombing runs (which was going to be last of the day) I found myself low, slow, and with the wrong head doing the thinking: I was going to drop a bomb, period. At about the time I figured I should get rid of the bomb, I saw trees ***above*** *my canopy. I immediately pulled real hard on the stick and, as Snake Said,*[2] *got an APC rate kicker, which put me level (I swore it was thirty degrees nose-down) with the top of the target pylon. At the same time, I heard this voice (the RSO's) saying, "95 feet at 6 o'clock, Two." And then almost immediately after, the same (now real mad) voice, "Negative Two, Foul Two." Hearing no reply - as I was fighting with a second rate kicker and dodging the tree tops just beyond the target area - , "Did you hear me, Two? That was a foul."*

I had heard him, but I was choking on fear, bile was coming up, and my eyeballs were stuck to the inside of my sun visor. "Gawd, that was close." Unknowingly, I had kept flying West, away from the range, and the Lead who had obviously seen (done?) it before, followed without saying anything. When he figured I had somewhat recovered, he nicely asked me if I would mind switching frequencies and then he led me back home.

I could hardly get out of the aircraft, but I did. In the debrief, there was not much more said than to be more careful the next time. And I always have been, ever since...honest! The sad part is that the Lead who had been very tolerant of my stupidity, later died in a mid-air collision with another one of our buddies. The other third of the French Connection became so affected by the loss that he quit to join a charter airline outfit as a non-flying executive. Me, I am still in the Air Force, relating scary stories.

* * * * * *

I can empathize with Roche in his consternation over the activation of the kicker, as I had a similar event happen to me when I was flying F–104Gs with the Fighter Weapons School in Arizona, and this was by far the most critical emergency that I ever experienced in the aircraft. In early 1981, I was leading a Weapons School surface attack mission involving high-speed, low angle pop-up deliveries on one of the manned ranges. On recovery from the second pass during a 5 degree, 500 knot

Above: *The Starfighter got back...this time. Dramatic evidence of birdstrike damage.*

[1] 5000 feet above the ground.

[2] A reference to the "Snake Sez" cartoons of Lockheed test pilot "Snake" Reaves, which were sprinkled sporadically throughout his excellent SURE Reports. These reports provided very useful tips on flying the Starfighter under different aerodynamic conditions.

simulated CBU delivery, the aircraft began an uncommanded, rapid nose low pitch oscillation. During the first two large oscillations, the APC system fired, forcing the nose of the aircraft even lower. More bad news, because the emergency disconnect "paddle switch" on the stick had no effect. At that point I momentarily considered ejection, but immediately decided that I was out of the operating envelope of the seat. While physically overpowering four more kicks of the stick with one hand,[1] I was able to reach back with the other and turn the guarded APC switch to "off" by feel. I finally recovered the jet at less than 50 feet and remember seeing a very large desert cactus filling the front windscreen on the pullout. Later investigation revealed that the whole nightmare had been caused by an insidious break in the wiring in the stabilizer trim actuator and the pitch servo disconnect. During "G" loading, the wires separated, and unloading reconnected the wires. This malfunction was also greatly amplified by the fully-functioning APC system. It was only after I had turned the APC system off that the oscillations ceased. I firmly believe that it was only my intimate knowledge of the Starfighter, based on a great deal of accumulated experience, that saved my life that day. Though I received a very nice Commendation from the United States Air Force for, in their words, "his superior airmanship and prompt reaction to this grave in-flight emergency, which undoubtedly prevented the loss of an aircraft and averted possible injury", I must hasten to assure the reader that my actions were motivated by a completely selfish desire to continue breathing, and had nothing to do with trying to save the jet. In fact, had I felt that I had been within safe ejection parameters, I would not have hesitated to "jettison the aircraft". I, like virtually everyone who flew the '104, had long since come to the conclusion that, under certain emergency conditions, the aircraft was not worth a plug nickel, and that given these conditions, the decision to eject would have to be near-reflex.

* * * * * *

The *intentional* deactivation of the APC system on missions involving dynamic maneuvering close to the ground was an extremely emotional issue throughout the Starfighter era. While no one doubted the utility of the system at high altitude, where airspace for recovery was generally not a problem, the '104 community was effectively divided on the usefulness of the system in the air-to-ground arena. Some felt that the system saved lives by preventing an aerodynamic pitch-up, while others maintained that the cure was worse than the disease; in other words, that activation of the stick "kicker" at low altitude exacerbated a pilot's problems by "kicking him into the ground". Wally Peel, who flew '104s with 441 Squadron during the twilight years of the program, suggests that this procedural controversy followed the CF–104 to its operational grave...

I had the pleasure/displeasure/honour of conducting the last kicker study of the Starfighter era, when we had yet another pilot hit a tree after inducing kicker activation during recovery from a practice weapons delivery against a tactical target. While researching the background of the "kicker debate", the most surprising fact that came to light was that most of the previous studies, and APC usage rules, were based for the most part only on emotional views. Very little effort had been made to assess the system's operation objectively, particularly its impact on pilots who were attempting to appease the system by making their recoveries more gentle [2]. Some of the APC viewpoints and procedures promulgated over the years were falsely predicated on the supposition that the system was not working properly. It was seen to be not only the cause of at least one death, but was often viewed as an unnecessary system, good only for striking great fear into the hearts of many '104 pilots. In fact, in the case of the last pilot who hit a tree, subsequent investigation revealed that he could easily have recovered the aircraft, except that he was ***gently*** *pulling on the stick in order to avoid a second activation of the kicker.*

Thus over the years, there was a variety of inconsistent logic applied to rules written in Flying Orders as to when and where to deactivate the system. Regardless of the controversy, when the APC system was engaged and the kicker fired, the additional loss of altitude was excessive and ***could*** *prove fatal. During my study, it was discovered that the German Air Force had modified their Starfighters such that the additional hydraulic pressure, which abruptly forced the horizontal stabilizer pitch change during the activation of the kicker, was bled off more quickly. This significantly reduced the additional altitude lost after the kicker fired.[3] In fact, this modification was incorporated in the CF–104 fleet for its last two years of service. The final legislation on the issue was that the APC was to remain* ***on at all times*** *to protect against the possibility of pitch-up.*

In spite of the physical modification and the final rules, the emotion and debate centering around this system will undoubtedly continue to be the subject of heated discussion by some Starfighter pilots until memories of the kicker fade into history.

Sometimes during critical emergencies in the CF–104, when skill and cunning had all been used up, it didn't hurt to have a little Divine Intervention. Ian Struthers, who flew Starfighters in Europe with 441 Squadron from 1975 until 1978, thinks that this may well have happened to him...

On Friday, June 27th, 1975, after waiting for the last sorties to launch, Capt. John Evans (Officer in Charge Wing Operations Centre) and I taxied out in aircraft 104658 enroute to Denmark for a "dirty weekend". As this was John's first Starfighter trip and he had spent his career in the back seat of Voodoos, I was not about to have any bad mouth with regards to the performance of the '104. Consequently, I planned a burner climb to Flight Level 230 on the normal SID [4] departure for Runway 22.

The weather was about 1500 feet and 3 miles in haze; the type of cloud that you can see straight down from 20,000 feet, but nothing forward. We had a full fuel load with pylon tanks and the takeoff and clean-up went by the book. As we passed through 14,000 feet, still in burner, and just prior to the right turn that brings you back overhead, a large bang was heard, a noticeable loss of thrust was felt, and to my horror, the EGT [5] was pegged past 1000°C. My immediate reaction was to pull the throttle to idle and turn left back towards the base. John asked if there was a problem (he knew that there was) and if he could assist. I replied in a rather high voice, that all was not up to scratch and we had to make an emergency return to base.

At idle power the engine instruments were normal, and while I felt certain that we had experienced a compressor stall for which the checklist calls for engine shut-down, I believed that since the indications were now normal that action would be somewhat imprudent. I then advanced the power towards 100% and the engine stalled again at 86%. Meanwhile I was talking to radar, had the Tacan needle slightly offset to the left and established my gliding speed at 260 Knots with takeoff flap. This produced a rate of descent of approximately 3200 feet per minute, and any further back pressure on the stick to decrease this only caused a rapid decrease in airspeed and increase in the rate of descent. I was not a happy camper!

On reduction to idle power, once again, the engine cleared itself to normal parameters. This time, I advanced the power to 85% and left it there. It held for about two to three minutes and then compressor stalled again. I advised radar that I would have to jettison my tip and

[1] One finds an unusual amount of physical strength under the circumstances!
[2] In point of fact, with a *normally* operating APC system, the pilot could physically overpower the stick kicks and recover from the ensuing dive.

pylon tanks, and as I was about to push the external jettison button I noticed a French village below. I waited until I couldn't stand it any longer, then jettisoned the tanks. To my surprise, I could see the tip tanks go almost straight out from the aircraft, and not back as I had anticipated. John, meanwhile, advised me that all the tanks had separated cleanly. The engine compressor stalled again and I set 82% which held for the time being. With the departure of the fuel tanks, the rate of descent eased off somewhat to between 2500 and 2800 feet per minute. When I visually saw the runway, I felt confident that we were in a good position and I planned an initial touch-down point of half way down the runway.

As I started the turn to final, I felt stick shaker and initially thought, "No problem, it's just the dual." Then I quickly realized that we no longer had fuel tanks and therefore the stick shaker indication was valid. Because my height seemed more than adequate, I decided to lower the gear and it came down without any problem. I continued the turn on light stick shaker and realized that while our height was good, I would not be able to make the turn to line up with the runway. The only option I could think of was to use Land flap, which I then selected. The good news was that it worked beautifully, the stick shaker went away and the turn rate increased so that I was able to line up with the approach end of Runway 22. The bad news was that the added drag increased my rate of descent tremendously and I could see that we were going to hit short. I then automatically firewalled the throttle and low and behold, it worked! We touched down about 12 inches past the threshold, much to my delight, and John's as well I might add. To this day, I believe that the big hand of God gave me that extra half mile to the runway. The technical side of the explanation was that because Land flaps have boundary layer flow, which utilizes bleed air from the 17th stage of the compressor, this allowed the engine to operate without another compressor stall.

The trip was 15 minutes long and as we rolled to a stop to be met by the Base Commander, Col. Roddick, Sgt. Brown (the NCO in charge of the Wing Operations Centre) was heard to comment to John Evans..."Besides that Sir, how did you enjoy your first Starfighter trip?"

The final investigation showed that a 5/8" bolt had trashed the engine. However, it was not from the aircraft. The checklist was also revised to reflect that if the engine clears at idle after a compressor stall, do not shut the engine down and attempt a re-light!

As usual, Air Traffic Control, the firefighters and all others did a great job and were there when we needed them.

EJECTION SEAT

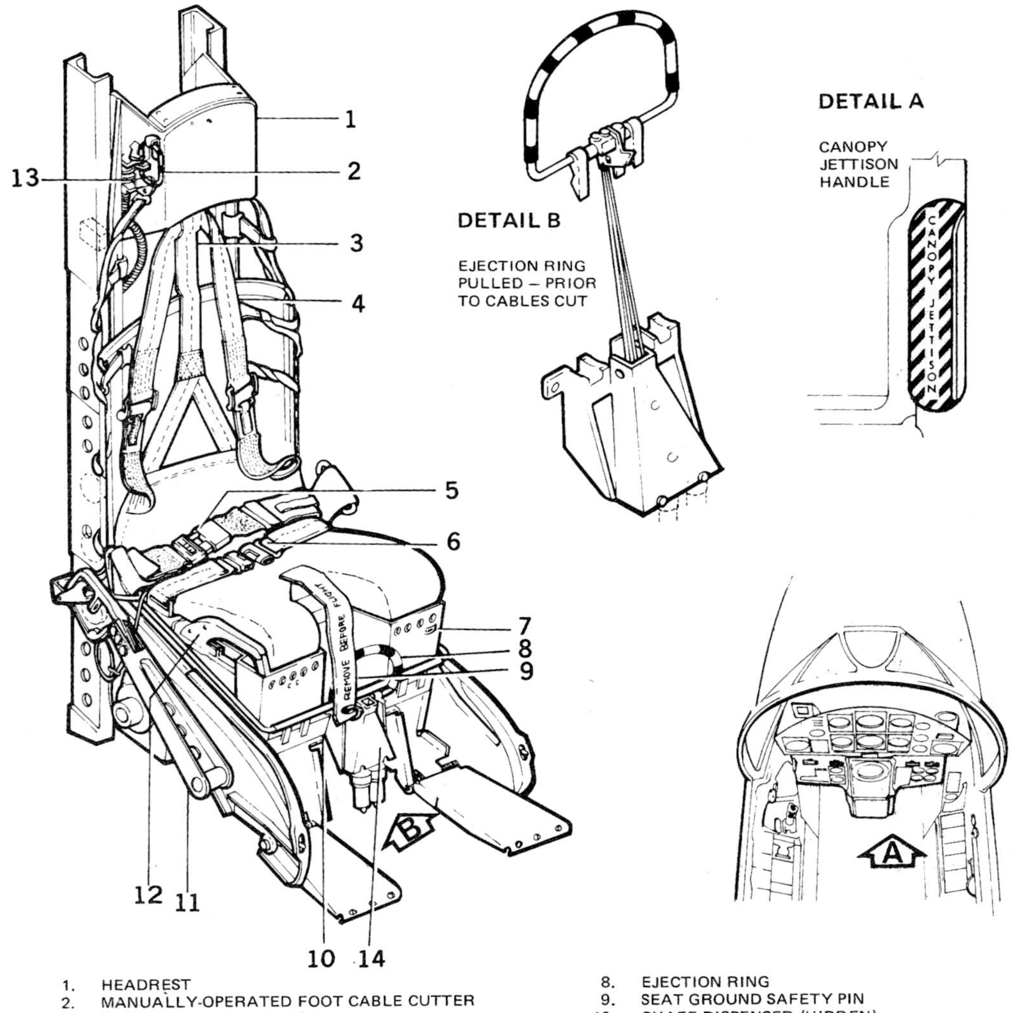

1. HEADREST
2. MANUALLY-OPERATED FOOT CABLE CUTTER
3. PILOT – SEAT SEPARATOR
4. SHOULDER HARNESS
5. RPI LAP BELT
6. SURVIVAL KIT ATTACHMENT STRAP
7. OXYGEN SYSTEM FLOW TESTER CONTROLS
8. EJECTION RING
9. SEAT GROUND SAFETY PIN
10. CHAFF DISPENSER (HIDDEN)
11. KNEE GUARD (STOWED POSITION)
12. SURVIVAL KIT RELEASE HANDLE
13. OXYGEN MASK HOSE STOWAGE PLUG
14. EJECTION RING CABLE CUTTER (HIDDEN)

[3] The author was flying an aircraft with this modification when his previously-described incident occurred.
[4] Standard Instrument Departure
[5] Exhaust Gas Temperature

COLD LAKE
104783
FORCES ARMEES CANADIENNES
CAF 872

War Stories and Miscellaneous Ramblings

- photo by Bill Johnson

Squadron exchanges with representative units from other NATO nations were a favourite social and professional pastime during the CF–104 era, and each line squadron had an exchange of sorts almost every year. Sometimes these exchanges evolved into longer-term relationships, as was the case between 421 Squadron and 341 Jagdbombergeshwader of the Luftwaffe at Memmingen. These two units were formally established as sister squadrons in March of 1974, and forged lasting ties of friendship and professional cooperation dating from that time. This pairing concept eventually developed into a practical working relationship, and in 1975 a program was initiated whereby each of the squadrons would send one pilot to the other unit for a three-day period of operational integration. This program reaped tremendous benefits in terms of mutual education, and was destined to occur several times each year for many years. However, twinning with a NATO neighbour meant acceptance of some of their quainter customs, some of which could be a true endurance test, as described in the 421 Squadron Official History...

Lieutenant-Colonel Herb Sievert, CO, and the Squadron Operations Officer, Major Ross Huckle, participated in a Mini Exchange to the Memmingen sister squadron in May, 1978. Like all pilots who exchange with 341 Squadron, they were invited to participate in the Squadron's demolition exercise, known as the Bavarian Triathalon, which tests the known abilities of trained fighter pilots. In competition against time and a 341 Squadron representative, the 421 duo was required to sniff twenty centimeters of snuff per nostril in a two-minute period, followed by a two-minute break. Then, they chug-a-lugged two litres of beer each (or as much as they could in a three-minute time period). Following another short break, they were tested on their ability to hammer eight nails of varying lengths into a piece of wood within a certain period of time. Victory fell to the well-trained Canadian pilots in the hard-fought battle.

But not all the quaint customs were merely social, and some fundamental differences in the way different nationalities did business were experienced by Gord Hatch during a deployment to Spain in 1983...

In 1983, the Spanish Air Force indicated an interest in a limited simultaneous squadron exchange with the Canadians at Baden. This event was to be in addition to the normal non-simultaneous mass exchanges assigned to the Baden squadrons. Initially there was little interest because of the multitude of tasks that the squadrons were supporting, but it was finally agreed that 441 Squadron would organize the deployment to Madrid and 421 Squadron would plan the hosting at Baden. The deployed group would consist of two pilots from each 1 CAG Squadron, and a collection of servicing personnel.

In August 1983, a liaison visit to Spain was carried out to finalize the details of what would be the first Canadian-Spanish exchange. The 1.8 hour trip was a fair stretch for even a four-tanked machine when one considers the fuel used for the usual French air traffic control detours and required altitude changes. Because of the bi-country agreement that had the USAF sharing the Madrid Torrejon Base, the aircraft were required to land across town at a small transport base. The crews were then given a spirited drive through Madrid to Torrejon.

The meetings went well, and the proposed departure into France the following day would have been on time until it was discovered that the locals were still trying to get the two drag chutes down to a size and shape that would allow insertion into the drag chute box. Needless to say, it required a number of repackings and a good deal of brute force.

The actual exchange took place from October 2, 1983 to October 7, 1983. The deployed group aircrew were Major Gord Hatch and Captain Mark Holmes from 441 Squadron, Captains Andre Deschamps and Wally Niemi from 421 Squadron and Captains Al Stephenson and Bill Huckstep from 439 Squadron. Four aircraft equipped with tip and pylon tanks made the trip, while support personnel and equipment came by CC–130 Hercules. On arrival, the pylon tanks were taken off the two aircraft designated for ACM, while the two to be used for low level navigation and tactical training were left with both their pylon and tip tanks.

The schedule was planned so that the six pilots would rotate through the four aircraft and all get to fly some Dissimilar Air Combat Training (DACT) and low level tactical sorties. The first sorties were real eye openers. For the hosts, the building of accurate attack maps with precise timing and tactics was unheard of. They all knew where so-called targets such as dams, bridges and railyards were located, and they would just fly there to carry out simulated attacks. We had been led to believe that we could use their maps. After the first planning phase, they discovered that we had actually cut up a fair number of maps for our mission. We were told that maps were not to be cut but were to be used with pencil lines and then folded. After the sortie had been flown, the marks were to be erased and the undamaged maps put back in their drawers. For pilots used to hacking up route and run-in maps by the dozen, it was a rude awakening.

Another shock was the effect of the pecking order within the squadron. After the first DACT sortie, we discovered that there would not be a debriefing because it would mean a loss of face for their senior pilots who repeatedly used a "knock-it-off" call when a CF–104 called a shot. The fact that ground attack CF–104 aircraft with tip tanks were coming back with good gun film of F–4 aircraft was more than they could believe. As the week progressed, we also realized that our system of letting the most qualified pilot lead the mission, regardless of rank, was also beyond their comprehension.

The Spaniards were superb hosts and fêted the visitors to a first class banquet the night before the departure. They had not, however, counted on 441 Squadron for a challenge to eat raw eggs. After the required demonstrations, which included the 421 and 439 stalwarts, only a few of the locals distinguished themselves with stellar performances.

Near the end of the deployment, the wing commander reminded us that the host squadron had flown F–104 aircraft in the day interceptor role prior to receiving the F–4C aircraft. On the wall was a plaque noting that the squadron had flown some 15,000 hours without an "A" category accident. A few remarks were also made about the German and Canadian accident record, and in reply it was pointed out to him that the four CF–104s ***on the line*** *had between them more than 16,000 hours without an accident.*

Emulating the customs of others can often lead to hilarious results. Pat Barrett flew '104s with 441 Squadron from 1974 until 1977, then as Group Flight Safety Officer at the Headquarters in Lahr until 1979. In 1975, the era of "piano burning for fun and profit" was in its heyday, and Pat recalls a particularly expensive exchange with the RAF that summer...

441 Squadron's June 1975 exchange with 14 Squadron, RAF Bruggen, was memorable for, among other things, an introduction to the RAF pastime of burning pianos. As it turned out, 441 stalwarts provided the first demo, but unlike the Brits, whose habit it was to acquire an over-the-hill instrument for their project, 441 chose a fully operational one; the Bruggen Officers' Mess piano no less, which in the course of the "meet-and-greet" went up in flames on the Mess lawn.

The extra-high profile that this event soon took on was the result of plain bad luck in that the Station Commander's wife had a piano recital scheduled in the Mess for the following morning.

During the subsequent visit of 14 Squadron to Baden-Soellingen, the RAF returned the favour with a midnight conflagration featuring the Officers' Mess baby grand on the street outside the front door. This event attracted, among others, the fire department, a streaker, and eventually the A-R-M-Y who were less-than-pleased seeing the abuse of their "table"[1]*. A major effort ensued over the following days involving all sorts of high rollers attempting to soothe the ruffled grunts.*

No book on the CF–104 era would be complete without mentioning the "grand-daddy" of all the exchanges, the annual NATO Tiger Meet, of which 439 Squadron was a perennial member in good standing. While the stories associated with Tiger Meets are legion, perhaps the most infamous of these gatherings was the 1975 iteration, hosted by 52 Squadron of the Luftwaffe at Leck in Northern Germany. Jim McCullough describes this memorable event in depth...

The trip to Leck originated from Lahr where 439 (Tiger) Squadron, along with the other 1 CAG squadrons, had been deployed because the runway lighting system at Soellingen was being upgraded. After arriving at Lahr by bus and visiting the Meteorological Office, I was delighted to learn that the weather between Lahr and Leck was "clear and a million", and would remain that way throughout the day. Based on that forecast, I planned a low level route between Lahr and Leck. After completing my mission planning I was informed, by a pilot not scheduled to attend Tiger Meet, that the Leck weather had "gone clampers". I discounted his comment for three reasons. First, the weatherman who presented the weather briefing was extremely confident of what to expect enroute and on arrival. (The "Met Man" was so confident that I should have been suspicious.) Second, I attributed the pilot's comment concerning a deteriorating weather situation to be one of sour grapes. Third, McWillie (who was sitting on the throne) heard the deteriorating weather comment and declared it to be incorrect. Who knows more about anything than McWillie, especially when he's sitting on the throne?

Airborne and enroute to Leck, the weather began to deteriorate, and by the time we reached the Bingen area, the distance between ground and cloud base was extremely limited with visibility reduced in rain to about as far forward as the gunsight. At that point, I made the decision to close up the formation, stroke the burners, and get the four '104s "On Top" because there was no other logical place to go. Thirty thousand plus feet later we arrived "On Top" and proceeded to Leck between some classic anvil-shaped clouds protruding through the stratus. An inauspicious beginning to a number of inauspicious events that collectively form my recollection of "Tiger Meet '75".

Of the many unusual events that took place at Tiger Meet '75 that are etched clearly in my mind, the traditional Tiger Meet flypast has to qualify as the damnedest thing I have ever participated in during my thirty-three year military career.

Technically, the 1975 Tiger Meet flypast never took place because when the GAF authorities at Leck requested authority for the flypast, it was denied. Therefore, at a predetermined time, thirty-odd aircraft in Vic sections of fives and boxes of four were just going to "happen to take off, work the same radio frequency, and, by the way, this section is red, this section is green..."

In order to ensure maximum safety during this non-event, a number of sections would be led by GAF G–91s flown by pilots who were familiar with the area. Unfortunately, these individuals failed to arrive at the non-briefing for the non-flypast. In order to absorb the time, a series of sexually explicit adult films were screened. When it was time to depart the briefing room, we were extended several final pieces of advice by an Italian pilot who lectured us on the dangers of jetwash from flying too high relative to the aircraft in front and how, if we flew too low, it would look terrible. His dissertation was greeted by many with "you got it, Luigi".

After proceeding to the '104s and starting, I now had four aircraft running and nowhere to go. Fortunately, at that point a GAF type handed me a message that read, "follow G–91 3296". In spite of the dispersal area of Leck Air Base being like a forested maze, very soon after beginning to taxi I spotted G–91 3296. Everything was now under control because I knew that 3296 was being flown by the squadron commander and that we were the first section. Best to be close to the front of the pack in big flypasts!

We took off with the G–91 rolling as a single and the four '104s rolling as two-plane elements. We joined up in a five-plane vic at 360 knots. This meant we flew with takeoff flap down, and with each turn a degree of rudder was required. The problem being that at 360 Knots, when a G–91 puts on 30 degrees of bank, it turns; a '104 under the same conditions simply flies straight ahead with one wing low!

The first post takeoff indication we had that it was not going to be a swell trip was when we met a GAF RF–4 beak-to-beak over the Isle of Sylt. That caused a slight delay in re-establishing the formation and rebuilding confidence. The purpose of the RF–4 was to photograph the non-existent Tiger Meet flypast.

After the excitement caused by the RF–4, everything settled down nicely. In fact, the formation was going so smoothly that the leader

Above: *441 Squadron's piano exchange team at RAF Station Bruggen in 1975. The Chief Torch, LCol John Hutt, expresses financial embarassment. Left to right: Jim Maurstad, Gus Youngson, Ian Struthers, Laurie Hawn, John Hutt, Bruce Stott, Ted Lee and Pat Barrett.*

[1] Army officers stationed at Baden-Soellingen, lacking their own "Pilot's Bar", habitually used the piano as their "stand-up" luncheon table during noon-hour in the Officers' Mess.

104838
LECK GAF
52
TIGER MEET
75
TIGER MEET '76
NATO
TIGER MEET '77
UPPER HEYFORD
31 Smd
KLEINE
BROGEL
NATO TIGER MEET 1978

decided we should expand the exercise to include an overflight of Hussum Air Base to show them what they were missing. It was over Hussum that things really "got off the rails"!

To fully understand the event, it must be appreciated that the flypast included Belgique, Italian, RAF, German and Canadian aircraft. What is significant is that one of the RAF aircraft was flown by an American exchange officer with a German navigator in the back seat, who was just along for the ride. This particular RAF aircraft, along with three other Gnats, were in Vic formation on a GAF G–91 which was piloted by a Lieutenant whose formation qualification, as Lead, was limited to two-plane elements.

It was over Hussum Air Base that a speed change occurred, the separation between sections disappeared, and a mid-air collision was the result. An RAF Gnat collided with an Italian F–104S that was, prior to the speed change, two sections in trail ahead of the Gnat.

Dave Jurkowski, another member of the fabled Canadian flight of four that day, describes what happened next . . .

Sometime well into the join up, I heard a stream of excited, high pitched Italian. After a measured pause, we heard, ". . . Ahhh, Lecka Tower . . . Lecka Tower . . . ahhhh . . . Tiger Green hasa middair collisionne . . . we declare emergency-! . . . butta first . . . we make a low pass!" Well, our stalwart lead, Major Jim McCullough, did the right thing . . . casually winding his watch and whistling a popular strain, he led us away from whatever it was that might have happened. To make a long story short, an American Exchange Officer flying an RAF Gnat with a German Nav in the back seat literally drove his nose up the tail pipe of an Italian F–104S in an 18–plane,, unauthorized formation in Germany! Everyone lived! (But maybe not in their own air force anymore).

The Gnat lost its radios and TACAN over Hussum Air Field (they landed between the taxiway and the active runway) and the Italian 104 lost some J–79 nozzle feathers and the rear half of one tip tank.

As for my acquiring the photo of the perpetrator of this event,[1] *it happened on my swan-song before leaving Germany in 1977. You must understand that both damaged aircraft were whisked away in a heart-beat lest someone admit evidence. Well, I was able to retrieve a record of the "non-event" in a public bar in Cambrai, France almost two years later. Frank Birchall, Guy Dutil, Don Anderson and I were welcomed most sociably by 1/12 Squadron, FAF-a Mystère unit at Cambrai. That evening, downtown, the French CO demanded to be thrown over the bar as was the Canadian custom (we were reliably informed). Not wanting to hurt the CO's feelings or the proprietor's glassware, we gently rolled him over the bar and kept everyone's honour intact. Not so. Mind afixed and eyes aglaze, the French CO decided to do it himself. Taking a 30 foot bead amidst chairs and tables, he sprinted out of the dark recesses of the pub and vaulted over the bar to the sound of broken glass, splashing spirits and the nervous laughter of the owner. "VOILA!" the CO exclaimed. Despite our abject apologies and protestations of innocence,*

[1] The Gnat aircraft.

the CO assuaged our concerns by declaring that the owner was once in the FAF and, therefore, it was OK to wreck his bar because he really didn't mind. "The owner understands!", he lied. Well, the owner was in the FAF alright; he was the FAF photographer at the Leck Tiger Meet in question. After a carafe of the finest house scotch, he let me keep the print, which hung over his bar. Voila indeed!

And so ended the "Great Flypast Caper" of the '75 Meet. However, Jim McCullough has other lasting impressions of these exciting times...

While at Tiger Meet '75, I roomed with an extremely outgoing personality. On the evening of arrival, the Canadians were hosted by a GAF Major and his wife; the Major's wife was an artist. Over the mantle of their fireplace hung one of her paintings, depicting the bust of an old mariner which had been painted using various shades of blue. My roommate asked if the painting was for sale. It was, but as my roommate was informed, it was a very expensive picture being priced at DM2000. My roommate's only reaction was that he was amazed they would consider selling it so cheaply - of course he would purchase the painting. (It's possible my roommate may have had more than one drink at this time.) Anyway, the deal was closed, but no cash changed hands.

I was awakened early the next morning by my roommate who demanded that I inform him that he hadn't purchased a painting the previous evening. I informed him that I couldn't do that. He then said, "OK, then tell me I didn't pay DM2000 for it." I informed him that I couldn't do that either. My roommate then declared that "we" had a problem. I assured him that "we" didn't have a problem, but rather "he" had a problem. He then went into speed-thinking mode and came up with a masterful plan. The essence of it was that Helen (the wife/artist) would have forgotten about the sale. However, to finesse the plan... he concluded that we needed wheels and flowers. Dwayne Lucas, our Servicing Officer, had wheels, and with wheels we could get to a florist and then deliver the flowers. We arrived at the florists where my roommate ordered enough flowers for a Mafia Funeral. Enroute to deliver the goods, I was briefed in detail by my roommate that we would simply deliver them and leave; and that not one word was to be uttered about the painting. The flowers were gratefully accepted. We were asked if we would have a drink. Of course we would. Care to have another drink? Of course we would. Events were going exactly as briefed until my roommate got carried away and said, "Now, Helen... about the picture." As it turned out, they wanted to give my roommate the painting, which he wouldn't accept.

Canada's attitude towards the Meets in general was decidedly different from some of the other European participants, as Jim explains in closing on this subject...

The aspect of annual Tiger Meets that set Canadians apart from other participants was that we went to fly and always attempted to launch several times a day. Certainly, the Canadians took full advantage of the festivities. However, we also got some excellent experience through concentrated exposure to areas over which we did not operate on a daily basis. So, yes, there were a lot of strange happenings associated with Tiger Meets, but there were also some excellent fellowship and flying experience to be gained. Tiger Meets were well worth whatever it cost 1 CAG to support the deployments.

Without a doubt, the most prestigious event to occur at Baden-Soellingen during the Starfighter era was the presentation of Squadron Colours to all three squadrons of 1 CAG by His Royal Highness Prince Philip on the 4th of May, 1973. The criteria for the award of Colours is twenty-five years of service, or particularly meritorious operations. The Colours are always presented by either a member of the Royal Family, or their appointed representative. The 421 Squadron History elaborates on the significance of these symbols...

The practice of consecrating Colours is of very long standing, and because of the religious significance, the Colour becomes not only a sign of loyalty and achievement, but also a sign and symbol of fellowship with God. After service, Colours are laid up in a public or sacred building, an indication of the reverence in which they are held. They are saluted by all soldiers and always move under an armed guard. They are, in fact, a squadron's most prized possessions.

For each squadron, its Colour is the shrine of its traditions, a memorial to the devotion and sacrifices of the men of the squadron in years gone by, and an inspiration to those who serve. The Colour is to be honoured as a symbol of the trust which the Sovereign places in the squadron, and as an emblem of its achievements.

In fact, an entire gala weekend was planned around this august event, and no-one there at the time will ever forget the intense planning (down to the last minutia) and preparation for these ceremonies. Couth and decorum are not traits which come easily to fighter pilots, and thus the Base Commander, Colonel A.J. Bauer, thought that mandatory "curtsey parades" in the Mess prior to the Big Day were required for the squadron officers and their wives to get their manners proficiency levels up to a suitable standard for meeting "The Prince". Who there at that time could also forget the pristine F–86 Sabre that had been painstakingly placed on a pedestal at the front gate just in time for this event, only to have the supporting steel rod fracture and the Sabre thunder in on its nose from fifteen feet! They managed to get it repaired (though not remounted) in time, but it looked like several Engineering Officers were going to have strokes before all was put right.

Participating in the 4th of May ceremony were over 450 officers and men of the three squadrons, and members of both the CFB Ottawa Pipe Band and the Canadian Forces Central Band. To add to the pomp and circumstance, gunners from the Royal

Above: *Perpetrator of the 1975 Tiger Meet Great Midair Caper just after landing at Leck. He added new meaning to the phrase "losing your radio", as it had actually fallen out of the nose!*

- photo courtesy of Dave Jurkowski

Canadian Horse Artillery fired a 21–gun Royal Salute, and a mass formation of 36 Starfighters flew majestically overhead.

Other festivities included a reception and luncheon with Prince Philip following the parade, and a fabulous Air Display on the following day, featuring both the celebrated Red Arrows of the RAF flying Gnats and the Patrouille de France in their Fouga Magisters. Both teams seemed to realize that they were playing to a very critical audience, and both of them gave one of the most spectacular performances of their respective careers.

However, one of the most successful and yet controversial happenings of the weekend centred around the 36–plane flypast, and it can be truly said that Sam Firth, CO of 417 Squadron at the time and flypast leader, reached legend status in the Air Force that day.

To regress slightly, the parade went off without a hitch, and was beautifully orchestrated on the ground with Prince Philip such that, by him being prompted to do things at just the right times, twelve aircraft from each squadron were passing directly overhead the parade square at the exact second that the Prince was dropping that particular squadron's Colour into the kneeling recipient's scabbard. For the finale, the second that hands were shooting upward in the Royal Salute, 36 '104s thundered overhead in perfect symmetry. It was all incredibly dramatic, and there was scarcely a dry eye to be seen. Nevertheless, very few people realize (nor are they meant to) that while the airborne formation is responsible for arriving on the scene within a few seconds of a given time of day, the fine tuning of what happens on the parade square is done by the key players on the ground, either by speeding up the proceedings, or slowing them down when appropriate. Here, hats must be doffed to His Royal Highness, who played his part with great precision, dignity and élan. What none of the spectators knew, however, was that the stately 36–plane flypast they ultimately witnessed had almost become a complete débâcle due to a misinterpretation of timing. Apparently, Sam Firth had inadvertently chopped a minute from the final run-in and actually had to weave the entire formation out over France to gain back the time. Anyone who has flown in a precision gaggle of this size will know that it is anything but maneuverable, and the slightest untoward movement has a tremendous "ripple effect" on those flying at the fringes. In fact, some of the pilots were in afterburner to keep up, while others were at idle power with the speed brakes out, just to maintain position in these unexpected turns! Sam Firth elaborates in his own words...

The alignment of the parade, ceremony, and dias necessitated a run-in from West to East, which of course meant that we had to fly into France. The French airspace control authorities obliged us by giving up a small pocket of airspace - not really sufficient, but on the other hand, it was not insufficient either. I worked out a procedure which allowed us to accomplish the mission quite safely, and with sufficient time checks to enable us to arrive over the designated point when expected. We operated out of Lahr with forty plus aircraft in order to get thirty-six going, and the operation went extremely well. The maintainers were absolutely first class, briefings and practices went well, and there was really nothing to be concerned about whatsoever. May 4th was the day of the event, and accordingly at the appropriate time, everyone fired up.

The 36 aircraft were initially broken into three groups of twelve, in vic formation and boxes of four, to arrive over the parade one minute apart to coincide with the presentation of the colours by Prince Philip to the junior officer on each Squadron. The timing for this was quite straightforward and had worked well in the practice, so there was no reason to believe it would work otherwise when the day came. In any case, we took off, formed up, and headed along our appointed route. I flew over with the first twelve '104s on the first go, and a minute later we had the second twelve, and then the third bunch. The timing was precise, and we swung out over the somewhat confined French airspace to form up the 36 airplanes for the grande finale when they had the Royal Salute to end the ceremony.

The airspace meant that I had to fly an oblong pattern of two-minute legs, while the others were forming up in a diamond-shaped 36-plane formation. I was flying a dual, as I had been throughout all the practices, with a pilot in the back who was a time checker, i.e., responsible for ensuring that we were over our marks, and the time was proceeding correctly, in case (and this seems somewhat humorous now) the watch I had in front of me and my own wristwatch packed up. In any case, it was handy to have him along because it was another check for me, and all I had to do was concentrate on flying as gently as I could in order that the other 35 guys I had along would have an easier task.

I was outbound on the last orbital leg, when from out of the back seat of my aircraft came the statement that I was a minute late. Without further ado, I commenced a turn, and 30 degrees into the turn I realized that the information given to me was in error, and that I was indeed on time. Now, however, I was 40 degrees into the turn, and with 35 aircraft behind you, there is not much you can do. From here on in, I had to lose one minute, and I had to wing it. I rolled out and decided to fly for 20 seconds before turning back to the initial point for the run-in. This heading, as it turned out, took us in the direction of the French Army firing range at Bitche. Fortunately, they were not firing that day - whether they were on a wine break or not, I don't know! In any case, we passed over the outskirts of the range, then turned away and back towards the IP. On the way back, I realized that I should probably have flown back for about 30 seconds vice 20, because the turn took me closer to Baden and the IP point. However, once I was there, there was nothing I could do. We were in takeoff flap configuration, and I reduced my own airspeed to 320 knots. In the debriefing afterwards, John Hutt told me that he saw 285 knots pass through his airspeed indicator at one point; nevertheless, it seemed to be a safe airspeed at 320 knots, and that is what I held.

I approached the IP point and had about a 40 degree turn now in order to go over it and straighten out for the run-in, which was about two minutes and that was all. We got over there all right, and I was heading right for the airfield, but with all the previous activity and reduction in airspeed, I still didn't make it, and crossed over the airfield about 8 seconds early.

That wasn't good... it would have been better to have been 8 seconds late; however, I was told by people on the ground that you would not have noticed the difference as far as the parade or the flypast was concerned, although I am not sure that Colonel Arnie Bauer would agree with that.[1]

A couple of months later, back in Cold Lake, Colonel Bauer arrived to do some rocket firing and bomb dropping. During a luncheon on a bad weather day, I had taken the map that I had used for the flypast and had it framed, appropriate comments put on it, and presented it to him. While making the presentation, I mentioned that I would be known from now on as Colonel Sammy Zigzag, because of the path I took in trying to arrive back at the IP on time for the run-in.

The chaps took it pretty well... they must have wondered what the hell was going on until the next day during the debriefing. It is sixteen years years since that happened. I don't believe it really screwed up the ceremony, as I have mentioned, and if it has given people a good laugh, so much the better. At the time, however, it was anything but funny to me, and I only wish I had ignored the information I had received from the back seat. I knew that we were on time, and even now I can't tell you why I turned - it just escapes me. However, that's the way it goes.

[1] As mentioned, those on the ground adjusted the parade timing accordingly.

* * * * * *

Exercise Alerts were the source of many colourful stories. As I'm sure is true in war, they were a curious dichotomy of intense activity, punctuated by stretches of extreme boredom; the latter predominantly during the long enforced stays in the bunker as the exercise geared down to a finish. When people are tired and bored, they look for something to break the tedium, and fighter pilots are no exception. Thus, it came to pass late in 1974 that Paul Rackham got the champion idea of blackening both of his Flight Commander's gas mask eyepieces during the late hours of an Alert. As the flying wound down, much more time was spent in the bunker and the frequent donning of gas masks was the norm since the exercise placed considerable emphasis on self-protection in a chemically hostile environment. Paul had prepped some of us on his stunt; we could hardly wait until the next simulated gas attack...

Now Reg Kendrick, Paul's Flight Commander, was a prince of a chap, a fine pilot, and a well-respected supervisor, but as an authority figure his credibility was somewhat in question at that moment as he sat there, a muffled little voice coming out of this mound of blacked-out rubber saying over and over, "I'm gonna *get* you guys for this..." Perhaps you had to be there, as the saying goes, but this childish prank did wonders for morale at a time when it was needed most, and typifies the high spirits that pervaded the Air Group during the CF–104 era.

Nonetheless, some highjinks were considerably more complex in both structure and repercussions...

During another Alert in the mid-seventies, Cec Hume at 421 Squadron also thought a self-generated exercise input would make life more interesting. He had been scheduled to fly on a four-plane bombing range mission which was to be led by Larry Crabb and also included another Squadron pilot named Harv Wregget. The pre-flight briefing was being monitored by John England, the Group TacEval Officer. At an early stage of the briefing, Cec slipped Harv a note which read as follows... "EXERCISE, EXERCISE, EXERCISE. Act deranged and refuse to fly." Thinking that the "exercise input" had originated with John England, Harv put on an Academy Award performance of a pilot going off the deep end and breaking down under stress. Larry Crabb was horrified; he couldn't believe what he was hearing and seeing. The Squadron went as far as to summon the padre to counsel Harv, and inform him that "it was OK to kill a commie," but Harv would not be swayed and was eventually hauled off in a white sports coat for "exercise psychiatric evaluation". However, when Harv eventually found out that the exercise input had come from Hume and *not* the TacEval shop, he swore revenge. In fact, he did a masterful job of biding his time, and just when Cec felt he could stop looking over his shoulder, Harv struck. Since very few Canadians living on the German economy had telephones, Alert recalls were accomplished through a personal notification system, which usually meant that some nameless face showed up ringing your doorbell at a God-awful hour of the night. Harv did a deal with Cec's recaller, such that Cec was roused from an extremely deep sleep in the early hours of a Sunday morning, immediately following a Squadron thrash. As Cec hared into the Squadron Building in the dead of night and soon realized that he was an Alert force of one, he did not need to be a rocket scientist to realize that he had been well and truly had. Revenge, according to Harv, was sweet.

Speaking of Alert recalls, Heather Bashow tells this story about which the author has very little recollection. The reasons should be intuitively obvious...

You really had to feel sorry for the poor guys... Alerts could be called at any time, and were most often called in the middle of the night. Untimely as they always seemed to be, one occasion was particularly memorable in that it was called in the wee small hours of a Sunday morning, after the year's Tri-Squadron party. Common I am sure to most of the squadron members, David was in the very first hour of a sound sleep that he had assumed would last for quite some time. Instead, I awoke to hear the doorbell in the dark that Sunday morning, and realized I was the only one in the room in anything resembling a functioning state. Wearily, I acknowledged the unpopular sod at the door, and returned to the bedroom to try and find some semblance of the alert pilot they were requiring from somewhere within the snoring, wine-saturated lump burrowed beneath the sheets. David doesn't awaken quickly, so when he leapt from the bed as I reached down to touch him, I knew all was not as it appeared. Sure enough, up on initiative, down on judgement, he began to get dressed... in his mess kit. I softly suggested they might be expecting him in a flying suit? His semi-conscious response was, "Ahh fuck it... they'll know who I am." I patiently explained that perhaps the missing name tag wasn't exactly the point here... and eventually he saw reason, and grumpily redressed in appropriate attire. As I understand it, very little flying was done on this particular Alert.

It was certainly understandable for the groundcrew to expect their aircrew to be properly attired for flight. Nonetheless, the coup that the author narrowly failed to pull off in the preceeding story was accomplished in a splendid manner by two Starfighter pilots in 1970. Dave McIntosh explains...

When the squadrons were cut back in 1970, the surplus aircraft were stored at Lahr. It was eventually decided to ferry them all to Prestwick, Scotland for storage/repair/sale, or whatever came up, and a lot of the testing and ferrying work was done by the 1 CAG HQ Air Staff. Some of the aircraft tested fully serviceable after sitting on the ground for several months, but most of them had minor unserviceabilities. Basically, the aircraft had to test "serviceable for ferry flight" which left some latitude... they required a good engine, airframe, TACAN, and enough radio channels to get from Lahr to Prestwick. Normally the flights were made in two or four plane sections, with the leader getting the aircraft that was "most serviceable". There were no major incidents, and all of the aircraft eventually made it to Prestwick.

*One day, two Headquarters pilots dropped off two singles at Prestwick and picked up a Baden T–33 to fly back. They were to attend a Mess Dinner in Baden that night, but the flight was delayed and the idea of missing a Mess Dinner was **not** to be considered. Their only problem was that their mess kits were in Lahr, and time was running out. When the T–33 eventually landed at Baden after a short stop in Lahr, a staff car was there to meet the crew. They climbed out of the aircraft in mess kit, brushed themselves off, put hats on, gave the groundcrew a snappy salute, and drove off... leaving the young man standing there, screwdriver in hand and mouth open, wondering what the hell was going on.*

* * * * * *

One very real hazard of flying fighters in the Central Region of Europe was the potential for getting lost and inadvertently straying over the wrong side of the political border. This *did* happen to both sides from time to time, and even included some intentional straying in the form of defections from behind the Iron Curtain. On the NATO side, an air defence advisory was issued on Guard frequency, known as a Brass Monkey call, when friendly aircraft inadvertently strayed too far East. The idea when you heard this call was to verify your position, and if the call then applied to you, turn tail and "get out of Dodge" as quickly as possible. Certainly, none of the strayings by NATO aircraft were intended to be provocative and it is highly unlikely that Warsaw pact incursions were intended to be provocative either, though both sides tested the Air Defence system in one form or another on occasion. For a tactical fighter pilot working at low level in less-than-stellar weather with occasionally questionable on-board navigation systems, infrequent errors on ***both*** sides were inevitable. In the eighties, when the CF–104s were ungraded with the excellent LW–33 system, border violations would no longer be a problem. The technology had arrived to prevent a mistake of that nature from happening, and the professionalism of the 1 CAG pilots demanded that there would not be repeat occurrences of the unintentional strayings of earlier years. However, the antiquated LN–3 system was very prone to providing completely erroneous bearing and distance information during one form of insidious failure, and if this happened, a CF–104 pilot could be in serious trouble. Laurie Hawn relates one such occurrence and again, a brief glossary is provided:

Buffer Zone - An area of neutral, protected airspace between West Germany and the Warsaw Pact nations.
Radalt - Radar altimeter
SOC - Sector Operations Centre (a NATO air defence controlling agency)
FAC - Forward Air Controller

Brass Monkey? - Who said brass Monkey?

April 23, 1973 was a beautiful day over Central Europe. It was warm and sunny and the vis was uncharacteristically unlimited. Having come home from leave a couple of days early, I decided to wander down to the 441 Foxes Den and see what was happening with the campaign to hold off the godless Communist plague. I figured to at least bag a free lunch and continue my domination of the Boss, Al "Honker" Young, at the old Ace-Deuce board. The day was to prove far more interesting, and embarrassing, than that.

The first plaintive "c'mon mahone-chucker" (the desperate cry of one who must rely on luck over skill) had barely blurted from Honker's lips when Clancy walked in. "Hey, Hawnski, how'd you like a trip? Burroughs is sick and we're in the middle of a Close Air Support exercise with the Belgian Army up north." (The exercise was called Sky Blue, matching the day.) Two thoughts immediately flashed across my mind - "I'd do anything to take a trip from Burroughs", and "Clancy is far too big to turn down". So I leapt from my chair, leaving the Boss pathetically claiming victory by default; and dug some flying gear out of my locker.

As power-on time was imminent, Clancy gave me the two-minute special briefing. "Take IP Orange to the end of the route. The target area is another 30 miles north, so climb to about ten thousand and contact the Belgique FAC on 233.4. They're using a portable radar to get us into the target area. Give him a couple of passes from this IP (Handing me a 1:50,000 map) and have fun. You'll have lots of gas left, so do what you want after that." This was sure going to beat the hell out of taking all the Boss' money.

Off I went to my Silver Sliver, and blasted into the blue Baden sky with a kick-in-the-ass from my trusty J–79. "Man, what a great day!" I moseyed uneventfully along IP Orange, watching the contrails as the duty-Phantom at the Karlsruhe intersection got carved (again) while he studied his How-to-Fly book. Near the end of the IP route (about 120 miles north), I put the map away and climbed to ten thousand. The FAC came up on the first call (this was a good day), radar identified me and vectored me toward the IP. The target was some Belgian armour in a tree line approximately two minutes east of the IP. Even I could find the IP on a day like this, and I pushed up to 540 for the run-in. The FAC got me in sight, and with a couple of "left 10, right 20s", I made a rooster tail in their mussel soup. (I wonder when we're going to get a radalt?) "Merde Chaude" my new friend proclaimed (must be a fighter pilot doing his penance); "let's do that again from the same IP." With more fighters coming behind, the FAC instructed me to clear the target area eastbound before turning south after the second attack.

"This is great! I've got a bag of gas left, a clear blue sky, and nothing to do but look for someone to carve." What I didn't appreciate was that the target was already in the Buffer Zone as I meandered eastbound at about 5,000 feet, dutifully squawking with my transponder. Sans map from present position to the end of IP Orange, I figured to do a rough point-to-point on the INS back to the route; and then fly

Above: *Occasionally, colourful personalities "tried the '104 on for size". Here Judy Lamarsh goes flying with Pat Barrett of 441 Squadron.*

it backward to Soellingen. (BIG mistake!) For the next five-to-ten minutes, I trolled generally east-southeast, in accordance with the INS bearing and distance from home. About the time I should have been seeing the railroad junction at the end of IP Orange, I began to have some doubts. It just didn't look right. As gas was now to the point that I should have been heading for home anyway, I decided to climb and tune in Frankfurt TACAN.

As I levelled off at 20,000 feet (Oh, for the freedom of 1973 again!), the TACAN settled down. "070 for 95 miles? Nah, can't be." Retune it; same result. "Jeeesus; that's not where I thought I was! There were no "Brass Monkey" calls; I must be down in the corner where the border turns east near Fulda." With my day still only partially ruined, I turned towards Soellingen still squawking at 20,000 feet. Just east of Frank-

- photo by Bill Johnson

furt, another very strange thing happens. I get jumped by two USAFE[1] F–4s fer crissake! Now this was very un-American in those days; you could never get those guys to react. "Damn Yanks, they never want to fight when I've got gas. I'll just put it up to Mach .99 on the way home and they'll bugger off." Smoking home now, I do a few check turns to make sure the Double-Uglies have given up. Seeing none, I slow the jet to turn initial for 04. As I'm about to turn the last 45 to initial, something catches my peripheral vision. "Gawdam, where did he come from?" There's a Phantom with Hahn AFB markings (ironic, no?) pulling into close echelon. About a mile out and a mile back is another one. My day now approaching ruination, I do not have the presence of mind to call "initial with three". Instead I wonder where the hell 070 for 95 really is. The Yanks break off and I can almost hear their snickering above my mounting panic. No longer the Cool Commie Killer, I check the INS terminal error in the line and it says 090 for 150 miles. ""Holy Shit! I was doing a point-to-point on somewhere in Czechoslovakia!"

Sweating profusely, I go into Mission Planning and confirm, to my chagrin, that 070 for 95 puts me just south of Erfurt (one of their bigger MiG–21 bases). I have just spent about fifteen minutes overflying East Germany at from 5,000 to 20,000 feet, squawking my brains out. "Boss, you'd better come and have a look at this." Rrrrring! "Yes, Ajax Ops? Where was I just now? Well… I… er…" What follows is not pretty. I talk to Lahr Radar and they tell me they watched the whole chase as the F–4s ran me down at about 1.3 Mach. After promising never to whip his ass at Ace-Deuce again if he'll help me; I leave the Boss at the polite request of Colonel A.J. for an interview.

Apparently, SOC 4 was also not having a brilliant day. Military radar had not seen me crossing the border in either direction. Rhein Radar just happened to have two F–4s on a cross-country when they picked me up with the civil radar. The Yanks were only too happy to ID a high-speed target exiting the East Zone. Although I never did get any confirmation, "SOCski Fourski" must have been having a wine lunch-

[1] United States Air Force Europe.

eon that day as well. As bad as my day turned out, it could have been even more interesting had I actually found someone to bounce..."Ahah, Tally-Ho. Let's just sneak up on that guy and gun his tits off. What the hell is that, an F–5? Doesn't look like a Mirage. Uh oh..."

As a postscript, a few folks actually lost their jobs in SOC 4 and I still have a souvenir copy of Gen. Theriault's Reproof. I've also enjoyed other peoples' accounts over the years that had me racing out on the deck with MiGs in hot pursuit firing Atolls at my Capitalist heinie. A final postscript occurred in the O'Club at Luke AFB several years later. I'm standing in the crowded bar on a Friday night having a beer with a USAF Major named Jay Calloway who's flying '104s. Turns out he flew F–4s from Hahn between '71 and '74. I said, "You didn't happen to see a '104 coming out of the East Zone in April '73, did you?" "Was that you?" "Yeah, was that you?" I've been looking for you for years." "Hey, I told them that I couldn't really tell your markings, but I thought you were German." "Yeah, sure; what are you drinking?"

Laurie was certainly not the only CF–104 pilot to make an inadvertent, unauthorized aerial sight-seeing tour of Warsaw Pact real estate. While the next contributor prefers anonymity, the astute reader will grasp that this event occurred a significant amount of time prior to Laurie Hawn's incident...

Whither Goest?

Even flying the magnificent Zip in the Strike days got a little boring from time to time. There were a limited number of navigation routes, too many landings at home base, great maintenance (so you never got scared silly by things going wrong in the air), not much formation, and very little opportunity to measure yourself against others or even your ability to do your war task realistically. It was easy to get overconfident or blasé.

So one morning at Met Briefing, I barely listened to The Liar droning on about a 50 knot wind at 1000 feet AGL (Above Ground Level). Who ***cares****? The Groundspeed Readout wasn't afraid of a 50 knot wind. It could figure things out. Who needs liars?*

The Black Forest was in the clouds, and so was most of southern Germany, east to about Erfurt near the Air Defence Identification Zone (ADIZ). No big deal. The rules were to remain visual at all time, but if everybody did that, nobody would ever do any mission training except for maybe a day or two each July. The rules were broken regularly, and pretty well everyone knew that they were, but like I keep saying, no big deal. Low level flight in cloud had its dangers, but most pilots found them to be minimal and just pressed on.

At the time of this incident (for lack of a better word), there was a program to mix the CPMs (Combat Profile Missions - we used to call them maps) of both 3 and 4 Wings. Unfortunately there was quite a big difference in the way each Wing made its CPMs, and the mixing program was an attempt to at least make the pilots of either Wing able to use the maps of the other in a pinch. Again, no big deal. I had been at 4 Wing for a couple of years, and if I couldn't handle any route we had, even if the map had been made by a blind person, well, don't even think about it; no problem. I filed for Route 408, which hacked over Gaggenau and then headed due east for about eight or nine minutes towards Czechoslovakia before a screeching left turn toward the north paralleling the ADIZ. It was said that 4 ATAF was always apprised when a 408 Route was filed, and that it monitored Warsaw Pact (WP) reaction to a high speed eastbound target. This thought crossed my mind later in the mission.

Anyhow, the CPM I grabbed happened to be a 3 Wing map, and I didn't catch that instead of the 4 Wing normal cruise of 450 knots groundspeed, this one was done at 540 knots. I picked up a preprogrammed Station Storage Unit (SSU) [1]. How spoiled we had become!

With my white scarf blowing in the wind, I taxied and found my radar to be unserviceable. No big deal. I decided I would use the higher of the safety altitudes, guaranteeing at least 1500 feet ground clearance even if I couldn't see the ground, which I was sure would be the case at least until I broke out of cloud about eight minutes after hacking my stopwatch at the start of the route. If I didn't break out of cloud, I would pull the old "180 and punch up out of it" trick. No sweat.

Wouldn't you know it! An INS fault light - no Groundspeed Readout. No big deal. I'll just peg the Indicated Airspeed at the groundspeed required, 540, and fly for eight minutes... no VFR after eight minutes? Mission over.

Cleared for takeoff - better close this canopy and make sure I don't catch my scarf in it as it closes. Scarves like this cost money!

Gear up, flaps up - leave the burner in to hit 540 before the hack. Ah, there it is, Gaggenau. Peg 540 on the Airspeed Indicator (ASI) and hack on heading 090, right over Gaggenau. Slip up to the safety height and into the soup. No sweat. Just as scheduled. Sure do miss the radar picture, though.

Coming up to decision time - almost eight minutes after hack. Hey! I'm out of it and in the clear, just like the liar said. Now, I should have a sharp left turn in a minute or so. Let's see, what's on the ground that's also on the map? Hmmm. Nothing. Maybe I better make the left turn anyhow, as I should be getting pretty close to that ADIZ.

Whoops. What are those aircraft? F–84s? Who had those anymore? Biafra, maybe? Hey...them is MiG–19s - two elements, and I think those are ATOLLS [2] I see. Oh oh, that first element is too close, and they're almost pointing at me. Let's hang a hard right and speed this machine up a bit. Full burner. Oops, there's another element, almost ready to point at me. If I keep this up, they're going to turn me deeper and deeper into Czechoslovakia, where my razor sharp fighter pilot brain had figured out I was. 540 knots instead of 450 knots for eight minutes, fifty knots of tail wind, high enough above ground level at the safety altitude I had flown for Czechoslovak radar to see me. What an ass I had been!

But there would be time later for ego analysis. The trick now was to get these scum away from me and to get back to the boredom and tedium of 4 Wing without upsetting the 4 ATAF Air Defence weenies, which meant keeping down low getting back into Germany. NATO air defences were notoriously lousy at catching WP intruders, so why should they be able to catch me?

Just plugging in the burner distanced me from both MiG-19 elements, and diving for the weeds helped a bit too. Levelling off at about seven inches AGL, I left the burner in for a while. There were probably complaints to the Burgermeisters of a couple of towns I couldn't miss, and I hoped no-one tried to phone 4 ATAF or even 4 Wing to comment on it. At that point, my concern was my own reputation. The nasty intentions of the MiGs, who by now were far behind, were no longer on my mind.

Back at Soellingen, I landed the machine, called in "red" for radar and INS, and waited for Sputnik to take me back to the Squadron where I feared the worst. Get there. Light up (everybody smoked in those days). Nothing. No call to the CO's office or Wing Ops. Nothing. Well, wait a while. Something will boil up. Nothing. I had lucked out. Nobody but me and a bunch of MiG–19 slack asses, and maybe a WP Air Defence Tech or two, ever knew what had gone on that day.

Several years later and a few drinks into the evening, I related the story to a colleague, which I think was therapeutic for me. It certainly was when he told me of a similar situation - different circumstances, but the bottom line was the same - fooling around in someone else's airspace. Did I learn anything from this escapade? Yes. I took more care in flight preparation. More importantly, I realized that the '104 could become involved, unarmed and outnumbered, and come out of it unscathed. All you had to do was go home. Quickly.

[1] An electronically programmed route plot which was inserted like a cassette into the aircraft's inertial navigation system.
[2] Infra red missiles.

* * * * * *

Any pilot who has flown the Starfighter has vivid recollections of his first flight in the jet. To say that it was exciting, even on the most routine of occasions, would be a massive understatement. However Marty Abbott, who flew with 439 Squadron from from 1975 until 1978, had far more excitement on his first CF–104 trip than anyone should *ever* have. Marty explains...

This is a story about my first trip in a '104, my first flight at twice the speed of sound, and the first time that I learned the true meaning of the word "terror". I remember it all quite vividly.

My determination to fly the '104 arose when I was sixteen. In 1969, I was on a summer job surveying in remote northern Alberta. While wading through waist deep muskeg, dragging a surveyor's chain, the silence of the wilderness was shattered when a '104 came shrieking by 100 feet overhead, standing on its wing. It came and went within three or four seconds, but it left an unforgettable impression on a youthful mind that had long been fascinated with flight. If I was going to be anything in life, it had to be a fighter pilot flying '104s. After finishing high school, I joined up, graduating through R.O.T.P. at university, earned my wings, and as fate would have it, was awarded the only '104 posting on my wings course. I was twenty-one and life was more than perfect, but I was destined to slop through the muskeg once again. On November 7, 1974.

Immediately after wings graduation at Cold Lake, Alberta, I was sent down to the '104 training unit, 417 Squadron, at the old American–built SAC site just off the end of Runway 12. The air was filled with the ear-splitting thunder of '104s pounding down the runway for takeoff. This was exciting stuff; I was about to join the ranks of the real fighter pilots who flew these incredible machines. I wandered up the alert tube into the squadron building and peered into the operations room. There stood Gord Todd, the squadron maintenance test pilot. I sauntered up to the Ops desk which was occupied by a huge mountain of a man, Major Clancy Sheldrup, the Ops Officer for the day. "Who the hell are you, and what are you doing in my squadron building?" he growled. He cut short my explanation and ordered me to get my ass over to 4 Hangar right away. I was going on my first '104 trip. It was a CF–104 dual and Gord needed a backseater. It was to be an air test for a newly overhauled engine. My heart rate picked up.

I ran downstairs and grabbed a parachute, and spurs (which attach your feet to the ejection seat to prevent your lower legs from being cut off by the canopy rail in an ejection). I grabbed the rest of my gear and galloped over to 4 Hangar. Gord was already doing the walk-around on the aircraft and told me to get strapped in. It took me several minutes to attach myself to the various lanyards, cables, hoses, straps, clasps and buckles which are necessary for the proper functioning of the ejection seat. No sooner had I finished than Gord began the wind up of the engine. He went through the customary post-start checks and then off we taxied to the active runway.

We lined up at the end of Runway 12. Gord ran up the J–79 engine and stood on the brakes while he did the engine checks. The '104 lurched and bucked and screamed like a banshee. It did not like being held back. There clearly was a lot more power in this beast than the CF–5s that I had just finished flying. The outside air temperature had dropped that morning to -20°C, which made for plenty of thrust. Gord released the brakes and advanced the throttle to afterburner. The '104 jumped forward and hurtled down the runway. The acceleration was phenomenal. It made CF–5s look like mopeds. After just a few seconds of takeoff roll, Gord rotated and slapped up the gear handle almost simultaneously. We were airborne, and by the time we reached the end of the runway we were doing 450 knots and still accelerating! At 550 knots, Gord yarded the stick back and pulled 4 "Gs" to the near vertical. We climbed this way until we reached 35,000 feet, a few seconds later. Jesus, things were happening fast. The adrenaline was flowing and my heart rate picked up again. It was to pick up a lot more.

The air test required a Mach run to be followed by a series of throttle slams and other checks. Gord pointed the machine northeast and wound her up to Mach 2.2. The J–79 was howling and went in a normal overspeed of 103% rpm. I could still feel the acceleration as we hit Mach 2.0 - there was plenty of engine thrust to push us faster, but the airframe was at its limits for heat from air friction. Gord pulled the power back out of afterburner and commenced a climbing turn back towards base. He pulled 6 Gs" to bleed off some speed - my body then weighed 1200 pounds and felt like it, as I could barely lift my hand to reposition the oxygen mask that was tearing off my face with the "G" force. We were at 38,000 feet and pointed towards base. The high "G" turn did not bleed off much speed as we were still coasting along at Mach 1.6. Gord began the engine checks and pulled the power all the way back to idle, about 83% rpm at that altitude and speed. He then slammed the throttle all the way up to full military power, to check the time required for the engine to wind back up to 100%. We both watched the rpm gauge. It did not move. After a few more seconds, it still did not move. I looked at the throttle. It was still at full military power but the engine was at flight idle. Come on engine! Nothing! Gord exclaimed,

Above: *"Chimp" receives blast from Chief – 421 Squadron completed a squadron exchange with a Royal Netherlands Air Force Squadron at Twente in May 1985. As usual the Chimp, Captain Harry Mueller, was in the thick of things upholding Squadron spirit. After having won the outdoor crud game and being rescued from his unexpected swim in the base cesspool, he reported to the "Chief" for debriefing. As can be seen LCol Sanford was less than impressed with the Chimp's appearance and odor. As punishment, he was forced to remain as squadron "stud" for another four months as rumours of his upcoming wedding forced many a Rhine Valley Fraulein into a state of deep depression.*

- photo courtesy of Ivan Sanford

"Oh shit!" My heart really began thumping.

We still had plenty of airspeed and altitude. So we had some time, or so we thought, to sort out this problem. Gord tried every possible throttle movement. Idle, full military, sector afterburner, full afterburner. Nothing. The engine was stuck in flight idle. The engine tracked with the throttle movement, but not the rpm. "Check your throttle!" Gord yelled. "Check your circuit breakers!" he yelled again. Nothing was amiss. Our speed began to fall off quickly. Gord lowered takeoff flap and held the minimum glide speed of 240 knots. I then understood the expression, "the '104 glides like a piano". It seemed like we were going almost straight down compared to the other military aircraft I had flown. The ground was coming up to us at an alarming rate. The altimeter was unwinding relentlessly. Gord radioed, "Cold Lake Tower, Deadeye 25!" in an urgent tone. "Deadeye 25, Cold Lake, go ahead," was the calm reply; to which Gord responded, "We're on the 040 radial at 40 miles, declaring an emergency. Our engine is at idle and will not respond to throttle movements!" "Roger Deadeye 25, squawk emergency for a positive ID," replied the tower. Gord cranked the selector button on the IFF/SIF to emergency, a device which highlighted our aircraft to ground radars. It also set off alarm bells on ground radar whenever selected to emergency, and I envisaged all the bells getting some attention down there.

We then tried desperate things. Gord flamed out the engine and re–lit it. It re–lit all right, but at the rpm to which it decreased after being flamed out. The rpm was so low at that point that the generators fell off the line. We lost all electrical power, our main radios and IFF/SIF. The instrument panel went blank, with numerous cross hairs, "off" flags, and frozen instruments. Gord deployed the ram air turbine and we got emergency electrical power that gave us some instruments. We tried the emergency UHF radio to call Cold Lake again and update our position.

It did not work. Things were not going well. I wondered whether my ejection seat would work as advertised. The stories of ejectees with broken necks and quadriplegia flashed through my mind. We were just then falling through 10,000 feet. Below us was a myriad of lakes. They had told us in the weather briefing that morning that the lakes in the area had a thin layer of ice. If we ejected into a lake, we would not live more than two or three minutes. Avoid lakes at all costs. Yeah, sure. There are more lakes up there than land. I called out the altitudes to Gord in 1000-foot increments. My heart was thumping furiously. My eyes were wide.

About 2000 feet above ground, Gord calmly stated, "Let's get the fuck out of here!" I had to go first so I already had my hand on the ejection seat D–ring between my legs. I pressed my back against the ejection seat. I pulled the D–ring its full travel. The explosive bolts on either side of the canopy blew it off, and the spur cables slammed my legs back into the seat. The rocket fired almost simultaneously. The rocket on the '104 ejection seat accelerates to 90 mph in six-tenths of a second. To call it a rocket is a misnomer - it's really a large cannon shell. And sure enough, it felt like I was hit from behind by a Mack truck travelling 90 mph. The wind was knocked out of me. I felt my head driven into my shoulders and my mid-section collapse as the seat went up the rails. I then hit the wind blast. It felt like hitting a brick wall. How can air be so hard? I tumbled backwards violently. My helmet partially ripped off but was held on by my oxygen mask, which was pulled down around my neck. The "butt-snapper" on the ejection seat fired and kicked my body away from the seat. The parachute opened with a resounding crack. Because I was still doing well over 200 knots at that point, my body was snapped like a bullwhip. My family jewels felt like they were propelled into my throat. The whole process took less than two seconds.

Suddenly everything was quiet. I looked up and saw this huge tri-coloured chute above me. None of the risers were tangled. I could hear my racing heart pounding in my ears. The D–ring was still in my right hand - I had a death grip on it. The cable cutters had automatically cut away from the ejection seat. I looked to the right and saw a tremendous kaboom as Gord ejected out of the doomed '104. His parachute opened and snapped him like a rag doll. I became transfixed on the '104. It was gliding straight towards a nearby lake, in absolute silence. It whacked into the lake and skipped along in pieces. The force was so great that a wall of water appeared to rise from the lake and hang in the air for the longest time. I probably had so much adrenaline pumping through me at that point that things were happening in slow motion.

I turned my head to see what was going on below me. To my horror, I saw something tangled and bloody hanging out of my mouth. It was my tongue, or what was left of it. I must have bitten through it. I quickly stuffed it back in my mouth so I didn't have to look at it. My flying suit was ripped to shreds by the wind blast. Then to my further horror, I found that I was directly over the center of a lake, 1000 feet up. "There is no fucking way I am going to freeze to death in a frigging lake in northern Alberta," I resolved to myself. I reached up and grabbed the two front risers of the parachute and heaved on them with what strength I had left. This rapidly increased my rate of descent. It was clear I was not going to make the shore of the lake. I reached down to release my survival pack to inflate the dinghy. Then I noticed that the wind seemed to pick up as I got nearer the ground and was blowing me towards shore. I reached up and pulled down on the risers again. It looked like I was going to clear the lake! But as I was going through two hundred feet, I noticed hundreds of branchless dead trees pointing up like toothpicks. Big toothpicks. "Christ, I'm going to be impaled on a dead tree!", I thought. I crossed my legs and arms in front of me and brought my knees up to my chest. The survival pack underneath me might provide some protection. I banged through the dead trees and several snapped off, tearing right through my Mae West. I was unhurt by the trees, but instead of hitting solid ground, I broke through ice and was submerged up to my neck, in ice cold muskeg.

I dog-paddled and flailed through the broken ice and muck to a soggy hummock. I was shivering uncontrollably and started rifling through my seat pack for the URT–503, the emergency beacon. If they did not pick me up soon, I would die of exposure. My hands were numb and I could not tear open the heavy gauge plastic bag which contained the beacon. I tried to tear it with my teeth, but my teeth felt painfully sensitive. I couldn't feel my teeth with what was left of my tongue, so I stuck my finger in my mouth. I was missing several fillings, which must have been banged out by the force of the ejection. I then fished out my survival knife which amazingly was still velcroed to my leg in the torn pocket of my flying suit. I cut open the bag and pulled out the antenna to start the beacon, but the test light did not come on. The beacon was defective! I swore a blue streak, then looked to the horizon to see how far solid ground was in case I had to spend the night. It was at least a half mile, and I would die long before I got there. I rifled through the survival pack for the signal mirror and flares. I then realized I might not have pulled out the antenna the last half inch to start the beacon. I pulled out the antenna with my teeth and saw the light come on. I was elated.

Within minutes, a CF–5 located me and appeared overhead. In what seemed like hours, but was really fifteen minutes, I heard the thumping of the rescue helicopter. It came straight towards me and passed about 50 feet to the west and continued on as though it had never

Photos at right: *How it looked from the air... 36 plus their shadows over the Rhine. And how it looked from the ground... HRH Prince Philip presents the Colors to the Baden Squadrons in 1973.*

seen me. I was stunned. Didn't they see me? Didn't those pricks know that I was going to die of exposure? My wet flying suit clung to my frigid body. The helicopter then turned around and came back towards me. I fired flares like crazy. It saw me but it could not land because of the dead trees towering above me. The crewman lowered the sling, but unfortunately could not get it closer than 20 feet away. As soon as the sling touched the muskeg, I half-swam and scrambled through the ice and muck. The winch dragged me out of the muskeg, but the cable snagged on a dead tree on the way up. They had to lower me back into the muskeg to unsnag it. On the second try, I made it to the helicopter's skid. The downwash from the rotor blades pummelled the hell out of me and chilled my wet body to the bone. The noise was deafening. I dragged myself up on the skid and a crewman, leaning out precariously, grabbed me. I flopped onto the helicopter floor in a puddle of mud and water. I looked up and saw one of the base doctors strapped into the back seat. He had a motion-sick green face, and a trail of vomit all down the front of his flying suit. "Are you okay?" he croaked. I snickered, and said something to the effect that he was a useless tit. With a moan, he closed his eyes and let his head fall back onto the cargo netting behind him, mouth breathing. Must have been a tough ride in the helicopter.

We then went and picked up Gord, who had landed half a mile away in a rather pleasant forest glade. He had a roaring fire going, with a lean-to half built, and was reclined on his survival sleeping bag. The only thing missing was an R.V. and some hot dogs. They flew us back to the base hospital where doctors poked, prodded and x-rayed us for a couple of days.

So ended my first trip in a '104, for which I received a Mach 2 pin, and a caterpillar pin from the makers of my parachute. They recovered the engine and it was determined to have been defectively rebuilt.

The ejection did nothing to quench my thirst for flying the '104; I went on to fly another 900 trips in the machine on a tour of duty in Europe. The terror I experienced punching out could never match the exhilaration of a tree top low level tactical mission at 600 knots, a supersonic mock dog fight with Luftwaffe F–4 Phantoms, or strafing old tanks with the 4000 rounds per minute gatling gun at the Suippes weapons range in France. It was the most exciting period of my life, and not a day goes by without thoughts of the exhilaration of flying the '104. It will always be in a class by itself.

* * * * * *

The CF–104 era of fighter operations featured no shortage of colourful characters, but one of the most colourful of all wasn't even a Canadian. His real name was Max Something-or-other; nobody really seemed to know for sure; but one and all knew him by his nickname, Sputnik. One cannot discuss 421 and 441 Squadrons during the Starfighter days without mentioning this individual. In Sputnik, we had a fireplug of a middle-aged German with a penchant for baseball caps who was the perennial duty driver for Central Dispersal. Sputnik spoke no known language (including German) with any recognizable degree of fluency, and was probably the World's Worst Driver. Many is the fighter pilot who has had his life flash before his eyes while in the safe-keeping of Sputnik as he careened his merry way hither and yon. This was *always* done with his hair (what there was of it) on fire and accompanied by an unintelligible tirade of guttural-something mixed with pidgin English, as he gleefully scattered anything that dared approach his path. He was an utterly fearless, mission-oriented individual whose only goal was to get his terrified charges from Point A to Point B, preferably "via direct". He had little or no concern for the more mundane things in life, such as traffic lights, stop signs, curbs, pedestrians, etc.; and woe betide the hapless soul (including the Base Commander) who parked in his official parking spot. His favourite expression was "Sputnik nicht boom boom"... whatever *that* meant.

He was very much a man of mystery. He had apparently been around as long as the base, or at least as long as anyone could remember. Rumour had it that he drove snow plows for the German Army in Norway during the war (the mind boggles), but that rumour was never confirmed. At any rate, Sputnik was a colourful character, and he occupies a very special place in the history of the Starfighter era. At 439 Squadron down in South Dispersal, we were often green with envy, for we had no such legend. The man was held in such high esteem by the inmates at Central Dispersal that when he retired on July 4th, 1975, Laurie Hawn, Ian Struthers, Rick Wall and Pat Barrett from 441 Squadron did a special flypast for him to honour the occasion.

* * * * * *

The loss of an aircraft is never cause for celebration, but that was almost the case on March 5, 1975 when Ian Struthers and Ted Lee of 441 Squadron trashed 104666 on takeoff at Baden-Soellingen. To fully appreciate the significance of this remark, the reader must understand that 666 was the perennial Hangar Queen; a jet that spent the vast majority of its time being purged of one malfunctioning gremlin after another. The maintainers hated it with a passion, and the anti-Christ symbology of the three sixes in its number block was not lost on them. They called it, among other things, Triple Sick and The Evil One. Ian Struthers tells the story of the demise of this legendary aircraft...

On the morning of March 5, 1975, I taxied out in aircraft 104666, a dual commonly referred to by the aircrew as Triple Six, but more commonly and not so affectionately as Triple Pig, or The Jet from Hell by the groundcrew. I was Number Four on a bombing mission to Suippes Range in France, and as I was relatively new to 441 Squadron, this was the Suippes Range Checkout in my Combat Ready phase training. Captain Ted Lee was my check pilot in The Pit (back seat). It was a beautiful day, warm, good visibility and little cloud. The aircraft was loaded with pylon tanks and a bomb dispenser, which placed it close to its maximum all-up weight. We lined up on Runway 04 with my jet on the extreme right-hand side. Lead and Two rolled normally, followed by Number Three and myself shortly thereafter. We rotated at approximately 205 knots in good position, when a large bang was heard and the aircraft shook violently. As this is probably the most critical phase of flight in the Starfighter, and believing that an engine malfunction was the most likely culprit (which I could not verify by looking inside the cockpit at the engine instruments because of my formation position on Number Three) I elected to abort the takeoff. Ted in the back had noticed black pieces of "something" flying about on the right side, and before he was able to advise me of a tire failure, I had already chopped the throttle to idle. Ted advised the tower that we were aborting and with about 3000 feet of runway left and around 215 knots on the clock, I jumped on the brakes. At around 200 knots, I pulled the drag chute and I could feel it deploy, but then it felt as if it had blown off. In fact, it hung in there beautifully but the inertia of the jet at that speed and weight was awesome. I tried to steer to the centre of the runway, then deployed the tail-hook. The aircraft did not want to slow down, and as the barrier approached extremely quickly, my reflexes placed the throttle to cut-off. Wrong,[1] *as this killed the hydraulics, which control the brakes and the nosewheel steering. While the brakes were not particularly effective, what with only a square aluminum mass remaining on the right side, the nosewheel steering had been doing a sterling job of getting me to where I needed to be; namely, the centre of the barrier cable. With the loss of*

[1] Correct for an aircraft on fire, but not otherwise.

nosewheel steering, the aircraft swung rapidly to the right through about 30 degrees. I immediately selected emergency brakes and stood on the left one, as the barrier was no longer out in front of the aircraft. The nose slowly came back to the left and I remember thinking, "OK, we're just going to make it. I'll catch the barrier just where the tape meets the barrier cable." This would have worked, except that the right pylon tank went under the tape, was torn off, and immediately blew up. The ***bad*** *news was that due to this unforeseen event, we failed barrier engagement and had a huge fireball. The* ***good*** *news was that we were still going 185 knots and left the fireball behind! Not to be outdone, the left pylon tank was then sliced open by a runway light and dispensed JP–4 at an appropriate rate, allowing the fire to follow us. As we then left the runway at high speed, about 15 degrees off its heading, the landing gear, not seeing the humor in this situation, decided to depart the scene... leaving me to try to control the beast as we then bounced from one tip tank to the other (neither tip lost any fuel). As I then watched the pitot boom bending back and forth during its contact with the ground, I started thinking about that old pilot joke that talked about the next step in a circumstance like this being the tasting of dirt, and suddenly the joke wasn't all that funny! However, throughout this entire sequence, even though we certainly had sufficient speed, I must admit that never once did ejecting enter my mind.*

When we came to a grinding halt, I noticed with horror that the back of the aircraft was on fire and that there was no noticeable movement from Ted. My first thoughts were, "I do not want to burn" and "I must hurry to help Ted." I opened the canopy normally as opposed to jettisoning it (though we were supposed to jettison if airframe damage was suspected) and with my helmet, parachute and, much to my chagrin, also my seat-pack, I jumped out and attempted to land on my feet and then roll. This plan failed miserably as the extra weight from the seat pack on my butt caused me to go straight in on my head!

Ted, fascinated by the ride, realized that I was already in the process of exiting the jet and proceeded to follow the checklist verbatim. He pulled the canopy emergency jettison handle, and the plexiglass hood went straight up and straight back down again, trapping him inside the rear cockpit. He then unstrapped all his goodies, including his parachute, and stood on the seat pushing the canopy up with his back. He just managed to move it about fifteen to twenty inches, then jumped through without a scratch! He then stopped to assist me in my own egress, as I was still lying on the ground, stunned, in need of help, and absorbed in the sound of the practice bombs cooking off in what was left of the somewhat-modified bomb dispenser. The trusty firefighters, as always, were there within two minutes to extinguish the fire and to safety the aircraft, or what remained of it.

Triple Pig was not to fly again, much to the delight of the groundcrew, who for months later would offer to buy me a beer for reducing their workload in the maintenance shops. The initial cause of the accident was the failure of the sidewall of a brand new tire, which blew at around 190 knots. Engineering studies determined that the aircraft was beyond economical repair, and the cockpit area was then sent to AETE to determine the cause of the incorrect separation of the rear canopy.

There, it was discovered that tests had never been done on the canopy separation from a dual aircraft on the ground. In fact, they found that had the checklist been followed and had I jettisoned the front canopy, which was differently shaped that that of the single-seat aircraft, my top torso would have been cut in half when it came back down in a half-turn and struck the ejection seat with its forward edge!

Pat Barrett, who had been Ted's Number Three that day, had an additional observation to make on this particular accident...

Sometime previously, during an early morning launch just after a shower had gone through the Base, Andy, the tower controller, called a fire on one of our aircraft during the takeoff roll. It turned out to be Bruce Reid, who subsequently jettisoned his tip tanks over France and came back in for an immediate heavyweight landing. No indication of fire was ever found, and the general opinion was that Andy had seen some afterburner reflections in the pooled water on the runway. In any event, in the aftermath of the Triple Six conflagration where the same tower controller was on duty, Laurie Hawn from 441 Squadron confronted Andy soon after in the bar at the Officers' Mess and said, "Now Andy, ***that*** *was a fire!"*

Speaking of Pat Barrett, the author is grateful to him for the following "snapshot vignettes" of events in 1 CAG during the latter half of the seventies...

Spring '75 - Don Myles (CO 441 Squadron) has a sense of humor failure when upon arrival for line-up on Runway 22 with four bombers for Pampa Range, he found four bombers on the taxiway ahead of him (from 439 Squadron) with the same call sign, also going to Pampa. A quick check with our Ops revealed that Laurie Hawn had traded the period to 439 and then forgotten about it. Don taxied his four back to the dispersal and shut down... not a word - and not a sign of Hawn when we got back to the Squadron building.

September 9, 1975 – On Ed McGillivray's second bailout, where he landed in sight of the autobahn between Baden-Soellingen and Lahr, the first person to reach him in the field, of all the people and traffic on that major European artery, was Jack Orr, a 441 Squadron pilot. We were operating temporarily out of Lahr at that time and many of the pilots were commuting.

January '76 – On a four-plane Attack training mission, Dale Purcell, who was leading and Gus Youngson, his Number Three, manage to switch their maps while signing out the aircraft at servicing. Hilarious radio transmission ensued as they attempted to sort it all out

Photo, above: *Triple Six's last ride. 5 March, 1975.*

Photo, below: *Circa 1970. LCol Bruce Burgess, CO 439 Squadron, receives congratulations and heartfelt thanks from Sputnik on the occasion of being the first person to ever understand a single phrase this ace driving legend has uttered. Col Kaufman, Baden's Base Commander, obviously can't believe it either...*

Above: *The "Tijuana Taxi" soars above the clouds in 1983.*

Below: *Oops, back to the drawing board… the first 441 Squadron "Checkerbird" was something less than aesthetic perfection.*

Above: *AETE's 104 704 thunders over the northern Alberta landscape.*

Below: *104 709 and three Cold Lake companions head for the bombing range at high level in 1970. The open bomb rack was a Canadian innovation to supplement the limited MNIA bomb dispenser available outside of Europe and the Air Division.*

in the air.

May 28, 1976 – George Landry, after leading a four-plane onto Siegenburg from an unusual and non-standard direction was asked by a rather incredulous range tower controller how the visibility was. "You'd never know it by my navigation, Siegenburg, but actually it's quite good."

May 30, 1977 – During a mixed mess dinner in the Black Forest Officers' Mess at Lahr for legless Second World War ace Douglas Bader, Jim Gale acting as Mr. Vice (the event coordinator) inadvertently says, "Ladies and gentlemen, we will now take a ten-minute break to stretch our legs."[1]

October '77 - George Landry leads an extremely successful mass attack on Hahn Air Force Base. Unfortunately, the target was Spangdahlem Air Force Base. Operations (441 Squadron) had screwed up.

Summer '77 - Ted Bain lands his Starfighter at Baden-Soellingen. Unfortunately, all his radio transmissions for permission to land were to Lahr tower.

March 7, 1978 - Don Robinson from 439 Squadron ejected from 104838 near Memmingen. This was a late bailout following a series of compressor stalls and a gradual power loss. Consequently, the aircraft, seat, canopy and Don all landed in a field in close proximity and only seconds apart, to the great astonishment and fright of a young lady and the horse she was riding, virtually in the midst of it all. The owners subsequently claimed that this caused the horse a severe case of apoplexy, and threatened to sue "big time".

* * * * * *

Though the Starfighter was very much a crowd pleaser at a host of airshows, not everyone shared the general enthusiasm of the air-minded public for the jet on *all* occasions. Dave McIntosh explains...

In 1967, five of us were sent to Ottawa to provide a CF–104 formation for the Centennial Airshow which was taking place at Rockcliffe. During one of the practices, we had a close brush with a helicopter on our run-in... he was holding in the wrong place. On show day, we started our final run-in to the show site, and our Lead asked the helicopter for his position. "I'm hiding behind a chimney in Hull," he replied. Another lesson learned.

While on an "incentive display mission" to CFB Moose Jaw in September 1968, Dave pitched up a '104 in the circuit while trying to avoid a Tutor jet trainer that just happened to be "in the wrong place at the wrong time". In a way, the same thing could be said for Dave's life insurance agent...

When I had my infamous tangle with a Tutor at Moose Jaw and had to bail out, one of the first people to visit me was Squadron Leader Al Simpson, RCAF, Retired, who had previously sold me a life insurance policy. He stated that he happened to be in Moose Jaw on a promotional tour, and on behalf of the Company he was glad that I was OK... otherwise the Company would have had to pay out a whole lot of money. It's really nice to feel wanted.

* * * * * *

Cross-country navigation proficiency missions were one of the more delightful mandatory flying requirements of the CF–104 era. Not only did 1 CAG pilots have the opportunity to practice Instrument Flight Rules in strange and exotic places, but these sojourns provided ample opportunity to soak up all the local culture after arrival. However, *getting* to some of these exotic garden spots was not always straightforward, as Marty Abbott explains concerning a 1976 visit to Greece...

It was to be a dirty weekend in Athens... we were always looking for exotic places to visit on weekends. Greece had been on our list for some time, but the war between that country and Turkey over Cyprus had prevented visits to these NATO allies for some time. Eventually, our embassy in Athens managed to acquire diplomatic approval for a four-plane of '104s from 439 Squadron to deploy from our base in Baden-Soellingen, Germany to Tanagra, Greece, over a long weekend in November 1976. Guy Dutil was to lead this gaggle, which included Keith Robbins, Dan Bouchard and myself.

The trip had to be done in two hops: Baden-Soellingen to downtown Italy, via France; and from Italy over the heel of the boot (on an airway which gave a wide berth to Albania) across the Ionian Sea to Tanagra, on the Aegean coast of Greece. Our '104s had recently had the M–61 gatling gun installed, at the expense of a significant amount of internal fuel. The leg across the Ionian Sea was barely possible fuel-wise before the installation of the gun and could now only be done if we stripped the aircraft of their MN–1A bomb dispensers and pylon sway-braces. Pylon tanks would have solved our problems, but the squadron could not afford the removal of four aircraft from the flying program for two days while the tanks were uploaded and tested. Besides, we were not going to let a tight fuel situation prevent us from inflicting a weekend of terror on Athens. All our fuel calculations assumed that the weather and Italian air traffic control would cooperate. Having regard to our previous experiences with Italian meteorologists and Roma Controlla, we knew that such assumptions could well be untenable, but we were not about to admit this to one another.

So off we launched in our Starfighters, ammo cans stuffed with duty free booze to trade to the natives, flying suits bulging with enough Drachmas to keep us out of jail.

The weather was perfect on our first hop to Grossetto, Italy. I was relieved at this, as on start–up my stripped aircraft went unserviceable, and I was left with the choice of not going or taking a machine with sway-braces and bomb dispenser. Such choices are easily made by fighter pilots, particularly young ones. If the weather was this good over the Ionian Sea, then perhaps the excess drag would not matter. Wishful thinking.

After arriving in Grossetto, I confirmed that my machine was burning more fuel per mile than the others. My rough calculations indicated that I would arrive in Tanagra with 1100 lbs. of fuel. Emergency fuel was 1000 lbs. in a '104, so no sweat. Little did I know that tight fuel would be a boring problem compared to what was in store for us.

While our aircraft were being refueled in Grossetto, we stopped by Operations to check the weather for the next hop. Luigi said the weather was severe clear across the Ionian Sea and that only scattered cloud existed over downtown Greece. Luigi also said that Roma Controlla would permit us to climb directly on course; our fuel situation would not permit anything else. It all sounded too good to be true. It was. Luigi was wrong. About everything.

Off we launched again in our flush-riveted weekend fun-jets. Lead called us over to Roma Controlla frequency and things began going wrong right away. Roma Controlla wanted us to turn 180 degrees and climb to altitude opposite the direction in which we wished to go! Our snivelling and whining was to no avail. Our intended course was to take us over Rome but there was apparently too much civilian traffic to tolerate four fighters, so we climbed north; and even though we lied about our altitude to get an early turn back on course, plenty of precious fuel had been wasted. As we crossed the coastline, Roma Controlla stopped talking to us, although we were still in Italian airspace. Shortly thereafter, our TACAN broke lock so we were navigating by dead reckoning. Again, not unusual for Italy, but not much fun when things

[1] Sir Douglas apparently loved it.

aren't going all that well.

Our next problem began about 100 nautical miles out over the Ionian Sea. There, our radar painted a huge squall line of very solid-looking cumulonimbus cloud lying at right angles to our direction of travel. Worse yet, the squall line appeared to be topped at 35,000 feet. We were then at 28,000 feet. To fly through cumulonimbus in a jet fighter is to court disaster. Our only choice was to turn back or climb. We of course chose to climb, and as no one was talking to us, we did so without clearance.

We slowly staggered up to 37000 feet. The '104 literally wallows at that altitude subsonic, and we could not waste fuel using afterburner to go supersonic. The turbulence over the squall line became severe enough to bang us around our cockpits, making aircraft control a delicate matter - our APC gauges showed that we were dangerously near pitch-up. Of greater concern was the fuel we were burning to maintain altitude. Full military power was required and we still had a lower Mach number than we did at 28,000 feet. All this was disconcerting, particularly because we still did not have a TACAN lock-on from Greece and were unsure how far we had to go. The visibility then started decreasing in haze, so we closed up our Finger Four formation to a couple of hundred feet.

No sooner had we closed formation than I noticed a large blip at the top of my radar scope. In two, one-second sweeps of the antennae, the blip had come halfway down the scope, meaning that we were closing on something at a terrific rate. I was about to bring to Lead's attention when he yelled, "Break left!". Instinctively, I snatched the control column hard left and pulled as much as I dared without pitching the machine up. A PanAm Boeing 707 streaked past 50 feet to my right, in the opposite direction. It was close enough that I could see the blur of passengers' faces in the windows. This trip was not going well.

At this point, I concluded that even if we did make it to Greece, we would probably be arrested as soon as an irate PanAm pilot finished screaming at Greek air traffic control. Lead then wisely decided to squawk emergency on our IFF/SIF and switched us over to guard frequency. We had to find out where we were, pronto. We did not want to wander into Albanian airspace or bailout over the Mediterranean south of Greece, or run into another airliner.

Unfortunately, we could not raise anyone on guard other than Araxos Tower (in southern Greece) who told us in broken English not to clutter up the frequency as it was for emergencies only! Other calls on regular air traffic control frequencies went unanswered.

We eventually picked up the coastline on radar and were relieved to find that we had not drifted north over Albania. However, our Greek friends had apparently forgotten to turn on their TACAN, and there was solid undercast which appeared to cover the entire Greek peninsula. With no navigational aids and no air traffic controller who would talk to us, we wondered how we were going to find a place to land in the few minutes of flying time remaining.

When we crossed the coastline, Lead called us over to Tanagra tower frequency and to our amazement, we were eventually answered. To our dismay, the only English the tower controller appeared to know were the words "Cleared to land". We still had to find the airfield. When we estimated that we were halfway or more across the Greek peninsula we started a descent - if the fuel lasted, we might be able to make the Aegean Sea and thereby hopefully break through the undercast without running into anything, presuming the undercast did not extend to sea level.

After some tense moments descending through cloud with only

Above: *Eric Thurston taxis in after a performance at the Moose Jaw Air Show in 1973.*

- photo by Bill Johnson

Above: *Pleasing shot of the Alberta Arrows in line-abreast formation, 1977.*

Below: *Photo courtesy of John Bradley.*

Photo by Bill Johnson

our radar to guide us, we broke through the undercast and found ourselves a few miles off the eastern coast of Greece. We quickly turned inland and with our maps were able to locate where the airfield should be. By this time my fuel gauge indicated 600 pounds, which was well below emergency fuel (the '104 fuel gauge is notoriously inaccurate below 600 pounds). If I did not land within two or three minutes, I would have to eject. Shortly, we sighted the airfield, but our friend in the tower could not give us any information as to which runway was active - only the words, "Cleared to land". I committed myself to landing on the nearest runway. I entered final turn knowing that if I flamed out, it was highly unlikely that the ejection seat would be of any use, given the '104s rate of descent in final turn.

Much to my relief, I touched down with the engine still running. After taxiing into the dispersal area, I shut down and noted that the fuel gauge indicated less than 400 pounds of fuel. If it was correct, I had had about three minutes flying time to spare.

In my preoccupation with my own plight, I had failed to notice the fifteen or so scruffy military fellows who had come to greet us, armed with machine guns. The jig was up. We silently climbed out of sweat-soaked cockpits and were directed to a waiting van. I could not believe that word of our near–miss had travelled so fast, but it looked like we were going to spend some time in a dingy Greek jail. I wondered if anyone had our embassy's phone number.

The van took us directly to a run-down Base Operations building where we were immediately ushered into the Base Commander's office. None of our hosts, up to that point, were able to speak English, but the Base Commander had no such inability. We were flabbergasted when he welcomed us to his base and poured us a large glass of some foul Greek liquor, which we gulped down. It eventually dawned on us that he had no knowledge of our joust with the airliner, and we were not about to educate him. Before it was probably polite to do so, we excused ourselves, quickly bundled into a beat-up bus (supplied, along with an interpreter, by the accommodating Base Commander!) and dog-tracked into Athens at high speed. We figured we might as well have some fun until the news caught up with us.

*It never did, which led us to believe that the PanAm 707 wasn't where **it** was supposed to be either. As for the weekend in Athens and the return trip, that's another story altogether.*

This next story probably won't do a great deal to enhance the fighter pilot's square-jawed image with the general public. Still, human beings (even fighter pilots) are not infallible and like the man says, "when ya gotta go, ya gotta go". Ralph Annis elaborates…

I must claim what is perhaps a unique experience that I hope never happens to anyone else. On one early morning flight, I had a target on the Atlantic Coast of France, a long haul from Zweibrucken, even in the '104. Half way to the target, I realized I had not had my regular morning crap and that I was going to be hard pressed to get home in time. I continued to the target, turned and started home, but there was no way I could make it. I pulled up to 7000 feet, kicked in the autopilot and started undressing. I jammed my helmet up on the cowl and started to take off my Mae West when the helmet fell down and kicked out the autopilot. I did this two more times during my efforts in the small cockpit. My Mae West came next, followed by the parachute. My one-piece flying suit and knickers were lowered to my ankles and pushed to the floor of the cockpit. I took off my T-shirt and that, along with some maps, became the repository of my bodily function. After this strength-draining exercise, I sat back in the cockpit just relaxing in the sun as the aircraft passed over Zweibrucken. Heading due east, I thought what would happen if someone saw me on radar heading for the Iron Curtain, scrambled someone to intercept me, and I was seen sitting in the cockpit nude! Thinking they would probably ship me back home for reasons of insanity, I quickly dressed, turned and landed. I exited the aircraft holding my T-shirt as a little bag to the questioning glances of the ground crew.

Of all my experiences during two tours of flying the CF–104, both enjoyable and terrifying, that one sticks in my mind above all others. ***PER ARDUA AD ASTRA.***

* * * * * *

The vast majority of a fighter pilot's career in peacetime consists of practicing, hopefully as realistically as possible, his craft for war. The exercises seem to be endless, and everything is either "simulated this" or "simulated that". Small wonder that after repeated sessions of crying wolf, it is sometimes difficult for a warrior in peacetime to be persuasive when a non-simulated event occurs. Lawrence Sianchuk explains…

It was March 16th, 1981, and the mission was a four-plane upgrade trip in which I was flying chase on Bob Lawrence, who was upgrading to Element Lead in the Number Three position. Henry Raffel (a.k.a. "The Hawk") was in my back seat on his first trip as a Combat Ready (CR) pilot in Germany. He had just completed the rigourous 439 Tiger Squadron training syllabus and I had done his check ride on the morning launch in the same aircraft, CF–104 665. He had, of course, been in the front seat on that mission and the simulated emergency that I had presented him with as a part of the trip was a birdstrike on his Lead, Gord Wallis. Henry had told Gord to eject ("Exercise, Exercise, Exercise!") just as he got to the top of the zoom with no re–light, and we then pushed up the power and went home. Having passed the test, Henry walked out of the debriefing and immediately experienced one of those little annoyances that went with becoming the newest CR pilot on the squadron - no priority on the scheduling board. As a result, the best he could manage for the second lift was a ride in my back seat.

The mission launched and set sail for Bavaria via the Hornisgrinde tower. Perhaps the plan should have been reconsidered when we all had to "avoid the last known position" as a result of getting into the old nose-high-low-airspeed-formation-ballistic-in-cloud manoeuvre not five minutes off the end of the runway! But we just decided that we'd never do that again and pressed on.

So there we were, in Card formation, heading 270 degrees Magnetic on the run-in to the third planned target, which was just north of Leipheim. Since it was bird season, we were limited to 510 KTAS (Knots True Airspeed), which meant about 500 KIAS (Knots Indicated Airspeed). The Lead Element was 15 seconds ahead of us and I was just starting to close up with Bob for his attack. There were showers in the area and, at this time, there was one about ten–to–fifteen miles ahead of us. I was looking forward trying to determine whether the shower was on or past the target when I spotted a "buzzard" - the German version of a hawk - as it flashed past the left side of the cockpit. It was so close that it did not get past the left intake, and although I believe the J–79 could probably have survived at our enroute cruising speed of 420 KIAS, three pounds of bird at 500 KIAS was just a bit too much for the compressor blades. Before I could really contemplate how fortunate it was that the buzzard hadn't come through my windshield, I found myself with the classic compressor stall - a loud buzzing in the back end and the EGT (Exhaust Gas Temperature) somewhere up around 800 degrees Centigrade with RPM rapidly unwinding.

I chopped the throttle, zoomed, called birdstrike to Bob, and told Henry to get Leipheim (a Luftwaffe air base) on the TACAN. The engine settled down nicely at idle power, but when I tried to move the throttle back up, it stalled again. I went to idle and tried once more with the same result. We needed about 87% to keep airborne and the best I could get was in the low 70s. By this time, the TACAN had locked on and showed 12 miles to Leipheim. At about 1500 feet above ground at 220 KIAS with the aircraft just over the top of the zoom, the increasing nose-low attitude that I was having to adopt to maintain airspeed made it intuitively obvious that we were not going to be able to glide into Leipheim that day. In fact, all I could see out the front was a large forest. I decided to eject, and since the backseater had to go first in the '104 dual, I called, "Henry, this is not looking too good - prepare to eject…eject, eject, eject."

Now, one must consider Henry's state of mind at this point in time. First of all, he had just completed some two years of intensive flying training in which numerous simulated airborne emergencies had been practiced, always with the prefix, "exercise, exercise, exercise". As I began the zoom, he had been occupied with dialing in the TACAN and did not have total situation awareness as I was too busy to stop and explain things. Finally, with the sudden rush of activity, there was really no time for any air of urgency to develop in the cockpit in spite of the imminent severe landing to which the aircraft was now committed.

As a result, Henry was left with some doubt as to my intentions since my tone of voice was rather matter-of-fact, and caused him to wonder if we were just doing a simulated emergency for which I had forgotten the routine prefix of "exercise, exercise, exercise". However, the emergency procedure concerning ejection calls was very clear (one did not forget to say "exercise, exercise, exercise" when practicing) and it was obvious that something was wrong. He therefore decided to make just one last input to satisfy his doubts - and so it happened that my order to eject was greeted by momentary silence followed by an incredulous voice which called from the backseat:

"You mean for real?!?!..."

Henry later told me that it was only a rhetorical question which would allow him to say to a subsequent Board (as to why he had ejected from a perfectly serviceable aircraft) that yes, he had had some doubts, but the captain of the aircraft did order the ejection and so he didn't wait around for the answer. The evidence supports this as, before I could yell, "Get the hell out of here!", there was a reassuring explosion from the backseat and I was left wondering whether or not I had strapped in properly as I pulled the ejection handle myself...

The subsequent Board of Inquiry commended us for making timely ejections.

Being a member of an air accident Board of Inquiry was an onerous task, and a lot of inspired excuse-making has transpired over the years in order to attempt to avoid this duty. It used to be that if you were an eyewitness to a crash, you could not be a member of the Board. However, it didn't always work that way, as Dave Jurkowski explains...

I vividly remember, for three reasons, the time Ed McGillivray leapt out of his brain-dead CF–104 shortly after take off from Lahr: the wreckage hit a cemetery; despite having witnessed the ejection and crash, I was still required to be the aircrew member for the Board (a myth quickly dies); and Ed did incredible work keeping his crippled aircraft flying for as long as he did.

Ed took off in formation in the early morning Rhine haze. Shortly after gear up, he heard and felt a loud bang and got a fire light; but fire could not be confirmed by his wingman, Captain Joel Paton. Setting himself up for a quick square pattern back to the base, he got a SLOW LIGHT and a T2 RESET condition, which was a complete non-sequitur under those conditions. As a result, he lost throttle control. We later determined that, even though throttle movement had no effect on RPM, he actually had limited control of his slowly increasing speed with his variable nozzle. Unable to slow to gear lowering speed around base leg, chance solved his problem for him, with considerable overkill. The OIL LOW LEVEL caution came on and Ed had no choice but to fire the Emergency Nozzle Closure System (ENCS). As a result, he now lost complete control of his thrust. With speed now rapidly decreasing and a less than ideal runway alignment into a low hazy sun, he turned to the West and ejected. Two swings and Ed was throwing his helmet around in a spargel patch as if it was his fault! In a nutshell, he underwent eleven red page emergencies (including ejection) in 7 minutes, 42 seconds. Later, in the flight simulator, several others tried to cope with the same number of emergencies: they couldn't. Luckily the cemetery inmates remained interred and one Captain Eddie McGillivray was picked up by Captain Jack Orr who was driving along the autobahn to Lahr. All ended well, but the Board was reopened some years later because, despite scientific analysis suggesting the contrary, we all felt the compressor casing had failed. The cause of this accident remains a mystery to this day.

* * * * * *

When one speaks of the flight simulator to a fighter pilot, he will invariably categorize it as a love-hate relationship. Love, because emergency procedures and systems operations assiduously practiced in the simulator to perfection very frequently saved lives and aircraft when the Real Thing happened in the air. Hate, because the average emergency drills portion of a session in this technological marvel tended to be a sadistic ritual, during which the simulator instructors took a perverse glee in making their pilot victims sweat bullets as they conjured up every miniscule thing that could possibly go wrong with the aircraft. The average 1.5 hours of CF–104 simulator mission seemed to last about seven days. Gord Hatch reflects on the overall impact and value of this trainer to the CF–104 program...

I suppose that in its day, the CF–104 Operational Flight and Tactics Trainer (OFTT) was a state-of-the-art machine. However, the rows of steam-driven analog computers would today compare unfavourably with most desk top home computers. Except for heat generation, the OFTT would not come out on top in very many categories. To put the OFTT into perspective though, one must remember that the CF–104 Starfighter was a very complex aircraft and it was replacing some pretty basic machines. Experienced pilots and pipeliners alike were, for the most part, coming from aircraft such as the T–33 and F–86. The CF–104 OTU at Cold Lake had the task of converting these Sabre jocks into potential Third World War aces, and the OFTT was a major factor in the success of the program.

Most students had only flown aircraft with simple hydraulic, electrical and navigation systems. This equipment basically either worked or did not work, and there were few backup options. Now, for instance, instead of a simple manual control system with an aileron boost or a single hydraulic control system with a backup electrical pump to cope with, the pilot was faced with complexity. The CF–104 had two so-called independent hydraulic control systems plus a Ram Air Turbine (RAT) driven pump that could pressurize one of the main systems. It also had a complex Utility system as part of a main system. The electrical system was another marvel. Most pilots went from aircraft that had a battery, one generator, and at best, a back-up inverter. The Starfighter with its battery, two generators, a complex, interwoven, almost redundant system of busses, fixed frequency hydraulic driven generator and a RAT backup generator was a fair challenge.

Above: *Ed McGillivray's '779 in a German cemetery, 1975. The people most directly affected by this crash were long since past caring...*

Navigation systems also took a bit of a technology leap. From aircraft with ADF only, or aircraft with both TACAN and ADF, the move to a machine with a TACAN and an inertial navigation system was a big step. This aircraft not only knew where home plate was, but could also get you quite close to a number of other places. If that wasn't enough, the pilot had a backup Dead Reckoning (DR) mode that, given the wind velocity, could do most inertial functions reasonably well. As a last resort, there was a Compass Only mode that would give standby attitude and heading information to the main attitude indicator with about the same accuracy as the earlier aircrafts' main systems.

For an all–weather Strike role, this machine had another marvel: a ground-mapping radar. This technology was new to all but a few pilots who had escaped from the Clunk (CF–100) world, and even those pilots normally had help from the rear cockpit. The radar unit seemed to have a mode for every situation, a knob or a switch for every finger not already in use, and it initially humbled more than a few pilots.

Although the OFTT originally had a projected runway environment that appeared during the landing phase as the aircraft came through approach minimums, most of the simulator flying was "on the dials". This made learning the system more difficult because without either a good instrument cross–check or the use of the autopilot, many OFTT sorties ended with a prang. The OFTT did however provide the means to safely learn how to manage the Starfighter systems and to keep abreast of changes.

The OFTT training therefore must be given much of the credit for the success of the overall CF–104 program. Most pilots graduated from the OTU with a good understanding of the Starfighter systems and some idea of how to manage them. The long–term success of the CF–104 era however must be shared by the high reliability of the actual aircraft. Based on experience as an OFTT instructor, it was obvious that once on a squadron, a good number of CF–104 pilots allowed their knowledge to slip away. While the professional drivers would periodically review the Aircraft Operating Instructions and checklist to ensure that they could react in a timely manner to a malfunction, those without that initiative lived in a self-inflicted world of mystery. For them, the OFTT pre–sortie discussion was a major embarrassment, and actual time in "the box" was often a confusing one of simple problems made into compound emergencies by inappropriate action.

The OFTT was also a chance to display creativity, and many instructors left their mark. Birdstrikes were popular and usually called for some good hits with a stick on the side of the cockpit before the inevitable compressor stall. One instructor actually brought in a dead chicken to smack against the windshield for realism. Another put a waste basket of burning rags under the machine before lighting up the fire light. More than one Strike pilot practicing his "actual" route noted "adult" movies being shown on the screen in front of the windscreen as he approached the TRP. A recce pilot was impressed with a hydraulic malfunction until he was told the mess on his flying suit was actually from a leaking headset liquid-filled ear cup!

Over the long years that the OFTT machines were used, the task of keeping them both serviceable and up-to-date required long hours of dedicated service by the assigned technicians. In the early days of eight operational CF–104 squadrons in the Air Division, the machines were on a fairly busy schedule. Routine maintenance, snag repair and system modifications had to be worked into the periods of the day when the machine wasn't needed. Many evening repair shifts virtually worked through the night to ensure that the following days schedule could be met. Without their dedication, the program could not have worked.

With the demise of the all-weather Strike role, the ability of "the box" to provide realistic operational training was greatly reduced. No longer were pilots required to work with the dual timers, special weapons control panel and variable range radar cursors. Instead, operationally they only needed to practice conventional weapons selections and malfunctions, and eventually learn the sights and sounds of the radar warning receiver. The early eighties introduction of the LW–33 Nav/Attack system into the CF–104 singles made the OFTT even more obsolete. "The box" retained the original LN–3 system and began to more closely resemble the front seat of the dual than the single as which it had started life.

When the last sorties were flown in early 1986 at Baden, many pilots did not know that the OFTT originally had cockpit motion, a cockpit enclosing thermal shield and radar modes that were covered over when visitors were looking into the cockpit. Few could visualize the secrecy of the "actual" strike routes that required the destroying of the glass plate on which the route had been traced during an OFTT flight. "The box" was tired, but it had done its job.

* * * * * *

War stories of life and CF–104 operations at Decimomannu abound, and would fill a book in their own right. Gord Hatch reflects on the changing nature of the Sardinia deployment over the years, and recalls that the flight proficiency of the "occasional flyers" on staff at Decci perhaps wasn't always all that it *should* have been...

The use of Sardinia for weapons training over the years went through many changes. In the Strike days, there were one week camps, week-and-a-half camps, and full two–week camps supporting a year round schedule. The Ground Attack squadrons for years were not involved in Sardinia training. In the 1980s, camps were sporadic and only made use of range time surplus to the normal users' requirements. These latter deployments were generally squadron deployments that used prepositioned aircraft and CC–130 transports for the squadron rotations. However, back in the sixties, the camp was usually made up from pilots from all three Wings, and it was a good chance to socialize with the less fortunate from the other bases and squadrons. Normally, each pilot brought an aircraft, and usually there was a dual brought for radar training and qualification. The permanent Sardinia staff relied on deployment aircraft for all of their flying.

During one such deployment, the dual 660 came from 3 Wing and, as was normally the practice, it had been chosen because of its good serviceability record. However, soon after the flying started, any dual missions scheduled after the first launch each day were scrubbed due to the lack of an aircraft. On investigation, it was discovered that on each sortie that the dual had flown, there had been a nosewheel shimmy on landing; and although the techs had done everything they could to rectify the problem, it was to no avail.

One morning, the back–seater was one of the 3 Wing pilots who had brought the aircraft to camp and was quite puzzled at the problems being encountered. On recovery, the aircraft did experience a beauty of a shimmy, but what had not been mentioned before was that the front seat pilot, one of the permanent Sardinia staff, was landing at approximately 200 knots and just slamming the nose onto the runway so that he could get the drag chute out to avoid overtaking the aircraft ahead. After some discussion, the aircraft was inspected and put back on the line as serviceable. With other pilots it the front seat, it continued to come back serviceable.

George Miller has many fond memories of Decci as a staffer there, and now elaborates on how Canadians coped with some of the quainter customs of the area...

One of the best remembered functions by old Decci hands was the annual New Year's Levy, billed "The Kissing of the Pig". At the entrance to the levy was a large, fat roasted pig on a platter complete with apple in mouth, held by two of the Club stalwarts. To gain entrance, one

had to kiss the vital part of the pig's posterior. It, however, was covered in mustard, and it proved difficult indeed to muster the courage to plant the kiss after the revelling of the late night before. The levy always ended with initiation into the Polar Bear Club whereby everyone en masse went for a dip in, by this time of year, the ice cold Med.

Another function often recalled was "Mystery Night", an evening that for weeks had been advertised as surprise entertainment of the first order. On that evening, everyone had to be in the Maple Leaf House by 1930 hours, at which time the door would be closed to further entry. The organizers expected 100 people, but were faced with 220. A sequence of excellently planned happenings then occurred, the highlight of which was a 95 km train ride north to Alghero. The train, with live music and bar on each car, was completely reserved, and was the only train running in Sardinia at that time of night. In Alghero, a banquet and dance ensued. The crowning touch that will never be forgotten by those who took part was that the organizers had told everyone that the train was merely taking them on a circuitous route to the other side of the city of Cagliari! Place signs enroute, and even in Alghero, were covered so as not to give the plot away. Everyone was too interested in partying to pay attention, and at the end of it all, at the 5:00 a.m. "egg-in-the-hole" breakfast back at Maple Leaf House, they could not believe where they had been!

During each deployment, pilots had to be given refresher sea survival training. This consisted of two half-days of lectures and an afternoon undergoing water drills in the Poetto Bay. A ski barge and Boston Whaler were the school's fleet, and the staff consisted of the instructor (resident weapons officer with sea survival instructor qualification) and up to five especially trained volunteer airmen. All were scuba trained. Drills were no piece of cake, especially for those who could not swim, and there were no exemptions. One of the most challenging drills involved stepping off backwards from an approximate seven foot platform on the ski barge wearing black-out goggles, and immediately on entering the water being towed by the Boston Whaler via cable attached to the parachute harness. The forerunner of the present quick-release box often took an extraordinary amount of effort to open under the pressure exerted on the box by the towing action. Due to the often desperate pilot's contortions to activate the release, the pilot's body would sometimes without warning dart underwater. Sheer panic would then result in such superhuman strength that the infernal release gave way. Nevertheless, the drill was accomplished and the fearful reputation of the exercise maintained. Hundreds of German Luftwaffe pilots were also given sea survival training by the Canadians. Germany's air force finally established a parallel facility directly beside the Canadian school in 1968.

A famous anecdote comes to mind that exemplified the good-natured esprit between air and ground crews on deployment. It occurred at an outdoor evening barbecue hosted by the groundcrew on their final night prior to a rotation back to Germany following a three-month stay. A Corporal, who was as well known for his excellent trade ability as his practical jokes, set the aircrew up beautifully for the "big one". In impeccable manner, he served wine and a platter of large cheese squares to the aircrew. Paying little attention to inspecting the food, due to the only light being that from the fire, but commenting on the tastiness of the cheese, most had two or three pieces. After it was totally consumed except for one large piece held by the perpetrator, attention was called and the cheese square placed on a log in the fire so that all could see it. The cheese simply dissolved into a swarm of maggots. What he had served was the Sardinian delicacy, known to the natives as magotty cheese. There were few aircrew stomachs that could stand the sight,

Above: *Rene Serrao and Jake Miller (in the CF-101) collectively thrilled audiences with their formation teamwork across the nation in 1967. They performed a precision aerial ballet that was second to none. This shot was taken at Abbotsford, B.C.*

- photo by Bill Johnson

knowing that similar action was taking place internally. Needless to say, the practical joker had to run for his life.

During his tenure as Personnel Administration Officer at Decci between 1964 and 1966, Dave Girling was also privileged to acquire many fond memories of life on Sardinia at the time. Here are but two of them, the first of which became known as the Great Alitalia Caper...

Deployment to Decci was not popular among most of the groundcrew in Air Division. Deployments were usually for six weeks but occasionally extended to eight or more weeks, usually because air transport was not available to effect a rotation. During the summer of 1966, air transport was in particularly short supply, and after almost 10 weeks of deployment the crew deployed at Decci was becoming restless. With "Service Air" resources clearly unavailable for some time to come, the situation called for exceptional action. It was decided that a commercial charter would be made, and an Alitalia Viscount was contracted forthwith. One sunny Sunday morning, the Viscount arrived at Elmas, the civil airport which served Cagliari. The departing deployment crew were loaded aboard, obviously delighted with the unaccustomed standard of service and comfort. The aircraft departed for Strassbourg where the replacement crew waited for the return trip.

Those of us on staff at Decci at the time were pleased that the rotation could finally be accomplished with what appeared to be a perfect solution. Until the flight returned, however, we had no idea that the charter contract with Alitalia had for some reason included all normal airline charter services, including full beverage service. Our first indication that anything was amiss came just after the aircraft came to a stop at Elmas. The external airstair was moved to the aircraft door... the door opened, and one extremely bedraggled stewardess emerged... her blouse no longer tucked into her skirt, and her hair in disarray. She stepped out onto the airstair and leaned against the outside of the fuselage with one wrist pressed against her forehead. She truly looked as if she had never expected to see the sun and fresh air again. From the aircraft emerged a group who were clearly in the midst of a great party; a group considerably subdued at the start of work on Monday morning!

On August 13, 1965, Flight-Lieutenant Al Seitz of 422 Squadron, Baden-Soellingen, departed Decci one Friday afternoon to redeploy to Baden. Just past the northern coast of Sardinia, he experienced a total hydraulic failure, and with the aircraft in a slight left bank and slightly nose-down attitude, and with the Mach approaching .92, Al ejected. With great misfortune, he landed in the water after having been separated from his dinghy. Fortunately, the crew of a small fishing boat, the Cao Brothers, saw Al descending in his parachute, and set off immediately to rescue him. Despite the Cao Brothers prompt action, Al was in the rather heavy seas for half an hour or more, and would not have lasted must longer. They took him to their home port of Porto Torres at the north end of the island from whence Al was med–evaced by helicopter through Decci to the Italian Military Hospital in Cagliari for observation and a short convalescence before returning to Baden.

422 Squadron later decided to honour the crew and owner of the boat that rescued Al, and a Dining-In was organized for this purpose at Decci. On the appointed day, the CO's staff car was despatched to Porto Torres to bring them to the base. 422 Squadron arrived en masse in a fleet of '104s and T–33s. We determined later from our driver that the four guests of honour had been severely into the red wine during the drive to Decci, and by the time they arrived at the Mess for the dinner, they were quite loaded. Their condition continued to deteriorate rapidly as they discovered a particular affinity for Canadian Club. Al and the senior 422 Squadron officers made a valiant effort to extend words of thanks and appreciation. However, their efforts were interrupted by frequent hugs and kisses for Al, and by the owner of the boat demonstrating an incredible back flip/roll from a perch atop the water cooler in the corner of the dining room. Difficult indeed to hold people's attention in the face of such determined diversions! All four guests of honour made the trip, from Mess to barracks, horizontal in the back of my Opel station wagon.

Bill Turnbull remembers the Decci deployments as well, particularly from the vantage point of a Reconnaissance pilot determined to keep honour and dignity intact while immersed in a sea of Strike pilots...

Working with the Italian Air Force was always an interesting experience. When the Base ran out of maintenance money, the conscripts would steal light bulbs from our quarters, ignoring any valuables that might be lying around. When the Canadian Detachment Commander and the Italian Base Commander were at odds, we would sometimes feel the heat, such as the time I was interrogated by the Italian secret police for taking photographs near the base - of scenery, I might add.

Occasionally, the range would, without notice, be declared closed; usually about the time a four-plane section was checking in with the controllers. We were always very unhappy with inaccurate range scoring and tried to install a photographic scoring system which the Italians went to great lengths to sabotage. I assume they perceived it as an insult, a threat, or both. For example, they suddenly decided to level the range with a bulldozer just after cameras and connecting cables had been laid out on the ground. Needless to say, the cables were found neatly chopped into one-foot lengths. We abandoned the project.

The two weeks of concentrated range work usually ended with a Combat Profile Mission (CPM) which terminated in a "Shape" drop at the range. The camp participants would each throw some money in the pot, to be collected by the one who achieved the most accurate delivery in terms of distance and "splash" time. The Strike pilots really became incensed when one of the recce pilots took their money. I did it, and it was easy. We were probably more proficient at low level visual navigation than they were, and that was really the key to the exercise.

Before flying any CPM which traversed the interior of Sardinia, we were briefed to avoid certain towns in the mountains. These were reportedly home to the local "bandidos" and aircraft had, it was said, taken small arms fire when flying in those areas. Kidnapping seemed to be the main source of bandido revenue, but this was practiced in a very honourable way. The victims were always returned unharmed once the ransom was paid. Those amateurs who tried to break into the business, only to panic and kill their hostages, were quickly dispatched by the bandidos themselves, according to local legend. The stories have a certain credibility for amateurs really gave the business a bad reputation.

When sporadic redeployments to Decci were resurrected by the CF–104 community in the early eighties, they lacked the intensity of effort that had characterized the Canadian presence on Sardinia during the sixties. Mostly, they deployed to do Dissimilar Air Combat Training in the area's excellent electronically-instrumented training area, known as the Air Combat Maneuvering Range Instrumented (ACMRI). Occasionally, they would also do some air-to-ground proficiency weapons deliveries at Capo Frasca Range, but only as very limited opportunities became available. Still, the deployments provided ample opportunity to demonstrate native skill and cunning, not to mention an occasional strong dose of good luck, as Gord Hatch reiterates...

During one of the later Sardinia deployments, one of the missions that came up was a 2 vs 2, CF–104 against RAF F–4s. After the face-to-face briefing, one of the Brit pilots jibed that the Canadians should clean their mirrors. The uncharacteristic taunt was a little premature. Due to a bowser driver work-to-rule squabble, only one CF–104, piloted by Rick Gelinas, was fuelled in time for the planned departure. The F–

4 pair was also reduced to one with a ground abort, and the first engagement was inconclusive. As the two aircraft (1 F–4, 1 CF–104) repositioned, Rick was joined by his late arriving winger. The F–4 coming down from the north thought that he was west of both Starfighters, and his hard turn east to meet the first aircraft he spotted turning into him, put him quickly into the gun sight of Rick turning in from the west. It was over so fast that the Brits were dumb-struck. The ensuing debriefing in the ACMRI trailer was more of a Brit backseater assassination than what could be termed meaningful discussion.

Mike Savard of 441 Squadron had the honour of being a member of the last CF–104 deployment to Decci, in October 1983. Supervisors on any flying establishment are always expected to lead by example, and the Canadian Starfighter community was no exception. Here is a classic case where stern words of caution from management to the troops backfired somewhat. The setting is the Ops building shortly after the pilot's arrival, and the briefer is Major Graham Larke, the Detachment Commander. Mike explains...

Graham emphasized the importance of local procedures and insisted on the fact that far too many overstresses had been recorded, necessitating a great deal of extra work for the groundcrew. At the conclusion of the briefings, the Commanding Officer, LCol. Betts stood up and re-emphasized the importance of self-discipline and the burden of overstresses.

Whether the "calzonnes", the red wine or the age..., the cause will remain undetermined, but in the span of two days, the CO and two majors, including yours truly, had exceeded the allowable "G" loading. Ironic you say! Perhaps funny today, but awfully embarrassing at the time. The boys had behaved well, but the adults had not done so great (Gord Hatch kept his cool and his reputation remained unscathed).

Nevertheless, this deployment was a very valuable experience which, for most of the pilots, represented a first crack at ACMRI. I think that it was fitting for the last Canadian '104 Squadron to be the last at Decci.

* * * * * *

Neil Gillespie had a distinguished flying career in CF–104s, both at 421 Squadron as an "original" in the early sixties, then later at 417 Squadron in the early seventies. The author is grateful to The Golden King of the Skies[1] for the following vignettes, based on his Starfighter experiences over the years.

It was thirty below at Cold Lake in the winter of '63. Tom Swifties were in vogue. What's a Tom Swifty? It's a word play that combines a situation with a suitable adverb. For example, "Look what this slicing machine had done to the end of my arm," the butcher said off-handedly.

*Conrad Platz was in trouble. He reported his emergency on the radio and indicated that his nozzles had failed open, and that he couldn't get them closed or maintain altitude. A voice from the nether interposes on the UHF, "Mayday Mayday, said **Condescendingly**". Platz landed OK... well, as OK as Platz ever could land.*

The experimental bombing exercise at Decci was to assess the accuracy of delivering a MK–106 from a 1000 foot AGL level supersonic approach, the idea being to find a less complicated escape than the LADD manoeuvre presented. Naturally, there were no ballistic tables, and it was pretty much a "That Looks About Right" release. After several dry supersonic passes, Delta One, JT Price, delivered live, and his bomb came nowhere close to even hitting the island of Sardinia. Delta Two

Above: *An armament technician does a gun harmonization check on a '104 at Baden-Soellingen in 1974.*

[1] Otherwise known as the Prince of Niceness and Decency.

called in Hot, and his bomb landed at the foot of the scoring tower, whereupon the Italian scoring crew, probably rattled by the supersonic bombs and the near miss, transmits, "Hey, Delta Two... thatsa bomba verra verra short and verra verra danger. For Delta section, thissa range she'sa close, you go home now, an donna come back. Verra verra danger." When JT informed the range tower that the airfield itself was temporarily closed, and that Delta section might as well hang around the range until the airfield opened, the range tower replied, "She'sa no matter. For Delta section, thissa range isa closa, closa, closa. You go home now." I was Delta Two...

It was a live (2000 lb. blivit) [1] *drop on Vliehors,*[2] *and the visibility was bad in haze. High tide was making pickup of the target on radar difficult. Golden King pickles on a reasonable return, LADDs, and enters the escape manoeuvre. Vliehors Range says, "You have pickled on a Soviet ELINT (which we subsequently learned occasionally moored on the bombing approach), and it looks like you might have a shack.*[3] *We suggest you get the hell out of here as quickly as possible." (It wasn't a shack, but the bomb landed right beside the ELINT, which recovered it... what does a Russian do with 2000 pounds of concrete and a wet parachute?)*

421 Squadron Grostenquin - early '64. Squadron pilot Don McKay, now with the Peoples' Airline, was your typical pipe smoker snob, and gassed us all with his fumes. When we would ask him to smoke outside or not at all, he would lecture us on how much money he spent on his expensive tobacco, and that we should be pleased with the aroma. A plan arose.

Whenever McKay went flying, we would break into his locker, dump some of his tobacco out of the pouch, and replace it was a like amount of shavings from the pencil sharpener. We couldn't wait for his comments after the first time we did this, but we were disappointed. He just sucked on his pipe, orgasing all over the place about what pleasure it was giving him.

The locker break-ins went on until we were certain the contents of the tobacco pouch was 100% shavings, but McKay kept telling us that we didn't know what we were missing. Actually, it didn't smell any worse than 100% tobacco!

I don't know if McKay still smokes, but if he smokes anything other than pencil sharpener shavings, he's wasting his money.

***Harry Stroud, The King of Karlsruhe** - The TACAN let–down for 4 Wing had its penetration turn over Karlsruhe, and the city was overflown at about 4500 feet AGL at the bottom of the approach. An engine failure over Karlsruhe would almost certainly call for bailout.*

We discussed this in the Squadron one day, and Harry Stroud was part of the group; in fact I recall him speaking loudest on the subject. The decision was simple. Engine failure, bail out. No ifs, ands, or buts. Get out of it! Who had the engine failure, just as discussed? Stroud. Does he bail out? Not when he said it should happen. Harry steered his Zip to the outskirts with a bit of hydraulics available from his windmilling engine, and then bailed out at about 50 feet, barely making it, and injuring himself. He was fêted in the Karlsruhe papers as a Herc, and I guess he was. I've heard he's now the King of Smoke, B.C.

***Tuck it in there, Three!** - Like Tinkers to Evers to Chance, certain threesomes fit together. The threesome I'm thinking about is closer to, say, W.C. Fields, Hitler, and the Boston Strangler, but they did fit Bad actors each of them, although time has tamed their acts. These days we can even discern trace indications of rational human behaviour in the two of us still kicking. This story is about one morning in the life of the third, who isn't. Paul Rackham died in a CF–104 accident at Bodo Norway in May, 1973.*

Paul and a few other 1 CAG pilots were in Cold Lake on Reverse Augmentation in the fall of 1973. Aircraft serviceability was low at the time, and all available daylight hours had to be used to maintain the syllabus, which meant 0600 takeoffs, and this tale concerns one such mission.

The pre-dawn weather was clear with visibility about a zillion miles and zero wind. The leaves on the trees in the area had recently changed colour, and a huge red ball of sun poked over the eastern horizon as the four-ship section slipped through the silky sky at around a hundred feet. It was a 540 knot mission, but there wasn't a hint of a bump in the air. The Loose Arrow formation was easy to fly and a pleasure to maintain. The beauty of the situation can only be really appreciated by someone who's been there, and this one was classic. The mission was briefed no-radio, but, apparently overwhelmed by the sheer beauty of the moment, Paul broke the rules to blurt out over the UHF, "Some silly bugger's actually paying us to do this".

The arrival of a new fighter type of aircraft in an operating theatre is like waving a red flag in front of a bull to a bunch of fighter pilots. Everyone wants to be first to capture the "new kid on the block" on film, *gunsight* film, that is. Hank Morris remembers one such incident...

1975 Eagle Encounter
(or the trailing edge of technology meets the leading edge)

While returning from an upgrading trip in Bavaria low level with Major Jake Newlove on my wing, we spotted a couple of contrails at about 10 - 15 miles. A quick check of fuel, and we decided to go after them. In those days of almost unrestricted flight, we stroked the burner and accelerated quickly above the smog. As we closed, the two dots quickly took on the shape of fighters in a Trail formation. The lead aircraft was a "double ugly" F–4, and in Trail a strange, sleek-looking aircraft with twin vertical stabilizers and almost glowing in a phosphorescent eggshell blue. We came out of burner simultaneously, somewhat in awe of being in the presence of a higher form of life or extraterrestrial. "It's the Eagle!" Jake's voice crackled over the radio. Basic instincts quickly took over those of curiosity, and immediately we pressed forward in our Double Attack formation.

The F–15 Eagle, obviously on a demonstration flight, picked me up coming in and turned toward me, while Jake slid in behind the F–15, claiming a "camera kill". We broke off, heading for Baden-Soellingen, ecstatic that we had recorded the first F–15 "kill" in Europe.

Upon landing, the gun camera film was gingerly carried away to be processed with instructions that it be handled with TLC. We were dismayed to find out that there was no film, due to the camera circuit breakers being left out. Another golden moment lost...the one that got away.

* * * * * *

Friday night beer calls were an institution during the Starfighter era; an opportunity to blow off steam, relieve pent-up frustrations, and theoretically, to tell The Boss just exactly what you thought of him (this was called feedback) without fear of him taking notes. Theoretically, that is. The drinking could be done without fear of having to fly the next day, which was just as well since, as CF–104 pilots both worked hard and played hard, Friday nights were *definitely* in the latter category. A lot of problems were solved at beer calls, and a lot of brain cells "bit the dust" as well. Larry Crabb elaborates...

Beer Call

Who can forget the age-old tradition of everyone on squadron proceeding to the Mess at about 1700 hours Friday to be served by Bob and René. The "Grunts" stayed out front, but the three squadrons mingled together in the back-bar. Shortly after 1800, each Squadron plus their associates and guests would proceed to the Squadron table for

[1] A simulated nuclear weapon made of concrete.
[2] A practice bombing range just off the Dutch coast.
[3] Direct hit.

the usual eating and drinking, tell war stories, and throw the odd bun, etc. at the other Squadrons, and then head for the crud table. There are a thousand stories, but some were unique.

In '72 or '73, the streaking craze started in North America. We wanted to introduce it to Europe. Paul Beaulieu plus a couple of others left the table as if to go to the back bar. They rushed around to the kitchen entrance, stripped, pulled their shorts over their heads, and streaked through the dining room. Unfortunately, Paul was going so fast that he could not negotiate the corner at the Base Commander's table. He slammed into the back of one of the chairs, leaving imprints with his knackers. As the room roared with laughter, all you could see was this bent-over individual gasping for air, barely creeping out of the Mess. It was about an hour before Paul returned to the table.

During my tenure as CO of 441 Silver Fox Squadron, one of the traditions on Friday night was to have the youngest pilot act as the "egg-Meister", whose task it was to administer a raw egg to our unsuspecting guests at the table. He would put on a demonstration, and then we would sing a song while these individuals would try to force down the egg. Believe me, many an egg was regurgitated onto the table. One night, we were hosting four USAF F–15 pilots, led by a Major who had been a POW in Vietnam. He was the only one who was able to keep the egg down. He whispered to his Lieutenant, who shortly returned with a needle and thread. He stood up, and after several chug-a-lugs, he gave a little speech of thanks; but as he was talking, he took the needle and shoved it through his cheek, pulled the needle out through his mouth, and started a see-saw motion with the thread as he talked. Needless to say, he received a rousing ovation for this one-upmanship. Suddenly, he hollered for silence, turned to me and said, "Now it's your turn." The other squadrons loved it because they knew he had me. I was sure everyone could hear my heart frantically pounding, but I knew I had to respond to the challenge. I reached over, pulled the needle and thread from his mouth, and with very shaky hands, worked it through my cheek... but in my nervousness, it also came out through the corner of my lip! Through the applause, Rob Porter, my Deputy Commanding Officer (DCO), looked up at me and said, "Boss, you have balls as big as footballs, but a brain the size of a pea!" So true.

Practice bombing in the CF–104 was quite an art form compared to today's "smart" systems, which essentially make everyone an ace bomber. One had to juggle all the permutations and combinations of target tracking, wind allowance, altitude, airspeed, dive angle, and "G" loading. In addition, just getting the practice bomb dispenser doors open and the correct bomb type away could be fraught with the potential for failure, as Gord Hatch relates...

In Europe, the MK–106 and BDU–33 practice bombs were carried in the MN1A dispenser. With its clam-shell doors closed, it was a very secure way to lug the bombs around the countryside. The MN1A was carried on the centreline rack and was configured so that the pilot used the same cockpit switch positions for a practice bomb as would be used for an actual weapon. This was possible because, located in the lower electrical bay, there was a switch with two positions...MN1A and Normal. It was to be checked during the pilot's preflight, and should have been found lock-wired in the appropriate position. There was at least one case of an aircraft with ejection cartridges installed and the switch left in the Normal position during an MN1A training sortie. Unfortunately, the ballistics for the full dispenser are not the same as for the individual practice bombs, and it was an unscorable projectile when it inadvertently jettisoned.

Those pilots who got into the CF–104 program late did not suffer the original frustration of trying to figure out if the MN1A doors were open, closed, or in between. The final configuration with a two-position Open/Closed switch and an indicator light to show when the doors were open was a real treat. The system used in the 1960s was a little more difficult, and some pilots never did figure it out. Again, it seemed to be tied to making actual weapon selections and it was all geared to the DCU9/A control.[1] *To close the doors on the ground or in the air, the controller was quickly moved from* Ground *to* Safe *to* Ground. *This action made the MN1A think that a bomb had been released, so it then closed the doors. Once the doors were closed, the controller was moved to* Safe *and the solenoid allowed to cool. To open the doors, the switch moved back to the* Ground *position and when a bomb was dropped, the doors would close on their own. Once the doors had time to close, the switch was put back to* Safe *and left there until the next bomb was needed. The problem was that if on the run–in to the target the pilot went to open the doors and he found the control still in the* Ground *position from the previous pass, he had to select* Safe *and wait long enough for the solenoid to cool before going back to* Ground *to open the doors. The final kicker was that if after a release, the controller was taken out of the* Ground *position before the doors were fully closed, they would just stop where they were. From a partial position, they had to be first closed using the* Ground/Safe/Ground *plus cooling cycle before they could be opened. The above was all done without the help of an indicator light to let the pilot know if he had succeeded.*

During the Ground Attack days, at least in the early 1980s, the normal MN1A load was four MK–106s and two BDU–33 practice bombs. The BDUs were always in the 5 and 6 bomb positions so that the section lead could brief a common sequence for the events to be flown,

Above: *Wally Peel and Pierre Rochefort being silly at TAM '82. Wally's attire is somewhat of an overstatement.*

[1] Part of the nuclear weapons arming circuitry.

and so that the armourers could have a standard load. After a number of bomb-related incidents, it became common practice after a sortie to visually confirm that the correct number of bombs, if any, were still in the dispenser. After one particular sortie where the intent was to drop the two BDUs, then two MK–106s, the visual check showed a BDU still in place, plus only one of the two MK–106s. As the intervalometer had correctly stepped to the number 3 position and four bombs had been dropped, something was not right. Possibly there was a reason for the unscorable-at-six BDU pass and the very long MK–106, since the ballistic properties of each bomb type were very different, and a bomb-sight setting meant for a BDU (when actually releasing a MK–106 - and vice versa) would make for a spectacular impact error.

On top of all the normal things that could go wrong with switches and bomb sequencing, there was always the "gremlin factor", or problems caused by stray electrical voltages. Pat Barrett recalls one such occurrence on Siegenburg Range…

During a Siegenburg bombing mission in 1976, the range tower was unable to spot any of Clark Little's BDU–33s. To his great surprise on returning to Baden-Soellingen, Clark found his bomb dispenser empty. In the ensuing days, his BDUs turned up in various locations in Bavaria in the general vicinity of Siegenburg - in a farmer's attic, and so on. It was eventually determined that a stray electron was pickling off a BDU every time the control column UHF transmit button was used.[1] *Immediately thereafter, use of this button for radio transmissions was banned while doing weapons releases.*

Generally speaking, the CF–104's cockpit design was ergonomically very pleasing, especially for its day, with practically every switch, gauge, button and light being right where the pilot would most appreciate it. I say *practically*, because there were some glaring exceptions. The most notable was the External Stores Jettison Button, or "Panic Button", as it was more frequently called. This circuit was always electrically "hot", and upon activation, cleaned the wing of all external stores except the pylons and the Twin Stores Carrier, if mounted. Naturally, this included the tip tanks, which came sailing off in a splendid fashion. The *bad* news was that this button had only a paper guard over it, and was located precariously close to the engine throttle. An errant extended index finger on a throttle slammed rapidly into afterburner range would break the paper cover[2] and depress the jettison button, with spectacular results! Pat Barrett tells of just such a happening...

Jim Gale was leading a three-plane proficiency Attack mission into central Germany on March 31, 1977. They were flying out of Lahr, and returning to Baden-Soellingen after completion of a Southern Safari exercise. The first target was in a forested area near Ramstein. During the final run-in, after I as Number Two had been signalled in to close formation for the Attack phase, the Section was bounced and someone called, "extend!"[3] *At this point, Jim shoved the throttle plus a mittful of maps into afterburner range... in the process, jettisoning his tip tanks - literally right before my very eyes!*

*I took a photo, which is probably the only one of a "clean" aircraft with a bomb dispenser. The shot was taken while we were motoring up and down the Rhine Valley burning off fuel, and while Jim was preoccupied with explaining (at **great** length) to Operations on the radio just what had occurred.*

Jim Gale now provides his own recollection of the events…

The Squadron CO, Lieutenant-Colonel John Hutt, was my trusty number three that day. On his panic call to "break left", I immediately rammed in full afterburner, with my throttle hand full of maps and my fingers fully extended. Shortly thereafter, I was surprised to hear my winger (Pat Barrett) transmit, "Lead, you'd better roll out; you've lost your tips!" At the time, we were flying somewhere between Ramstein and Zweibrucken, over rolling terrain that was heavily forested and broken by many scattered villages and roads. We orbited the area for several minutes, hoping to spot the location where the tanks went in, but without success. Needless to say, after landing back at Soellingen, a few nervous hours elapsed before a ground party from base was able to confirm that the tanks had impacted safely in a forested area and had caused no damage, except to the nerves of a German logging crew who were working nearby as the tanks came crashing down through the trees.

When we were bounced, my wingman was able to clearly identify the attacker as a Canadian CF–104 (not surprising, considering the range to which he had let the bogey close), but back at base it was impossible to single out any one likely suspect from the large number of single-ship missions that had been airborne at the time. Obviously, no one was prepared to publicly declare himself as the attacker. Nonetheless, about three weeks after the incident, at a Friday night beer call, I was secretively approached by a rather sheepish squadron-mate who admitted, with a good deal of embarassment and apology, that he had been the culprit. He was, however, quick to confirm that jettisoning tip tanks with a bogey at gun range was a highly effective evasive tactic, and one that had totally watered his eyes.

There seemed to be no limit to the amount of ingenuity demonstrated by the armament technicians during the CF–104 era, but it was seemingly impossible to make a change that was completely gremlin-proof (and perhaps, idiot-proof). Gord Hatch explains…

Some clever lad realized that the "panic button", designed to quickly clear the aircraft of external stores, was also to be used as a last method to jettison hung ordnance. As this use would also cause the unavoidable loss of the tip tanks, a simple wiring change was done to add a switch that would temporarily isolate the tip tank jettison circuit from the "panic button" circuit. A switch was eventually installed with a red guarded cover and label. Although there is no record of this switch being used as intended, it was used with spectacular results. A section of aircraft with rocket pods briefed that the tip saver switch would be activated to allow the use of the panic button to jettison the empty pods.

All went well for three aircraft, but the fourth aircraft lost both the spent rocket pods, plus the tips. Interestingly, the tip saver switch was adjacent to the pylon jettison switch. The pylon jettison switch will not do anything if a store is on the pylon, but if it is activated or reactivated after the store is gone, the pylons will be jettisoned. The incident aircraft was seen to jettison its pylons while taxiing in after the sortie. No electrical fault was found and the squadrons went back to using the selective jettison modes for non-critical stores release.

* * * * * *

The Decci Bus, or "Drunk Bus" that Dave Girling mentioned earlier did yeoman service at Baden as a general utility "jack-of-all-trades" vehicle. However, its main *raison d'être* was to provide safe transport home to Friday night beer call attendees who had partaken of a few ales. To this end, a rotating schedule was set up amongst the various Base units, who in turn provided a Duty Driver for the evening. Generally speaking, this self-policing system worked very well, *except* on one occasion when an order from a superior was taken just a little too literally. Pat Barrett elaborates…

A story in frequent re-tell when I arrived at 441 Squadron in mid-'74 had to do with one particular squadron pilot who, having made himself obnoxious (though not particularly impaired) at probably his first beer call, was given the following order by the CO, Don Myles:

"Go home… and take the Drunk Bus!"

This order he took quite literally, and as a consequence, the Drunk Bus disappeared for the weekend…safely driven by this Squadron

[1] There were two methods, once airborne, to transmit on the UHF radio. The primary method, both air and ground, was to use the transmit button on the throttle. The secondary method was a control stick transmit button, which only worked when airborne, and controlled the nose wheel steering on the ground.

[2] The Americans and Germans actually had a hinged metal cover over their "panic button". Why we didn't, I'll never know.

[3] The call to accelerate and get out of Harm's Way.

neophyte to his home somewhere in the Schwarzwald.

* * * * * *

The attainment of 1000 flying hours on aircraft type is a "Big Deal" to a fighter pilot. Due to relatively-constrained annual flying time accumulation in comparison with transport or maritime pilot peers, this figure represents several years of intensive flying. Furthermore, since fighter-type missions tend to be of short duration, the sortie activity level is usually very brisk, and 1000 flying hours often represents *at least* that many takeoffs and landings. In short, the 1000 hours mark is a coveted plateau; a moment to be savoured, and if possible, recorded appropriately in a fighter pilot's career. Sometimes the preening was all for naught though, as happened to Larry Crabb on his 1000 hour trip when he was CO of 441 Squadron...

On Monday, I would be flying my 1000th hour in the Starfighter. Dave Owen decided that we needed a Checkerbird to commemorate the event. On Sunday, all the squadron pilots assembled near the HAS,[1] *where Dave had stockpiled the supplies. He had gone to the school and cleaned them out of black and white poster paint. We would paint the aircraft all white, and then when dry, use a large cardboard stencil to paint over it in black to form the checkers. We mixed the white paint in large garbage cans. Unfortunately, we found out that it was too runny, and therefore we had to scrounge large quantities of flour to thicken it, since we were out of white paint. It was a beautiful sunny Sunday, and the hours quickly passed. When we were finished, we hid the end result in a HAS to maximize the "surprise factor" on the Base the next day. Monday morning, we all breathed a sigh of relief that there was no rain forecast, since the poster paint would have washed off. I would lead a four-plane with my Checkerbird, and Dave would follow in the dual with a photographer to record the occasion. Before departure, I made a tour of the 439 Squadron dispersal to let Baz Lawlor (the CO) and the Tigers see a "real aircraft". We launched on a tour of Bavaria, did some low approaches at German bases, viewed the beautiful Alps, while all the time I mentally prepared myself for the ultimate picture. Everyone has their aircraft photographed against the Hohenzollern Castle, but I wanted a coup. I would have my picture taken against the Olympic Tower in Munich! I hacked near Chemsee and came in on a low-level route to pass to the north side of the tower, wondering if the airport radar was tracking me, which could have resulted in an airspace violation. All went as planned. We hustled home, jubilant, and I received a great soaking from the fire truck. The film was quickly developed, but much to my dismay, the ultimate picture was a flop; it only showed the Checkerbird against a large concrete background, the base of the tower. Dave had hesitated to move out and climb in order to take in the whole tower! I had put my instrument ticket on the line for nothing.*

A sequel to this story... the weather remained good, so most 441 pilots got to fly the aircraft. On Thursday, we decided to wash the paint off. What a disaster! Underneath every black rectangle, the sun's radiation had baked the white flour mixture into the camouflage paint. In order to remove this mixture, it actually required removal of the painstakingly-applied camouflage underneath. Needless to say, the Base Aircraft Maintenance Officer was furious that he had to repaint the aircraft!

* * * * * *

During the CF–104 era, there were many opportunities to participate in rather unusual multi-national trials with the aircraft. One such happening was the beacon bombing trials, in which less-sophisticated Attack aircraft such as the Starfighter were mated with those of a greater all-weather Attack capability. The idea was to fly close formation on the more sophisticated aircraft, and release weapons on his command to put a greater ordnance weight-of-effort on a target. Hank Morris recalls the beacon bombing trials...

Beacon Bombing in Bavaria, circa 1975

In November 1975, I was in charge of a deployment which included Dave Jurkowski and twelve technicians to Erding air base, near

Above: *441 did an early unit checker aircraft in the late-sixties. Note the unusual serial number!*

[1] Hardened Aircraft Shelter.

ANADA
FORCE
ARMÉE

Munich for Exercise Salty Target. Fighter bombers from various NATO Air Forces were involved.

We flew on the wing of an F–111 and a U.S. F–4 to practice the effectiveness of beacon bombing. Inert 500 pound bombs and 25 pound practice bombs (BDUs) were used. The target was a bunker at Grafenwoelhr Range and Dave and I flew on an Upper Heyford F–111, a multi-engined Attack aircraft. Because of the time of year, we spent a lot of time on the ground. Although Graf was not too far away, the route at 7500 feet was circuitous, and the USAF "one star" in charge of the operation from Ramstein was "overly cautious" about the whole operation. In fact, he seemed obsessed with the fuel consumption of the Canadian CF-104s, so much so that Dave repeatedly got into the books sharpening his pencil before each flight to extract a few more pounds of gas. At one of the final briefings, the General gave us his usual pep talk and again asked me for assurances that we had enough gas for the flight. I retorted that we did indeed, but that if anything untoward occurred, we would declare an emergency and conduct a single engine approach into the nearest airfield. He smiled, reassured, but quickly realized as the other pilots guffawed that he had been had. Dave and I presented him with a photo at the end of the exercise. The bombing went well and scores were well within NATO qualifying parameters from the rarified altitude of 7500 feet and always in cloud.

* * * * * *

The fruits of recognition are often akin to being a double-edged sword, complete with advantages and disadvantages. Dave Jurkowski recalls how one "returning warrior" was just a mite too presumptive concerning what he obviously felt was suitable recognition for his efforts...

Cash Returns to Canada

Captain Cash Poulson - Fighter Pilot Extraordinaire - was about to repatriate to Canada in the late '70s. Lugging baggage, wife and kids through the hot, sultry summer serpentine of the Lahr Canada Customs Boutique, Cash groaned a muttered expletive when the Customs Officer glared at him, even though Cash and company were buried ten back in the sweltering pack.

"You there! Bring your bags up here to this counter!"

"Just great!", thought Cash expensively.

Photos: *1. Armament technicians load practice 20mm ammunition into a CF-104 prior to a weapons training sortie. 2. 104 763, 417 Squadron's distinctively painted Starfighter for the OTU stand-down in 1983 drones majestically above a cloud layer at Cold Lake.*

He struggled forward.

"Your name Poulson?", the agent asked, eyeing Cash's name tag.

"Yeah," Cash bleated uncharacteristically.

"Well, C'mon in here, park your bags. You're through customs and there's going to be a flypast of '104s for you."

"I should hope so!" retorted CASH POULSON - FIGHTER PILOT EXTRAORDINAIRE - quickly regaining his composure.

Cash, now in full control of the Aircraft Movements Unit, strides outside to await the tribute. With typically impeccable timing, two smoking CF–104s, lead by Major Ross Huckle of 421 Squadron, streaked low over the brilliantly white Boeing parked on the Lahr ramp. Actually a pussycat at heart, Cash stood to attention, saluted, and no doubt slightly moist-eyed, briefly reminisced about the tremendous operational fighter tour which was about to come quickly to a close.

Watching the black smoke trails recede into the summer haze, Cash noticed the Baden Rube Band formed up at the base of the Boeing stairs. Having enjoyed schnapps, bratwurst, lederhosen, feathered hats and very close bonds with German fishing and hunting clubs and the Baden Rube Band, this was too much for this sentimentalist-at-heart.

"Think I'll go and inspect the Baden Rube Band."

Cash went up the front rank exchanging pleasantries with the strangely quiet members of the band and, as he was about to start the next rank, he caught a glimpse of a glaring Lieutenant-General Ramsey Withers, who seemed to have joined the inspection party of one. Horrorstruck (for a nano-second at least) Cash devined his faux pas.

Well, to make a long story short, Cash waited until the smoking lamp was lit, somewhere over France around level-off, before he slithered up to apologize to the General. But before Cash could say anything, General Withers looked over his glasses and said, "Cash..."

"He knows my name!" Cash thought.

"Cash, I don't know whether the flypast was for you and the band was for me, or vice versa. But let's just call it even, shall we?" the General suggested.

* * * * * *

One of the greatest fears of a fighter pilot is getting stuck with something you don't want in terms of ordnance. Several types of munitions are considered unsafe for landing with once they have been externally armed and taken aloft, and napalm certainly falls into that category. Frank Birchall flew '104s with 439 Squadron during the latter half of the seventies, and he remembers some harrowing moments at Pampa Range in Belgium while he tried desperately to shed a very unwelcome companion...

While I appreciate that I won't get the entire Starfighter community to agree with me, I flew the CF–104 at the right time, the right place, the right squadron, and with the right people. The period 1975 to 1979 on 439 Squadron boasted a fighter pilot roster second-to-none. Names like Bill Fuoco, Ian Morrice, Bernie Reid, Dave Jurkowski, Keith MacDonald, Dave Bashow, Brian Croft, Don Robinson, and certainly Jim McCullough. Jim was assigned to me as my monitor pilot for the three-month upgrade period to combat readiness. I learned more in those three months that I did in my remaining four years in Europe. Not surprising then that my story has to do with Jim and I flying together...

On January 23, 1976, Jim was leading me on a two-ship bombing trip to Pampa Range in northern Belgium. This was to be my first live weapons drop since arriving in Europe, and my fangs were out. The mission profile would consist of one dry pass, followed by one hot pass and the simultaneous release of the two napalm bombs, carried one under each wing. The weather was typically European-winter and I remember thinking as we departed Baden under Special Visual Flight Rules (CVFR) conditions, that it wasn't much better than my Instrument Flight Rules (IFR) limits allowed for flight. Jim was unconcerned, and with only minor deviations, we arrived at Pampa right on ETA for our range period.

Visibility was good (?)...barely three miles in haze and fog, and the split for spacing and the dry pass were uneventful. Jim then called for "switches hot" and he proceeded to "pickle" both cannisters right on target. Now the "sprogs" turn... peer pressure was at maximum, my mouth was dry and my heart was racing. Obviously, I wanted to shine. The target was acquired, altitude was 50 feet, airspeed was 450 knots... all was set. I pickled and heard a reassuring thud as the weapons released...or so I thought. At that moment, the aircraft rolled and yawed mildly to the right, and I then discovered that the right-hand bomb had not released. CONCERN!! I advised Lead, safetied up my armament switches, and motored around the bombing pattern while we figured out what to do. Together, we went through the arming sequence again, I called "in hot", and again, no luck. Jim then got on the radio to Baden through Kleine Brogel airfield to consult the oracles back at home base. Basically, there was nothing more to do except to try the emergency all-jettison button. The trip to Pampa and return in good weather allowed for only about three passes on the range, due to fuel constraints. Bingo fuel [1] was generally about 2800 pounds for this mission, and I was almost at that state. PANIC!! By now, the adrenaline was really flowing and I was most anxious to get rid of the jellied gasoline under my right wing. If this procedure didn't work, I was going to have to land with this unstable, volatile weapon, which was in a very unpredictable safety state. Furthermore, I would have to do it at Kleine Brogel airfield just seven miles to the north of the range, since my fuel state with the increased drag of the hung bomb would not allow me to return to Baden. Kleine Brogel might not consider a potential conflagration all over their runway to be a particularly NATO-neighbourly act! Rolling in on what was going to be, one way or another, my last pass, Jim coolly reminded me that I should be at a thousand feet and 350 knots, or ***jettison*** *limits, instead of the weapons delivery parameters of 450 knots and 50 feet, for which I was striving. An awful lot of TLAR (that looks about right) was used on that run to eyeball the right spot to jettison.*

Finally, I pickled... RELIEF!! Everything went; the napalm straight down, and the two empty tip tanks floated to impact the target area "unscorable at twelve o'clock". Jim and I then discussed recovering at Kleine Brogel, but when he learned that I had the same fuel as he did, not to mention that I was now flying the aircraft in its most aerodynamically-clean configuration,[2] he decided to bring us home.

Just before landing, Jim advised 439 Squadron to come outside and look at the flypast, mentioning that he was leading the new standard CF–104 configuration for operational missions in Europe! We then landed uneventfully, but this trip gave me a lot to talk about for some time.

Half the battle in becoming a successful fighter pilot is to have one's priorities in order, and to be able to think fast on one's feet in unusual circumstances. Remember that jolly extrovert Ross Huckle from 421 Squadron...the champion of the Bavarian Triathlon? Dave Granger, who also flew '104s with 421 during the same period certainly does...

Ross was at Siegenburg Range one day when his tip tanks fell off/auto-jettisoned on a bomb pass. 1 CAG was having one of the highly-competitive Top Gun competitions, and a bomb drop at Siegenburg was part of the scenario, as per usual. On Huck's pass, the tip tank bolt failed and the auto-jettison system worked as advertised; ***both*** *tip tanks jettisoned [3]. The range officer radioed that the tanks had indeed departed the jet. But Huck was "going for the gold" and his radio reply is a classic... "Forget the tip tanks...just give me my bomb score."*

Ross was just as quick on the mike in a later incident...Most Air

[1] Fuel state at which an immediate cessation of training and a return to base is usually necessary to ensure an adequate fuel reserve for landing.

[2] i.e., nothing hanging on or from it, except wing pylons.

[3] This was to preclude an unacceptable asymmetrical weight condition from occuring, and a resulting dangerous rolling moment.

Traffic Control agencies will query an unexpected aircraft accidentally entering their control zones. When Huck did this one day at one of the European American bases and was asked to identify himself, he came back with, "My name is Bob Stickley, and I'm from 439 Squadron." Honour among thieves?

Allied exchange pilots added a great deal of lustre to the CF–104 program over the years. They brought with them a vast wealth of collective experience, as well as their own unique personalities and national perceptions. Harald Riedel, whose experiences with Rick Wall have been described earlier in this book, recalls flying at Cold Lake, as seen through the eyes of a German Air Force fighter pilot...

In the summer of 1979 I was posted, as the first Luftwaffe pilot, to CFB Cold Lake to fly the CF–104 with 417 Squadron. I had spoken earlier to some Canadian pilots in Germany and had been warned... "Cold Lake is not the end of the world... but you can see it from there."

Even though I had flown the Starfighter in Germany since 1971, I was very much impressed by the aggressiveness and professionalism of the Canadian pilots. The same holds true for the quality of student training in the Squadron, and I have to confess that I learned quite a lot. When I reflect back on the day-to-day flying with 417, the thing that comes to my mind first are the extra low level navigation missions at 100 feet we could fly to the north of the Base; something one can do in Germany only ***once****! Also I remember the high percentage of Air Combat Missions which were part of both student training and staff proficiency in those latter years of CF–104 operations. In the Luftwaffe, Air Combat in the F–104 had been discontinued in the seventies, for flight safety reasons. I still marvel at the area of the tactical range (huge by German standards) with its numerous targets and close proximity to the Base; as well as the controlled bombing range at Jimmy Lake, only five minutes flying time away. Once the instrumented ACM range was established in the airspace above the tactical range, flying a CF–104 out of Cold Lake with 417 Squadron became an unrestricted paradise on earth for a true fighter pilot.*

Above: *Though user-friendly, CF-104 switchology was not idiot-proof. Inadvertently jettisoned wing pylons and Twin Stores Carriers at Baden in 1984.*

Above: *The 441 Squadron flight line at Baden on a hazy day in 1985.*

In retrospect, I must honestly say that those four years with the OTU were the highlight of my flying career. Additionally, my family and myself learned a lot about Canada, Canadians, and the nature of life so close to the end of the world. I would go back in a heartbeat and I consider myself lucky to have been the only German pilot to exchange with 417 Squadron, flying a demanding aircraft in an unfettered environment, which one cannot find elsewhere in the western world.

Keith Cotner, a USAF pilot, flew the '104 with 417 Squadron from 1977 until 1980. A post (and future) F–4 Phantom driver, Keith reflects on his experiences with the diminutive Starfighter...

The '104 was the sleekest, fastest, most responsive airplane that I have ever flown. I remember the first time that I sat in the cockpit. It was snug for my 200 pound 6'2" frame - especially wearing a winter flying suit and mukluks, but the cockpit was well-organized and everything was at my fingertips. The switchology was logical - a forerunner to the human-engineered cockpits of today.

Flying with the Canadian Armed Forces at Cold Lake was refreshing and rewarding. The Canadians' attitude toward flying was slightly different than that to which I was accustomed. In Canada, the most important aspect of flying was hands-on training. Experience, in terms of actual flying hours, was the key to improvement. There, a pilot's primary job was to fly airplanes... and fly we did. I got over 800 hours in my three years at Cold Lake. That was the most concentrated flying I have done in my career and I never equalled it again.

We flew the airplane hard, and improvised when the '104 didn't quite meet our expectations. A classic example was when we took our shiny, silver training airplanes to Red Flag. When the desert sun reflected off the bright fuselages, every bandit in the war could see us for miles. Bagshaw, Campbell, and others said, "This isn't any fun", and promptly went to an art supply store to find a solution. When Baggy described to the store owner that he wanted to camouflage an airplane to blend in with the Nevada desert, the owner said that would be easy, and quickly worked out the necessary mixture of colours. The owner was a bit taken aback when Baggy announced that he wanted several gallons of each type of paint. He apparently thought Baggy was going to paint a model airplane and not four fully grown fighters! The next part was just as innovative... they used water soluble paint and splashed it on

Above: *Hank Morris, Dave Jurkowski and "Beacon Bombing in Bavaria", 1975. Note the spare bomb in Hank's leg pocket.*
- photo courtesy of Dave Jurkowski

with mops and brooms. (It doesn't rain in the desert, and we were able to wash it off when the exercise was done.) It worked great, and 417 Squadron was hard to find in the desert war.

I also learned the most about aerial combat in the '104. Now that sounds odd, since the '104 was not a great turning airplane and not renowned for its air-to-air prowess. After flying the F–4 in Weapons School, I thought I knew how to handle a jet in the aerial battle. All the same techniques applied to the '104, but with its higher wing loading and stick kicker, it taught me how important finesse and a light touch was at high angles of attack. There were many times when all I needed was to pull the nose just a little bit more to get a missile or gun shot. If I pulled too quick or too much, the stick kicker would engage and all nose position would be lost, quickly turning an advantage into an equal or disadvantageous fight. Flying the '104 in air-to-air also taught me the edge provided by a small fighter aircraft. Many times, we could get unseen entries into a fight, and also "kills", merely by sneaking up on people. That was a rare event in the F–4.

I'll never forget the day I got to take my wife Sally on a high speed taxi ride. The Squadron commander, Larry Best, was gracious about giving us the opportunity, and Sally was very excited about the prospect. I was going to show her how the F–104 would give you a kick in the ass when you lit the afterburner. I wanted to do it right, so I got into the performance tables to compute how fast I could accelerate and still stop the airplane with the drag chute in the remaining runway. I gave myself a 1000 foot buffer just for good measure. The taxi ride was scheduled at the end of the flying day so as not to interfere with training flights. Sally and I spent the afternoon talking about what we were going to do (the flight briefing), getting her suited up with flight gear, and sitting in the simulator. As the afternoon trips were landing, I noticed that there were some duals available that were not going to fly again. I asked if we could take one of those in order to get finished early. There was a bit of a delay, but the word came back that I was to take Larry Best's airplane when he landed. He was the last to land, and when we passed him on the way out to the airplane, he wished us well with a silly smirk. I preflighted quickly, got Sal strapped in, jumped in the front, and got power on. Then I got a surprise... there was only 300 pounds of fuel in the tanks! For what I wanted to do, it would take at least 300 to 400 pounds of gas. I quickly looked around the ramp for another airplane, and they were all in the process of being towed in. I quickly decided I could do it with a much shorter burner run and a quick taxi back. Everything went smoothly with no delays, and the burner kick impressed Sally, even though it was of shorter duration than I wanted. I was watching the gas gauge like a hawk because I didn't want to explain how I flamed out on my last Starfighter operation. However, as I was taxiing back with the gauge at 100 pounds, I knew I had it made. But just as I approached the cross runway, Tower asked me to hold for the incoming Dakota on a five mile final! I couldn't believe it! Those few minutes were the longest of my life, and my eyes were glued to the fuel gauge. The Dak landed and I made it safely back, but there couldn't have been enough gas left to drive a motor scooter around the block. It was an anxious time for me in aviation, and I hadn't even been airborne! Larry Best later bought me a drink at the bar, and he couldn't stop laughing. All Sally could say was that it was great. Well dear, I'm glad it was good for you...

The European squadrons also received their fair share of exchange pilots. However, only American and British officers were posted to CF-104s in 1 CAG and this was done on a rotational basis by squadrons. Gary Blake was a USAF pilot who served with distinction as Flight Commander, then Deputy Commanding Officer of 439 Squadron from 1972 until 1975. He was very much a novelty in the USAF, since he came to the Canadian phase of his service life with over 2000 hours in Starfighter time already! In all, he would acquire 2900 flying hours in the '104, including combat service in Vietnam and with the air forces of eight different countries. Gary recalls some of his experiences with the Canadians in Europe...

I guess the assumption was that because I had over 2000 hours of F–104 time that I must be an expert in all phases of '104 flight. There was a "slight" difference between flying a low level in Arizona and Germany. Imagine using the edge of a forest as a turn point! On one particular day, after about 30 minutes of "flying the forests", I realized that I had no idea where in the hell I was. Assuring myself that I was only temporarily disoriented, I assumed a southeasterly course which hopefully would get me close to Baden. I was at about 500 feet AGL when I flew right over top of a well camouflaged runway! A call came up on guard, "Canadian '104 over Buchel, we appreciate your flypast, but next time please give us a call first."

In far too short a time, I was scheduled for my qualification ride, along with my flight lead check. The winds nearly did me in, and I also got to takeoff using the southerly-headed runway at Baden for the first time. I thought I had memorized my favourite start point in the forest north of the Base, but it didn't look the same after the sweeping, 180 degree turn made after takeoff. I got about two miles south of course on the very first leg and was desperately looking for the beloved Hohenzollern Castle [1] to get me back on track, when a subtle burst of words came over the radio sotto voce, *"Pssst...castle on the left." Sure as hell, there it was. I was soon back on course, and the rest of the mission went very well. Also, I know the check pilot never heard Dan Graham, my wingman, say "castle on the left" because he whispered!*

Being an American, my favourite CF–104 tale concerns an American base in Europe, namely Bitburg. It was a cold and miserable day. I was flying as Number Two in an eight-plane flight, and I was giving a fellow named Chalky LeBlanc his flight lead check. The mission was a mass attack on the USAFE base at Bitburg, provided in support of their annual NATO TacEval. Chalky did very well. We flew a low level route, did an excellent airfield attack on Bitburg, formed up, pitched out, and landed there in **visual** *conditions. Upon landing, we learned that not an aircraft had "turned a wheel" at Bitburg that day as they were below their own instrument flying weather minimums!*

One of our more efficient practices was always carrying a loaded practice bomb dispenser on all low level navigation missions. When a flight approached one of the conventional gunnery ranges, they would call them, and if the range wasn't busy, enter the pattern and drop some practice bombs. Fred Kenney did this solo one day, and before he landed I got a call from the range saying that they suspected he had inadvertently released a BDU–33 practice bomb on the crosswind leg of the pattern, and that the BDU–33 had gone through a German's house. After Fred landed, we decided that it couldn't possibly have been him, and informed the range. About an hour later, I received a call stating that when the bomb went through the kitchen, it severed the electrical cord to the clock at precisely the time Fred was in the pattern. We were caught with our "bombs down".

I have to mention Tiger Meets... One of the more memorable statements to come out of one of them was from our US Army Liaison Officer, Lou Eason. On the last day of this particular Meet, hosted by a German squadron, Lou was standing with Jim McCullough on the deck of a ship as it cruised down the Rhine River. Slightly feeling the effects of the past few days, he looked at Jim and stated, "I will be kind of glad when this Tiger Meet is over and I can get back to a more structured lifestyle."

[1] The Hohenzollern Castle, ancestral home of the crown princes of Prussia, rises majestically on its own hill, separated distinctively from the main Swabian Jura range. It was an excellent track check point during the Starfighter era.

Relegated to gate guardian duties, 104 785 bears mute testimony to its past in front of CFB Baden-Soellingen, West Germany.

Looking very natty in its civilian color scheme, 104 633 now flies with the Combat Jets Flying Museum, based in Houston, Texas.

"Renee" was CF104D '632 in Canadian service. It is now the pride of Northern Lights Aircraft Inc. in Montgomery, Alabama.
- photo courtesy of Tom Archer

Epilogue - What now remains

Though the CF–104 Starfighter no longer graces the skies of Canada or Central Europe, a surprising number are still airworthy. Naturally, the vast majority of those still flying soldier on with the Turk Hava Kuvvertleri, the Turkish Air Force. Since the transfer in 1986, three of the initial 39 flyable single-seaters have crashed, all due to engine problems. However, those aircraft have been replaced by refurbishing several of the non-flyable spares also transferred in 1986. The Turks now operate the most diverse Starfighter fleet in the world, flying not only the Canadian variants, but also F–104Gs and the all-weather interceptor F–104S model, built by Aeritalia in Italy.

Two flyable CF–104Ds may still be seen in the United States, and they are John Hutt's old friends '632 and '633 from his Palmdale days in 1961. Both of these aircraft performed yeoman service at the OTU for the first dozen years of their military careers, and both were part of the 22 aircraft sale to Norway in 1973. In July, 1986, '633 was sent in a container from Sola Air Station to Gothenburg, Sweden, and then by boat to California. It was then purchased by Jim Robinson and the Combat Jets Flying Museum, based in Houston, Texas. Looking very natty in its red, white, blue and silver paint scheme, it regularly thrills airshow audiences throughout the southwestern United States. '632 is alive and well in Montgomery, Alabama; the proud flagship of Northern Lights Aircraft, operating out of Dannelly Field Airport. This private business provides high-performance aircraft and specialized flight programs to the aerospace industry using both the '104 and a two-seat Hawker Hunter. Tom Archer, a former Marine aviator and graduate of the United States Navy

Test Pilot School, is Vice President of Flight Research and Development, and as Chief Test Pilot has a job that makes former '104 pilots green with envy. He alternates between flying the Hunter and the Starfighter, and though he is very fond of them both, they are certainly "birds of different feathers". Tom talks about his recent experiences with '632...

Prior to flying the F–104, I had some erroneous preconceived notions about the airplane that were a long time in forming. As a child, I built a model of the Starfighter and often wondered what it would be like to fly. My chances of ever finding out first hand diminished as I joined the U.S. Marine Corps, a service that surely would not provide the opportunity. One of my classmates in test pilot school was an Italian Air Force pilot, Carlo Magrassi, who flew F–104s operationally. I delighted in the anecdotes of his experiences in the airplane. I was most appalled, however, at the thought of a final approach speed of 190 knots, gluttonous fuel consumption, stick kicker activation close to the ground, uncontrollable pitch-up, and the glide characteristics of a greased crowbar. Just looking at the point design features of the airplane led me to the assumption that the F–104 would prove to be squirrelly to handle, especially when slow.

Once out of the USMC and employed by Northern Lights Aircraft, Inc., my opportunity to fly the Starfighter finally came. The company purchased CF–104D s/n 12632 from the Norwegian Air Force in December 1988. Although in pristine condition upon delivery, the airplane was overhauled and reassembled prior to its maiden flight on May 16, 1989. Mr. Wolfgang Czaia, a former Luftwaffe F–104 test pilot, was at the controls; and although he hadn't flown the airplane in 19 years, he flew as though he'd been born in an F–104.

Shortly thereafter came my long-awaited chance to fly the Starfighter, under Wolfgang's tutelage. I was pleasantly surprised by the airplane's exceptional handling qualities. After just one flight, the "missile with a man in it" myth was dispelled. I found the acceleration and climb performance exhilarating, but was quick to realize the unforgiving nature of the '104 in the low speed and high angle of attack regime. My definition of "low speed" changed too, as I encountered airframe buffet at less than 2 "Gs" with speed below 350 KIAS (clean), which at first encounter was quite alarming. Although I went to great lengths to prepare myself for the rapid acceleration during takeoff, including several high speed taxi runs, I found myself several miles behind the '104 during my first takeoff roll. My left hand was spring loaded to raise the gear immediately after lift off (gear speed 260 KIAS) and to raise the flaps above 300 KIAS, but I was unable to capture the climb speed of 450 KIAS for the full afterburner climb to the working altitude. I finally reined the Starfighter in at 525 KIAS, and then at Wolfgang's direction, had to half-roll the airplane to prevent shooting through the assigned altitude.

On subsequent flights, I found the roll sensitivity and steady state roll rate to be comparable to the T–38 and A–4, which is, in the present vernacular, "eye watering". Pitch sensitivity, although not as pronounced, is high as well. The aircraft is extremely sensitive to applications of trim (which move the entire control surface), and smooth trim adjustments came only with practice. The stick forces are high with absolute centering, moderate breakout force and steep force gradients, with good control harmony between aileron and elevator. With the artificial rate damping provided by the Stability Augmentation System, the airplane exhibits positive static stability, convergent dynamic modes, and good damping in all axes. Subsonic turn performance at military power (non-afterburning) did not exceed my preconceived expectations. Sustained "G" capability at 21,000 pounds, .85 Mach, and 30,000 feet is less than 1.5 "G". On one such occasion, having to tighten a turn to remain within the working area, the aircraft lost 2000 feet during 180 degrees of turn. As expected, with low sustained "G" capability, turn rates are paltry, and turn radii are enormous. The landing pattern covers more ground than I was accustomed to, but excellent speed stability and the attributes of the flight control system facilitate hitting the pattern check points. However, the somewhat abrupt control inputs customarily employed by some pilots at landing pattern speeds generate commensurate airframe shudder, stick shaker, and attendant adrenaline rush. Even with the high final approach (170 KIAS minimum) and landing speed (150 KIAS minimum) and considerations for stopping the airplane, the landing technique is conventional and the '104 touches down nicely. Nose wheel steering, "bullet proof" anti-skid brakes, and a drag chute all contribute to allaying any anxiety over landing roll-out.

While conducting a weapon system test in the '104, I was required to accelerate from .9 Mach to the maximum speed available over an 80 mile course at 30,000 feet. The acceleration was begun with 4000 pounds of fuel, and in full afterburner. I could actually **see** *the fuel gauge needle move! Flying on top of an overcast, I momentarily diverted my attention to confirm my position, and at Mach 1.6 was alerted by the master caution audio tone. The low fuel light (1275 ± 250 pounds fuel) had illuminated after having covered 75 nautical miles in 5.5 minutes, and the airplane had guzzled 2700 pounds of fuel! The run was planned to terminate over the field, so I retarded the throttle to idle and descended through the 15,000 foot overcast, to land with the planned 1000 pounds remaining and a healthy respect for the Starfighter's appetite for fuel.*

Recently, I flew the '104 following a three and a half month hiatus from the airplane. During the absence, I flew the Hawker Hunter almost exclusively, conducting spin training for U.S. Navy test pilots. The Hunter is possessed of excessively light control forces, poor centering characteristics, almost no breakout force, weak roll rate damping, and 1950's vintage acceleration and climb performance. The aircraft additionally exhibits docile stall characteristics and relatively impressive instantaneous turn performance. Having become accustomed to the Hunter's slow takeoff acceleration, the '104's bolt down the runway was once again quite stimulating. The 30 knot surface wind across the irregular terrain produced a pronounced momentary shudder at 400 KIAS which, at first impression, seemed to be a pre-stall buffet. A couple of aileron rolls produced an almost dizzying effect after the docile rolls of the Hunter. The comparatively high control forces made stick movement seem like an effort, and upon returning to the field, the unexpectedly large turn radius caused me to overshoot the runway on line up for the break. The final approach speed, although relatively excessive, was easy to maintain and, following speed brake extension and a slight power reduction, a small pitch attitude increase (flare) prior to landing produced a comfortable touchdown. With the high surface wind down the runway, moderate braking, and no drag chute, the landing roll was approximately 5000 feet. It was good to be back in the '104.

As for the remainder of the Norwegian CF–104s, the last operational mission for these aircraft was flown by General O. Aamoth in '637 on April 22, 1983. Four were lost due to accidents, four are in museums, and three have been given to schools. The fate of the Danish CF–104s roughly mirrors that of their Norwegian counterparts, though none remain in flying condition anywhere in the world. All were withdrawn from flying service in the first half of the eighties. Two of the aircraft were lost in crashes, five were donated to museums, two are being used as gate guardians, six are utilized as airfield decoys, and the remainder serve as testbeds for Aircraft Battle Damage Repair.

The Canadian fleet have scattered to the winds... Several serve as gate guardians at CFB Baden-Soellingen, CFB Cold Lake, CFB Lahr, and CFB Trenton. An aircraft marked '872, which is actually a composite of aircrafts '803 and '816, is mounted on a pedestal in front of the Base Headquarters at Cold Lake. Additionally, '702 is mounted on a pylon beside the access road to the Base, just inside the town of Grand Centre. Other aircraft, though presently in storage at Mountainview, will become gate guardians at CFB Edmonton and CFB North Bay.

For the viewing public, the record-breaking '700 from centennial year now resides in the foyer of the new National Aviation Museum in Ottawa, and one other single-seater will eventually be placed in a museum in Winnipeg. Furthermore, the Maritimes have not been overlooked in the ultimate disposition process. The Atlantic Canada Aviation Museum (ACAM) in Armdale near Halifax is dedicated to the preservation of Canada's aviation heritage, and they are very proud of the Starfighter they have on display. John Christie, Vice-President of the Museum, explains how the museum came to acquire '783...

At present, the only genuine Canadair CF–104 on display in any Canadian Museum is 104783. A 417 Squadron bird, she spent her entire career at Cold Lake. The acquisition of this aircraft goes back to a visit which our recovery chairman (Mike Whitehead) and I made to CFB Mountainview in the spring of 1987. Among the aircraft stored there were a number of single and dual '104s - some in warpaint, others in natural metal. All were in various stages of disassembly, but two stood out - 104646 and 194783. They were potential museum material. Most of these aircraft were assigned to the Aircraft Battle Damage Repair (ABDR) program, but reflecting on the sad remnants of 104701 (the first Canadair built Starfighter) when it was scrapped out, I resolved to try and save one of these unique machines.

It was a lengthy process to convince the various powers that be that ACAM should have a '104. Many letters, phone calls, and meetings - and not a little scheming - paid off when staff from the Hon. Paul Dick's office called to say we could have one on the condition that ACAM assumed all preparation and delivery costs. The deal was struck, and shortly afterwards 104783 was selected.

In April 1988, thanks to the generous support of Brigadier General Colin Curleigh, I was flown to Mountainview in a VU–32 T–33 to inspect '783, and to commence the planning of her delivery to Halifax. My pilot was Captain Craig Furlong, appropriately a '104 driver earlier in his career. Craig's reaction was similar to many other '104 people who have since visited '783. He quietly walked around her, inspecting closely here and there, behaving like someone meeting an old and respected friend again. My reaction was more euphoric, coloured by the stark realization that, while small as fighters go, '783 was still a lot of aircraft. We took our time noting dimensions, general condition, and what was missing. At that time she was without wings, engine, radome, seat, several instruments and control boxes, but was otherwise in excellent shape, and obviously the pick of the litter! I was shown some of the missing parts and assured that everyone would do their best to make her as complete as possible.

Back home again, the delivery planning began in earnest. Eventually it was agreed that the best method was by flatbed, the aircraft on its landing gear, engine installed. Everything else could be tucked around it. Negotiations with Canadair had resulted in a commitment to underwrite delivery costs. They were as excited as ourselves to be involved in the recovery of this part of their heritage.

By June 1989, everything was ready. The trip to the Museum took three full days. The driver, ex-air force himself, took his time to minimize wear and tear. He was periodically called on his C.B. by people inquiring about the nature of his load. His response became "I've quit the Air Force, and I'm taking me plane with me!"

Above: *104 783, the proud star of the Atlantic Canada Aviation Museum in Armdale, Nova Scotia, near Halifax.*

- photo by John Christie

717
105

8.786

Late in the afternoon of the third day, the Owen-Davis Trucking vehicle pulled onto the apron at IMP Aerospace, and what a sight! The last few miles were in a light rain, and '783 was gleaming. She had suffered nary a scratch in transit. Offloading the next day was a media event. Not wanting to damage her, the ACAM crew exercised great care. Once we figured out how the specialized slings worked, the aircraft was quickly on terra firma again.

Now began the initial reassembly process. '783 was the ultimate model kit. The AMDU/Field Aviation people had done a tremendous job, carefully packaging parts and associated bolts and washers into specific sets. Study of the CFTOs and the neat packaging made assembly both simple and self-evident. Nevertheless, reassembly went much smoother thanks to the assistance of some IMP employees who had worked on '104s during their service time.

Two weeks later, essentially complete except for wings, '783 made the quarter-mile tow to the museum. Shortly afterwards, AMDU sent down a quantity of missing parts which were duly installed. Litton Systems found an LN–3 INS, CFB Summerside sent over a pair of rocket pods, and the folks in Trenton rounded up a dozen CRV–7s. As she now sits, '783 looks ready for action.

In October 1989, the Museum hosted a turnover party to celebrate the '104's arrival, and to honour the people associated with her. A crowd of 150, including representatives of government, business, military and ex-104 people, enjoyed the customary speeches and presentations. Highlighted by the "flying" arrival of '783, piloted by LCol. Hank Morris dressed in 421 garb and '104 spurs, the event was a great success. Many of the '104 people gave press interviews and acted as "tour" guides for those less familiar with the aircraft. Cadets present enjoyed sitting in '783 and having her secrets revealed by men who had flown her.

Acquisition of '783 had been a long and taxing process. However, as I watch the ex-'104 people's delight and quietly emotional reaction, I know it has all been worth it. Where else could Cecil Hume place his young son in the cockpit of a '104 he had flown, or Eric Thurston carry out a last pre-flight walkaround? Ralph Annis sat in the cockpit for a long time and never said a word - he just looked around, touching a switch here and a control there - remembering.

That is now '783's purpose - to educate the young, wow others with her sleek lines and stubby wings, dispel myths, highlight the achievements of the CF–104s and those associated with them. But perhaps best of all, '783 enables the Hank Morris', Fred Beliveaus, and Dave Trasks, if only for a moment, to touch their pasts.

So much for the ultimate disposition of these marvellous aircraft, but what of the locations from which they flew? Baden-Soellingen is the hub of the resurrected 1 Canadian Air Division with its three squadrons of CF–18 Hornets. Lahr, just 26 miles to the south on the E–4 autobahn, is the home of 444 Tactical Helicopter Squadron, and is the peacetime Air Transport Group hub in West Germany. Several units of the 4th Canadian Mechanized Brigade Group (4CMBG) also call the airfield home. In wartime, the airfield becomes an active fighter base, shared by augmenting CF–18 forces as well as other Allied aircraft. Roughly 40 miles to the northeast, Zweibrucken remains an active USAFE base, and hosts the 26th Tactical Reconnaissance Wing, which flies the aging, but still potent, RF–4 Phantom.

Grostenquin, France is now but a memory as a fighter base, its splendid runway resembling the surface of the moon. Apparently, the French Air Force felt the runway surface (which had been impervious to Roy deWolfe's touch-and-goes) was so robust that it would be an excellent candidate for the practical trials of the Durandal penetration bomb.

Marville... When 1 Wing packed their bags and headed east in 1967, they took as much of the Marville base infrastructure with them as possible, since it was all Canadian owned. Some splendid artifacts (from an old French chateau) which had been part of the Base Officer's Mess, were temporarily placed in storage, then later incorporated into the Chateau Room of the refurbished Officers' Mess at Moose Jaw in 1970. Marville had a life after the Canadian departure though, and Dave Ghyselincks revisited this historic site while he was flying Alpha-Jets on an exchange tour with the French Air Force in 1985...

I was an exchange instructor at the French Air Force advanced flying training unit in Tours, France, flying the Franco-German Alpha-Jet. The unit held a secondary role of Offensive Air Support, and was war-tasked to deploy on short notice eastbound. We practiced this role twice a year and 40 annual flying hours were reserved for each IP to conduct Offensive Air Support (OAS) training sorties, including air-to-ground range practice. In mid-March 1985, the unit was ordered to stand-down pilot training the following week in order to conduct a Tac-eval.

Shortly after we reported for duty on Monday morning, March 18th, two of the three squadrons at Tours were ordered to deploy with twelve aircraft each to Marville, in North-Eastern France. We were a bit surprised by this destination as the last time any of us had flown over the place a few weeks back, it was covered with sheep. There were no approach plates to be had, and no information listed in the Enroute Supplement.

By noon, maps had been made and a training mission briefed for the move. Our airplanes were ready and uploaded with the 30 mm gun-packs. We received new VFR approach plates, with non-precision IFR plates to be issued in Marville. A portable TACAN had been flown in the previous day along with a control tower and a quad radar. A refueling point had been established with large bladders, also dropped in by Transall transport. Although the airfield was quite accessible by road, the FAF was treating this as a completely air-deployed exercise.

We landed at about 1430 local time, and taxied to the northwest dispersal where the refuelling point had been set up. With the Alpha-Jets, it was just a question of taxiing up to the nearest bladder, shutting down, and going for a 10 minute walk while the crews ran the portable gas powered fuel pumps. We then cranked up again, in twos and fours, for the long taxi to the northeast marguerite. Some engineers were putting up the last few meters of new base perimeter fencing, while the Army battalion assigned to base defence were busy sighting their guns and laying concertina wire.

There were no hardened aircraft shelters on the airfield. The French Tactical Air Force had negotiated over the previous months to

Opposite page:

1. *Two duals in storage at Mountainview, Ontario in 1989.*
- DND photo by Cpl Nelson Levesque

2. *'717 in Norwegian service, accompanied by a RNoAF F-5.*
- Royal Norwegian Air Force photo

3. *CF-104 '786 was the last Canadian Starfighter to be delivered to the Turks, 7 May 1986. It is still flying with the Turkish Air Force at the time of publication.*
- photo by Turkish Air Force

4. *'771 in Danish colors, seen at Karup AB on 15 January, 1982.*
- Royal Danish Air Force photo

Official Heraldry of the CF-104 Era

SQUADRON
417
417
ESCADRILLE
SUPPORTING LIBERTY AND JUSTICE

SQUADRON
421
421
ESCADRILLE
BELLICUM CECINERE

SQUADRON
422
422
ESCADRILLE
THIS ARM SHALL DO IT

SQUADRON
427
427
ESCADRILLE
FERTE MANUS CERTAS

SQUADRON
430
430
ESCADRILLE
CELERITER CERTOQUE

SQUADRON
434
434
ESCADRILLE
IN EXCELSIS VINCIMUS

SQUADRON
439
439
ESCADRILLE
FANGS OF DEATH

SQUADRON
441
441
ESCADRILLE
STALK AND KILL

SQUADRON
444
444
ESCADRILLE
STRIKE SWIFT STRIKE SURE

repurchase the maneuvering surfaces of this former Canadian Air Force Base from the local township who now owned it. The administrative area had been turned into an industrial park in this depressed region of France; it housed a furniture maker and an ultralight aircraft manufacturer, as well as a print shop and various other small enterprises. Many of the barrack blocks I looked into had been gutted of their inside walls and were now harbouring hundreds of sheep. A mess hall had been partially converted into a small restaurant for the noontime trade generated by the few dozen employees on the site.

The airfield proper had remained in use as an uncontrolled, privately owned airport for the town of Montmedy. The only traffic for the last twenty years or so had been light piston-engined aircraft. Now the sound of jet aircraft was back. I was astonished at the smoothness of bunker, and soon had a portable generator going to give us heat, light and radios. One of the two old bunker rooms was for ops/mission-planning, and the other was for sleeping. It was surprising to see how well this structure had withstood the last two decades with absolutely no maintenance; again it was only swept clean for our use. A portable kitchen was parked in the southeast marguerite, where the other squadron was hiding, to feed us breakfast and lunch; the usual late evening French supper was catered at a restaurant in Montmedy.

We flew two trips a day on March 19th, 20th and 21st, the last trip being the return to Tours. I believe the FATAC continues to operate the airfield as a dispersal base now, mostly for Jaguars, rotating four aircraft in for a week or so each month. This is certainly a better fate for this fine base than the pockmarked surfaces of Grostenquin, which became the

the runway when we landed; it was better than our home field. It had obviously been built to a very high standard because all that was required prior to our arrival was some heavy sweeping. We could not use the field at night or in poor weather due to the lack of any lighting. Apparently, this runway had incorporated a heating system to combat freezing precipitation, but just as for the airfield lighting, the wiring had long ago been scavenged for the high scrap value of its copper.

In the northeast marguerite, our twelve aircraft were covered with camouflage netting and scattered on hard-stands around the single standing structure; an old hangar with large washed-out numerals on its sides marked "439 SQN"! I had a look inside; it was filled with grain, but could have been usable. We set up operations in the old squadron

runway cratering munitions test range for the FAF. If Grostenquin's runway was built as well as Marville's, it must have been a real challenge to penetrate!

And so we come to the end of the story. The CF–104 Starfighter , the people that were associated with her, and the events that occurred during her tenure of service combined to form a very special era. Though she never had to fire her guns in anger during Canadian service, she stood proud vigil on continuous duty for 25 years in Canadian colours. She was a real lady, and she will be missed…

Photo by Bill Johnson

Above : *Bill Card climbs aboard for a mission at the 1976 TWM in Twenthe, Holland. He would die in a training accident at Cold Lake just a little over a year later.*
Inset Above (from left to right) : *The intrepid airmen, TAM '76. L to R - Capt Roy Patterson (#4), Maj Hank Morris (spare), Maj Jim McCullough (#2 - Team leader), Capt Walt Pirie (#3), Capt Bill Card (Lead); The equally - intrepid maintainers; L to R - WO Don Hawes (Maintenance), Lt Dwayne Lucas (Maintenance Officer), WO Bruce Stag (Armament).*

Inset below (from right to left) : *Gord Hatch gets inverted just for the fun of it enroute to Turkey in '883 on 9 April 1986; The famous drunk bus looking very operational in its final paint scheme, circa 1980. - Photo by Pat Barrett*

1 CAG

1 CAG

1 CAG

HATCH

APPENDIX 1
CF-104 Era Commanders

OFFICERS COMMANDING 1 AIR DIVISION HQ (METZ, FRANCE AND LAHR, GERMANY)

AVM L.E. Wray	Sep 58 - Jul 63
AVM D.A.R. Bradshaw	Jul 63 - Jul 66
AVM R.J. Lane	Aug 66 - Jul 69
LGen D.C. Laubman	Jul 69 - Aug 70

COMMANDING OFFICERS 1 WING (MARVILLE, FRANCE AND LAHR, GERMANY)

G/C A.F. Avant	Aug 63 - Jul 66
G/C R.G. Christie	Jul 66 - Dec 68
Col A.J. Pudsey	Dec 68 - Jun 70

COMMANDING OFFICER 2 WING (GROSTENQUIN, FRANCE)

G/C E.R. Johnston	Nov 63 - Jul 64

COMMANDING OFFICERS 3 WING (ZWEIBRUCKEN, GERMANY)

G/C V.L. Berg	Jul 60 - Jul 63
G/C D.C. Laubman	Aug 63 - Aug 66
G/C K.E. Lewis	Aug 66 - Jan 68
Col W.J. Marsh	Feb 68 - Jul 69
LCol R.K. Trumley	Jul 69 - Aug 69

COMMANDING OFFICERS 4 WING (BADEN-SOELLINGEN, GERMANY)

G/C J.J. Jordan	Sep 61 - Jul 65
G/C C. Allison	Aug 65 - Oct 68
Col F.G. Kaufman	Oct 68 - Jul 70

OFFICERS COMMANDING 1 CANADIAN AIR GROUP (LAHR, GERMANY)

BGen M.F. Doyle	Aug 70 - Oct 71
BGen K.E. Lewis	Oct 71 - Jul 73
BGen G.C.E. Theriault	Jul 73 - Jun 75
BGen J.P.A. Cadieux	Jun 75 - Aug 77
BGen W.G. Paisley	Aug 77 - Jul 80
BGen P.D. Manson	Jul 80 - Aug 81
BGen B.R. Campbell	Aug 81 - Jul 83
BGen D. Huddleston	Jul 83 - Mar 86

BASE COMMANDERS BADEN-SOELLINGEN, GERMANY

Col F.G. Kaufman	Jul 70 - Jun 71
Col A.J. Bauer	Jul 71 - May 74
Col J. H. Roddick	Jul 74 - Aug 76
Col D.P. Wightman	Sep 76 - Aug 77
Col A.B.H. Bosman	Aug 77 - Jul 80
Col J.L. Frazer	Jul 80 - Jul 83
Col D.F. McIntosh	Jul 83 - Jul 85
Col. A.M. DeQuetteville	Jul 85 - Mar 86

APPENDIX 2
CF-104 Era Commanding Officers

6 S/R OTU

W/C K.C. Lett	Oct 61 - Jun 64
W/C W.G. Paisley	Jul 64 - Jul 65
W/C R.G. Middlemiss	Jul 65 - Aug 67
W/C K.J. Thorneycroft	Aug 67 - Jul 70

427 Squadron

W/C R.G. Middlemiss	Dec 62 - Feb 64
W/C J.R. Knight	Feb 64 - Jul 65
W/C J.F. Dunlop	Jul 65 - Sept 65
S/L J.A.C. Tousignant	Sep 65 - May 66
W/C P.J.S. Higgs	May 66 - Sep 67
W/C R.E. Carruthers	Sep 67 - Jan 68
W/C T. Reid	Jan 68 - Jul 70

434 Squadron

W/C O.B. Philp	Apr 63 - Dec 65
W/C J.A.G.F. Villeneuve	Dec 65 - Mar 67

430 Squadron

W/C H.R. Knight	Sep 63 - Jan 64
S/L M.A.J. White	Feb 64 - Jun 64
W/C A.J. Bauer	Jul 64 - Jul 66
W/C W.G. Paisley	Jul 66 - Oct 66
W/C J.W. Whitely	Nov 66 - Apr 67
W/C J.A.G.F. Villeneuve	May 67 - May 69
LCol W. Niemy	Jun 69 - May 70

422 Squadron

W/C W.H.F. Bliss	Jul 63 - Aug 66
W/C W.J. Stacey	Aug 66 - Jul 67
W/C R.C. Scott	Jul 67 - Jun 69
LCol D.P. Wightman	Jun 69 - Jul 70

444 Squadron

W/C K.J. Thorneycroft	May 63 - Jan 66
S/L G.C.E. Theriault	Jan 66 - Aug 66
W/C R.H. Annis	Aug 66 - Apr 67

421 Squadron

S/L G.C.E. Theriault	Nov 63 - Feb 64
W/C J.B. Lawrence	Feb 64 - Apr 67
W/C R.H. Annis	Apr 67 - Aug 68
Maj R. Riddell	Aug 68 - Dec 68
LCol B.A. Oxholm	Dec 68 - Jul 71
LCol C.L. Viger	Jul 71 - May 73
Maj L. Crabb	May 73 - Aug 73
LCol G. Fitzsimmons	Aug 73 - Jul 75
LCol B.L.M. Smith	Jul 75 - Jun 77
LCol H.A. Sievert	Jun 77 - Jul 78
LCol B. Kadonoff	Jul 78 - Jul 80
LCol D.F. Holman	Jul 80 - Jun 82
Maj J.L.D. Gauthier	Jun 82 - Aug 82
LCol I.G. Sanford	Aug 82 - Jul 85
Maj E.G. Thurston	Jul 85 - Oct 85

439 Squadron

S/L J.L. Frazer	Mar 64 - Nov 66
W/C S.P. Gulyas	Nov 66 - Jan 68
LCol I.H. Firth	Jan 68 - Apr 70
LCol B.T. Burgess	Apr 70 - May 72
Maj M.I. Chesser	May 72 - Jul 72
LCol J.A. Holt	Jul 72 - Aug 74
LCol P.L. DeSmedt	Aug 74 - Jun 68
LCol F.S. Sutherland	Jun 76 - Jun 78
LCol F.K. Lawlor	Jun 78 - Jul 80
LCol W.J. Anderson	Jul 80 - Jul 82
LCol L.G. Hill	Jul 82 - Nov 84

441 Squadron

W/C R.M. Edwards	Dec 63 - Oct 65
W/C J.F. Dunlop	Oct 65 - Aug 68
LCol P.D. Manson	Aug 68 - Jun 69
LCol B.T. Burgess	Jul 69 - May 70
LCol W. Niemy	May 70 - Jun 70
LCol D.P. Wightman	Jul 70 - Jul 71
LCol A. Young	Jul 71 - Jul 73
LCol D. Myles	Aug 73 - Jul 77
LCol R.J. Saulnier	Jul 77 - Jul 79
LCol L.J. Crabb	Jul 79 - Jul 81
LCol C.W. Wilson	Jul 81 - Aug 83
LCol K.R. Betts	Aug 83 - Aug 85
LCol G.H. Adamson	Aug 85 - Mar 86

1 CAG Maintenance Squadron / 1 Air Maintenance Squadron

LCol H.E. Hendrickson	CO 1 CAG Maint Sqn	May 73 - Jul 74
LCol G.D. Bennett	CO 1 CAG Maint Sqn	Jul 74 - Aug 76
LCol L. Vermeersch	CO 1 CAG Maint Sqn	Aug 76 - Aug 78
LCol G.G. Kemp	CO 1 CAG Maint Sqn	Aug 78 - Jul 80
LCol L.E. Johnson	CO 1 CAG Maint Sqn	Jul 80 - Aug 83
LCol D.C. Gilliland	CO 1 Air Maint Sqn	Aug 83 - Jul 84
LCol R.T. Linton	CO 1 Air Maint Sqn	Jul 84 - Mar 86

417 Squadron

LCol H.L. Graves	Jul 70 - Jul 72
Col J.H. Firth	Jul 72 - Jul 74
LCol A.B.H. Bosman	Jul 74 - Jul 76
LCol P.L. DeSmedt	Jul 76 - Jul 78
LCol L.F. Best	Jul 78 - Jul 80
LCol J.H. Newlove	Aug 80 - Jul 83

APPENDIX 3
CF-104 Aircraft Disposition

Note : F = fatal
N = non-fatal

NO.	TYPE	SERIAL #	DATE	UNIT	REMARKS
1.	CF-104D MK.1	104631	Nov 7/74	417 OTS Cold Lake	Engine failure on test flight due to foreign object damage. Pilots ejected safely. Capt. G.R. Todd. Lt. M.G. Abbott. N.
2.	CF-104D MK.1	104632	1973		Sold to RNoAF. Now civil registry USA. Montgomery, Alabama.
3.	CF-104D MK.1	104633	1973		Sold to RNoAF. Now civil registry USA. Houston, Texas.
4.	CF-104D MK.1	104634			Aircraft Battle Damage Repair instructional airframe
5.	CF-104D MK.1	104635	May 27/68	417 OTS Cold Lake	Engine failure during flight. Both pilots ejected safely. Capt. W.L. Worthy. Capt. J.M. Denard. N.
6.	CF-104D MK.1	104636	1986		Transferred to Turkey
7.	CF-104D MK.1	104637	1973		Sold to RNoAF. At 334 Squadron, Bodo Air Station. The aircraft is maintained in close to flyable status.
8.	CF-104D MK.1	104638	1986		Transferred to Turkey
9.	CF-104D MK.1	104639			Aircraft Battle Damage Repair instructional airframe
10.	CF-104D MK.1	104640	Dec 3/82	417 Sqn. Cold Lake	Mid-air collision while on a formation proficiency mission. Pilot did not eject. Capt. D.R. Owen. F.
11.	CF-104D MK.1	104641			Aircraft Battle Damage Repair instructional airframe
12.	CF-104D MK.1	104642	1986		Transferred to Turkey
13.	CF-104D MK.1	104643			Aircraft Battle Damage Repair instructional airframe
14.	CF-104D MK.1	104644			Aircraft Battle Damage Repair instructional airframe
15.	CF-104D MK.1	104645			Aircraft Battle Damage Repair instructional airframe
16.	CF-104D MK.1	104646			Pedestal Monument. CFB Trenton.
17.	CF-104D MK.1	104647	Dec 3/82	417 Sqn. Cold Lake	Mid-air collision while on a formation proficiency mission. Pilot did not eject. Capt. J.L.A. Tremblay. F.
18.	CF-104D MK.1	104648			Aircraft Battle Damage Repair instructional airframe
19.	CF-104D MK.1	104649	Nov 17/77	417 Sqn. Cold Lake	Aircraft struck ground during air combat training. Neither pilot ejected. Capt. W.D. Card. Capt. D.B. Breen. F.
20.	CF-104D MK.1	104650	1986		Transferred to Turkey
21.	CF-104D MK.1	104651	Jun 24/80	417 Sqn. Cold Lake	Engine failure due to bird strike. Both pilots ejected successfully. Capt. R.W. Wall. Capt. H. Riedel (GAF). N.
22.	CF-104D MK.1	104652			Aircraft Battle Damage Repair instructional airframe
23.	CF-104D MK.2	104653			Aircraft Battle Damage Repair instructional airframe

NO.	TYPE	SERIAL #	DATE	UNIT	REMARKS
24.	CF-104D MK.2	104654	1973		Sold to RDAF. Now in Air ForceTechnical School, Vaerlose AB.
25.	CF-104D MK.2	104655	1973		Sold to RDAF. Aircraft Battle Damage Repair, Karup AB.
26.	CF-104D MK.2	104656	Mar 4/77	1 CAG Baden	Aircraft struck ground on low level training mission. Neither pilot ejected. Capt. J.O. Shaw. Capt. D.M. Danko. F.
27.	CF-104D MK.2	104657	1973		Sold to RDAF. Now in Danish Aviation Museum, Billund.
28.	CF-104D MK.2	104658	1986		Transferred to Turkey
29.	CF-104D MK.2	104659	Sep 1/65	1 Wing Marville	Engine failure due to birdstrike. Both occupants ejected safely. F/L J.E. Greidanaus. Capt. C.F. Summers. N.
30.	CF-104D MK.2	104660	1973		Sold to RDAF. Now a decoy at Tirstrup AB.
31.	CF-104D MK.2	104661	1986		Transferred to Turkey
32.	CF-104D MK.2	104662	1973		Sold to RDAF. Aircraft Battle Damage Repair, Skrydstrup AB.
33.	CF-104D MK.2	104663	Oct 7/70	1 CAG Baden	Engine failure during flight. Both occupants ejected safely. Maj. W. Bain. Capt. L.A. O'Brien. N.
34.	CF-104D MK.2	104664	1973		Sold to RDAF. Aircraft Battle Damage Repair, Aalborg AB.
35.	CF-104D MK.2	104665	Mar 16/81	439 Sqn. Baden	Compressor stall due to birdstrike. Both occupants ejected safely. Capt. L. A. Sianchuk. Lt. H. Raffel. N.
36.	CF-104D MK.2	104666	Mar 5/75	1 CAG Baden	Abort due to tire rupture and subsequent loss of control. Both pilots successfully abandoned aircraft. Capt. L.E. Lee. Capt. K.I. Struthers. N.
37.	CF-104D MK.2	104667	1973		Sold to RDAF. Now in North Zealand Aviation Museum, Slangerup.
38.	CF-104D MK.2	104668	Oct 27/71	1 CAG Baden	Complete engine disintegration and fire due to foreign object damage. Both pilots ejected safely. Capt. D.O. Lunquist. Capt. P.M. Davis. N.
39.	CF-104	104700			Aircraft used for world altitude record attempt - 1967. Now in National Air Museum, Ottawa.
40.	CF-104	104701			Write off (cannibalization)
41.	CF-104	104702			Write off - On pedestal, Grand Centre, Alberta.
42.	CF-104	104703	1971		Sold to RDAF. Now a decoy at Karup AB. Renumbered 704 in Danish service since RDAF already had a 703.
43.	CF-104	104704			Aircraft Battle Damage Repair instructional airframe
44.	CF-104	104705	Dec 11/81	AETE Cold Lake	Aircraft struck frozen lake surface on low level tactical mission. Pilot ejected safely. Maj. G.W. Nicks. N.
45.	CF-104	104706			Aircraft Battle Damage Repair instructional airframe
46.	CF-104	104707	May 22/62	6 STR OTU Cold Lake	During takeoff, the canopy opened. Also, loss of thrust due to nozzle pump failure. Pilot ejected safely. F/L. J.G. Aiken. N.
47.	CF-104	104708	Apr 27/65	3 Wing Zweibrucken	Aborted takeoff and subsequent aircraft destruction. Pilot evacuated aircraft. F/L P.L. O'Donovan. N.

NO.	TYPE	SERIAL #	DATE	UNIT	REMARKS
48.	CF-104	104709	Sep 5/69	1 Wing Lahr	Loss of control during formation takeoff. Pilot ejected safely. Capt. K.J. Chatfield. N.
49.	CF-104	104710	Jun 17/70	417 OTS Cold Lake	Aircraft struck trees on practice weapon delivery. Pilot ejected safely. Capt. D.V. Koski. N.
50.	CF-104	104711	1986		Transferred to Turkey
51.	CF-104	104712	Nov 25/61	Canadair Montreal	Aircraft crashed and burned after pilot lost control during a routine check of automatic pitch system. Likely rigging problem. Pilot ejected safely. Mr. B. Flemming. N.
52.	CF-104	104713	1986		Transferred to Turkey
53.	CF-104	104714	Feb 12/76	1 CAG Baden	Aircraft impacted crest of ridge on low level radar navigation mission. Pilot did not eject. Maj. G.A. Hermanson. F.
54.	CF-104	104715	Dec 11/74	1 CAG Baden	Massive in-flight control restriction due to unidentified foreign object damage. Pilot ejected safely. Capt. F.G. Youngson. N.
55.	CF-104	104716	1986		Transferred to Turkey
56.	CF-104	104717	1973		Sold to RNoAF. Given to Sola School.
57.	CF-104	104718	Apr 14/70	4 Wing Baden	Mid-air collision in cloud on instrument approach. Pilot ejected safely. Capt. J.M. Hivon. N.
58.	CF-104	104719	May 27/63	4 Wing Baden	Engine flamed out on an initial acceptance flight. Pilot ejected safely. F/L L.A. Tapp. N.
59.	CF-104	104720	Aug 17/73	1 CAG Baden	Aircraft struck trees on a practice tactical weapons delivery. Pilot ejected safely. Capt. J.E. McGillivray. N.
60.	CF-104	104721	Jan 7/70	4 Wing Baden	Massive control malfunction in the landing pattern. Pilot did not eject. Capt. K.M. Wright. F.
61.	CF-104	104722	Jun 10/71	417 OTS Cold Lake	Control problems due to failure of #2 hydraulic system. Pilot ejected safely. Capt. J.M. Westrop. N.
62.	CF-104	104723	Mar 25/71	417 OTS Cold Lake	Structural breakup due to inadvertent overstress during air combat manoeuvring. Pilot ejected safely. Capt. R.A. Heston. N.
63.	CF-104	104724	Sep 24/68	417 OTS Cold Lake	Aircraft pitched up while avoiding another aircraft. Pilot ejected safely. Capt. D. MacIntosh. N.
64.	CF-104	104725	Jun 9/65	6 STR OTU Cold Lake	Pilot lost control due to undetermined technical malfunction on final approach. Pilot ejected safely. F/O G.W. Sanderson. N.
65.	CF-104	104726	Jan 14/69	417 OTS Cold Lake	Aircraft struck ground on night low level navigation training mission. Pilot did not eject. Lt. R.B. Kaiser. F.
66.	CF-104	104727	Aug 9/65	6 STR OTU Cold Lake	Engine fire during flight. Pilot ejected safely. F/O D.S. Scott. N.
67.	CF-104	104728	Jun 19/63	6 STR OTU Cold Lake	Aircraft struck ground after takeoff, probably due to open canopy. Pilot ejected at too low altitude. F/L W.G. Hollingshead. F.
68.	CF-104	104729	Jan 18/68	1 Wing Lahr	Aircraft struck ground during low level photo recce mission. Pilot did not eject. F/O J.W. Holmes. F.

NO.	TYPE	SERIAL #	DATE	UNIT	REMARKS
69.	CF-104	104730	1973		Sold to RNoAF. Now in Air Force Museum, Sola, Norway.
70.	CF-104	104731			Pedestal Monument. CFB North Bay
71.	CF-104	104732	Apr 30/82	417 Sqn. Cold Lake	Loss of control during air combat training. Pilot ejected safely. Capt. D. Ghyselincks. N.
72.	CF-104	104733	1986		Transferred to Turkey
73.	CF-104	104734	Jul 18/67	1 Wing Lahr	Compressor stall due to birdstrike. Pilot ejected safely. F/L G.R.S. King. N.
74.	CF-104	104735	1986		Transferred to Turkey
75.	CF-104	104736	Nov 4/67	6 STR OTU Cold Lake	Engine failure during flight. Pilot ejected safely. S/L J.E. Greatrix. N.
76.	CF-104	104737	1986		Transferred to Turkey
77.	CF-104	104738	Aug 13/65	4 Wing Baden	Engine failure during flight. Pilot ejected safely. F/L E.A. Seitz. N.
78.	CF-104	104739	1986		Transferred to Turkey
79.	CF-104	104740	Apr 3/68	1 Wing Lahr	Aircraft crashed into side of hill on low level recce mission. Pilot did not eject. Capt. R.C. Archibald. F.
80.	CF-104	104741	Nov 15/68	417 OTS Cold Lake	Engine failure due to birdstrike. Pilot ejected safely. Lt. J.A.M. Lemire. N.
81.	CF-104	104742	Aug 10/62	6 STR OTU Cold Lake	Loss of thrust during touch-and-go. Pilot ejected but sustained fatal injuries when parachute disintegrated in aircraft fire area. F/L J.R. Mulhall. F.
82.	CF-104	104743	1986		Transferred to Turkey
83.	CF-104	104744	May 18/83	417 Sqn. Cold Lake	Aircraft impacted ground during air-to-air firing mission. Pilot did not eject. Capt. S.M. Ritchie. F.
84.	CF-104	104745	Oct 21/66	6 STR OTU Cold Lake	Engine failure due to birdstrike. Pilot ejected safely. F/L R.R. Challoner. N.
85.	CF-104	104746	Dec 7/66	6 STR OTU Cold Lake	Aircraft crashed during night low level radar navigation mission. Pilot did not eject. F/L H.W. Robbins. F.
86.	CF-104	104747	1986		Transferred to Turkey
87.	CF-104	104748	May 21/67	1 Wing Lahr	Thrust loss on takeoff. Pilot ejected safely. S/L M.R. MacGregor. N.
88.	CF-104	104749	Mar 2/84	1 CAG Baden	Aircraft destroyed in hangar fire.
89.	CF-104	104750			Aircraft Battle Damage Repair instructional airframe
90.	CF-104	104751	1986		Transferred to Turkey
91.	CF-104	104752	Mar 5/64	6 STR OTU Cold Lake	Engine failure on low level bombing run, probably due to birdstrike. Pilot ejected safely. F/O A. Doran. N.
92.	CF-104	104753			Pedestal Monument. Western Canada Museum, Winnipeg
93.	CF-104	104754	Feb 21/79	417 Sqn. Cold Lake	Aircraft struck side of a mountain during a tactical egress. Pilot did not eject. Capt. B. B. Reid. F.

NO.	TYPE	SERIAL #	DATE	UNIT	REMARKS
94.	CF-104	104755	1973		Sold to RN0AF
95.	CF-104	104756	1986		Transferred to Turkey
96.	CF-104	104757	1971		Sold to RDAF. Now a decoy at Tirstrup AB.
97.	CF-104	104758	1971		Sold to RDAF. Now a decoy at Tirstrup AB.
98.	CF-104	104759	1973		Sold to RN0AF. Now in Norwegian Technical Museum.
99.	CF-104	104760	1986		Transferred to Turkey
100.	CF-104	104761	1986		Transferred to Turkey
101.	CF-104	104762	Jun 9/81	421 Sqn. Baden	Aircraft struck trees on simulated tactical delivery. Pilot ejected safely. Lt. K.G. Cranfield. N.
102.	CF-104	104763			Pedestal Monument. CFB Edmonton
103.	CF-104	104764	Nov 1/63	6 STR OTU Cold Lake	Failure of main fuel control unit. Pilot ejected safely. F/L C.W. Gehman. N.
104.	CF-104	104765	Aug 19/69	417 OTS Cold Lake	Engine failure due to birdstrike. Pilot ejected safely. Capt. G.F. Ball. N.
105.	CF-104	104766	1973		Sold to RN0AF
106.	CF-104	104767	Jan 10/64	6 STR OTU Cold Lake	Mid-Air collision in formation. Pilot ejected safely. F/O B.L. Smith. N.
107.	CF-104	104768	Mar 30/67	6 STR OTU Cold Lake	Engine failure due to birdstrike immediately after takeoff. Pilot ejected safely. F/L H.J. Rowe. N.
108.	CF-104	104769	May 4/73	417 OTS Cold Lake	Aircraft hit trees of practice weapons delivery. Pilot ejected safely. Capt. J.B. Croll. N.
109.	CF-104	104770	1986		Transferred to Turkey
110.	CF-104	104771	1971		Sold to RDAF. Now a decoy at Karup AB.
111.	CF-104	104772	Apr 18/73	417 OTS Cold Lake	Aircraft struck ground during tactical weapons delivery. Pilot did not eject. Capt. J.K. Salter. F.
112.	CF-104	104773	1986		Transferred to Turkey
113.	CF-104	104774			Aircraft Battle Damage Repair instructional airframe
114.	CF-104	104775	Nov 16/77	417 Sqn. Cold Lake	Aircraft struck ground on a formation low level training mission. Pilot did not eject. Maj. J.M.A. Coutu. F.
115.	CF-104	104776	1986		Transferred to Turkey
116.	CF-104	104777	Feb 18/63	6 STR OTU Cold Lake	Aircraft struck the surface of a lake during a high speed low level turn. Pilot did not eject. F/L D.H. McElmon. F.
117.	CF-104	104778	Jun 25/64	6 STR OTU Cold Lake	Compressor stall on low level flight. Pilot ejected safely. F/L W. G. Baker. N.
118.	CF-104	104779	Sep 9/75	421 Sqn. Baden	Engine fire on takeoff. Pilot ejected safely. Capt. J.E. McGillivray. N.

NO.	TYPE	SERIAL #	DATE	UNIT	REMARKS
119.	CF-104	104780	1986		Transferred to Turkey
120.	CF-104	104781	Nov 6/69	1 Wing Lahr	Aircraft struck top of hill on low level mission. Ejection unsuccessful. Lt. R. Fetchyshyn. F.
121.	CF-104	104782	Apr 2/69	417 OTS Cold Lake	Engine failure due to foreign object damage. Pilot ejected safely. Maj. W.L. Worthy. N.
122.	CF-104	104783			Atlantic Canada Aviation Museum, Halifax
123.	CF-104	104784			Pedestal Monument. CFB Lahr
124.	CF-104	104785			Pedestal Monument. CFB Baden-Soellingen
125.	CF-104	104786	1986		Transferred to Turkey
126.	CF-104	104787	1986		Transferred to Turkey
127.	CF-104	104788	1986		Transferred to Turkey
128.	CF-104	104789	May 27/74	417 OTS Cold Lake	Compressor stall at low level due to bird strike. Pilot ejected safely. Maj. E.S. Andrichuk. N.
129.	CF-104	104790			Aircraft Battle Damage Repair instructional airframe
130.	CF-104	104791	Sep 11/67	4 Wing Baden	Aircraft struck sea during bombing competition. Pilot did not eject. F/L R.S. Dunn. F.
131.	CF-104	104792			Aircraft Battle Damage Repair instructional airframe
132.	CF-104	104793	Oct 24/63	3 Wing Zweibrucken	Struck ground on night training exercise. Pilot did not eject. F/L H.B. Sheasby. F.
133.	CF-104	104794	Sep 11/63	3 Wing Zweibrucken	Engine Nozzle problems. Pilot ejected at too low altitude. F/L D.O. Schneider. F.
134.	CF-104	104795	1986		Transferred to Turkey. Subsequently destroyed in flying accident.
135.	CF-104	104796	1986		Transferred to Turkey
136.	CF-104	104797	1973		Sold to RN0AF. Subsequently destroyed in flying accident July 29, 1975.
137.	CF-104	104798	Mar 4/66	3 Wing Zweibrucken	Aircraft crashed into heavily forested hill on low level flight. Pilot did not eject. F/L D.C. Lawson. F.
138.	CF-104	104799			Aircraft Battle Damage Repair instructional airframe
139.	CF-104	104800	1973		Sold to RN0AF. Given to Asphaugen School at Bodo.
140.	CF-104	104801	1973		Sold to RN0AF. Presently on display at Flesland Air Station (property of Defence Museum).
141.	CF-104	104802	Jul 23/63	3 Wing Zweibrucken	Crashed into sea after practice weapon delivery. F/L R.J. Prescott. F.
142.	CF-104	104803	Sep 4/62	Canadair Montreal	Hit tree on final approach. Pilot ejected safely. F/L L.S. Lumsdaine. N. Some components displayed as 12872 at Cold Lake

NO.	TYPE	SERIAL #	DATE	UNIT	REMARKS
143.	CF-104	104804	Jul 23/71	1 CAG Baden	Severe compressor stall in transit to an exercise area. Pilot ejected safely. Lt. D.J. Burroughs. N.
144.	CF-104	104805			Aircraft Battle Damage Repair instructional airframe
145.	CF-104	104806	1986		Transferred to Turkey
146.	CF-104	104807	Nov 27/80	421 Sqn. Baden	Engine failure in flight due to improper maintenance. Pilot ejected safely. Capt. R. Harrison. N.
147.	CF-104	104808	1986		Transferred to Turkey
148.	CF-104	104809	May 1/64	3 Wing Zweibrucken	Nozzle failure on GCA approach. Pilot ejected safely. F/L D. E. Wilson. N
149.	CF-104	104810	1986		Transferred to Turkey
150.	CF-104	104811	May 11/64	3 Wing Zweibrucken	Disconnect of rudder linkage during flight. Pilot ejected safely. F/L L.S. Bentham.
151.	CF-104	104812	1971		Sold to RDAF. Now a decoy at Karup AB.
152.	CF-104	104813	May 22/83	439 Sqn. Baden	Aircraft departed controlled flight during an air display. Pilot ejected safely. Capt. A.J. Stephenson. N.
153.	CF-104	104814	1971		Sold to RDAF. Now at Egeskov Veteran Museum, Fyn.
154.	CF-104	104815	1986		Transferred to Turkey
155.	CF-104	104816	Jul 24/63	3 Wing Zweibrucken	Destroyed in hangar fire, Zweibrucken. With components of 104803, displayed as 12872 at Cold Lake
156.	CF-104	104817	Jul 5/65	3 Wing Zweibrucken	Engine failure during flight. Pilot ejected safely. F/L D.C.K. Thom. N.
157.	CF-104	104818	1973		Sold to RN0AF
158.	CF-104	104819	1971		Sold to RDAF. Crashed near Vilsund Sept. 5/78 due to horizontal stabilizer break-up in jetwash during ACM. Pilot ejected safely.
159.	CF-104	104820	Mar 21/66	3 Wing Zweibrucken	Severe compressor stall due to birdstrike. Pilot ejected safely. F/L J.M. Ayres. N.
160.	CF-104	104821	Jan 10/83	439 Sqn. Baden	Engine failure due to foreign object damage. Pilot ejected safely. Capt. T.F. Klassen. N.
161.	CF-104	104822			Aircraft Battle Damage Repair instructional airframe
162.	CF-104	104823	Jun 16/71	1 CAG Baden	Mid-air collision shortly after takeoff. Pilot ejected safely. Maj. M.I. Chesser. N.
163.	CF-104	104824	1986		Transferred to Turkey
164.	CF-104	104825	1971		Sold to RDAF. Now a gate guardian at 726 Squadron, Aalborg AB.
165.	CF-104	104826	1986		Transferred to Turkey
166.	CF-104	104827	Jul 29/82	439 Sqn. Baden	Mid-air collision while on training mission. Pilot ejected safely. Col. J.L. Frazer. N.

NO.	TYPE	SERIAL #	DATE	UNIT	REMARKS
167.	CF-104	104828	Apr 14/70	4 Wing Baden	Mid-air collision in cloud on instrument approach. Pilot ejected safely. Maj. M.D. Thom. N.
168.	CF-104	104829	Aug 18/78	421 Sqn. Baden	Engine failure due to birdstrike. Pilot ejected safely. Capt. R. Bollinger. N.
169.	CF-104	104830	Jun 16/83	441 Sqn. Baden	Compressor stall due to ricochet during a strafe pass. Pilot ejected safely. Capt G.W. Bayles. N.
170.	CF-104	104831	Jul 9/69	4 Wing Baden	In-flight fire due to foreign object damage. Pilot ejected safely. Capt. J.R. Dunlop. N.
171.	CF-104	104832	1971		Sold to RDAF. Now a gate guardian at 723 Squadron, Aalborg AB.
172.	CF-104	104833	1973		Sold to RNOAF. Subsequently destroyed in flying accident Aug. 10/78.
173.	CF-104	104834	Apr 27/70	1 Wing Lahr	Multiple compressor stalls at high level due to engine foreign object damage. Pilot ejected safely. Capt. D.R. Graham. N.
174.	CF-104	104835			Aircraft Battle Damage Repair instructional airframe
175.	CF-104	104836	1973		Sold to RNOAF
176.	CF-104	104837	1986		Transferred to Turkey
177.	CF-104	104838	Mar 7/78	439 Sqn. Baden	Engine failure due to series of compressor stalls. Pilot ejected safely. Capt. B. M. Robinson. N.
178.	CF-104	104839	1986		Transferred to Turkey. Subsequently destroyed in flying accident.
179.	CF-104	104840	Jul 25/78	439 Sqn. Baden	Aircraft crashed into side of hill during close air support mission. Pilot did not eject. Capt. G. Power. F.
180.	CF-104	104841	1986		Transferred to Turkey
181.	CF-104	104842	1986		Transferred to Turkey
182.	CF-104	104843			Aircraft Battle Damage Repair instructional airframe
183.	CF-104	104844	Aug 7/64	4 Wing Baden	Aircraft struck hill in deteriorating weather. Pilot did not eject. F/L I.W. MacLean. F.
184.	CF-104	104845	1986		Transferred to Turkey
185.	CF-104	104846	1971		Sold to RDAF. Now in Danish Aviation Museum, Billund.
186.	CF-104	104847	1986		Transferred to Turkey
187.	CF-104	104848	1986		Transferred to Turkey
188.	CF-104	104849	Oct 27/64	1 Wing Marville	Engine failure due to birdstrike. Pilot ejected safely. S/L J.L. Frazer. N.
189.	CF-104	104850	1973		Sold to RNOAF
190.	CF-104	104851	1971		Sold to RDAF. Now used for crash recovery training, Aalborg, AB.
191.	CF-104	104852	Oct 5/67	3 Wing Zweibrucken	Aircraft crashed into hill while on low level mission. Pilot did not eject. S/L D.J. Misselbrook. F.

NO.	TYPE	SERIAL #	DATE	UNIT	REMARKS
192.	CF-104	104853	Sep 16/65	3 Wing Zweibrucken	Engine failure due to compressor disintegration at high speed. Pilot ejected safely. F/L K. D. Castle. N.
193.	CF-104	104854	Apr 25/69	1 Wing Lahr	Severe cockpit damage after birdstrike. Pilot ejected safely. Capt. R.E. White. N.
194.	CF-104	104855	1971		Sold to RDAF. Used for NBCW training at Army Engineering and NBC School, Farum Barracks.
195.	CF-104	104856	Nov 16/64	3 Wing Zweibrucken	Engine failure due to inadequate maintenance. Pilot ejected safely. F/L H.R. Stroud. N.
196.	CF-104	104857	Oct 23/73	1 CAG Baden	Aircraft impacted hill on low level navigation exercise. Pilot did not eject. Capt. D.L. McCullough. F.
197.	CF-104	104858	Jan 27/64	2 Wing Grostenquin	Engine nozzle failure at low level. Pilot ejected safely. F/L L.G. Van Vliet. N
198.	CF-104	104859	Aug 27/80	441 Sqn. Baden	Loss of control due to flap structural break-up on practice bomb delivery. Pilot ejected safely. Maj. R.W. Porter. N.
199.	CF-104	104860	1973		Sold to RN0AF. Subsequently destroyed in flying accident June 8/79.
200.	CF-104	104861	Oct 24/70	1 CAG Baden	Aircraft flew into ground shortly after takeoff. Pilot did not eject. Lt. L.S. Hebetler. F.
201.	CF-104	104862	1986		Transferred to Turkey
202.	CF-104	104863	1986		Write off
203.	CF-104	104864	May 10/73	1 CAG Baden	Aircraft pitched up in landing pattern. Pilot ejected, but too late for parachute deployment. Capt. P.J. Rackham. F.
204.	CF-104	104865	1986		Transferred to Turkey
205.	CF-104	104866	1986		Transferred to Turkey. Subsequently destroyed in flying accident.
206.	CF-104	104867	Oct 28/66	4 Wing Baden	Aircraft pitched up during handling exercise. Pilot ejected safely. F/O R.J. Zemek. N.
207.	CF-104	104868	Mar 2/84	1 CAG Baden	Aircraft destroyed in hangar fire.
208.	CF-104	104869	1986		Transferred to Turkey
209.	CF-104	104870	1973		Sold to RN0AF
210.	CF-104	104871	Jun 11/65	4 Wing Baden	Compressor stall shortly after takeoff. Pilot ejected safely. F/O D.M. Caldwell. N.
211.	CF-104	104872	Mar 11/74	417 OTS Cold Lake	In-flight fire while on radar final. Pilot ejected safely. Maj. W.H. Blatter. N.
212.	CF-104	104873	1986		Transferred to Turkey
213.	CF-104	104874	Jun 19/68	4 Wing Baden	Aircraft went out of control while in the circuit for landing. Pilot ejected but with insufficient time to effect parachute deployment. Capt. R.J.Swanston. F.
214.	CF-104	104875	Jul 20/67	4 Wing Baden	Aircraft pitched up due to pilot disorientation. Pilot ejected but sustained fatal injuries due to seat malfunction. F/O R.J. Zemek. F.

NO.	TYPE	SERIAL #	DATE	UNIT	REMARKS
215.	CF-104	104876	Oct 23/63	4 Wing Baden	Engine fire on final approach. Pilot ejected safely. F/L H.R. Venus. N.
216.	CF-104	104877	Jul 25/69	4 Wing Baden	Mid-air collision on training flight. Pilot did not eject. Capt. W.E. Brason. F.
217.	CF-104	104878	May 4/65	4 Wing Baden	Engine fire during flight. Pilot ejected safely. F/L R.C. Beehler. N.
218.	CF-104	104879	May 16/65	CEPE Prestwick	Aircraft struck sea on radar test flight. Pilot did not eject. F/L I.W. McKnight. F.
219.	CF-104	104880			Aircraft Battle Damage Repair instructional airframe
220.	CF-104	104881	Jul 25/69	4 Wing Baden	Mid-air collision on training flight. Pilot ejected safely. Lt. G.P. Ferris. N.
221.	CF-104	104882	1973		Sold to RN0AF
222.	CF-104	104883	1986		Transferred to Turkey
223.	CF-104	104884	Feb 24/65	4 Wing Baden	Engine fire during flight. Pilot ejected safely. S/L R.W. Spencer. N.
224.	CF-104	104885	Aug 3/67	4 Wing Baden	Control loss due to hydraulic system contamination. Pilot ejected safely. F/O L.B. Mealing. N.
225.	CF-104	104886	1973		Sold to RN0AF
226.	CF-104	104887	1971		Sold to RDAF. Crashed near Fjernitslev Aug. 18/82 due to total instrument failure. Pilot ejected safely.
227.	CF-104	104888	1971		Sold to RDAF. Now in Technical Museum, Aalborg.
228.	CF-104	104889	1973		Sold to RN0AF. Given to Oslo School of Trade.
229.	CF-104	104890	1973		Sold to RN0AF
230.	CF-104	104891	1986		Transferred to Turkey
231.	CF-104	104892	Jun 4/82	417 Sqn. Cold Lake	In-flight fire due to improper maintenance. Pilot ejected safely. Capt. K.G. Cranfield. N.
232.	CF-104	104893	1986		Transferred to Turkey
233.	CF-104	104894	Feb 8/65	4 Wing Baden	Aircraft crashed into ground on low level training exercise. Pilot did not eject. F/L J.N. Stacey. F.
234.	CF-104	104895	Mar 19/74	AETE Cold Lake	Compressor stall due to gun malfunction in flight. Pilot ejected safely. Maj. M.D. Johnson. N.
235.	CF-104	104896	1971		Sold to RDAF. Now in North Zealand Aviation Museum, Slangerup.
236.	CF-104	104897	Jul 15/68	3 Wing Zweibrucken	Oil system malfunction during flight. Pilot ejected safely. Capt. V.F. Gerden. N.
237.	CF-104	104898	Jun 25/68	1 Wing Lahr	Aircraft crashed into hill while on a photo recce mission. Pilot did not eject. Capt. A.S. Andree. F.
238.	CF-104	104899	1986		Transferred to Turkey

Index

CF-104 MAIN OPERATING AREA, CENTRAL EUROPE (1962-1986)

The CF-104 "Super" Starfighter

CENTRELINE PYLON AND BOMB DISPENSER

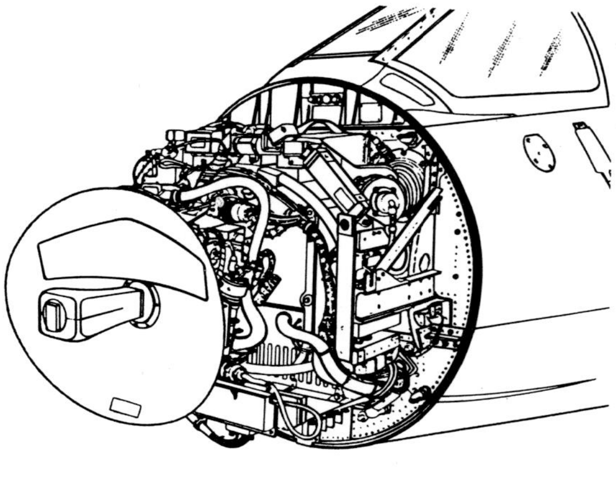

(1)

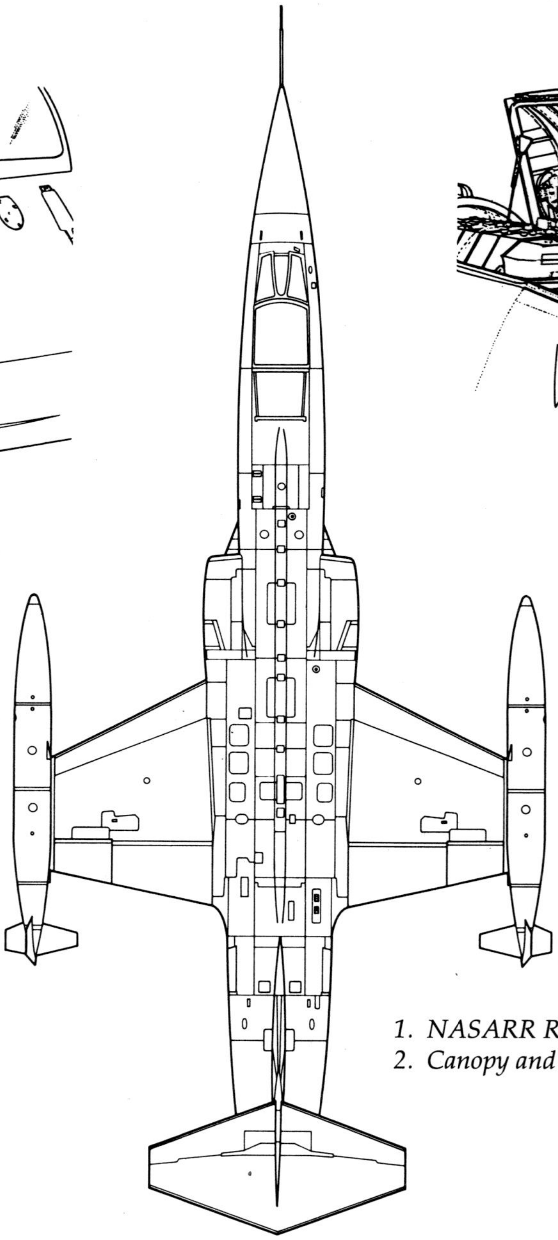

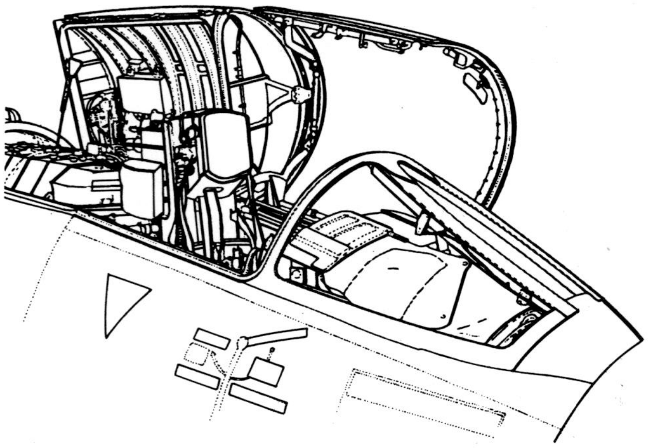

(2)

DIMENSIONS:

Span 21'11"
Length 54'9"
Height 13'6"

1. *NASARR R-24A North American Search and Ranging Radar*
2. *Canopy and open equipment bay*

TWO SEAT CF-104D
(LOCKHEED BUILT)

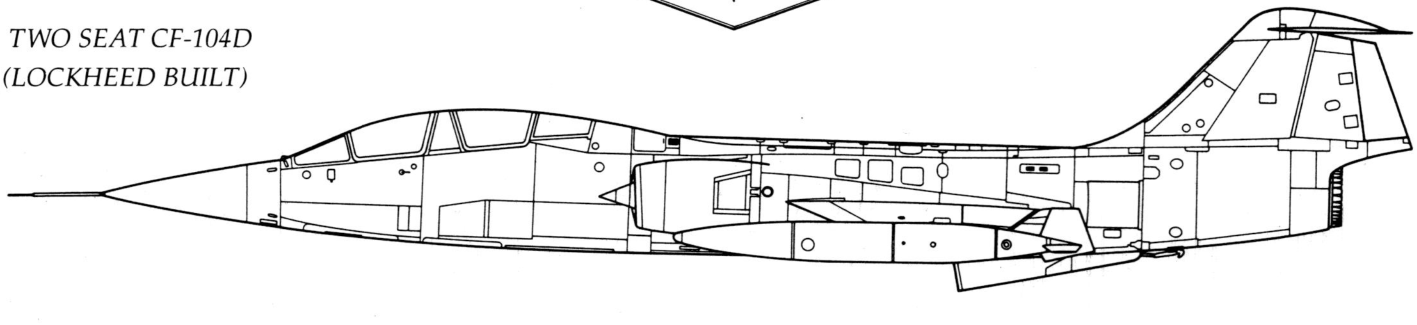

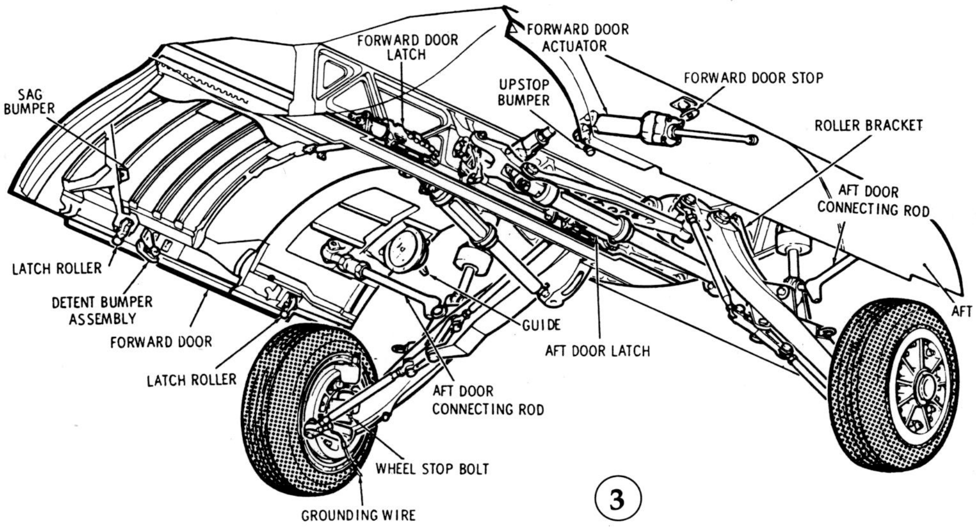

(3)

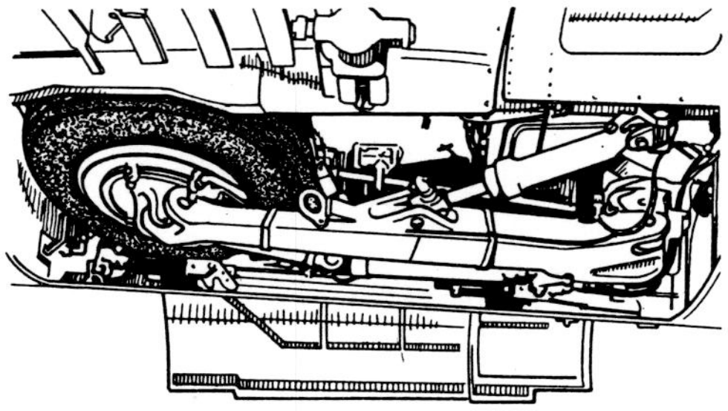

(4)

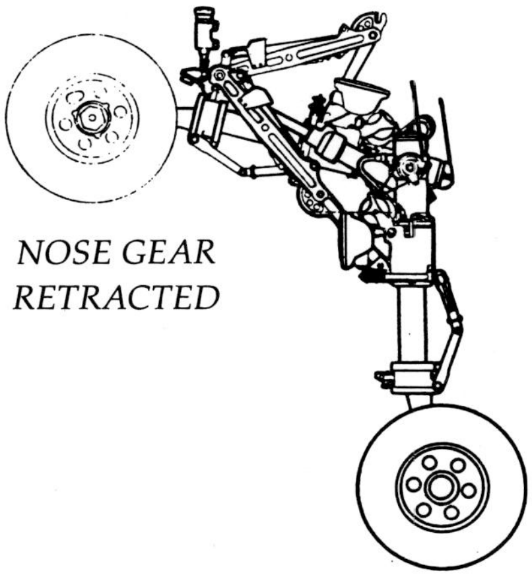

(5)

NOSE GEAR

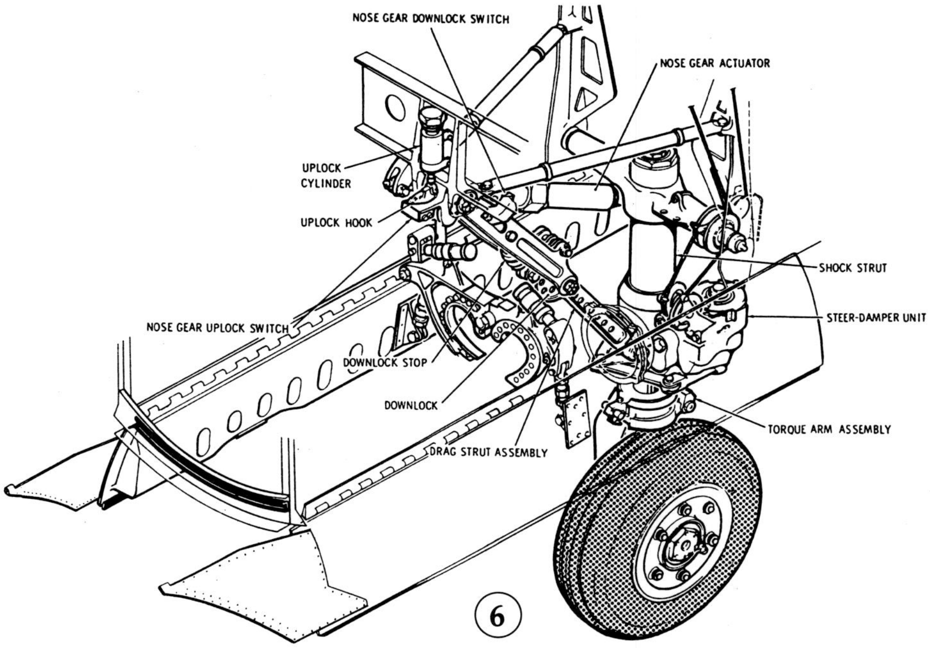

(6)

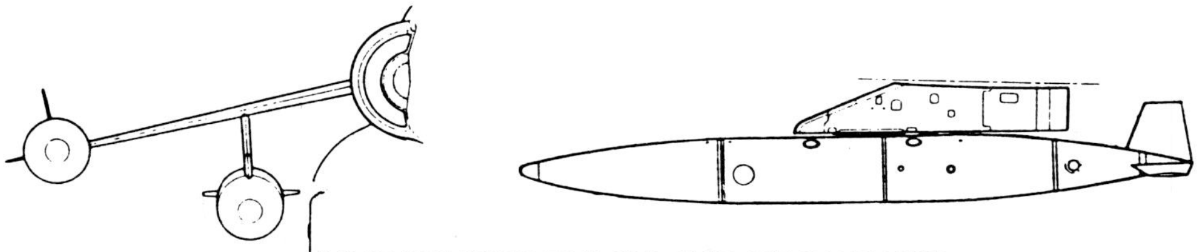

UNDERWING PYLON AND DROP TANK

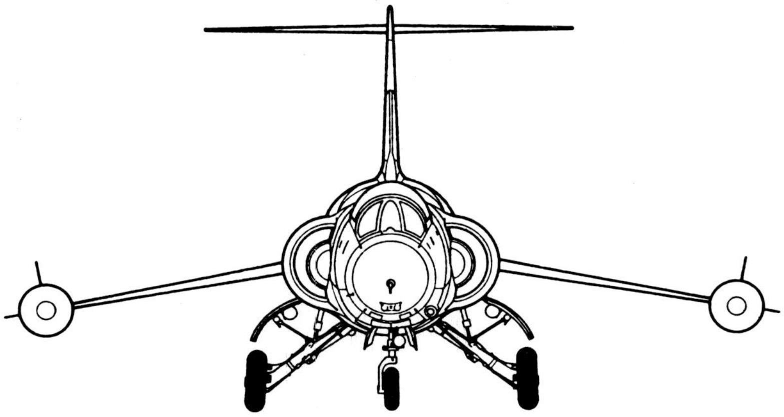

3. Main landing gear in detail
4. Main landing gear in retracted position
5. Nosewheel gear, depicted in both positions (Single-seat aircraft)
6. Nosewheel gear in detail

Drawing by Bob Migliardi, by permission of Sabre Models Publications, reworked by Chris Palimaka.